History Of Florence And Of The Affairs Of Italy

Niccolo Machiavelli

Contents

INTRODUCTION	7
BOOK I	11
CHAPTER I	11
CHAPTER II	16
CHAPTER III	23
CHAPTER IV	29
CHAPTER V	36
CHAPTER VI	42
CHAPTER VII	50
BOOK II	56
CHAPTER I	56
CHAPTER II	62
CHAPTER III	69
CHAPTER IV	75
CHAPTER V	83
CHAPTER VI	89
CHAPTER VII	95
CHAPTER VIII	101
CHAPTER IX	112
BOOK III	118
CHAPTER I	118
CHAPTER II	128
CHAPTER III	134
CHAPTER IV	141
CHAPTER V	148
CHAPTER VI	154
CHAPTER VII	160
BOOK IV	167
CHAPTER I	167
CHAPTER II	173
CHAPTER III	178
CHAPTER IV	184
CHAPTER V	191
CHAPTER VI	198
CHAPTER VII	204
BOOK V	211
CHAPTER I	211
CHAPTER II	217
CHAPTER III	225
CHAPTER IV	233
CHAPTER V	240
CHAPTER VI	247
CHAPTER VII	254
BOOK VI	260
CHAPTER I	260
CHAPTER II	267
CHAPTER III	274
CHAPTER IV	281
CHAPTER V	288
CHAPTER VI	295
CHAPTER VII	301
BOOK VII	307
CHAPTER I	307
CHAPTER II	317
CHAPTER III	325
CHAPTER IV	332
CHAPTER V	339
CHAPTER VI	345
BOOK VIII	352
CHAPTER I	352
CHAPTER II	359
CHAPTER III	367
CHAPTER IV	373
CHAPTER V	382
CHAPTER VI	388
CHAPTER VII	395

HISTORY OF FLORENCE AND OF THE AFFAIRS OF ITALY

BY
Niccolo Machiavelli

INTRODUCTION

Niccolo Machiavelli, the first great Italian historian, and one of the most eminent political writers of any age or country, was born at Florence, May 3, 1469. He was of an old though not wealthy Tuscan family, his father, who was a jurist, dying when Niccolo was sixteen years old. We know nothing of Machiavelli's youth and little about his studies. He does not seem to have received the usual humanistic education of his time, as he knew no Greek.[1] The first notice of Machiavelli is in 1498 when we find him holding the office of Secretary in the second Chancery of the Signoria, which office he retained till the downfall of the Florentine Republic in 1512. His unusual ability was soon recognized, and in 1500 he was sent on a mission to Louis XII. of France, and afterward on an embassy to Caesar Borgia, the lord of Romagna, at Urbino. Machiavelli's report and description of this and subsequent embassies to this prince, shows his undisguised admiration for the courage and cunning of Caesar, who was a master in the application of the principles afterwards exposed in such a skillful and uncompromising manner by Machiavelli in his Prince.

---

1 Villari, _Niccolo Machiavelli e i suoi tempi_, 2d ed. Milan, 1895-97, the best work on the subject. The most complete bibliography of Machiavelli up to 1858 is to be found in Mohl, _Gesch. u. Liter. der Staatswissenshaften_, Erlangen, 1855, III., 521-91. See also _La Vita e gli scritti di Niccolo Machiavelli nella loro Relazione col Machiavellismo_, by O. Tommasini, Turin, 1883 (unfinished). The best English translation of Machiavelli with which I am acquainted is: The Historical, Political, and Diplomatic writings of Niccolo Machiavelli, translated by Christian E. Detmold. Osgood & Co., Boston, 1882, 4 vols. 8vo.

The limits of this introduction will not permit us to follow with any detail the many important duties with which he was charged by his native state, all of which he fulfilled with the utmost fidelity and with consummate skill. When, after the battle of Ravenna in 1512 the holy league determined upon the downfall of Pier Soderini, Gonfaloniere of the Florentine Republic, and the restoration of the Medici, the efforts of Machiavelli, who was an ardent republican, were in vain; the troops he had helped to organize fled before the Spaniards and the Medici were returned to power. Machiavelli attempted to conciliate his new masters, but he was deprived of his office, and being accused in the following year of participation in the conspiracy of Boccoli and Capponi, he was imprisoned and tortured, though afterward set at liberty by Pope Leo X. He now retired to a small estate near San Casciano, seven miles from Florence. Here he devoted himself to political and historical studies, and though apparently retired from public life, his letters show the deep and passionate interest he took in the political vicissitudes through which Italy was then passing, and in all of which the singleness of purpose with which he continued to advance his native Florence, is clearly manifested. It was during his retirement upon his little estate at San Casciano that Machiavelli wrote The Prince, the most famous of all his writings, and here also he had begun a much more extensive work, his Discourses on the Decades of Livy, which continued to occupy him for several years. These Discourses, which do not form a continuous commentary on Livy, give Machiavelli an opportunity to express his own views on the government of the state, a task for which his long and varied political experience, and an assiduous study of the ancients rendered him eminently qualified. The Discourses **and** The Prince, written at the same time, supplement each other and are really one work. Indeed, the treatise, The Art of War, though not written till 1520 should be mentioned here because of its intimate connection with these two treatises, it being, in fact, a further development of some of the thoughts expressed in the Discorsi. The Prince, a short work, divided into twenty-six books, is the best known of all Machiavelli's writings. Herein he expresses in his own masterly way his views on the founding of a new state, taking for his type and model Caesar Borgia, although the latter had failed in his schemes for the consolidation of his power in the Romagna. The principles here laid down were the natural outgrowth of the confused political conditions of his time. And as in the Principe, as its name indicates, Machiavelli is concerned chiefly with the government of a Prince, so the Discorsi treat principally of the Republic, and here Machiavelli's model republic was the Roman commonwealth, the most successful and most enduring example of popular government. Free Rome is the embodiment of his political idea of the state. Much that Machiavelli says in this treatise is as true to-day and holds as good as the day it was written. And to us there is much that is of especial importance. To select a chapter almost at random, let us take Book I., Chap. XV.: "Public affairs are easily managed in a city where the body of the people is not corrupt; and where equality exists, there no principality can be established; nor can a republic be established where there is no equality."

No man has been more harshly judged than Machiavelli, especially in the two centuries following his death. But he has since found many able champions and the tide has turned. The Prince *has been termed a manual for tyrants, the effect of which has been most pernicious. But were Machiavelli's doctrines really new? Did he discover them? He merely had the candor and courage to write down what everybody was thinking and what everybody knew. He merely gives us the impressions he had received from a long and intimate intercourse with princes and the affairs of state. It was Lord Bacon, I believe, who said that Machiavelli tells us what princes do, not what they ought to do. When Machiavelli takes Caesar Borgia as a model, he in nowise extols him as a hero, but merely as a prince who was capable of attaining the end in view. The life of the State was the primary object. It must be maintained. And Machiavelli has laid down the principles, based upon his study and wide experience, by which this may be accomplished. He wrote from the view-point of the politician,--not of the moralist. What is good politics may be bad morals, and in fact, by a strange fatality, where morals and politics clash, the latter generally gets the upper hand. And will anyone contend that the principles set forth by Machiavelli in his* Prince *or his* Discourses *have entirely perished from the earth? Has diplomacy been entirely stripped of fraud and duplicity? Let anyone read the famous eighteenth chapter of* The Prince: "In what Manner Princes should keep their Faith," and he will be convinced that what was true nearly four hundred years ago, is quite as true to-day.

Of the remaining works of Machiavelli the most important is the *History of Florence* **written between 1521 and 1525, and dedicated to Clement VII. The first book is merely a rapid review of the Middle Ages, the history of Florence beginning with Book II. Machiavelli's method has been censured for adhering at times too closely to the chroniclers like Villani, Cambi, and Giovanni Cavalcanti, and at others rejecting their testimony without apparent reason, while in its details the authority of his** *History* **is often questionable. It is the straightforward, logical narrative, which always holds the interest of the reader that is the greatest charm of the** *History*. Of the other works of Machiavelli we may mention here his comedies the *Mandragola* **and** *Clizia*, and his novel *Belfagor*.

After the downfall of the Republic and Machiavelli's release from prison in 1513, fortune seems never again to have favoured him. It is true that in 1520 Giuliano de' Medici commissioned him to write his *History of Florence*, and he afterwards held a number of offices, yet these latter were entirely beneath his merits. He had been married in 1502 to Marietta Corsini, who bore him four sons and a daughter. He died on June 22, 1527, leaving his family in the greatest poverty, a sterling tribute to his honesty, when one considers the many opportunities he doubtless had to enrich himself. Machiavelli's life was not without blemish--few lives are. We must bear in mind the atmosphere of craft, hypocrisy, and poison in which he lived,--his was the age of Caesar Borgia and of Popes like the monster Alexander VI. and Julius II. Whatever his faults may have been, Machiavelli was always an ardent patriot and an earnest supporter of popular government. It is true that he was willing to accept a prince, if one could be found courageous enough and prudent enough to unite dismembered Italy, for in the unity of his native land he saw the only hope of its salvation.

Machiavelli is buried in the church of Santa Croce at Florence, beside the tomb of Michael Angelo. His monument bears this inscription:

"Tanto nomini nullum par eulogium."

And though this praise is doubtless exaggerated, he is a son of whom his country may be justly proud.

Hugo Albert Rennert.

BOOK I
CHAPTER I

Irruption of Northern people upon the Roman territories--Visigoths--Barbarians called in by Stilicho--Vandals in Africa--Franks and Burgundians give their names to France and Burgundy--The Huns--Angles give the name to England--Attila, king of the Huns, in Italy--Genseric takes Rome--The Lombards.

The people who inhabit the northern parts beyond the Rhine and the Danube, living in a healthy and prolific region, frequently increase to such vast multitudes that part of them are compelled to abandon their native soil, and seek a habitation in other countries. The method adopted, when one of these provinces had to be relieved of its superabundant population, was to divide into three parts, each containing an equal number of nobles and of people, of rich and of poor. The third upon whom the lot fell, then went in search of new abodes, leaving the remaining two-thirds in possession of their native country.

These migrating masses destroyed the Roman empire by the facilities for settlement which the country offered when the emperors abandoned Rome, the ancient seat of their dominion, and fixed their residence at Constantinople; for by this step they exposed the western empire to the rapine of both their ministers and their enemies, the remoteness of their position preventing them either from seeing or providing for its necessities. To suffer the overthrow of such an extensive empire, established by the blood of so many brave and virtuous men, showed no less folly in the princes themselves than infidelity in their ministers; for not one irruption alone, but many, contributed to its ruin; and these barbarians exhibited much ability and perseverance in accomplishing their object.

The first of these northern nations that invaded the empire after the Cimbrians, who were conquered by Caius Marius, was the Visigoths--which name in our language signifies "Western Goths." These, after some battles fought along its confines, long held their seat of dominion upon the Danube, with consent of the emperors; and although, moved by various causes, they often attacked the Roman provinces, were always kept in subjection by the imperial forces. The emperor Theodosius conquered them with great glory; and, being wholly reduced to his power, they no longer selected a sovereign of their own, but, satisfied with the terms which he granted them, lived and fought under his ensigns, and authority. On the death of Theodosius, his sons Arcadius and Honorius, succeeded to the empire, but not to the talents and fortune of their father; and the times became changed with the princes. Theodosius had appointed a governor to each of the three divisions of the empire, Ruffinus to the eastern, to the western Stilicho, and Gildo to the African. Each of these, after the death of Theodosius, determined not to be governors merely, but to assume sovereign dominion over their respective provinces. Gildo and Ruffinus were suppressed at their outset; but Stilicho, concealing his design, ingratiated himself with the new emperors, and at the same time so disturbed their government, as to facilitate his occupation of it afterward. To make the Visigoths their enemies, he advised that the accustomed stipend allowed to this people should be withheld; and as he thought these enemies would not be sufficient alone to disturb the empire, he contrived that the Burgundians, Franks, Vandals, and Alans (a northern people in search of new habitations), should assail the Roman provinces.

That they might be better able to avenge themselves for the injury they had sustained, the Visigoths, on being deprived of their subsidy, created Alaric their king; and having assailed the empire, succeeded, after many reverses, in overrunning Italy, and finally in pillaging Rome.

After this victory, Alaric died, and his successor, Astolphus, having married Placidia, sister of the emperors, agreed with them to go to the relief of Gaul and Spain, which provinces had been assailed by the Vandals, Burgundians, Alans, and Franks, from the causes before mentioned. Hence it followed, that the Vandals, who had occupied that part of Spain called Betica (now Andalusia), being pressed by the Visigoths, and unable to resist them, were invited by Boniface, who governed Africa for the empire, to occupy that province; for, being in rebellion, he was afraid his error would become known to the emperor. For these reasons the Vandals gladly undertook the enterprise, and under Genseric, their king, became lords of Africa.

At this time Theodosius, son of Arcadius, succeeded to the empire; and, bestowing little attention on the affairs of the west, caused those who had taken possession to think of securing their acquisitions. Thus the Vandals ruled Africa; the Alans and Visigoths, Spain; while the Franks and Burgundians not only took Gaul, but each gave their name to the part they occupied; hence one is called France, the other Burgundy. The good fortune of these brought fresh people to the destruction of the empire, one of which, the Huns, occupied the province of Pannonia, situated upon the nearer shore of the Danube, and which, from their name, is still called Hungary. To these disorders it must be added, that the emperor, seeing himself attacked on so many sides, to lessen the number of his enemies, began to treat first with the Vandals, then with the Franks; a course which diminished his own power, and increased that of the barbarians. Nor was the island of Britain, which is now called England, secure from them; for the Britons, being apprehensive of those who had occupied Gaul, called the Angli, a people of Germany, to their aid; and these under Vortigern their king, first defended, and then drove them from the island, of which they took possession, and after themselves named the country England. But the inhabitants, being robbed of their home, became desperate by necessity and resolved to take possession of some other country, although they had been unable to defend their own. They therefore crossed the sea with their families, and settled in the country nearest to the beach, which from themselves is called Brittany. The Huns, who were said above to have occupied Pannonia, joining with other nations, as the Zepidi, Eurili, Turingi, and Ostro, or eastern Goths, moved in search of new countries, and not being able to enter France, which was defended by the forces of the barbarians, came into Italy under Attila their king. He, a short time previously, in order to possess the entire monarchy, had murdered his brother Bleda; and having thus become very powerful, Andaric, king of the Zepidi, and Velamir, king of the Ostrogoths, became subject to him. Attila, having entered Italy, laid siege to Aquileia, where he remained without any obstacle for two years, wasting the country round, and dispersing the inhabitants. This, as will be related in its place, caused the origin of Venice. After the taking and ruin of Aquileia, he directed his course towards Rome, from the destruction of which he abstained at the entreaty of the pontiff, his respect for whom was so great that he left Italy and retired into Austria, where he died. After the death of Attila, Velamir, king of the Ostrogoths, and the heads of the other nations, took arms against his sons Henry and Uric, slew the one and compelled the other, with his Huns, to repass the Danube and return to their country; while the Ostrogoths and the Zepidi established themselves in Pannonia, and the Eruli and the Turingi upon the farther bank of the Danube.

Attila having left Italy, Valentinian, emperor of the west, thought of restoring the country; and, that he might be more ready to defend it against the barbarians, abandoned Rome, and removed the seat of government to Ravenna. The misfortunes which befell the western empire caused the emperor, who resided at Constantinople, on many occasions to give up the possession of it to others, as a charge full of danger and expense; and sometimes, without his permission, the Romans, seeing themselves so abandoned, created an emperor for their defense, or suffered some one to usurp the dominion. This occurred at the period of which we now speak, when Maximus, a Roman, after the death of Valentinian, seized the government, and compelled Eudocia, widow of the late emperor, to take him for her husband; but she, being of imperial blood, scorned the connection of a private citizen; and being anxious to avenge herself for the insult, secretly persuaded Genseric, king of the Vandals and master of Africa to come to Italy, representing to him the advantage he would derive from the undertaking, and the facility with which it might be accomplished. Tempted by the hope of booty, he came immediately, and finding Rome abandoned, plundered the city during fourteen days. He also ravaged many other places in Italy, and then, loaded with wealth, withdrew to Africa. The Romans, having returned to their city, and Maximus being dead, elected Avitus, a Roman, as his successor. After this, several important events occurred both in Italy and in the countries beyond; and after the deaths of many emperors the empire of Constantinople devolved upon Zeno, and that of Rome upon Orestes and Augustulus his son, who obtained the sovereignty by fraud. While they were designing to hold by force what they had obtained by treachery, the Eruli and the Turingi, who, after the death of Attila, as before remarked, had established themselves upon the farther bank of the Danube, united in a league and invaded Italy under Odoacer their general. Into the districts which they left unoccupied, the Longobardi or Lombards, also a northern people, entered, led by Godogo their king. Odoacer conquered and slew Orestes near Pavia, but Augustulus escaped. After this victory, that Rome might, with her change of power, also change her title, Odoacer, instead of using the imperial name, caused himself to be declared king of Rome. He was the first of those leaders who at this period overran the world and thought of settling in Italy; for the others, either from fear that they should not be able to hold the country, knowing that it might easily be relieved by the eastern emperors, or from some unknown cause, after plundering her, sought other countries wherein to establish themselves.

CHAPTER II

State of the Roman empire under Zeno--Theodoric king of the Ostrogoths--Character of Theodoric--Changes in the Roman empire--New languages--New names--Theodoric dies--Belisarius in Italy--Totila takes Rome--Narses destroys the Goths--New form of Government in Italy--Narses invites the Lombards into Italy--The Lombards change the form of government.

At this time the ancient Roman empire was governed by the following princes: Zeno, reigning in Constantinople, commanded the whole of the eastern empire; the Ostrogoths ruled Mesia and Pannonia; the Visigoths, Suavi, and Alans, held Gascony and Spain; the Vandals, Africa; the Franks and Burgundians, France; and the Eruli and Turingi, Italy. The kingdom of the Ostrogoths had descended to Theodoric, nephew of Velamir, who, being on terms of friendship with Zeno the eastern emperor, wrote to him that his Ostrogoths thought it an injustice that they, being superior in valor to the people thereabout, should be inferior to them in dominion, and that it was impossible for him to restrain them within the limits of Pannonia. So, seeing himself under the necessity of allowing them to take arms and go in search of new abodes, he wished first to acquaint Zeno with it, in order that he might provide for them, by granting some country in which they might establish themselves, by his good favor with greater propriety and convenience. Zeno, partly from fear and partly from a desire to drive Odoacer out of Italy, gave Theodoric permission to lead his people against him, and take possession of the country. Leaving his friends the Zepidi in Pannonia, Theodoric marched into Italy, slew Odoacer and his son, and, moved by the same reasons which had induced Valentinian to do so, established his court at Ravenna, and like Odoacer took the title of king of Italy.

Theodoric possessed great talents both for war and peace; in the former he was always conqueror, and in the latter he conferred very great benefits upon the cities and people under him. He distributed the Ostrogoths over the country, each district under its leader, that he might more conveniently command them in war, and govern them in peace. He enlarged Ravenna, restored Rome, and, with the exception of military discipline, conferred upon the Romans every honor. He kept within their proper bounds, wholly by the influence of his character, all the barbarian kings who occupied the empire; he built towns and fortresses between the point of the Adriatic and the Alps, in order, with the greater facility, to impede the passage of any new hordes of barbarians who might design to assail Italy; and if, toward the latter end of his life, so many virtues had not been sullied by acts of cruelty, caused by various jealousies of his people, such as the death of Symmachus and Boethius, men of great holiness, every point of his character would have deserved the highest praise. By his virtue and goodness, not only Rome and Italy, but every part of the western empire, freed from the continual troubles which they had suffered from the frequent influx of barbarians, acquired new vigor, and began to live in an orderly and civilized manner. For surely if any times were truly miserable for Italy and the provinces overrun by the barbarians, they were those which occurred from Arcadius and Honorius to Theodoric. If we only consider the evils which arise to a republic or a kingdom by a change of prince or of government; not by foreign interference, but by civil discord (in which we may see how even slight variations suffice to ruin the most powerful kingdoms or states), we may then easily imagine how much Italy and the other Roman provinces suffered, when they not only changed their forms of government and their princes, but also their laws, customs, modes of living, religion, language, and name. Any one of such changes, by itself, without being united with others, might, with thinking of it, to say nothing of the seeing and suffering, infuse terror into the strongest minds.

From these causes proceeded the ruin as well as the origin and extension of many cities. Among those which were ruined were Aquileia, Luni, Chiusi, Popolonia, Fiesole, and many others. The new cities were Venice, Sienna, Ferrara, Aquila, with many towns and castles which for brevity we omit. Those which became extended were Florence, Genoa, Pisa, Milan, Naples, and Bologna; to all of which may be added, the ruin and restoration of Rome, and of many other cities not previously mentioned.

From this devastation and new population arose new languages, as we see in the different dialects of France, Spain and Italy; which, partaking of the native idiom of the new people and of the old Roman, formed a new manner of discourse. Besides, not only were the names of provinces changed, but also of lakes, rivers, seas, and men; for France, Spain, and Italy are full of fresh names, wholly different from the ancient; as, omitting many others, we see that the Po, the Garda, the Archipelago, are names quite different from those which the ancients used; while instead of Caesar and Pompey we have Peter, Matthew, John, etc.

Among so many variations, that of religion was not of little importance; for, while combating the customs of the ancient faith with the miracles of the new, very serious troubles and discords were created among men. And if the Christians had been united in one faith, fewer disorders would have followed; but the contentions among themselves, of the churches of Rome, Greece, and Ravenna, joined to those of the heretic sects with the Catholics, served in many ways to render the world miserable. Africa is a proof of this; having suffered more horrors from the Arian sect, whose doctrines were believed by the Vandals, than from any avarice or natural cruelty of the people themselves. Living amid so many persecutions, the countenances of men bore witness of the terrible impressions upon their minds; for besides the evils they suffered from the disordered state of the world, they scarcely could have recourse to the help of God, in whom the unhappy hope for relief; for the greater part of them, being uncertain what divinity they ought to address, died miserably, without help and without hope.

Having been the first who put a stop to so many evils, Theodoric deserves the highest praise: for during the thirty-eight years he reigned in Italy, he brought the country to such a state of greatness that her previous sufferings were no longer recognizable. But at his death, the kingdom descending to Atalaric, son of Amalasontha, his daughter, and the malice of fortune not being yet exhausted, the old evils soon returned; for Atalaric died soon after his grandfather, and the kingdom coming into the possession of his mother, she was betrayed by Theodatus, whom she had called to assist her in the government. He put her to death and made himself king; and having thus become odious to the Ostrogoths, the emperor Justinian entertained the hope of driving him out of Italy. Justinian appointed Belisarius to the command of this expedition, as he had already conquered Africa, expelled the

Vandals, and reduced the country to the imperial rule.

Belisarius took possession of Sicily, and from thence passing into Italy, occupied Naples and Rome. The Goths, seeing this, slew Theodatus their king, whom they considered the cause of their misfortune, and elected Vitiges in his stead, who, after some skirmishes, was besieged and taken by Belisarius at Ravenna; but before he had time to secure the advantages of his victory, Belisarius was recalled by Justinian, and Joannes and Vitalis were appointed in his place. Their principles and practices were so different from those of Belisarius, that the Goths took courage and created Ildovadus, governor of Verona, their king. After Ildovadus, who was slain, came Totila, who routed the imperial forces, took Tuscany and Naples, and recovered nearly the whole of what Belisarius had taken from them. On this account Justinian determined to send him into Italy again; but, coming with only a small force, he lost the reputation which his former victories had won for him, in less time than he had taken to acquire it. Totila being at Ostia with his forces, took Rome before his eyes; but being unable to hold or to leave the city, he destroyed the greater part of it, drove out the citizens, and took the senators away from him. Thinking little of Belisarius, he led his people into Calabria, to attack the forces which had been sent from Greece.

Belisarius, seeing the city abandoned, turned his mind to the performance of an honourable work. Viewing the ruins of Rome, he determined to rebuild her walls and recall her inhabitants with as little delay as possible. But fortune was opposed to this laudable enterprise; for Justinian, being at this time assailed by the Parthians, recalled him; and his duty to his sovereign compelled him to abandon Italy to Totila, who again took Rome, but did not treat her with such severity as upon the former occasion; for at the entreaty of St. Benedict, who in those days had great reputation for sanctity, he endeavored to restore her. In the meantime, Justinian having arranged matters with the Parthians, again thought of sending a force to the relief of Italy; but the Sclavi, another northern people, having crossed the Danube and attacked Illyria and Thrace, prevented him, so that Totila held almost the whole country. Having conquered the Slavonians, Justinian sent Narses, a eunuch, a man of great military talent, who, having arrived in Italy, routed and slew Totila. The Goths who escaped sought refuge in Pavia, where they created Teias their king. On the other hand, Narses after the victory took Rome, and coming to an engagement with Teias near Nocera, slew him and routed his army. By this victory, the power of the Goths in Italy was quite annihilated, after having existed for seventy years, from the coming of Theodoric to the death of Teias.

No sooner was Italy delivered from the Goths than Justinian died, and was succeeded by Justin, his son, who, at the instigation of Sophia, his wife, recalled Narses, and sent Longinus in his stead. Like those who preceded him, he made his abode at Ravenna, and besides this, gave a new form to the government of Italy; for he did not appoint governors of provinces, as the Goths had done, but in every city and town of importance placed a ruler whom he called a duke. Neither in this arrangement did he respect Rome more than the other cities; for having set aside the consuls and senate, names which up to this time had been preserved, he placed her under a duke, who was sent every year from Ravenna, and called her the duchy of Rome; while to him who remained in Ravenna, and governed the whole of Italy for the emperor, was given the name of Exarch. This division of the country greatly facilitated the ruin of Italy, and gave the Lombards an early occasion of occupying it. Narses was greatly enraged with the emperor, for having recalled him from the government of the province, which he had won with his own valor and blood; while Sophia, not content with the injury done by withdrawing him, treated him in the most offensive manner, saying she wished him to come back that he might spin with the other eunuchs. Full of indignation, Narses persuaded Alboin, king of the Lombards, who then reigned in Pannonia, to invade and take possession of Italy.

The Lombards, as was said before, occupied those places upon the Danube which had been vacated by the Eruli and Turingi, when Odoacer their king led them into Italy; where, having been established for some time, their dominions were held by Alboin, a man ferocious and bold, under whom they crossed the Danube, and coming to an engagement with Cunimund, king of the Zepidi, who held Pannonia, conquered and slew him. Alboin finding Rosamond, daughter of Cunimund, among the captives, took her to wife, and made himself sovereign of Pannonia; and, moved by his savage nature, caused the skull of Cunimund to be formed into a cup, from which, in memory of the victory, he drank. Being invited into Italy by Narses, with whom he had been in friendship during the war with the Goths, he left Pannonia to the Huns, who after the death of Attila had returned to their country. Finding, on his arrival, the province divided into so many parts, he presently occupied Pavia,

Milan, Verona, Vicenza, the whole of Tuscany, and the greater part of Flamminia, which is now called Romagna. These great and rapid acquisitions made him think the conquest of Italy already secured; he therefore gave a great feast at Verona, and having become elevated with wine, ordered the skull of Cunimund to be filled, and caused it to be presented to the queen Rosamond, who sat opposite, saying loud enough for her to hear, that upon occasion of such great joy she should drink with her father. These words were like a dagger to the lady's bosom and she resolved to have revenge. Knowing that Helmichis, a noble Lombard, was in love with one of her maids, she arranged with the young woman, that Helmichis, without being acquainted with the fact, should sleep with her instead of his mistress. Having effected her design, Rosamond discovered herself to Helmichis, and gave him the choice either of killing Alboin, and taking herself and the kingdom as his reward, or of being put to death as the ravisher of the queen. Helmichis consented to destroy Alboin; but after the murder, finding they could not occupy the kingdom, and fearful that the Lombards would put them to death for the love they bore to Alboin, they seized the royal treasure, and fled with it to Longinus, at Ravenna, who received them favorably.

During these troubles the emperor Justinus died, and was succeeded by Tiberius, who, occupied in the wars with the Parthians, could not attend to the affairs of Italy; and this seeming to Longinus to present an opportunity, by means of Rosamond and her wealth, of becoming king of the Lombards and of the whole of Italy, he communicated his design to her, persuaded her to destroy Helmichis, and so take him for her husband. To this end, having prepared poisoned wine, she with her own hand presented it to Helmichis, who complained of thirst as he came from the bath. Having drunk half of it, he suspected the truth, from the unusual sensation it occasioned and compelled her to drink the remainder; so that in a few hours both came to their end, and Longinus was deprived of the hope of becoming king.

In the meantime the Lombards, having drawn themselves together in Pavia, which was become the principal seat of their empire, made Clefis their king. He rebuilt Imola, destroyed by Narses, and occupied Remini and almost every place up to Rome; but he died in the course of his victories. Clefis was cruel to such a degree, not only toward strangers, but to his own Lombards, that these people, sickened of royal power, did not create another king, but appointed among themselves thirty dukes to govern the rest. This prevented the Lombards from occupying the whole of Italy, or of extending their dominion further than Benevento; for, of the cities of Rome, Ravenna, Cremona, Mantua, Padua, Monselice, Parma, Bologna, Faenza, Forli, and Cesena, some defended themselves for a time, and others never fell under their dominion; since, not having a king, they became less prompt for war, and when they afterward appointed one, they were, by living in freedom, become less obedient, and more apt to quarrel among themselves; which from the first prevented a fortunate issue of their military expeditions, and was the ultimate cause of their being driven out of Italy. The affairs of the Lombards being in the state just described, the Romans and Longinus came to an agreement with them, that each should lay down their arms and enjoy what they already possessed.

CHAPTER III

Beginning of the greatness of the pontiffs in Italy--Abuse of censures and indulgences--The pope applies to Pepin, king of France, for assistance--Donation of Pepin to the pontiff--Charlemagne--End of the kingdom of the Lombards--The title of cardinal begins to be used--The empire passes to the Germans--Berengarius, duke of Fruili, created king of Italy--Pisa becomes great--Order and division of the states of Italy--Electors of the emperor created.

In these times the popes began to acquire greater temporal authority than they had previously possessed; although the immediate successors of St. Peter were more reverenced for the holiness of their lives, and the miracles which they performed; and their example so greatly extended the Christian religion, that princes of other states embraced it, in order to obviate the confusion which prevailed at that period. The emperor having become a Christian and returned to Constantinople, it followed, as was remarked at the commencement of the book, that the Roman empire was the more easily ruined, and the church more rapidly increased her authority. Nevertheless, the whole of Italy, being subject either to the emperors or the kings till the coming of the Lombards, the popes never acquired any greater authority than what reverence for their habits and doctrine gave them. In other respects they obeyed the emperors or kings; officiated for them in their affairs, as ministers or agents, and were even sometimes put to death by them. He who caused them to become of more importance in the affairs of Italy, was Theodoric, king of the Goths, when he established the seat of his empire at Ravenna; for, Rome being without a prince, the Romans found it necessary, for their safety, to yield obedience to the pope; his authority, however, was not greatly increased thereby, the only advantage being, that the church of Rome was allowed to take precedence of that of Ravenna. But the Lombards having taken possession, and Italy being divided into many parts, the pope had an opportunity of greater exertion. Being as it were the head of Rome, both the emperor of Constantinople and the Lombards respected him; so that the Romans, by his means, entered into league with the Lombards, and with Longinus, not as subjects, but as equals. Thus the popes, at one time friends of the Greeks, and at another of the Lombards, increased their own power; but upon the ruin of the eastern empire, which occurred during the time of Heraclius, their influence was reduced; for the Sclavi, of whom we spoke before, again assailed Illyria, and having occupied the country, named it Sclavonia, after themselves; and the other parts were attacked by the Persians, then by the Saracens under Mohammed, and lastly by the Turks, who took Syria, Africa, and Egypt. These causes induced the reigning pope, in his distress, to seek new friends, and he applied to the king of France. Nearly all the wars which the northern barbarians carried on in Italy, it may be here remarked, were occasioned by the pontiffs; and the hordes, with which the country was inundated, were generally called in by them. The same mode of proceeding still continued, and kept Italy weak and unsettled. And, therefore, in relating the events which have taken place from those times to the present, the ruin of the empire will be no longer illustrated, but only the increase of the pontificate and of the other principalities which ruled Italy till the coming of Charles VIII. It will be seen how the popes, first with censures, and afterward with these and arms, mingled with indulgences, became both terrible and venerable; and how, from having abused both, they ceased to possess any influence, and were wholly dependent on the will of others for assistance in their wars.

But to return to the order of our narration. Gregory III. occupied the papacy, and the kingdom of the Lombards was held by Astolphus, who, contrary to agreement, seized Ravenna, and made war upon the pope. On this account, Gregory no longer relying upon the emperor of Constantinople, since he, for the reasons above given, was unable to assist him, and unwilling to trust the Lombards, for they had frequently broken their faith, had recourse to Pepin II., who, from being lord of Austria and Brabant, had become king of France; not so much by his own valor as by that of Charles Martel, his father, and Pepin his grandfather; for Charles Martel, being governor of the kingdom, effected the memorable defeat of the Saracens near Tours, upon the Loire, in which two hundred thousand of them are said to have been left dead upon the field of battle. Hence, Pepin, by his father's reputation and his own abilities, became afterward king of France. To him Pope Gregory, as we have said, applied for assistance against the Lombards, which Pepin promised to grant, but desired first to see him and be honored with his presence. Gregory accordingly went to France, passing uninjured through the country of his enemies, so great was the respect they had for religion, and was treated honorably by Pepin, who sent an army into Italy, and besieged the Lombards in Pavia. King Astolphus, compelled by necessity, made proposals of peace to the French, who agreed to them at the entreaty of the pope--for he did not desire the death of his enemy, but that he should be converted and live. In this treaty, Astolphus promised to give to the church all the places he had taken from her; but the king's forces having returned to France, he did not fulfill the agreement, and the pope again had recourse to Pepin, who sent another army, conquered the Lombards, took Ravenna, and, contrary to the wishes of the Greek emperor, gave it to the pope, with all the places that belonged to the exarchate, and added to them Urbino and the Marca. But Astolphus, while fulfilling the terms of his agreement, died, and Desiderius, a Lombard, who was duke of Tuscany, took up arms to occupy the kingdom, and demanded assistance of the pope, promising him his friendship. The pope acceding to his request, the other princes assented. Desiderius kept faith at first, and proceeded to resign the districts to the pope, according to the agreement made with Pepin, so that an exarch was no longer sent from Constantinople to Ravenna, but it was governed according to the will of the pope. Pepin soon after died, and was succeeded by his son Charles, the same who, on account of the magnitude and success of his enterprises, was called Charlemagne, or Charles the Great. Theodore I. now succeeded to the papacy, and discord arising between him and Desiderius, the latter besieged him in Rome. The pope requested assistance of Charles, who, having crossed the Alps, besieged Desiderius in Pavai, where he took both him and his children, and sent them prisoners to France. He then went to visit the pontiff at Rome, where he declared, THAT THE POPE, BEING VICAR OF GOD, COULD NOT BE JUDGED BY MEN. The pope and the people of Rome made him emperor; and thus Rome began to have an emperor of the west. And whereas the popes used to be established by the emperors, the latter now began to have need of the popes at their elections; the empire continued to lose its powers, while the church acquired them; and, by these means, she constantly extended her authority over temporal princes.

The Lombards, having now been two hundred and thirty-two years in the country, were strangers only in name, and Charles, wishing to reorganize the states of Italy, consented that they should occupy the places in which they had been brought up, and call the province after their own name, Lombardy. That they might be led to respect the Roman name, he ordered all that part of Italy adjoining to them, which had been under the exarchate of Ravenna, to be called Romagna. Besides this, he created his son Pepin, king of Italy, whose dominion extended to Benevento; all the rest being possessed by the Greek emperor, with whom Charles was in league. About this time Pascal I. occupied the pontificate, and the priests of the churches of Rome, from being near to the pope, and attending the elections of the pontiff, began to dignify their own power with a title, by calling themselves cardinals, and arrogated so great authority, that having excluded the people of Rome from the election of pontiff, the appointment of a new pope was scarcely ever made except from one of their own number: thus on the death of Pascal, the cardinal of St. Sabina was created pope by the title of Eugenius II. Italy having come into the hands of the French, a change of form and order took place, the popes acquiring greater temporal power, and the new authorities adopting the titles of count and marquis, as that of duke had been introduced by Longinus, exarch of Ravenna. After the deaths of some pontiffs, Osporco, a Roman, succeeded to the papacy; but on account of his unseemly appellation, he took the name of Sergius, and this was the origin of that change of names which the popes adopt upon their election to the pontificate.

In the meantime, the Emperor Charles died and was succeeded by Lewis (the Pious), after whose death so many disputes arose among his sons, that at the time of his grandchildren, the house of France lost the empire, which then came to the Germans; the first German emperor being called Arnolfus. Nor did the Carlovingian family lose the empire only; their discords also occasioned them the loss of Italy; for the Lombards, gathering strength, offended the pope and the Romans, and Arnolfo, not knowing where to seek relief, was compelled to create Berengarius, duke of Fruili, king of Italy. These events induced the Huns, who occupied Pannonia, to assail Italy; but, in an engagement with Berengarius, they were compelled to return to Pannonia, which had from them been named Hungary.

Romano was at this time emperor of Greece, having, while prefect of the army, dethroned Constantine; and as Puglia and Calabria, which, as before observed, were parts of the Greek empire, had revolted, he gave permission to the Saracans to occupy them; and they having taken possession of these provinces, besieged Rome. The Romans, Berengarius being then engaged in defending himself against the Huns, appointed Alberic, duke of Tuscany, their leader. By his valor Rome was saved from the Saracens, who, withdrawing from the siege, erected a fortress upon Mount Gargano, by means of which they governed Puglia and Calabria, and harassed the whole country. Thus Italy was in those times very grievously afflicted, being in constant warfare with the Huns in the direction of the Alps, and, on the Neapolitan side, suffering from the inroads of the Saracens. This state of things continued many years, occupying the reigns of three Berengarii, who succeeded each other; and during this time the pope and the church were greatly disturbed; the impotence of the eastern, and the disunion which prevailed among the western princes, leaving them without defense. The city of Genoa, with all her territory upon the rivers, having been overrun by the Saracens, an impulse was thus given to the rising greatness of Pisa, in which city multitudes took refuge who had been driven out of their own country. These events occurred in the year 931, when Otho, duke of Saxony, the son of Henry and Matilda, a man of great prudence and reputation, being made emperor, the pope Agapito, begged that he would come into Italy and relieve him from the tyranny of the Berengarii.

The States of Italy were governed in this manner: Lombardy was under Berengarius III. and Alfred his son; Tuscany and Romagna were governed by a deputy of the western emperor; Puglia and Calabria were partly under the Greek emperor, and partly under the Saracens; in Rome two consuls were annually chosen from the nobility, who governed her according to ancient custom; to these was added a prefect, who dispensed justice among the people; and there was a council of twelve, who each year appointed rectors for the places subject to them. The popes had more or less authority in Rome and the rest of Italy, in proportion as they were favorites of the emperor or of the most powerful states. The Emperor Otho came into Italy, took the kingdom from the Berengarii, in which they had reigned fifty-five years, and reinstated the pontiff in his dignity. He had a son and a nephew, each named Otho, who, one after the other, succeeded to the empire. In the reign of Otho III.,

Pope Gregory V. was expelled by the Romans; whereupon the emperor came into Italy and replaced him; and the pope, to revenge himself on the Romans, took from them the right to create an emperor, and gave it to three princes and three bishops of Germany; the princes of Brandenburg, Palatine, and Saxony, and the bishops of Magonza, Treveri, and Colonia. This occurred in the year 1002. After the death of Otho III. the electors created Henry, duke of Bavaria, emperor, who at the end of twelve years was crowned by Pope Stephen VIII. Henry and his wife Simeonda were persons of very holy life, as is seen by the many temples built and endowed by them, of which the church of St. Miniato, near Florence, is one. Henry died in 1024, and was succeeded by Conrad of Suabia; and the latter by Henry II., who came to Rome; and as there was a schism in the church of three popes, he set them all aside, and caused the election of Clement II., by whom he was crowned emperor.

CHAPTER IV

Nicholas II. commits the election of the pope to the cardinals--First example of a prince deprived of his dominions by the pope--Guelphs and Ghibellines--Establishment of the kingdom of Naples--Pope Urban II. goes to France--The first crusade--New orders of knighthood--Saladin takes from the Christians their possessions in the east--Death of the Countess Matilda--Character of Frederick Barbarossa--Schism--Frederick creates an anti-pope--Building of Alexandria in Puglia--Disgraceful conditions imposed by the pope upon Henry, king of England--Reconciliation of Frederick with the pope--The kingdom of Naples passes to the Germans--Orders of St. Dominic and St. Francis.

Italy was at this time governed partly by the people, some districts by their own princes, and others by the deputies of the emperor. The highest in authority, and to whom the others referred, was called the chancellor. Of the princes, the most powerful were Godfred and the Countess Matilda his wife, who was daughter of Beatrice, the sister of Henry II. She and her husband possessed Lucca, Parma, Reggio, Mantua, and the whole of what is now called THE PATRIMONY OF THE CHURCH. The ambition of the Roman people caused many wars between them and the pontiffs, whose authority had previously been used to free them from the emperors; but when they had taken the government of the city to themselves, and regulated it according to their own pleasure, they at once became at enmity with the popes, who received far more injuries from them than from any Christian potentate. And while the popes caused all the west to tremble with their censures, the people of Rome were in open rebellion against them; nor had they or the popes any other purpose, but to deprive each other of reputation and authority.

Nicholas II. now attained the papacy; and as Gregory V. had taken from the

Romans the right to create an emperor, he in the same manner determined to deprive them of their share in the election of the pope; and confined the creation to the cardinals alone. Nor did this satisfy him; for, having agreed with the princes who governed Calabria and Puglia, with methods which we shall presently relate, he compelled the officers whom the Romans appointed to their different jurisdictions, to render obedience to him; and some of them he even deprived of their offices. After the death of Nicholas, there was a schism in the church; the clergy of Lombardy refused obedience to Alexander II., created at Rome, and elected Cadolo of Parma anti-pope; and Henry, who hated the power of the pontiffs, gave Alexander to understand that he must renounce the pontificate, and ordered the cardinals to go into Germany to appoint a new pope. He was the first who felt the importance of spiritual weapons; for the pope called a council at Rome, and deprived Henry of both the empire and the kingdom. Some of the people of Italy took the part of the pope, others of Henry; and hence arose the factions of the Guelphs and the Ghibellines; that Italy, relieved from the inundations of barbarians, might be distracted with intestine strife. Henry, being excommunicated, was compelled by his people to come into Italy, and fall barefooted upon his knees before the pope, and ask his pardon. This occurred in the year 1082. Nevertheless, there shortly afterward arose new discords between the pope and Henry; upon which the pope again excommunicated him, and the emperor sent his son, also named Henry, with an army to Rome, and he, with the assistance of the Romans, who hated the pope, besieged him in the fortress. Robert Guiscard them came from Puglia to his relief, but Henry had left before his arrival, and returned to Germany. The Romans stood out alone, and the city was sacked by Robert, and reduced to ruins. As from this Robert sprung the establishment of the kingdom of Naples, it seems not superfluous to relate particularly his actions and origin. Disunion having arisen among the descendants of Charlemagne, occasion was given to another northern people, called Normans, to assail France and occupy that portion of the country which is now named Normandy. A part of these people came into Italy at the time when the province was infested with the Berengarii, the Saracans, and the Huns, and occupied some places in Romagna, where, during the wars of that period, they conducted themselves valiantly. Tancred, one of these Norman princes, had many children; among the rest were William, surnamed Ferabac, and Robert, called Guiscard. When the principality was governed by William, the troubles of Italy were in some measure abated; but the Saracens still held Sicily, and plundered the coasts of Italy daily. On this account William arranged with the princes of Capua and Salerno, and with Melorco, a Greek, who governed Puglia and Calabria for the Greek emperor, to attack Sicily; and it was agreed that, if they were victorious, each should have a fourth part of the booty and the territory. They were fortunate in their enterprise, expelled the Saracens, and took possession of the island; but, after the victory, Melorco secretly caused forces to be brought from Greece, seized Sicily in the name of the emperor, and appropriated the booty to himself and his followers. William was much dissatisfied with this, but reserved the exhibition of his displeasure for a suitable opportunity, and left Sicily with the princes of Salerno and Capua. But when they had parted from him to return to their homes, instead of proceeding to Romagna he led his people towards Puglia, and took Melfi; and from thence, in a short time, recovered from the Greek emperor almost the whole of Puglia and Calabria, over which provinces, in the time of pope Nicholas II. his brother Robert Guiscard was sovereign. Robert having had many disputes with his nephews for the inheritance of these states, requested the influence of the pope to settle them; which his holiness was very willing to afford, being anxious to make a friend of Robert, to defend himself against the emperor of Germany and the insolence of the Roman people, which indeed shortly followed, when, at the instance of Gregory, he drove Henry from Rome, and subdued the people. Robert was succeeded by his sons Roger and William, to whose dominion not only was Naples added, but all the places interjacent as far as Rome, and afterward Sicily, of which Roger became sovereign; but, upon William going to Constantinople, to marry the daughter of the emperor, his dominions were wrested from him by his brother Roger. Inflated with so great an acquisition, Roger first took the title of king of Italy, but afterward contented himself with that of king of Puglia and Sicily. He was the first who established and gave that name to this kingdom, which still retains its ancient boundaries, although its sovereigns have been of many families and countries. Upon the failure of the Normans, it came to the Germans, after these to the French, then to the Aragonese, and it is now held by the Flemish. About this time Urban II. became pope and excited the hatred of the Romans. As he did not think himself safe even in Italy, on account of the disunion which prevailed, he directed his thoughts to a generous enterprise.

With his whole clergy he went into France, and at Anvers, having drawn together a vast multitude of people, delivered an oration against the infidels, which so excited the minds of his audience, that they determined to undertake the conquest of Asia from the Saracens; which enterprise, with all those of a similar nature, were afterward called crusades, because the people who joined in them bore upon their armor and apparel the figure of a cross. The leaders were Godfrey, Eustace, and Baldwin of Bouillon, counts of Boulogne, and Peter, a hermit celebrated for his prudence and sagacity. Many kings and people joined them, and contributed money; and many private persons fought under them at their own expense; so great was the influence of religion in those days upon the minds of men, excited by the example of those who were its principal ministers. The proudest successes attended the beginning of this enterprise; for the whole of Asia Minor, Syria, and part of Egypt, fell under the power of the Christians. To commemorate these events the order of the Knights of Jerusalem was created, which still continues, and holds the island of Rhodes--the only obstacle to the power of the Mohammedans. The same events gave rise to the order of the Knights Templars, which, after a short time, on account of their shameless practices, was dissolved. Various fortunes attended the crusaders in the course of their enterprises, and many nations and individuals became celebrated accordingly. The kings of France and England joined them, and, with the Venetians, Pisans, and Genoese, acquired great reputation, till the time of Saladin, when, by whose talents, and the disagreement of the Christians among themselves, the crusaders were robbed of all that glory which they had at first acquired; and, after ninety years, were driven from those places which they had so honorably and happily recovered. After the death of Urban, Pascal II. became pope, and the empire was under the dominion of Henry IV. who came to Rome pretending friendship for the pontiff but afterward put his holiness and all his clergy in prison; nor did he release them till it was conceded that he should dispose of the churches of Germany according to his own pleasure. About this time, the Countess Matilda died, and made the church heir to all her territories. After the deaths of Pascal and Henry IV. many popes and emperors followed, till the papacy was occupied by Alexander III. and the empire by Frederick, surnamed Barbarossa. The popes during this period had met with many difficulties from the people of Rome and the emperors; and in the time of Barbarossa they were much increased. Frederick possessed military talent, but was so full of pride that he would not submit to the pontiff. However, at his election to the empire he came to Rome to be crowned, and returned peaceably to Germany, where he did not long remain in the same mind, but came again into Italy to subdue certain places in Lombardy, which did not obey him. It happened at this time that the cardinal St. Clement, of a Roman family, separated from Alexander, and was made pope by some of the cardinals. The Emperor Frederick, being encamped at Cerma, Alexander complained to him of the anti-pope, and received for answer, that they were both to go to him, and, having heard each side, he would determine which was the true pope. This reply displeased Alexander; and, as he saw the emperor was inclined to favor the anti-pope, he excommunicated him, and then fled to Philip, king of France. Frederick, in the meantime, carrying on the war in Lombardy, destroyed Milan; which caused the union of Verona, Padua, and Vicenza against him for their common defense. About the same period the anti-pope died, and Frederick set up Guido of Cremona, in his stead. The Romans, from the absence of the pope, and from the emperor being in Lombardy, had reacquired some authority in Rome, and proceeded to recover the obedience of those places which had been subject to them. And as the people of Tusculum refused to submit to their authority, they proceeded against them with their whole force; but these, being assisted by Frederick, routed the Roman army with such dreadful slaughter, that Rome was never after either so populous or so rich. Alexander now returned to the city, thinking he could be safe there on account of the enmity subsisting between the Romans and the emperor, and from the enemies which the latter had in Lombardy. But Frederick, setting aside every other consideration, led his forces and encamped before Rome; and Alexander fled to William, king of Puglia, who had become hair of that kingdom after the death of Roger. Frederick, however, withdrew from Rome on account of the plague which then prevailed, and returned to Germany. The cities of Lombardy in league against him, in order to command Pavia and Tortona, which adhered to the imperial party, built a city, to be their magazine in time of war, and named in Alexandria, in honor of the pope and in contempt of Frederick.

Guido the anti-pope died, and Giovanni of Fermo was appointed in his stead, who, being favored by the imperialists, lived at Montefiascone. Pope Alexander being at Tusculum, whither he had been called by the inhabitants, that with his authority he might defend them from the Romans, ambassadors came to him from Henry, king of England, to signify that he was not blamable for the death of Thomas a Becket, archbishop of Canterbury, although public report had slandered him with it. On this the pope sent two cardinals to England, to inquire into the truth of the matter; and although they found no actual charge against the king, still, on account of the infamy of the crime, and for not having honored the archbishop so much as he deserved, the sentence against the king of England was, that having called together the barons of his empire, he should upon oath before them affirm his innocence; that he should immediately send two hundred soldiers to Jerusalem, paid for one year; that, before the end of three years, he should himself proceed thither with as large an army as he could draw together; that his subjects should have the power of appealing to Rome when they thought proper; and that he should annul whatever acts had been passed in his kingdom unfavorable to ecclesiastical rule. These terms were all accepted by Henry; and thus a great king submitted to a sentence that in our day a private person would have been ashamed of. But while the pope exercised so great authority over distant princes, he could not compel obedience from the Romans themselves, or obtain their consent that he should remain in Rome, even though he promised to intermeddle only with ecclesiastical affairs.

About this time Frederick returned to Italy, and while he was preparing to carry on new wars against the pope, his prelates and barons declared that they would abandon him unless he reconciled himself with the church; so that he was obliged to go and submit to the pope at Venus, where a pacification was effected, but in which the pope deprived the emperor of all authority over Rome, and named William, king of Sicily and Puglia, a coadjutor with him. Frederick, unable to exist without war, joined the crusaders in Asia, that he might exercise that ambition against Mohammed, which he could not gratify against the vicars of Christ. And being near the river Cydnus, tempted by the clearness of its waters, bathed therein, took cold, and died. Thus the river did a greater favor to the Mohammedans than the pope's excommunications had done to the Christians; for the latter only checked his pride, while the former finished his career. Frederick being dead, the pope had now only to suppress the contumacy of the Romans; and, after many disputes concerning the creation of consuls, it was agreed that they should elect them as they had been accustomed to do, but that these should not undertake the office, till they had first sworn to be faithful to the church. This agreement being made, Giovanni the anti-pope took refuge in Mount Albano, where he shortly afterward died. William, king of Naples, died about the same time, and the pope intended to occupy that kingdom on the ground that the king had left only a natural son named Tancred. But the barons would not consent, and wished that Tancred should be king. Celestine III., the then pope, anxious to snatch the kingdom from the hands of Tancred, contrived that Henry, son of Frederick should be elected emperor, and promised him the kingdom on the condition that he should restore to the church all the places that had belonged to her. To facilitate this affair, he caused Gostanza, a daughter of William, who had been placed in a monastery and was now old, to be brought from her seclusion and become the wife of Henry. Thus the kingdom of Naples passed from the Normans, who had been the founders of it, to the Germans. As soon as the affairs of Germany were arranged, the Emperor Henry came into Italy with Gostanza his wife, and a son about four years of age named Frederick; and, as Tancred was now dead, leaving only an infant named Roger, he took possession of the kingdom without much difficulty. After some years, Henry died in Sicily, and was succeeded in the kingdom by Frederick, and in the empire by Otho, duke of Saxony, who was elected through the influence of Innocent III. But as soon as he had taken the crown, contrary to the general expectation, he became an enemy of the pope, occupied Romagna, and prepared to attack the kingdom. On this account the pope excommunicated him; he was abandoned by every one, and the electors appointed Frederick, king of Naples, emperor in his stead. Frederick came to Rome for his coronation; but the pope, being afraid of his power, would not crown him, and endeavored to withdraw him from Italy as he had done Otho. Frederick returned to Germany in anger, and, after many battles with Otho, at length conquered him. Meanwhile, Innocent died, who, besides other excellent works, built the hospital of the Holy Ghost at Rome. He was succeeded by Honorius III., in whose time the religious orders of St. Dominic and St. Francis were founded, 1218. Honorius crowned Frederick, to whom Giovanni, descended from Baldwin, king of Jerusalem, who commanded the remainder of the Christian army in Asia and still held that title, gave a daughter in marriage; and, with her portion, conceded to him the title to that kingdom: hence it is that every king of Naples is called king of Jerusalem.

CHAPTER V

The state of Italy--Beginning of the greatness of the house of Este--Guelphs and Ghibellines--Death of the Emperor Frederick II.--Manfred takes possession of the kingdom of Naples--Movements of the Guelphs and Ghibellines in Lombardy--Charles of Anjou invested by the pope with the kingdom of Naples and Sicily--Restless policy of the popes--Ambitious views of pope Nicholas III.--Nephews of the popes--Sicilian vespers--The Emperor Rodolph allows many cities to purchase their independence--Institution of the jubilee--The popes at Avignon.

At this time the states of Italy were governed in the following manner: the Romans no longer elected consuls, but instead of them, and with the same powers, they appointed one senator, and sometimes more. The league which the cities of Lombardy had formed against Frederick Barbarossa still continued, and comprehended Milan, Brescia, Mantua, and the greater number of the cities of Romagna, together with Verona, Vicenza, Padua, and Trevisa. Those which took part with the emperor, were Cremona, Bergamo, Parma, Reggio, and Trento. The other cities and fortresses of Lombardy, Romagna, and the march of Trevisa, favored, according to their necessities, sometimes one party, sometimes the other.

In the time of Otho III. there had come into Italy a man called Ezelin, who, remaining in the country, had a son, and he too had a son named Ezelin. This person, being rich and powerful, took part with Frederick, who, as we have said, was at enmity with the pope; Frederick, at the instigation and with the assistance of Ezelin, took Verona and Mantua, destroyed Vicenza, occupied Padua, routed the army of the united cities, and then directed his course towards Tuscany. Ezelin, in the meantime, had subdued the whole of the Trevisian March, but could not prevail against Ferrara, which was defended by Azone da Este and the forces which the pope had in Lombardy; and, as the enemy were compelled to withdraw, the pope gave Ferrara in fee to this Azone, from whom are descended those who now govern that city. Frederick halted at Pisa, desirous of making himself lord of Tuscany; but, while endeavoring to discover what friends and foes he had in that province, he scattered so many seeds of discord as occasioned the ruin of Italy; for the factions of the Guelphs and Ghibellines multiplied,--those who supported the church taking the name of Guelphs, while the followers of the emperor were called Ghibellines, these names being first heard at Pistoia. Frederick, marching from Pisa, assailed and wasted the territories of the church in a variety of ways; so that the pope, having no other remedy, unfurled against him the banner of the cross, as his predecessor had done against the Saracens. Frederick, that he might be suddenly abandoned by his people, as Frederick Barbarossa and others had been, took into his pay a number of Saracens; and to bind them to him, and establish in Italy a firm bulwark against the church, without fear of papal maledictions, he gave them Nocera in the kingdom of Naples, that, having a refuge of their own, they might be placed in greater security. The pontificate was now occupied by Innocent IV., who, being in fear of Frederick, went to Genoa, and thence to France, where he appointed a council to be held at Lyons, where it was the intention of Frederick to attend, but he was prevented by the rebellion of Parma: and, being repulsed, he went into Tuscany, and from thence to Sicily, where he died, leaving his son Conrad in Suabia; and in Puglia, Manfred, whom he had created duke of Benevento, born of a concubine. Conrad came to take possession of the kingdom, and having arrived at Naples, died, leaving an infant son named Corradino, who was then in Germany. On this account Manfred occupied the state, first as guardian of Corradino, but afterward, causing a report to be circulated that Corradino had died, made himself king, contrary to the wishes of both the pope and the Neapolitans, who, however, were obliged to submit.

While these things were occurring in the kingdom of Naples, many movements took place in Lombardy between the Guelphs and the Ghibellines. The Guelphs were headed by a legate of the pope; and the Ghibelline party by Ezelin, who possessed nearly the whole of Lombardy beyond the Po; and, as in the course of the war Padua rebelled, he put to death twelve thousand of its citizens. But before its close he himself was slain, in the eightieth year of his age, and all the places he had held became free. Manfred, king of Naples, continued those enmities against the church which had been begun by his ancestors, and kept the pope, Urban IV., in continual alarm; so that, in order to subdue him, Urban summoned the crusaders, and went to Perugia to await their arrival. Seeing them few and slow in their approach, he found that more able assistance was necessary to conquer Manfred. He therefore sought the favor of France; created Louis of Anjou, the king's brother, sovereign of Naples and Sicily, and excited him to come into Italy to take possession of that kingdom. But before Charles came to Rome the pope died, and was succeeded by Clement IV., in whose time he arrived at Ostia, with thirty galleys, and ordered that the rest of his forces should come by land. During his abode at Rome, the citizens, in order to attach him to them, made him their senator, and the pope invested him with the kingdom, on condition that he should pay annually to the church the sum of fifty thousand ducats; and it was decreed that, from thenceforth, neither Charles nor any other person, who might be king of Naples, should be emperor also. Charles marched against Manfred, routed his army, and slew him near Benevento, and then became sovereign of Sicily and Naples. Corradino, to whom, by his father's will, the state belonged, having collected a great force in Germany, marched into Italy against Charles, with whom he came to an engagement at Tagliacozzo, was taken prisoner while endeavoring to escape, and being unknown, put to death.

Italy remained in repose until the pontificate of Adrian V. Charles, being at Rome and governing the city by virtue of his office of senator, the pope, unable to endure his power, withdrew to Viterbo, and solicited the Emperor Rodolph to come into Italy and assist him. Thus the popes, sometimes in zeal for religion, at others moved by their own ambition, were continually calling in new parties and exciting new disturbances. As soon as they had made a prince powerful, they viewed him with jealousy and sought his ruin; and never allowed another to rule the country, which, from their own imbecility, they were themselves unable to govern. Princes were in fear of them; for, fighting or running away, the popes always obtained the advantage, unless it happened they were entrapped by deceit, as occurred to Boniface VIII., and some others, who under pretense of friendship, were ensnared by the emperors. Rodolph did not come into Italy, being detained by the war in which he was engaged with the king of Bohemia. At this time Adrian died, and Nicholas III., of the Orsini family, became pontiff. He was a bold, ambitious man; and being resolved at any event to diminish the power of Charles, induced the Emperor Rodolph to complain that he had a governor in Tuscany favorable to the Guelphic faction, who after the death of Manfred had been replaced by him. Charles yielded to the emperor and withdrew his governor, and the pope sent one of his nephews, a cardinal, as governor for the emperor, who, for the honor done him, restored Romagna to the church, which had been taken from her by his predecessors, and the pope made Bertoldo Orsino duke of Romagna. As Nicholas now thought himself powerful enough to oppose Charles, he deprived him of the office of senator, and made a decree that no one of royal race should ever be a senator in Rome. It was his intention to deprive Charles of Sicily, and to this end he entered into a secret negotiation with Peter, king of Aragon, which took effect in the following papacy. He also had the design of creating two kings out of his family, the one in Lombardy, the other in Tuscany, whose power would defend the church from the Germans who might design to come into Italy, and from the French, who were in the kingdom of Naples and Sicily. But with these thoughts he died. He was the first pope who openly exhibited his own ambition; and, under pretense of making the church great, conferred honors and emolument upon his own family. Previous to his time no mention is made of the nephews or families of any pontiff, but future history is full of them; nor is there now anything left for them to attempt, except the effort to make the papacy hereditary. True it is, the princes of their creating have not long sustained their honors; for the pontiffs, being generally of very limited existence, did not get their plants properly established.

To Nicholas succeeded Martin IV., of French origin, and consequently favorable to the party of Charles, who sent him assistance against the rebellion of Romagna; and while they were encamped at Furli, Guido Bonatto, an astrologer, contrived that at an appointed moment the people should assail the forces of the king, and the plan succeeding, all the French were taken and slain. About this period was also carried into effect the plot of Pope Nicholas and Peter, king of Aragon, by which the Sicilians murdered all the French that were in that island; and Peter made himself sovereign of it, saying, that it belonged to him in the right of his wife Gostanza, daughter of Manfred. But Charles, while making warlike preparations for the recovery of Sicily, died, leaving a son, Charles II., who was made prisoner in Sicily, and to recover his liberty promised to return to his prison, if within three years he did not obtain the pope's consent that the kings of Aragon should be invested with the kingdom of Sicily.

The Emperor Rodolph, instead of coming into Italy, gave the empire the advantage of having done so, by sending an ambassador, with authority to make all those cities free which would redeem themselves with money. Many purchased their freedom, and with liberty changed their mode of living. Adolpho of Saxony succeeded to the empire; and to the papacy, Pietro del Murrone, who took the name of Celestino; but, being a hermit and full of sanctity, after six months renounced the pontificate, and Boniface VIII. was elected.

After a time the French and Germans left Italy, and the country remained wholly in the hands of the Italians; but Providence ordained that the pope, when these enemies were withdrawn, should neither establish nor enjoy his authority, and raised two very powerful families in Rome, the Colonnesi and the Orsini, who with their arms, and the proximity of their abode, kept the pontificate weak. Boniface then determined to destroy the Colonnesi, and, besides excommunicating, endeavored to direct the weapons of the church against them. This, although it did them some injury, proved more disastrous to the pope; for those arms which from attachment to the faith performed valiantly against its enemies, as soon as they were directed against Christians for private ambition, ceased to do the will of those who wished to wield them. And thus the too eager desire to gratify themselves, caused the pontiffs by degrees to lose their military power. Besides what is just related, the pope deprived two cardinals of the Colonnesi family of their office; and Sciarra, the head of the house, escaping unknown, was taken by corsairs of Catalonia and put to the oar; but being afterward recognized at Marseilles, he was sent to Philip, king of France, who had been excommunicated and deprived of the kingdom. Philip, considering that in a war against the pontiff he would either be a loser or run great hazards, had recourse to deception, and simulating a wish to come to terms, secretly sent Sciarra into Italy, who, having arrived at Anagnia, where his holiness then resided, assembled a few friends, and in the night took him prisoner. And although the people of Anagnia set him at liberty shortly after, yet from grief at the injury he died mad. Boniface was founder of the jubilee in 1300, and fixed that it should be celebrated at each revolution of one hundred years. In those times various troubles arose between the Guelph and Ghibelline factions; and the emperors having abandoned Italy, many places became free, and many were occupied by tyrants. Pope Benedict restored the scarlet hat to the cardinals of the Colonnesi family, and reblessed Philip, king of France. He was succeeded by Clement V., who, being a Frenchman, removed the papal court to Avignon in 1305.

CHAPTER VI

The Emperor Henry comes into Italy--The Florentines take the part of the pope--The Visconti originate the duchy of Milan--Artifice of Maffeo Visconti against the family of de la Torre--Giovanni Galeazzo Visconti, first duke of Milan--The Emperor Louis in Italy--John, king of Bohemia, in Italy--League against the king of Bohemia and the pope's legate--Origin of Venice--Liberty of the Venetians confirmed by Pepin and the Greek emperor--Greatness of Venice--Decline of Venice--Discord between the pope and the emperor--Giovanna, queen of Naples--Rienzi--The jubilee reduced to fifty years--Succession of the duke of Milan--Cardinal Egidio the pope's legate--War between the Genoese and the Venetians.

At this time, Charles II. of Naples died, and was succeeded by his son Robert. Henry of Luxemburg had been elected to the empire, and came to Rome for his coronation, although the pope was not there. His coming occasioned great excitement in Lombardy; for he sent all the banished to their homes, whether they were Guelphs or Ghibellines; and in consequence of this, one faction endeavoring to drive out the other, the whole province was filled with war; nor could the emperor with all his endeavors abate its fury. Leaving Lombardy by way of Genoa, he came to Pisa, where he endeavored to take Tuscany from King Robert; but not being successful, he went to Rome, where he remained only a few days, being driven away by the Orsini with the consent of King Robert, and returned to Pisa; and that he might more securely make war upon Tuscany, and wrest the country from the hands of the king, he caused it to be assailed by Frederick, monarch of Sicily. But when he was in hope of occupying Tuscany and robbing the king of Naples of his dominions, he died, and was succeeded by Louis of Bavaria. About the same period, John XXII. attained the papacy, during whose time the emperor still continued to persecute the Guelphs and the church, but they were defended by Robert and the Florentines. Many wars took place in Lombardy between the Visconti and the Guelphs, and in Tuscany between Castruccio of Lucca and the Florentines. As the family of Visconti gave rise to the duchy of Milan, one of the five principalities which afterward governed Italy, I shall speak of them from a rather earlier date.

Milan, upon recovering from the ruin into which she had been thrown by Frederick Barbarossa, in revenge for her injuries, joined the league formed by the Lombard cities for their common defense; this restrained him, and for awhile preserved alive the interests of the church in Lombardy. In the course of the wars which followed, the family of La Torre became very potent in that city, and their reputation increased so long as the emperor possessed little authority in the province. But Frederick II. coming into Italy, and the Ghibelline party, by the influence of Ezelin having grown powerful, seeds of the same faction sprang up in all the cities. In Milan were the Visconti, who expelled the La Torres; these, however, did not remain out, for by agreement between the emperor and the pope they were restored to their country. For when the pope and his court removed to France, and the emperor, Henry of Luxemburg, came into Italy, with the pretext of going to Rome for his crown, he was received in Milan by Maffeo Visconti and Guido della Torre, who were then the heads of these families. But Maffeo, designing to make use of the emperor for the purpose of expelling Guido, and thinking the enterprise not difficult, on account of the La Torre being of the contrary faction to the imperial, took occasion, from the remarks which the people made of the uncivil behavior of the Germans, to go craftily about and excite the populace to arm themselves and throw off the yoke of these barbarians. When a suitable moment arrived, he caused a person in whom he confided to create a tumult, upon which the people took arms against the Germans. But no sooner was the mischief well on foot, than Maffeo, with his sons and their partisans, ran to Henry, telling him that all the disturbance had been occasioned by the La Torre family, who, not content to remain peaceably in Milan, had taken the opportunity to plunder him, that they might ingratiate themselves with the Guelphs of Italy and become princes in the city; they then bade him be of good cheer, for they, with their party, whenever he wished it, were ready to defend him with their lives. Henry, believing all that Maffeo told him, joined his forces to those of the Visconti, and attacking the La Torre, who were in various parts of the city endeavoring to quell the tumult, slew all upon whom they could lay hands, and having plundered the others of their property, sent them into exile. By this artifice, Maffeo Visconti became a prince of Milan. Of him remained Galeazzo and Azzo; and, after these, Luchino and Giovanni. Giovanni became archbishop of Milan; and of Luchino, who died before him, were left Bernabo and Galeazzo; Galeazzo, dying soon after, left a son called the Count of Virtu, who after the death of the archbishop, contrived the murder of his uncle, Bernabo, became prince of Milan, and was the first who had the title of duke. The duke left Filippo and Giovanmaria Angelo, the latter of whom being slain by the people of Milan, the state fell to Filippo; but he having no male heir, Milan passed from the family of Visconti to that of Sforza, in the manner to be related hereafter.

But to return to the point from which we deviated. The Emperor Louis, to add to the importance of his party and to receive the crown, came into Italy; and being at Milan, as an excuse for taking money of the Milanese, he pretended to make them free and to put the Visconti in prison; but shortly afterwards he released them, and, having gone to Rome, in order to disturb Italy with less difficulty, he made Piero della Corvara anti-pope, by whose influence, and the power of the Visconti, he designed to weaken the opposite faction in Tuscany and Lombardy. But Castruccio died, and his death caused the failure of the emperor's purpose; for Pisa and Lucca rebelled. The Pisans sent Piero della Corvara a prisoner to the pope in France, and the emperor, despairing of the affairs of Italy, returned to Germany. He had scarcely left, before John king of Bohemia came into the country, at the request of the Ghibellines of Brescia, and made himself lord of that city and of Bergamo. And as his entry was with the consent of the pope, although he feigned the contrary, the legate of Bologna favored him, thinking by this means to prevent the return of the emperor. This caused a change in the parties of Italy; for the Florentines and King Robert, finding the legate was favorable to the enterprises of the Ghibellines, became foes of all those to whom the legate and the king of Bohemia were friendly. Without having regard for either faction, whether Guelph or Ghibelline, many princes joined them, of whom, among others, were the Visconti, the Della Scala, Filippo Gonzao of Mantua, the Carrara, and those of Este. Upon this the pope excommunicated them all. The king, in fear of the league, went to collect forces in his own country, and having returned with a large army, still found his undertaking a difficult one; so, seeing his error, he withdrew to Bohemia, to the great displeasure of the legate, leaving only Reggio and Modena guarded, and Parma in the care of Marsilio and Piero de' Rossi, who were the most powerful men in the city. The king of Bohemia being gone, Bologna joined the league; and the leaguers divided among themselves the four cities which remained of the church faction. They agreed that Parma should pertain to the Della Scalla; Reggio to the Gonzaga; Modena to the family of Este, and Lucca to the Florentines. But in taking possession of these cities, many disputes arose which were afterward in a great measure settled by the Venetians. Some, perhaps, will think it a species of impropriety that we have so long deferred speaking of the Venetians, theirs being a republic, which, both on account of its power and internal regulations, deserves to be celebrated above any principality of Italy. But that this surprise may cease when the cause is known, I shall speak of their city from a more remote period; that everyone may understand what were their beginnings, and the causes which so long withheld them from interfering in the affairs of Italy.

When Attila, king of the Huns, besieged Aquileia, the inhabitants, after defending themselves a long time, began to despair of effecting their safety, and fled for refuge to several uninhabited rocks, situated at the point of the Adriatic Sea, now called the Gulf of Venice, carrying with them whatever movable property they possessed. The people of Padua, finding themselves in equal danger, and knowing that, having became master of Aquileia, Attila would next attack themselves, also removed with their most valuable property to a place on the same sea, called Rivo Alto, to which they brought their women, children, and aged persons, leaving the youth in Padua to assist in her defense. Besides these, the people of Monselice, with the inhabitants of the surrounding hills, driven by similar fears, fled to the same rocks. But after Attila had taken Aquileia, and destroyed Padua, Monselice, Vicenza, and Verona, the people of Padua and others who were powerful, continued to inhabit the marshes about Rivo Alto; and, in like manner, all the people of the province anciently called Venetia, driven by the same events, became collected in these marshes. Thus, under the pressure of necessity, they left an agreeable and fertile country to occupy one sterile and unwholesome. However, in consequence of a great number of people being drawn together into a comparatively small space, in a short time they made those places not only habitable, but delightful; and having established among themselves laws and useful regulations, enjoyed themselves in security amid the devastations of Italy, and soon increased both in reputation and strength. For, besides the inhabitants already mentioned, many fled to these places from the cities of Lombardy, principally to escape from the cruelties of Clefis king of the Lombards, which greatly tended to increase the numbers of the new city; and in the conventions which were made between Pepin, king of France, and the emperor of Greece, when the former, at the entreaty of the pope, came to drive the Lombards out of Italy, the duke of Benevento and the Venetians did not render obedience to either the one or the other, but alone enjoyed their liberty. As necessity had led them to dwell on sterile rocks, they were compelled to seek the means of subsistence elsewhere; and voyaging with their ships to every port of the ocean, their city became a depository for the various products of the world, and was itself filled with men of every nation.

For many years the Venetians sought no other dominion than that which tended to facilitate their commercial enterprises, and thus acquired many ports in Greece and Syria; and as the French had made frequent use of their ships in voyages to Asia, the island of Candia was assigned to them in recompense for these services. While they lived in this manner, their name spread terror over the seas, and was held in veneration throughout Italy. This was so completely the case, that they were generally chosen to arbitrate in controversies between the states, as occurred in the difference between the Colleagues, on account of the cities they had divided among themselves; which being referred to the Venetians, they awarded Brescia and Bergamo to the Visconti. But when, in the course of time, urged by their eagerness for dominion, they had made themselves masters of Padua, Vicenza, Trevisa, and afterward of Verona, Bergamo, and Brescia, with many cities in Romagna and the kingdom of Naples, other nations were impressed with such an opinion of their power, that they were a terror, not only to the princes of Italy, but to the ultramontane kings. These states entered into an alliance against them, and in one day wrested from them the provinces they had obtained with so much labor and expense; and although they have in latter times reacquired some portions, still possessing neither power nor reputation, like all the other Italian powers, they live at the mercy of others.

Benedict XII. having attained the pontificate and finding Italy lost, fearing, too, that the emperor would assume the sovereignty of the country, determined to make friends of all who had usurped the government of those cities which had been accustomed to obey the emperor; that they might have occasion to dread the latter, and unite with himself in the defense of Italy. To this end he issued a decree, confirming to all the tyrants of Lombardy the places they had seized. After making this concession the pope died, and was succeeded by Clement VI. The emperor, seeing with what a liberal hand the pontiff had bestowed the dominions of the empire, in order to be equally bountiful with the property of others, gave to all who had assumed sovereignty over the cities or territories of the church, the imperial authority to retain possession of them. By this means Galeotto Malatesti and his brothers became lords of Rimino, Pesaro, and Fano; Antonio da Montefeltro, of the Marca and Urbino; Gentile da Varano, of Camerino; Guido di Polenta, of Ravenna; Sinibaldo Ordelaffi, of Furli and Cesena; Giovanni Manfredi, of Faenza; Lodovico Alidossi, of Imola; and besides these, many others in divers places. Thus, of all the cities, towns, or fortresses of the church, few remained without a prince; for she did not recover herself till the time of Alexander VI., who, by the ruin of the descendants of these princes, restored the authority of the church.

The emperor, when he made the concession before named, being at Tarento, signified an intention of going into Italy. In consequence of this, many battles were fought in Lombardy, and the Visconti became lords of Parma. Robert king of Naples, now died, leaving only two grandchildren, the issue of his sons Charles, who had died a considerable time before him. He ordered that the elder of the two, whose name was Giovanna or Joan, should be heiress of the kingdom, and take for her husband Andrea, son of the king of Hungary, his grandson. Andrea had not lived with her long, before she caused him to be murdered, and married another cousin, Louis, prince of Tarento. But Louis, king of Hungary, and brother of Andrea, in order to avenge his death, brought forces into Italy, and drove Queen Joan and her husband out of the kingdom.

At this period a memorable circumstance took place at Rome. Niccolo di Lorenzo, often called Rienzi or Cola di Rienzi, who held the office of chancellor at Campidoglio, drove the senators from Rome and, under the title of tribune, made himself the head of the Roman republic; restoring it to its ancient form, and with so great reputation of justice and virtue, that not only the places adjacent, but the whole of Italy sent ambassadors to him. The ancient provinces, seeing Rome arise to new life, again raised their heads, and some induced by hope, others by fear, honored him as their sovereign. But Niccolo, notwithstanding his great reputation, lost all energy in the very beginning of his enterprise; and as if oppressed with the weight of so vast an undertaking, without being driven away, secretly fled to Charles, king of Bohemia, who, by the influence of the pope, and in contempt of Louis of Bavaria, had been elected emperor. Charles, to ingratiate himself with the pontiff, sent Niccolo to him, a prisoner. After some time, in imitation of Rienzi, Francesco Baroncegli seized upon the tribunate of Rome, and expelled the senators; and the pope, as the most effectual means of repressing him, drew Niccolo from his prison, sent him to Rome, and restored to him the office of tribune; so that he reoccupied the state and put Francesco to death; but the Colonnesi becoming his enemies, he too, after a short time, shared the same fate, and the senators were again restored to their office. The king of Hungary, having driven out Queen Joan, returned to his kingdom; but the pope, who chose to have the queen in the neighborhood of Rome rather than the king, effected her restoration to the sovereignty, on the condition that her husband, contenting himself with the title of prince of Tarento, should not be called king. Being the year 1350, the pope thought that the jubilee, appointed by Boniface VIII. to take place at the conclusion of each century, might be renewed at the end of each fifty years; and having issued a decree for the establishment of it, the Romans, in acknowledgment of the benefit, consented that he should send four cardinals to reform the government of the city, and appoint senators according to his own pleasure. The pope again declared Louis of Tarento, king, and in gratitude for the benefit, Queen Joan gave Avignon, her inheritance, to the church. About this time Luchino Visconti died, and his brother the archbishop, remaining lord of Milan, carried on many wars against Tuscany and his neighbors, and became very powerful. Bernabo and Galeazzo, his nephews, succeeded him; but Galeazzo soon after died, leaving Giovan Galeazzo, who shared the state with Bernabo. Charles, king of Bohemia, was then emperor, and the pontificate was occupied by Innocent VI., who sent Cardinal Egidio, a Spaniard, into Italy. He restored the reputation of the church, not only in Rome and Romagna, but throughout the whole of Italy; he recovered Bologna from the archbishop of Milan, and compelled the Romans to accept a foreign senator appointed annually by the pope. He made honorable terms with the Visconti, and routed and took prisoner, John Agut, an Englishman, who with four thousand English had fought on the side of the Ghibellines in Tuscany. Urban V., hearing of so many victories, resolved to visit Italy and Rome, whither also the emperor came; after remaining a few months, he returned to the kingdom of Bohemia, and the pope to Avignon. On the death of Urban, Gregory XI. was created pope; and, as the Cardinal Egidio was dead, Italy again recommenced her ancient discords, occasioned by the union of the other powers against the Visconti; and the pope, having first sent a legate with six thousand Bretons, came in person and established the papal court at Rome in 1376, after an absence of seventy-one years in France. To Gregory XI., succeeded Urban VI., but shortly afterwards Clement VI. was elected at Fondi by ten cardinals, who declared the appointment of Urban irregular. At this time, the Genoese threw off the yoke of the Visconti under whom they had lived many years; and between them and the Venetians several important battles were fought for the island of Tenedos. Although the Genoese were for a time successful, and held Venice in a state of siege during many months, the Venetians were at length victorious; and by the intervention of the pope, peace was made in the year 1381. In these wars, artillery was first used, having been recently invented by the Dutch.

CHAPTER VII

Schism in the church--Ambitious views of Giovanni Galeazzo Visconti--The pope and the Romans come to an agreement--Boniface IX. introduces the practice of Annates--Disturbance in Lombardy--The Venetians acquire dominion on terra firma--Differences between the pope and the people of Rome--Council of Pisa--Council of Constance--Filippo Visconti recovers his dominion--Giovanna II. of Naples--Political condition of Italy.

A schism having thus arisen in the church, Queen Joan favored the schismatic pope, upon which Urban caused Charles of Durazzo, descended from the kings of Naples, to undertake the conquest of her dominions. Having succeeded in his object, she fled to France, and he assumed the sovereignty. The king of France, being exasperated, sent Louis of Anjou into Italy to recover the kingdom for the queen, to expel Urban from Rome, and establish the anti-pope. But in the midst of this enterprise Louis died, and his people being routed returned to France. In this conjuncture the pope went to Naples, where he put nine cardinals into prison for having taken the part of France and the anti-pope. He then became offended with the king, for having refused to make his nephew prince of Capua; and pretending not to care about it, requested he would grant him Nocera for his habitation, but, having fortified it, he prepared to deprive the king of his dominions. Upon this the king pitched his camp before the place, and the pope fled to Naples, where he put to death the cardinals whom he had imprisoned. From thence he proceeded to Rome, and, to acquire influence, created twenty-nine cardinals. At this time Charles, king of Naples, went to Hungary, where, having been made king, he was shortly afterward killed in battle, leaving a wife and two children at Naples. About the same time Giovanni Galeazzo Visconti murdered Bernabo his uncle and took the entire sovereignty upon himself; and, not content with being duke of Milan and sovereign of the whole of Lombardy, designed to make himself master of Tuscany; but while he was intent upon occupying the province with the ultimate view of making himself king of Italy, he died. Boniface IX. succeeded Urban VI. The anti-pope, Clement VI., also died, and Benedict XIII. was appointed his successor.

Many English, Germans, and Bretons served at this period in the armies of Italy, commanded partly by those leaders who had from time to time authority in the country, and partly by such as the pontiffs sent, when they were at Avignon. With these warriors the princes of Italy long carried on their wars, till the coming of Lodovico da Cento of Romagna, who formed a body of Italian soldiery, called the Company of St. George, whose valor and discipline soon caused the foreign troops to fall into disrepute, and gave reputation to the native forces of the country, of which the princes afterward availed themselves in their wars with each other. The pope, Boniface IX., being at enmity with the Romans, went to Scesi, where he remained till the jubilee of 1400, when the Romans, to induce him to return to the city, consented to receive another foreign senator of his appointing, and also allowed him to fortify the castle of Saint Angelo: having returned upon these conditions, in order to enrich the church, he ordained that everyone, upon vacating a benefice, should pay a year's value of it to the Apostolic Chamber.

After the death of Giovanni Galeazzo, duke of Milan, although he left two children, Giovanmaria and Filippo, the state was divided into many parts, and in the troubles which ensued Giovanmaria was slain. Filippo remained some time in the castle of Pavia, from which, through the fidelity and virtue of the castellan, he escaped. Among others who occupied cities possessed by his father, was Guglielmo della Scala, who, being banished, fell into the hands of Francesco de Carrera, lord of Padua, by whose means he recovered the state of Verona, in which he only remained a short time, for he was poisoned, by order of Francesco, and the city taken from him. These things occasioned the people of Vicenza, who had lived in security under the protection of the Visconti, to dread the greatness of the lord of Padua, and they placed themselves under the Venetians, who, engaging in arms with him, first took Verona and then Padua.

At this time Pope Boniface died, and was succeeded by Innocent VII. The people of Rome supplicated him to restore to them their fortresses and their liberty; but as he would not consent to their petition, they called to their assistance Ladislaus, king of Naples. Becoming reconciled to the people, the pope returned to Rome, and made his nephew Lodovico count of La Marca. Innocent soon after died, and Gregory XII. was created, upon the understanding to renounce the papacy whenever the anti-pope would also renounce it. By the advice of the cardinals, in order to attempt the reunion of the church, Benedict, the anti-pope, came to Porto Venere, and Gregory to Lucca, where they made many endeavors, but effected nothing. Upon this, the cardinals of both the popes abandoned them, Benedict going to Spain, and Gregory to Rimini. On the other hand, the cardinals, with the favor of Balthazar Cossa, cardinal and legate of Bologna, appointed a council at Pisa, where they created Alexander V., who immediately excommunicated King Ladislaus, and invested Louis of Anjou with the kingdom; this prince, with the Florentines, Genoese, and Venetians, attacked Ladislaus and drove him from Rome. In the head of the war Alexander died, and Balthazar Cossa succeeded him, with the title of John XXIII. Leaving Bologna, where he was elected, he went to Rome, and found there Louis of Anjou, who had brought the army from Provence, and coming to an engagement with Ladislaus, routed him. But by the mismanagement of the leaders, they were unable to prosecute the victory, so that the king in a short time gathered strength and retook Rome. Louis fled to Provence, the pope to Bologna; where, considering how he might diminish the power of Ladislaus, he caused Sigismund, king of Hungary, to be elected emperor, and advised him to come to Italy. Having a personal interview at Mantua, they agreed to call a general council, in which the church should be united; and having effected this, the pope thought he should be fully enabled to oppose the forces of his enemies.

At this time there were three popes, Gregory, Benedict, and Giovanni, which kept the church weak and in disrepute. The city of Constance, in Germany, was appointed for the holding of the council, contrary to the expectation of Pope John. And although the death of Ladislaus had removed the cause which induced the pope to call the council, still, having promised to attend, he could not refuse to go there. In a few months after his arrival at Constance he discovered his error, but it was too late; endeavoring to escape, he was taken, put into prison, and compelled to renounce the papacy. Gregory, one of the anti-popes, sent his renunciation; Benedict, the other, refusing to do the same, was condemned as a heretic; but, being abandoned by his cardinals, he complied, and the council elected Oddo, of the Colonnesi family, pope, by the title of Martin V. Thus the church was united under one head, after having been divided by many pontiffs.

Filippo Visconti was, as we have said, in the fortress of Pavia. But Fazino Cane, who in the affairs of Lombardy had become lord of Vercelli, Alessandria, Novara, and Tortona, and had amassed great riches, finding his end approach, and having no children, left his wife Beatrice heiress of his estates, and arranged with his friends that a marriage should be effected between her and Filippo. By this union Filippo became powerful, and reacquired Milan and the whole of Lombardy. By way of being grateful for these numerous favors, as princes commonly are, he accused Beatrice of adultery and caused her to be put to death. Finding himself now possessed of greater power, he began to think of warring with Tuscany and of prosecuting the designs of Giovanni Galeazzo, his father.

Ladislaus, king of Naples, at his death, left to his sister Giovanna the kingdom and a large army, under the command of the principal leaders of Italy, among the first of whom was Sforza of Cotignuola, reputed by the soldiery of that period to be a very valiant man. The queen, to shun the disgrace of having kept about her person a certain Pandolfello, whom she had brought up, took for her husband Giacopo della Marca, a Frenchman of the royal line, on the condition that he should be content to be called Prince of Tarento, and leave to her the title and government of the kingdom. But the soldiery, upon his arrival in Naples, proclaimed him king; so that between the husband and the wife wars ensued; and although they contended with varying success, the queen at length obtained the superiority, and became an enemy of the pope. Upon this, in order to reduce her to necessity, and that she might be compelled to throw herself into his lap, Sforza suddenly withdrew from her service without giving her any pervious notice of his intention to do so. She thus found herself at once unarmed, and not having any other source, sought the assistance of Alfonzo, king of Aragon and Sicily, adopted him as her son, and engaged Braccio of Montone as her captain, who was of equal reputation in arms with Sforza, and inimical to the pope, on account of his having taken possession of Perugia and some other places belonging to the church. After this, peace was made between the queen and the pontiff; but King Alfonzo, expecting she would treat him as she had her husband, endeavored secretly to make himself master of the strongholds; but, possessing acute observation, she was beforehand with him, and fortified herself in the castle of Naples. Suspicions increasing between them, they had recourse to arms, and the queen, with the assistance of Sforza, who again resumed her service, drove Alfonzo out of Naples, deprived him of his succession, and adopted Louis of Anjou in his stead. Hence arose new contests between Braccio, who took the part of Alfonzo, and Sforza, who defended the cause of the queen. In the course of the war, Sforza was drowned in endeavoring to pass the river Pescara; the queen was thus again unarmed, and would have been driven out of the kingdom, but for the assistance of Filippo Visconti, the duke of Milan, who compelled Alfonzo to return to Aragon. Braccio, undaunted at the departure of Alfonzo, continued the enterprise against the queen, and besieged L'Aquila; but the pope, thinking the greatness of Braccio injurious to the church, received into his pay Francesco, the son of Sforza, who went in pursuit of Braccio to L'Aquila, where he routed and slew him. Of Braccio remained Oddo, his son, from whom the pope took Perugia, and left him the state of Montone alone; but he was shortly afterward slain in Romagna, in the service of the Florentines; so that of those who had fought under Braccio, Niccolo Piccinino remained of greatest reputation.

Having continued our general narration nearly to the period which we at first proposed to reach, what remains is of little importance, except the war which the Florentines and Venetians carried on against Filippo duke of Milan, of which an account will be given when we speak particularly of Florence. I shall, therefore, continue it no further, briefly explaining the condition of Italy in respect of her princes and her arms, at the period to which we have now come. Joan II. held Naples, La Marca, the Patrimony and Romagna; some of these places obeyed the church, while others were held by vicars or tyrants, as Ferrara, Modena, and Reggio, by those of the House of Este; Faenza by the Manfredi; Imola by the Alidossi; Furli by the Ordelaffi; Rimini and Psaro by the Malatesti; and Camerino by those of Varano. Part of Lombardy was subject to the Duke Filippo, part to the Venetians; for all those who had held single states were set aside, except the House of Gonzaga, which ruled in Mantua. The greater part of Tuscany was subject to the Florentines. Lucca and Sienna alone were governed by their own laws; Lucca was under the Guinigi; Sienna was free. The Genoese, being sometimes free, at others, subject to the kings of France or the Visconti, lived unrespected, and may be enumerated among the minor powers.

None of the principal states were armed with their own proper forces. Duke Filippo kept himself shut up in his apartments, and would not allow himself to be seen; his wars were managed by commissaries. The Venetians, when they directed their attention to terra firma, threw off those arms which had made them terrible upon the seas, and falling into the customs of Italy, submitted their forces to the direction of others. The practice of arms being unsuitable to priests or women, the pope and Queen Joan of Naples were compelled by necessity to submit to the same system which others practiced from defect of judgment. The Florentines also adopted the same custom, for having, by their frequent divisions, destroyed the nobility, and their republic being wholly in the hands of men brought up to trade, they followed the usages and example of others.

Thus the arms of Italy were either in the hands of the lesser princes, or of men who possessed no state; for the minor princes did not adopt the practice of arms from any desire of glory, but for the acquisition of either property or safety. The others (those who possessed no state) being bred to arms from their infancy, were acquainted with no other art, and pursued war for emolument, or to confer honor upon themselves. The most noticed among the latter were Carmignola, Francesco Sforza, Niccolo Piccinino the pupil of Braccio, Agnolo della Pergola, Lorenzo di Micheletto Attenduli, il Tartaglia, Giacopaccio, Cecolini da Perugia, Niccolo da Tolentino, Guido Torello, Antonia dal Ponte ad Era, and many others. With these, were those lords of whom I have before spoken, to which may be added the barons of Rome, the Colonnesi and the Orsini, with other lords and gentlemen of the kingdoms of Naples and Lombardy, who, being constantly in arms, had such an understanding among themselves, and so contrived to accommodate things to their own convenience, that of those who were at war, most commonly both sides were losers; and they had made the practice of arms so totally ridiculous, that the most ordinary leader, possessed of true valor, would have covered these men with disgrace, whom, with so little prudence, Italy honored.

With these idle princes and such contemptible arms, my history must, therefore, be filled; to which, before I descend, it will be necessary, as was at first proposed, to speak of the origin of Florence, that it may be clearly understood what was the state of the city in those times, and by what means, through the labours of a thousand years, she became so imbecile.

BOOK II

CHAPTER I

The custom of ancient republics to plant colonies, and the advantage of it--Increased population tends to make countries more healthy--Origin of Florence--Aggrandizement of Florence--Origin of the name of Florence--Destruction of Florence by Totila--The Florentines take Fiesole--The first division in Florence, and the cause of it--Buondelmonti--Buondelmonti slain--Guelphs and Ghibellines in Florence--Guelphic families--Ghibelline families--The two factions come to terms.

Among the great and wonderful institutions of the republics and principalities of antiquity that have now gone into disuse, was that by means of which towns and cities were from time to time established; and there is nothing more worthy the attention of a great prince, or of a well-regulated republic, or that confers so many advantages upon a province, as the settlement of new places, where men are drawn together for mutual accommodation and defense. This may easily be done, by sending people to reside in recently acquired or uninhabited countries. Besides causing the establishment of new cities, these removals render a conquered country more secure, and keep the inhabitants of a province properly distributed. Thus, deriving the greatest attainable comfort, the inhabitants increase rapidly, are more prompt to attack others, and defend themselves with greater assurance. This custom, by the unwise practice of princes and republics, having gone into desuetude, the ruin and weakness of territories has followed; for this ordination is that by which alone empires are made secure, and countries become populated. Safety is the result of it; because the colony which a prince establishes in a newly acquired country, is like a fortress and a guard, to keep the inhabitants in fidelity and obedience. Neither can a province be wholly occupied and preserve a proper distribution of its inhabitants without this regulation; for all districts are not equally healthy, and hence some will abound to overflowing, while others are void; and if there be no method of withdrawing them from places in which they increase too rapidly, and planting them where they are too few the country would soon be wasted; for one part would become a desert, and the other a dense and wretched population. And, as nature cannot repair this disorder, it is necessary that industry should effect it, for unhealthy localities become wholesome when a numerous population is brought into them. With cultivation the earth becomes fruitful, and the air is purified with fires--remedies which nature cannot provide. The city of Venice proves the correctness of these remarks. Being placed in a marshy and unwholesome situation, it became healthy only by the number of industrious individuals who were drawn together. Pisa, too, on account of its unwholesome air, was never filled with inhabitants, till the Saracens, having destroyed Genoa and rendered her rivers unnavigable, caused the Genoese to migrate thither in vast numbers, and thus render her populous and powerful. Where the use of colonies is not adopted, conquered countries are held with great difficulty; districts once uninhabited still remain so, and those which populate quickly are not relieved. Hence it is that many places of the world, and particularly in Italy, in comparison of ancient times, have become deserts. This has wholly arisen and proceeded from the negligence of princes, who have lost all appetite for true glory, and of republics which no longer possess institutions that deserve praise. In ancient times, by means of colonies, new cities frequently arose, and those already begun were enlarged, as was the case with Florence, which had its beginning from Fiesole, and its increase from colonies.

It is exceedingly probable, as Dante and Giovanni Villani show, that the city of Fiesole, being situate upon the summit of the mountain, in order that her markets might be more frequented, and afford greater accommodation for those who brought merchandise, would appoint the place in which to told them, not upon the hill, but in the plain, between the foot of the mountain and the river Arno. I imagine these markets to have occasioned the first erections that were made in those places, and to have induced merchants to wish for commodious warehouses for the reception of their goods, and which, in time, became substantial buildings. And afterward, when the Romans, having conquered the Carthaginians, rendered Italy secure from foreign invasion, these buildings would greatly increase; for men never endure inconveniences unless some powerful necessity compels them. Thus, although the fear of war induces a willingness to occupy places strong and difficult of access, as soon as the cause of alarm is removed, men gladly resort to more convenient and easily attainable localities. Hence, the security to which the reputation of the Roman republic gave birth, caused the inhabitants, having begun in the manner described, to increase so much as to form a town, this was at first called the Villa Arnina. After this occurred the civil wars between Marius and Sylla; then those of Caesar, and Pompey; and next those of the murderers of Caesar, and the parties who undertook to avenge his death. Therefore, first by Sylla, and afterward by the three Roman citizens, who, having avenged the death of Caesar, divided the empire among themselves, colonies were sent to Fiesole, which, either in part or in whole, fixed their habitations in the plain, near to the then rising town. By this increase, the place became so filled with dwellings, that it might with propriety be enumerated among the cities of Italy.

There are various opinions concerning the derivation of the word Florentia. Some suppose it to come from Florinus, one of the principal persons of the colony; others think it was originally not Florentia, but Fluentia, and suppose the word derived from fluente, or flowing of the Arno; and in support of their opinion, adduce a passage from Pliny, who says, "the Fluentini are near the flowing of the Arno." This, however, may be incorrect, for Pliny speaks of the locality of the Florentini, not of the name by which they were known. And it seems as if the word Fluentini were a corruption, because Frontinus and Cornelius Tacitus, who wrote at nearly the same period as Pliny, call them Florentia and Florentini; for, in the time of Tiberius, they were governed like the other cities of Italy. Besides, Cornelius refers to the coming of ambassadors from the Florentines, to beg of the emperor that the waters of the Chiane might not be allowed to overflow their country; and it is not at all reasonable that the city should have two names at the same time. Therefore I think that, however derived, the name was always Florentia, and that whatever the origin might be, it occurred under the Roman empire, and began to be noticed by writers in the times of the first emperors.

When the Roman empire was afflicted by the barbarians, Florence was destroyed by Totila, king of the Ostrogoths; and after a period of two hundred and fifty years, rebuilt by Charlemagne; from whose time, till the year 1215, she participated in the fortune of the rest of Italy; and, during this period, first the descendants of Charles, then the Berengarii, and lastly the German emperors, governed her, as in our general treatise we have shown. Nor could the Florentines, during those ages, increase in numbers, or effect anything worthy of memory, on account of the influence of those to whom they were subject. Nevertheless, in the year 1010, upon the feast of St. Romolo, a solemn day with the Fiesolani, they took and destroyed Fiesole, which must have been performed either with the consent of the emperors, or during the interim from the death of one to the creation of his successor, when all assumed a larger share of liberty. But then the pontiffs acquired greater influence, and the authority of the German emperors was in its wane, all the places of Italy governed themselves with less respect for the prince; so that, in the time of Henry III. the mind of the country was divided between the emperor and the church. However, the Florentines kept themselves united until the year 1215, rendering obedience to the ruling power, and anxious only to preserve their own safety. But, as the diseases which attack our bodies are more dangerous and mortal in proportion as they are delayed, so Florence, though late to take part in the sects of Italy, was afterward the more afflicted by them. The cause of her first division is well known, having been recorded by Dante and many other writers; I shall, however, briefly notice it.

Among the most powerful families of Florence were the Buondelmonti and the Uberti; next to these were the Amidei and the Donati. Of the Donati family there was a rich widow who had a daughter of exquisite beauty, for whom, in her own mind, she had fixed upon Buondelmonti, a young gentleman, the head of the Buondelmonti family, as her husband; but either from negligence, or, because she thought it might be accomplished at any time, she had not made known her intention, when it happened that the cavalier betrothed himself to a maiden of the Amidei family. This grieved the Donati widow exceedingly; but she hoped, with her daughter's beauty, to disturb the arrangement before the celebration of the marriage; and from an upper apartment, seeing Buondelmonti approach her house alone, she descended, and as he was passing she said to him, "I am glad to learn you have chosen a wife, although I had reserved my daughter for you;" and, pushing the door open, presented her to his view. The cavalier, seeing the beauty of the girl, which was very uncommon, and considering the nobility of her blood, and her portion not being inferior to that of the lady whom he had chosen, became inflamed with such an ardent desire to possess her, that, not thinking of the promise given, or the injury he committed in breaking it, or of the evils which his breach of faith might bring upon himself, said, "Since you have reserved her for me, I should be very ungrateful indeed to refuse her, being yet at liberty to choose;" and without any delay married her. As soon as the fact became known, the Amidei and the Uberti, whose families were allied, were filled with rage, and having assembled with many others, connections of the parties, they concluded that the injury could not be tolerated without disgrace, and that the only vengeance proportionate to the enormity of the offence would be to put Buondelmonti to death. And although some took into consideration the evils that might ensue upon it, Mosca Lamberti said, that those who talk of many things effect nothing, using that trite and common adage, Cosa fatta capo ha. Thereupon, they appointed to the execution of the murder Mosca himself, Stiatti Uberti, Lambertuccio Amidei, and Oderigo Fifanti, who, on the morning of Easter day, concealed themselves in a house of the Amidei, situate between the old bridge and St. Stephen's, and as Buondelmonti was passing upon a white horse, thinking it as easy a matter to forget an injury as reject an alliance, he was attacked by them at the foot of the bridge, and slain close by a statue of Mars. This murder divided the whole city; one party espousing the cause of the Buondelmonti, the other that of the Uberti; and as these families possessed men and means of defense, they contended with each other for many years, without one being able to destroy the other.

Florence continued in these troubles till the time of Frederick II., who, being king of Naples, endeavored to strengthen himself against the church; and, to give greater stability to his power in Tuscany, favored the Uberti and their followers, who, with his assistance, expelled the Buondelmonti; thus our city, as all the rest of Italy had long time been, became divided into Guelphs and Ghibellines; and as it will not be superfluous, I shall record the names of the families which took part with each faction. Those who adopted the cause of the Guelphs were the Buondelmonti, Nerli, Rossi, Frescobaldi, Mozzi, Bardi, Pulci, Gherardini, Foraboschi,

Bagnesi, Guidalotti, Sacchetti, Manieri, Lucardesi, Chiaramontesi, Compiobbesi, Cavalcanti, Giandonati, Gianfigliazzi, Scali, Gualterotti, Importuni, Bostichi, Tornaquinci, Vecchietti, Tosinghi, Arrigucci, Agli, Sizi, Adimari, Visdomini, Donati, Passi, della Bella, Ardinghi, Tedaldi, Cerchi. Of the Ghibelline faction were the Uberti, Manelli, Ubriachi, Fifanti, Amidei, Infangati, Malespini, Scolari, Guidi, Galli, Cappiardi, Lamberti, Soldanieri, Cipriani, Toschi, Amieri, Palermini, Migliorelli, Pigli, Barucci, Cattani, Agolanti, Brunelleschi, Caponsacchi, Elisei, Abati, Tidaldini, Giuochi, and Galigai. Besides the noble families on each side above enumerated, each party was joined by many of the higher ranks of the people, so that the whole city was corrupted with this division. The Guelphs being expelled, took refuge in the Upper Val d'Arno, where part of their castles and strongholds were situated, and where they strengthened and fortified themselves against the attacks of their enemies. But, upon the death of Frederick, the most unbiased men, and those who had the greatest authority with the people, considered that it would be better to effect the reunion of the city, than, by keeping her divided, cause her ruin. They therefore induced the Guelphs to forget their injuries and return, and the Ghibellines to lay aside their jealousies and receive them with cordiality.

CHAPTER II

New form of government in Florence--Military establishments--The greatness of Florence--Movements of the Ghibellines--Ghibellines driven out of the city--Guelphs routed by the forces of the king of Naples--Florence in the power of the king of Naples--Project of the Ghibellines to destroy Florence opposed by Farinata degli Uberti--Adventures of the Guelphs of Florence--The pope gives his standard to the Guelphs--Fears of the Ghibellines and their preparations for the defense of their power--Establishment of trades' companies, and their authority--Count Guido Novello expelled--He goes to Prato--The Guelphs restored to the city--The Ghibellines quit Florence--The Florentines reform the government in favor of the Guelphs--The pope endeavors to restore the Ghibellines and excommunicates Florence--Pope Nicholas III. endeavors to abate the power of Charles king of Naples.

Being united, the Florentines thought the time favorable for the ordination of a free government, and that it would be desirable to provide their means of defense before the new emperor should acquire strength. They therefore divided the city into six parts, and elected twelve citizens, two for each sixth, to govern the whole. These were called Anziani, and were elected annually. To remove the cause of those enmities which had been observed to arise from judicial decisions, they provided two judges from some other state,--one called captain of the people, the other podesta, or provost,--whose duty it was to decide in cases, whether civil or criminal, which occurred among the people. And as order cannot be preserved without a sufficient force for the defense of it, they appointed twenty banners in the city, and seventy-six in the country, upon the rolls of which the names of all the youth were armed; and it was ordered that everyone should appear armed, under his banner, whenever summoned, whether by the captain of the people or the Anziani. They had ensigns according to the kind of arms they used, the bowmen being under one ensign, and the swordsmen, or those who carried a target, under another; and every year, upon the day of Pentecost, ensigns were given with great pomp to the new men, and new leaders were appointed for the whole establishment. To give importance to their armies, and to serve as a point of refuge for those who were exhausted in the fight, and from which, having become refreshed, they might again make head against the enemy, they provided a large car, drawn by two oxen, covered with red cloth, upon which was an ensign of white and red. When they intended to assemble the army, this car was brought into the New Market, and delivered with pomp to the heads of the people. To give solemnity to their enterprises, they had a bell called Martinella, which was rung during a whole month before the forces left the city, in order that the enemy might have time to provide for his defense; so great was the virtue then existing among men, and with so much generosity of mind were they governed, that as it is now considered a brave and prudent act to assail an unprovided enemy, in those days it would have been thought disgraceful, and productive only of a fallacious advantage. This bell was also taken with the army, and served to regulate the keeping and relief of guard, and other matters necessary in the practice of war.

With these ordinations, civil and military, the Florentines established their liberty. Nor is it possible to imagine the power and authority Florence in a short time acquired. She became not only the head of Tuscany, but was enumerated among the first cities of Italy, and would have attained greatness of the most exalted kind, had she not been afflicted with the continual divisions of her citizens. They remained under the this government ten years, during which time they compelled the people of Pistoria, Arezzo, and Sienna, to enter into league with them; and returning with the army from Sienna, they took Volterra, destroyed some castles, and led the inhabitants to Florence. All these enterprises were effected by the advice of the Guelphs, who were much more powerful than the Ghibellines, for the latter were hated by the people as well on account of their haughty bearing while in power, during the time of Frederick, as because the church party was in more favor than that of the emperor; for with the aid of the church they hoped to preserve their liberty, but, with the emperor, they were apprehensive of losing it.

The Ghibellines, in the meantime, finding themselves divested of authority, could not rest, but watched for an occasion of repossessing the government; and they thought the favorable moment come, when they found that Manfred, son of Frederick, had made himself sovereign of Naples, and reduced the power of the church. They, therefore, secretly communicated with him, to resume the management of the state, but could not prevent their proceedings from coming to the knowledge of the Anziani, who immediately summoned the Uberti to appear before them; but instead of obeying, they took arms and fortified themselves in their houses. The people, enraged at this, armed themselves, and with the assistance of the Guelphs, compelled them to quit the city, and, with the whole Ghibelline party, withdraw to Sienna. They then asked assistance of Manfred king of Naples, and by the able conduct of Farinata degli Uberti, the Guelphs were routed by the king's forces upon the river Arbia, with so great slaughter, that those who escaped, thinking Florence lost, did not return thither, but sought refuge at Lucca.

Manfred sent the Count Giordano, a man of considerable reputation in arms, to command his forces. He after the victory, went with the Ghibellines to Florence, and reduced the city entirely to the king's authority, annulling the magistracies and every other institution that retained any appearance of freedom. This injury, committed with little prudence, excited the ardent animosity of the people, and their enmity against the Ghibellines, whose ruin it eventually caused, was increased to the highest pitch. The necessities of the kingdom compelling the Count Giordano to return to Naples, he left at Florence as regal vicar the Count Guido Novallo, lord of Casentino, who called a council of Ghibellines at Empoli. There it was concluded, with only one dissenting voice, that in order to preserve their power in Tuscany, it would be necessary to destroy Florence, as the only means of compelling the Guelphs to withdraw their support from the party of the church. To this so cruel a sentence, given against such a noble city, there was not a citizen who offered any opposition, except Farinata degli Uberti, who openly defended her, saying he had not encountered so many dangers and difficulties, but in the hope of returning to his country; that he still wished for what he had so earnestly sought, nor would he refuse the blessing which fortune now presented, even though by using it, he were to become as much an enemy of those who thought otherwise, as he had been of the Guelphs; and that no one need be afraid the city would occasion the ruin of their country, for he hoped that the valor which had expelled the Guelphs, would be sufficient to defend her. Farinata was a man of undaunted resolution, and excelled greatly in military affairs: being the head of the Ghibelline party, and in high estimation with Manfred, his authority put a stop to the discussion, and induced the rest to think of some other means of preserving their power.

The Lucchese being threatened with the anger of the count, for affording refuge to the Guelphs after the battle of the Arbia, could allow them to remain no longer; so leaving Lucca, they went to Bologna, from whence they were called by the Guelphs of Parma against the Ghibellines of that city, where, having overcome the enemy, the possessions of the latter were assigned to them; so that having increased in honors and riches, and learning that Pope Clement had invited Charles of Anjou to take the kingdom from Manfred, they sent ambassadors to the pope to offer him their services. His holiness not only received them as friends, but gave them a standard upon which his insignia were wrought. It was ever after borne by the Guelphs in battle, and is still used at Florence. Charles having taken the kingdom from Manfred, and slain him, to which success the Guelphs of Florence had contributed, their party became more powerful, and that of the Ghibellines proportionately weaker. In consequence of this, those who with Count Novello governed the city, thought it would be advisable to attach to themselves, with some concession, the people whom they had previously aggravated with every species of injury; but these remedies which, if applied before the necessity came would have been beneficial, being offered when they were no longer considered favors, not only failed of producing any beneficial results to the donors, but hastened their ruin. Thinking, however, to win them to their interests, they restored some of the honors of which they had deprived them. They elected thirty-six citizens from the higher rank of the people, to whom, with two cavaliers, knights or gentlemen, brought from Bologna, the reformation of the government of the city was confided. As soon as they met, they classed the whole of the people according to their arts or trades, and over each art appointed a magistrate, whose duty was to distribute justice to those placed under him. They gave to each company or trade a banner, under which every man was expected to appear armed, whenever the city required it. These arts were at first twelve, seven major and five minor. The minor arts were afterward increased to fourteen, so that the whole made, as at present, twenty-one. The thirty-six reformers also effected other changes for the common good.

Count Guido proposed to lay a tax upon the citizens for the support of the soldiery; but during the discussion found so much difficulty, that he did not dare to use force to obtain it; and thinking he had now lost the government, called together the leaders of the Ghibellines, and they determined to wrest from the people those powers which they had with so little prudence conceded. When they thought they had sufficient force, the thirty-six being assembled, they caused a tumult to be raised, which so alarmed them that they retired to their houses, when suddenly the banners of the Arts were unfurled, and many armed men drawn to them. These, learning that Count Guido and his followers were at St. John's, moved toward the Holy Trinity, and chose Giovanni Soldanieri for their leader. The count, on the other hand, being informed where the people were assembled, proceeded in that direction; nor did the people shun the fight, for, meeting their enemies where now stands the residence of the Tornaquinci, they put the count to flight, with the loss of many of his followers. Terrified with this result, he was afraid his enemies would attack him in the night, and that his own party, finding themselves beaten, would murder him. This impression took such hold of his mind that, without attempting any other remedy, he sought his safety rather in flight than in combat, and, contrary to the advice of the rectors, went with all his people to Prato. But, on finding himself in a place of safety, his fears fled; perceiving his error he wished to correct it, and on the following day, as soon as light appeared, he returned with his people to Florence, to enter the city by force which he had abandoned in cowardice. But his design did not succeed; for the people, who had had difficulty in expelling him, kept him out with facility; so that with grief and shame he went to the Casentino, and the Ghibellines withdrew to their villas.

The people being victorious, by the advice of those who loved the good of the republic, determined to reunite the city, and recall all the citizens as well Guelph as Ghibelline, who yet remained without. The Guelphs returned, after having been expelled six years; the recent offences of the Ghibellines were forgiven, and themselves restored to their country. They were, however, most cordially hated, both by the people and the Guelphs, for the latter could not forget their exile, and the former but too well remembered their tyranny when they were in power; the result was, that the minds of neither party became settled.

While affairs were in this state at Florence, a report prevailed that Corradino, nephew of Manfred, was coming with a force from Germany, for the conquest of Naples; this gave the Ghibellines hope of recovering power, and the Guelphs, considering how they should provide for their security, requested assistance from Charles for their defense, in case of the passage of Corradino. The coming of the forces of Charles rendered the Guelphs insolent, and so alarmed the Ghibellines that they fled the city, without being driven out, two days before the arrival of the troops.

The Ghibellines having departed, the Florentines reorganized the government of the city, and elected twelve men who, as the supreme power, were to hold their magistracy two months, and were not called Anziani or "ancients," but Buono Uomini or "good men." They also formed a council of eighty citizens, which they called the Credenza. Besides these, from each sixth, thirty citizens were chosen, who, with the Credenza and the twelve Buono Uomini, were called the General Council. They also appointed another council of one hundred and twenty citizens, elected from the people and the nobility, to which all those things were finally referred that had undergone the consideration of the other councils, and which distributed the offices of the republic. Having formed this government, they strengthened the Guelphic party by appointing its friends to the principal offices of state, and a variety of other measures, that they might be enabled to defend themselves against the Ghibellines, whose property they divided into three parts, one of which was applied to the public use, another to the Capitani, and the third was assigned to the Guelphs, in satisfaction of the injuries they had received. The pope, too, in order to keep Tuscany in the Guelphic interest, made Charles imperial vicar over the province. While the Florentines, by virtue of the new government, preserved their influence at home by laws, and abroad with arms, the pope died, and after a dispute, which continued two years, Gregory X. was elected, being then in Syria, where he had long lived; but not having witnessed the working of parties, he did not estimate them in the manner his predecessors had done, and passing through Florence on his way to France, he thought it would be the office of a good pastor to unite the city, and so far succeeded that the Florentines consented to receive the Syndics of the Ghibellines in Florence to consider the terms of their recall. They effected an agreement, but the Ghibellines without were so terrified that they did not venture to return. The pope laid the whole blame upon the city, and being enraged excommunicated her, in which state of contumacy she remained as long as the pontiff lived; but was reblessed by his successor Innocent V.

The pontificate was afterward occupied by Nicholas III. of the Orsini family. It has to be remarked that it was invariably the custom of the popes to be jealous of those whose power in Italy had become great, even when its growth had been occasioned by the favors of the church; and as they always endeavored to destroy it, frequent troubles and changes were the result. Their fear of a powerful person caused them to increase the influence of one previously weak; his becoming great caused him also to be feared, and his being feared made them seek the means of destroying him. This mode of thinking and operation occasioned the kingdom of Naples to be taken from Manfred and given to Charles, but as soon as the latter became powerful his ruin was resolved upon. Actuated by these motives, Nicholas III. contrived that, with the influence of the emperor, the government of Tuscany should be taken from Charles, and Latino his legate was therefore sent into the province in the name of the empire.

CHAPTER III

Changes in Florence--The Ghibellines recalled--New form of government in Florence--The Signory created--Victory over the Aretins--The Gonfalonier of Justice created--Ubaldo Ruffoli the first Gonfalonier--Giano della Bella--New reform by his advice--Giano della Bella becomes a voluntary exile--Dissensions between the people and the nobility--The tumults composed--Reform of Government--Public buildings--The prosperous state of the city.

Florence was at this time in a very unhappy condition; for the great Guelphic families had become insolent, and set aside the authority of the magistrates; so that murders and other atrocities were daily committed, and the perpetrators escaped unpunished, under the protection of one or other of the nobility. The leaders of the people, in order to restrain this insolence, determined to recall those who had been expelled, and thus gave the legate an opportunity of uniting the city. The Ghibellines returned, and, instead of twelve governors, fourteen were appointed, seven for each party, who held their office one year, and were to be chosen by the pope. The Florentines lived under this government two years, till the pontificate of Martin, who restored to Charles all the authority which had been taken from him by Nicholas, so that parties were again active in Tuscany; for the Florentines took arms against the emperor's governor, and to deprive the Ghibellines of power, and restrain the nobility, established a new form of government. This was in the year 1282, and the companies of the Arts, since magistrates had been appointed and colors given to them, had acquired so great influence, that of their own authority they ordered that, instead of fourteen citizens, three should be appointed and called Priors, to hold the government of the republic two months, and chosen from either the people or the nobility. After the expiration of the first magistracy they were augmented to six, that one might be chosen from each sixth of the city, and this number was preserved till the year 1342, when the city was divided into quarters, and the Priors became eight, although upon some occasions during the interim they were twelve.

This government, as will be seen hereafter, occasioned the ruin of the nobility; for the people by various causes excluded them from all participation in it, and then trampled upon them without respect. The nobles at first, owing to their divisions among themselves, made no opposition; and each being anxious to rob the other of influence in the state, they lost it altogether. To this government a palace was given, in which they were to reside constantly, and all requisite officers were appointed; it having been previously the custom of councils and magistrates to assemble in churches. At first they were only called Priors, but to increase their distinction the word signori, or lords, was soon afterward adopted. The Florentines remained for some time in domestic quiet, during which they made war with the Aretins for having expelled the Guelphs, and obtained a complete victory over them at Campaldino. The city being increased in riches and population, it was found expedient to extend the walls, the circle of which was enlarged to the extent it at present remains, although its diameter was previously only the space between the old bridge and the church of St. Lorenzo.

Wars abroad and peace within the city had caused the Guelph and Ghibelline factions to become almost extinct; and the only party feeling which seemed occasionally to glow, was that which naturally exists in all cities between the higher classes and the people; for the latter, wishing to live in conformity with the laws, and the former to be themselves the rulers of the people, it was not possible for them to abide in perfect amity together. This ungenial disposition, while their fear of the Ghibellines kept them in order, did not discover itself, but no sooner were they subdued than it broke forth, and not a day passed without some of the populace being injured, while the laws were insufficient to procure redress, for every noble with his relations and friends defended himself against the forces of the Priors and the Capitano. To remedy this evil, the leaders of the Arts' companies ordered that every Signory at the time of entering upon the duties of office should appoint a Gonfalonier of Justice, chosen from the people, and place a thousand armed men at his disposal divided into twenty companies of fifty men each, and that he, with his gonfalon or banner and his forces, should be ready to enforce the execution of the laws whenever called upon, either by the Signors themselves or the Capitano. The first elected to this high office was Ubaldo Ruffoli. This man unfurled his gonfalon, and destroyed the houses of the Galletti, on account of a member of that family having slain one of the Florentine people in France. The violent animosities among the nobility enabled the companies of the Arts to establish this law with facility; and the former no sooner saw the provision which had been made against them than they felt the acrimonious spirit with which it was enforced. At first it impressed them with greater terror, but they soon after returned to their accustomed insolence, for one or more of their body always making part of the Signory, gave them opportunities of impeding the Gonfalonier, so that he could not perform the duties of his office. Besides this, the accuser always required a witness of the injury he had received, and no one dared to give evidence against the nobility. Thus in a short time Florence again fell into the same disorders as before, and the tyranny exercised against the people was as great as ever; for the decisions of justice were either prevented or delayed, and sentences were not carried into execution.

In this unhappy state, the people not knowing what to do, Giano della Bella, of a very noble family, and a lover of liberty, encouraged the heads of the Arts to reform the constitution of the city; and by his advice it was ordered that the Gonfalonier should reside with the Priors, and have four thousand men at his command. They deprived the nobility of the right to sit in the Signory. They condemned the associates of a criminal to the same penalty as himself, and ordered that public report should be taken as evidence. By these laws, which were called the ordinations of justice, the people acquired great influence, and Giano della Bella not a small share of trouble; for he was thoroughly hated by the great, as the destroyer of their power, while the opulent among the people envied him, for they thought he possessed too great authority. This became very evident upon the first occasion that presented itself.

It happened that a man from the class of the people was killed in a riot, in which several of the nobility had taken a part, and among the rest Corso Donati, to whom, as the most forward of the party, the death was attributed. He was, therefore, taken by the captain of the people, and whether he was really innocent of the crime or the Capitano was afraid of condemning him, he was acquitted. This acquittal displeased the people so much, that, seizing their arms, they ran to the house of Giano della Bella, to beg that he would compel the execution of those laws which he had himself made. Giano, who wished Corso to be punished, did not insist upon their laying down their arms, as many were of opinion he ought to have done, but advised them to go to the Signory, complain of the fact, and beg that they would take it into consideration. The people, full of wrath, thinking themselves insulted by the Capitano and abandoned by Giano della Bella, instead of going to the Signory went to the palace of the Capitano, of which they made themselves masters, and plundered it.

This outrage displeased the whole city, and those who wished the ruin of Giano laid the entire blame upon him; and as in the succeeding Signory there was an enemy of his, he was accused to the Capitano as the originator of the riot. While the case was being tried, the people took arms, and, proceeding to his house, offered to defend him against the Signory and his enemies. Giano, however, did not wish to put this burst of popular favor to the proof, or trust his life to the magistrates, for he feared the malignity of the latter and the instability of the former; so, in order to remove an occasion for his enemies to injure him, or his friends to offend the laws, he determined to withdraw, deliver his countrymen from the fear they had of him, and, leaving the city which at his own charge and peril he had delivered from the servitude of the great, become a voluntary exile.

After the departure of Giano della Bella the nobility began to entertain hopes of recovering their authority; and judging their misfortune to have arisen from their divisions, they sent two of their body to the Signory, which they thought was favorable to them, to beg they would be pleased to moderate the severity of the laws made against them. As soon as their demand became known, the minds of the people were much excited; for they were afraid the Signors would submit to them; and so, between the desire of the nobility and the jealousy of the people, arms were resorted to. The nobility were drawn together in three places: near the church of St. John, in the New Market, and in the Piazza of the Mozzi, under three leaders, Forese Adimari, Vanni de Mozzi, and Geri Spini. The people assembled in immense numbers, under their ensigns, before the palace of the Signory, which at that time was situated near St. Procolo; and, as they suspected the integrity of the Signory, they added six citizens to their number to take part in the management of affairs.

While both parties were preparing for the fight, some individuals, as well of the people as of the nobility, accompanied by a few priests of respectable character, mingled among them for the purpose of effecting a pacification, reminding the nobility that their loss of power, and the laws which were made against them, had been occasioned by their haughty conduct, and the mischievous tendency of their proceedings; that resorting to arms to recover by force what they had lost by illiberal measures and disunion, would tend to the destruction of their country and increase the difficulties of their own position; that they should bear in mind that the people, both in riches, numbers, and hatred, were far stronger than they; and that their nobility, on account of which they assumed to be above others, did not contribute to win battles, and would be found, when they came to arms, to be but an empty name, and insufficient to defend them against so many. On the other hand, they reminded the people that it is not prudent to wish always to have the last blow; that it is an injudicious step to drive men to desperation, for he who is without hope is also without fear; that they ought not to forget that in the wars the nobility had always done honor to the country, and therefore it was neither wise nor just to pursue them with so much bitterness; and that although the nobility could bear with patience the loss of the supreme magistracy, they could not endure that, by the existing laws, it should be in the power of everyone to drive them from their country; and, therefore, it would be well to qualify these laws, and, in furtherance of so good a result, be better to lay down their arms than, trusting to numbers, try the fortune of a battle; for it is often seen that the many are overcome by the few. Variety of opinion was found among the people; many wished to decide the question by arms at once, for they were assured it would have to be done some time, and that it would be better to do so then than delay till the enemy had acquired greater strength; and that if they thought a mitigation of the laws would satisfy them, that then they would be glad to comply, but that the pride of the nobility was so great they would not submit unless they were compelled. To many others, who were more peaceable and better disposed, it appeared a less evil to qualify the laws a little than to come to battle; and their opinion prevailing, it was provided that no accusation against the nobility could be received unless supported with sufficient testimony.

Although arms were laid aside, both parties remained full of suspicion, and each fortified itself with men and places of strength. The people reorganized the government, and lessened the number of its officers, to which measure they were induced by finding that the Signors appointed from the families, of which the following were the heads, had been favorable to the nobility, viz.: the Mancini, Magalotti, Altoviti, Peruzzi, and Cerretani. Having settled the government, for the greater magnificence and security of the Signory, they laid the foundation of their palace; and to make space for the piazza, removed the houses that had belonged to the Uberti; they also at the same period commenced the public prisons. These buildings were completed in a few years; nor did our city ever enjoy a greater state of prosperity than in those times: filled with men of great wealth and reputation; possessing within her walls 30,000 men capable of bearing arms, and in the country 70,000, while the whole of Tuscany, either as subjects or friends, owed obedience to Florence. And although there might be some indignation and jealousy between the nobility and the people, they did not produce any evil effect, but all lived together in unity and peace. And if this peace had not been disturbed by internal enmities there would have been no cause of apprehension whatever, for the city had nothing to fear either from the empire or from those citizens whom political reasons kept from their homes, and was in condition to meet all the states of Italy with her own forces. The evil, however, which external powers could not effect, was brought about by those within.

CHAPTER IV

The Cerchi and the Donati--Origin of the Bianca and Nera factions in Pistoia--They come to Florence--Open enmity of the Donati and the Cerchi--Their first conflict--The Cerchi head the Bianca faction--The Donati take part with the Nera--The pope's legate at Florence increases the confusion with an interdict--New affray between the Cerchi and the Donati--The Donati and others of the Nera faction banished by the advice of Dante Alighieri--Charles of Valois sent by the pope to Florence--The Florentines suspect him--Corso Donati and the rest of the Nera party return to Florence--Veri Cerchi flies--The pope's legate again in Florence--The city again interdicted--New disturbances--The Bianchi banished--Dante banished--Corso Donati excites fresh troubles--The pope's legate endeavors to restore the emigrants but does not succeed--Great fire in Florence.

The Cerchi and the Donati were, for riches, nobility, and the number and influence of their followers, perhaps the two most distinguished families in Florence. Being neighbors, both in the city and the country, there had arisen between them some slight displeasure, which, however, had not occasioned an open quarrel, and perhaps never would have produced any serious effect if the malignant humors had not been increased by new causes. Among the first families of Pistoia was the Cancellieri. It happened that Lore, son of Gulielmo, and Geri, son of Bertacca, both of this family, playing together, and coming to words, Geri was slightly wounded by Lore. This displeased Gulielmo; and, designing by a suitable apology to remove all cause of further animosity, he ordered his son to go to the house of the father of the youth whom he had wounded and ask pardon. Lore obeyed his father; but this act of virtue failed to soften the cruel mind of Bertacca, and having caused Lore to be seized, in order to add the greatest indignity to his brutal act, he ordered his servants to chop off the youth's hand upon a block used for cutting meat upon, and then said to him, "Go to thy father, and tell him that sword wounds are cured with iron and not with words."

The unfeeling barbarity of this act so greatly exasperated Gulielmo that he ordered his people to take arms for his revenge. Bertacca prepared for his defense, and not only that family, but the whole city of Pistoia, became divided. And as the Cancellieri were descended from a Cancelliere who had had two wives, of whom one was called Bianca (white), one party was named by those who were descended from her BIANCA; and the other, by way of greater distinction, was called NERA (black). Much and long-continued strife took place between the two, attended with the death of many men and the destruction of much property; and not being able to effect a union among themselves, but weary of the evil, and anxious either to bring it to an end, or, by engaging others in their quarrel, increase it, they came to Florence, where the Neri, on account of their familiarity with the Donati, were favored by Corso, the head of that family; and on this account the Bianchi, that they might have a powerful head to defend them against the Donati, had recourse to Veri de Cerchi, a man in no respect inferior to Corso.

This quarrel, and the parties in it, brought from Pistoia, increased the old animosity between the Cerchi and the Donati, and it was already so manifest, that the Priors and all well-disposed men were in hourly apprehension of its breaking out, and causing a division of the whole city. They therefore applied to the pontiff, praying that he would interpose his authority between these turbulent parties, and provide the remedy which they found themselves unable to furnish. The pope sent for Veri, and charged him to make peace with the Donati, at which Veri exhibited great astonishment, saying that he had no enmity against them, and that as pacification presupposes war, he did not know, there being no war between them, how peacemaking could be necessary. Veri having returned from Rome without anything being effected, the rage of the parties increased to such a degree, that any trivial accident seemed sufficient to make it burst forth, as indeed presently happened.

It was in the month of May, during which, and upon holidays, it is the custom of Florence to hold festivals and public rejoicings throughout the city. Some youths of the Donati family, with their friends, upon horseback, were standing near the church of the Holy Trinity to look at a party of ladies who were dancing; thither also came some of the Cerchi, like the Donati, accompanied with many of the nobility, and, not knowing that the Donati were before them, pushed their horses and jostled them; thereupon the Donati, thinking themselves insulted, drew their swords, nor were the Cerchi at all backward to do the same, and not till after the interchange of many wounds, they separated. This disturbance was the beginning of great evils; for the whole city became divided, the people as well as the nobility, and the parties took the names of the Bianchi and the Neri. The Cerchi were at the head of the Bianchi faction, to which adhered the Adimari, the Abati, a part of the Tosinghi, of the Bardi, of the Rossi, of the Frescobaldi, of the Nerli, and of the Manelli; all the Mozzi, the Scali, Gherardini, Cavalcanti, Malespini, Bostichi, Giandonati, Vecchietti, and Arrigucci. To these were joined many families of the people, and all the Ghibellines then in Florence, so that their great numbers gave them almost the entire government of the city.

The Donati, at the head of whom was Corso, joined the Nera party, to which also adhered those members of the above-named families who did not take part with the Bianchi; and besides these, the whole of the Pazzi, the Bisdomini, Manieri, Bagnesi, Tornaquinci, Spini, Buondelmonti, Gianfigliazzi, and the Brunelleschi. Nor did the evil confine itself to the city alone, for the whole country was divided upon it, so that the Captains of the Six Parts, and whoever were attached to the Guelphic party or the well-being of the republic, were very much afraid that this new division would occasion the destruction of the city, and give new life to the Ghibelline faction. They, therefore, sent again to Pope Boniface, desiring that, unless he wished that city which had always been the shield of the church should either be ruined or become Ghibelline, he would consider some means for her relief. The pontiff thereupon sent to Florence, as his legate, Cardinal Matteo d'Acquasparta, a Portuguese, who, finding the Bianchi, as the most powerful, the least in fear, not quite submissive to him, he interdicted the city, and left it in anger, so that greater confusion now prevailed than had done previously to his coming.

The minds of men being in great excitement, it happened that at a funeral which many of the Donati and the Cerchi attended, they first came to words and then to arms, from which, however, nothing but merely tumult resulted at the moment. However, having each retired to their houses, the Cerchi determined to attack the

Donati, but, by the valor of Corso, they were repulsed and great numbers of them wounded. The city was in arms. The laws and the Signory were set at nought by the rage of the nobility, and the best and wisest citizens were full of apprehension. The Donati and their followers, being the least powerful, were in the greatest fear, and to provide for their safety they called together Corso, the Captains of the Parts, and the other leaders of the Neri, and resolved to apply to the pope to appoint some personage of royal blood, that he might reform Florence; thinking by this means to overcome the Bianchi. Their meeting and determination became known to the Priors, and the adverse party represented it as a conspiracy against the liberties of the republic. Both parties being in arms, the Signory, one of whom at that time was the poet Dante, took courage, and from his advice and prudence, caused the people to rise for the preservation of order, and being joined by many from the country, they compelled the leaders of both parties to lay aside their arms, and banished Corso, with many of the Neri. And as an evidence of the impartiality of their motives, they also banished many of the Bianchi, who, however, soon afterward, under pretense of some justifiable cause, returned.

Corso and his friends, thinking the pope favorable to their party, went to Rome and laid their grievances before him, having previously forwarded a statement of them in writing. Charles of Valois, brother of the king of France, was then at the papal court, having been called into Italy by the king of Naples, to go over into Sicily. The pope, therefore, at the earnest prayers of the banished Florentines, consented to send Charles to Florence, till the season suitable for his going to Sicily should arrive. He therefore came, and although the Bianchi, who then governed, were very apprehensive, still, as the head of the Guelphs, and appointed by the pope, they did not dare to oppose him, and in order to secure his friendship, they gave him authority to dispose of the city as he thought proper.

Thus authorized, Charles armed all his friends and followers, which step gave the people so strong a suspicion that he designed to rob them of their liberty, that each took arms, and kept at his own house, in order to be ready, if Charles should make any such attempt. The Cerchi and the leaders of the Bianchi faction had acquired universal hatred by having, while at the head of the republic, conducted themselves with unbecoming pride; and this induced Corso and the banished of the Neri party to return to Florence, knowing well that Charles and the Captains of the Parts were favorable to them. And while the citizens, for fear of Charles, kept themselves in arms, Corso, with all the banished, and followed by many others, entered Florence without the least impediment. And although Veri de Cerchi was advised to oppose him, he refused to do so, saying that he wished the people of Florence, against whom he came, should punish him. However, the contrary happened, for he was welcomed, not punished by them; and it behooved Veri to save himself by flight.

Corso, having forced the Pinti Gate, assembled his party at San Pietro Maggiore, near his own house, where, having drawn together a great number of friends and people desirous of change, he set at liberty all who had been imprisoned for offenses, whether against the state or against individuals. He compelled the existing Signory to withdraw privately to their own houses, elected a new one from the people of the Neri party, and for five days plundered the leaders of the Bianchi. The Cerchi, and the other heads of their faction, finding Charles opposed to them, withdrew from the city, and retired to their strongholds. And although at first they would not listen to the advice of the pope, they were now compelled to turn to him for assistance, declaring that instead of uniting the city, Charles had caused greater disunion than before. The pope again sent Matteo d'Acquasparta, his legate, who made peace between the Cerchi and the Donati, and strengthened it with marriages and new betrothals. But wishing that the Bianchi should participate in the employments of the government, to which the Neri who were then at the head of it would not consent, he withdrew, with no more satisfaction nor less enraged than on the former occasion, and left the city interdicted for disobedience.

Both parties remained in Florence, and equally discontented; the Neri from seeing their enemies at hand, and apprehending the loss of their power, and the Bianchi from finding themselves without either honor or authority; and to these natural causes of animosity new injuries were added. Niccolo de' Cerchi, with many of his friends, went to his estates, and being arrived at the bridge of Affrico, was attacked by Simone, son of Corso Donati. The contest was obstinate, and one each side had a sorrowful conclusion; for Niccolo was slain, and Simone was so severely wounded that he died on the following night.

This event again disturbed the entire city; and although the Neri were most to blame, they were defended by those who were at the head of affairs; and before sentence was delivered, a conspiracy of the Bianchi with Piero Ferrante, one of the barons who had accompanied Charles, was discovered, by whose assistance they sought to be replaced in the government. The matter became known from letters addressed to him by the Cerchi, although some were of opinion that they were not genuine, but written and pretended to be found, by the Donati, to abate the infamy which their party had acquired by the death of Niccolo. The whole of the Cerchi were, however, banished,--with their followers of the Bianchi party, of whom was Dante the poet,--their property confiscated, and their houses pulled down. They sought refuge, with a great number of Ghibellines who had joined them, in many places, seeking fresh fortunes in new undertakings. Charles, having effected the purpose of his coming, left the city, and returned to the pope to pursue his enterprise against Sicily, in which he was neither wiser nor more fortunate than he had been at Florence; so that with disgrace and the loss of many of his followers, he withdrew to France.

After the departure of Charles, Florence remained quiet. Corso alone was restless, thinking he did not possess that sort of authority in the city which was due to his rank; for the government being in the hands of the people, he saw the offices of the republic administered by many inferior to himself. Moved by passions of this kind, he endeavored, under the pretense of an honorable design, to justify his own dishonorable purposes, and accused many citizens who had the management of the public money, of applying it to their private uses, and recommended that they should be brought to justice and punished. This opinion was adopted by many who had the same views as himself; and many in ignorance joined them, thinking Corso actuated only by pure patriotism. On the other hand, the accused citizens, enjoying the popular favor, defended themselves, and this difference arose to such a height, that, after civil means, they had recourse to arms. Of the one party were Corso and Lottieri, bishop of Florence, with many of the nobility and some of the people; on the other side were the Signory, with the greater part of the people; so that skirmishes took place in many parts of the city. The Signory, seeing their danger great, sent for aid to the Lucchese, and presently all the people of Lucca were in Florence. With their assistance the disturbances were settled for the moment, and the people retained the government and their liberty, without attempting by any other means to punish the movers of the disorder.

The pope had heard of the tumults at Florence, and sent his legate, Niccolo da Prato, to settle them, who, being in high reputation both for his quality, learning, and mode of life, presently acquired so much of the people's confidence, that authority was given him to establish such a government as he should think proper. As he was of Ghibelline origin, he determined to recall the banished; but designing first to gain the affections of the lower orders, he renewed the ancient companies of the people, which increased the popular power and reduced that of the nobility. The legate, thinking the multitude on his side, now endeavored to recall the banished, and, after attempting in many ways, none of which succeeded, he fell so completely under the suspicion of the government, that he was compelled to quit the city, and returned to the pope in great wrath, leaving Florence full of confusion and suffering under an interdict. Neither was the city disturbed with one division alone, but by many; first the enmity between the people and the nobility, then that of the Ghibellines and the Guelphs, and lastly, of the Bianchi and the Neri. All the citizens were, therefore, in arms, for many were dissatisfied with the departure of the legate, and wished for the return of the banished. The first who set this disturbance on foot were the Medici and the Guinigi, who, with the legate, had discovered themselves in favor of the rebels; and thus skirmishes took place in many parts of the city.

In addition to these evils a fire occurred, which first broke out at the garden of St. Michael, in the houses of the Abati; it thence extended to those of the Capoinsacchi, and consumed them, with those of the Macci, Amieri, Toschi, Cipriani, Lamberti, Cavalcanti, and the whole of the New Market; from thence it spread to the gate of St. Maria, and burned it to the ground; turning from the old bridge, it destroyed the houses of the Gherardini, Pulci, Amidei, and Lucardesi, and with these so many others that the number amounted to seventeen hundred. It was the opinion of many that this fire occurred by accident during the heat of the disturbances. Others affirm that it was begun willfully by Neri Abati, prior of St. Pietro Scarragio, a dissolute character, fond of mischief, who, seeing the people occupied with the combat, took the opportunity of committing a wicked act, for which the citizens, being thus employed, could offer no remedy. And to insure his success, he set fire to the house of his own brotherhood, where he had the best opportunity of doing it. This was in the year 1304, Florence being afflicted both with fire and the sword. Corso Donati alone remained unarmed in so many tumults; for he thought he would more easily become the arbitrator between the contending parties when, weary of strife, they should be inclined to accommodation. They laid down their arms, however, rather from satiety of evil than from any desire of union; and the only consequence was, that the banished were not recalled, and the party which favored them remained inferior.

CHAPTER V

The emigrants attempt to re-enter Florence, but are not allowed to do so--The companies of the people restored--Restless conduct of Corso Donati--The ruin of Corso Donati--Corso Donati accused and condemned--Riot at the house of Corso--Death of Corso--His character--Fruitless attempt of the Emperor Henry against the Florentines--The emigrants are restored to the city--The citizens place themselves under the king of Naples for five years--War with Uguccione della Faggiuola--The Florentines routed--Florence withdraws herself from subjection to King Robert, and expels the Count Novello--Lando d'Agobbio--His tyranny--His departure.

The legate being returned to Rome, and hearing of the new disturbance which had occurred, persuaded the pope that if he wished to unite the Florentines, it would be necessary to have twelve of the first citizens appear before him, and having thus removed the principal causes of disunion, he might easily put a stop to it. The pontiff took this advice, and the citizens, among whom was Corso Donati, obeyed the summons. These having left the city, the legate told the exiles that now, when the city was deprived of her leaders, was the time for them to return. They, therefore, having assembled, came to Florence, and entering by a part of the wall not yet completed, proceeded to the piazza of St. Giovanni. It is worthy of remark, that those who, a short time previously, when they came unarmed and begged to be restored to their country, had fought for their return, now, when they saw them in arms and resolved to enter by force, took arms to oppose them (so much more was the common good esteemed than private friendship), and being joined by the rest of the citizens, compelled them to return to the places whence they had come. They failed in their undertaking by having left part of their force at Lastra, and by not having waited the arrival of Tolosetto Uberti, who had to come from Pistoia with three hundred horse; for they thought celerity rather than numbers would give them the victory; and it often happens, in similar enterprises, that delay robs us of the occasion, and too great anxiety to be forward prevents us of the power, or makes us act before we are properly prepared.

The banished having retired, Florence again returned to her old divisions; and in order to deprive the Cavalcanti of their authority, the people took from them the Stinche, a castle situated in the Val di Greve, and anciently belonging to the family. And as those who were taken in it were the first who were put into the new prisons, the latter were, and still continue, named after it,--the Stinche. The leaders of the republic also re-established the companies of the people, and gave them the ensigns that were first used by the companies of the Arts; the heads of which were called Gonfaloniers of the companies and colleagues of the Signory; and ordered, that when any disturbance arose they should assist the Signory with arms, and in peace with counsel. To the two ancient rectors they added an executor, or sheriff, who, with the Gonfaloniers, was to aid in repressing the insolence of the nobility.

In the meantime the pope died. Corso, with the other citizens, returned from Rome; and all would have been well if his restless mind had not occasioned new troubles. It was his common practice to be of a contrary opinion to the most powerful men in the city; and whatever he saw the people inclined to do, he exercised his utmost influence to effect, in order to attach them to himself; so that he was a leader in all differences, at the head of every new scheme, and whoever wished to obtain anything extraordinary had recourse to him. This conduct caused him to be hated by many of the highest distinction; and their hatred increased to such a degree that the Neri faction to which he belonged, became completely divided; for Corso, to attain his ends, had availed himself of private force and authority, and of the enemies of the state. But so great was the influence attached to his person, that everyone feared him. Nevertheless, in order to strip him of the popular favor (which by this means may easily be done), a report was set on foot that he intended to make himself prince of the city; and to the design his conduct gave great appearance of probability, for his way of living quite exceeded all civil bounds; and the opinion gained further strength, upon his taking to wife a daughter of Uguccione della Faggiuola, head of the Ghibelline and Bianchi faction, and one of the most powerful men in Tuscany.

When this marriage became known it gave courage to his adversaries, and they took arms against him; for the same reason the people ceased to defend him, and the greater part of them joined the ranks of his enemies, the leaders of whom were Rosso della Tosa, Pazino dei Pazzi, Geri Spini, and Berto Brunelleschi. These, with their followers, and the greater part of the people, assembled before the palace of the Signory, by whose command a charge was made before Piero Branca, captain of the people, against Corso, of intending, with the aid of Uguccione, to usurp the government. He was then summoned, and for disobedience, declared a rebel; nor did two hours pass over between the accusation and the sentence. The judgment being given, the Signory, with the companies of the people under their ensigns, went in search of him, who, although seeing himself abandoned by many of his followers, aware of the sentence against him, the power of the Signory, and the multitude of his enemies, remained undaunted, and fortified his houses, in the hope of defending them till Uguccione, for whom he had sent, should come to his Relief. His residences, and the streets approaching them, were barricaded and taken possession of by his partisans, who defended them so bravely that the enemy, although in great numbers, could not force them, and the battle became one of the hottest, with wounds and death on all sides. But the people, finding they could not drive them from their ground, took possession of the adjoining houses, and by unobserved passages obtained entry. Corso, thus finding himself surrounded by his foes, no longer retaining any hope of assistance from Uguccione, and without a chance of victory, thought only of effecting his personal safety, and with Gherardo Bordoni, and some of his bravest and most trusted friends, fought a passage through the thickest of their enemies, and effected their escape from the city by the Gate of the Cross. They were, however, pursued by vast numbers, and Gherardo was slain upon the bridge of Affrico by Boccaccio Cavicciulli. Corso was overtaken and made prisoner by a party of Catalan horse, in the service of the Signory, at Rovezzano. But when approaching Florence, that he might avoid being seen and torn to pieces by his victorious enemies, he allowed himself to fall from horseback, and being down, one of those who conducted him cut his throat. The body was found by the monks of San Salvi, and buried without any ceremony due to his rank. Such was the end of Corso, to whom his country and the Neri faction were indebted for much both of good and evil; and if he had possessed a cooler spirit he would have left behind him a more happy memory. Nevertheless, he deserves to be enumerated among the most distinguished men our city has produced. True it is, that his restless conduct made both his country and his party forgetful of their obligation to him. The same cause also produced his miserable end, and brought many troubles upon both his friends and his country. Uguccione, coming to the assistance of his relative, learned at Remoli that Corso had been overcome by the people, and finding that he could not render him any assistance, in order to avoid bringing evil upon himself without occasion, he returned home.

After the death of Corso, which occurred in the year 1308, the disturbances were appeased, and the people lived quietly till it was reported that the Emperor Henry was coming into Italy, and with him all the Florentine emigrants, to whom he had promised restoration to their country. The leaders of the government thought, that in order to lessen the number of their enemies, it would be well to recall, of their own will, all who had been expelled, excepting such as the law had expressly forbidden to return. Of the number not admitted, were the greater part of the Ghibellines, and some of those of the Bianchi faction, among whom were Dante Alighieri, the sons of Veri de' Cerchi and of Giano della Bella. Besides this they sent for aid to Robert, king of Naples, and not being able to obtain it of him as friends, they gave their city to him for five years, that he might defend them as his own people. The emperor entered Italy by the way of Pisa, and proceeded by the marshes to Rome, where he was crowned in the year 1312. Then, having determined to subdue the Florentines, he approached their city by the way of Perugia and Arezzo, and halted with his army at the monastery of San Salvi, about a mile from Florence, where he remained fifty days without effecting anything. Despairing of success against Florence, he returned to Pisa, where he entered into an agreement with Frederick, king of Sicily, to undertake the conquest of Naples, and proceeded with his people accordingly; but while filled with the hope of victory, and carrying dismay into the heart of King Robert, having reached Buonconvento, he died.

Shortly after this, Uguccione della Faggiuola, having by means of the Ghibelline party become lord of Pisa and of Lucca, caused, with the assistance of these cities, very serious annoyance to the neighbouring places. In order to effect their relief the Florentines requested King Robert would allow his brother Piero to take the command of their armies. On the other hand, Uguccione continued to increase his power; and either by force or fraud obtained possession of many castles in the Val d'Arno and the Val di Nievole; and having besieged Monte Cataini, the Florentines found it would be necessary to send to its relief, that they might not see him burn and destroy their whole territory. Having drawn together a large army, they entered the Val di Nievole where they came up with Uguccione, and were routed after a severe battle in which Piero the king's brother and 2,000 men were slain; but the body of the Prince was never found. Neither was the victory a joyful one to Uguccione; for one of his sons, and many of the leaders of his army, fell in the strife.

The Florentines after this defeat fortified their territory, and King Robert sent them, for commander of their forces, the Count d'Andria, usually called Count Novello, by whose deportment, or because it is natural to the Florentines to find every state tedious, the city, notwithstanding the war with Uguccione, became divided into friends and enemies of the king. Simon della Tosa, the Magalotti, and certain others of the people who had attained greater influence in the government than the rest, were leaders of the party against the king. By these means messengers were sent to France, and afterward into Germany, to solicit leaders and forces that they might drive out the count, whom the king had appointed governor; but they failed of obtaining any. Nevertheless they did not abandon their undertaking, but still desirous of one whom they might worship, after an unavailing search in France and Germany, they discovered him at Agobbio, and having expelled the Count Novello, caused Lando d'Agobbio to be brought into the city as Bargello (sheriff), and gave him the most unlimited power of the citizens. This man was cruel and rapacious; and going through the country accompanied with an armed force, he put many to death at the mere instigation of those who had endowed him with authority. His insolence rose to such a height, that he stamped base metal with the impression used upon the money of the state, and no one had sufficient courage to oppose him, so powerful had he become by the discords of Florence. Great, certainly, but unhappy city! which neither the memory of past divisions, the fear of her enemies, nor a king's authority, could unite for her own advantage; so that she found herself in a state of the utmost wretchedness, harassed without by Uguccione, and plundered within by Lando d'Agobbio.

The friends of the king and those who opposed Lando and his followers, were either of noble families or the highest of the people, and all Guelphs; but their adversaries being in power they could not discover their minds without incurring the greatest danger. Being, however, determined to deliver themselves from such disgraceful tyranny, they secretly wrote to King Robert, requesting him to appoint for his vicar in Florence Count Guido da Battifolle. The king complied; and the opposite party, although the Signory were opposed to the king, on account of the good quality of the count, did not dare to resist him. Still his authority was not great, because the Signory and Gonfaloniers of the companies were in favor of Lando and his party.

During these troubles, the daughter of King Albert of Bohemia passed through Florence, in search of her husband, Charles, the son of King Robert, and was received with the greatest respect by the friends of the king, who complained to her of the unhappy state of the city, and of the tyranny of Lando and his partisans; so that through her influence and the exertions of the king's friends, the citizens were again united, and before her departure, Lando was stripped of all authority and send back to Agobbio, laden with blood and plunder. In reforming the government, the sovereignty of the city was continued to the king for another three years, and as there were then in office seven Signors of the party of Lando, six more were appointed of the king's friends, and some magistracies were composed of thirteen Signors; but not long afterward the number was reduced to seven according to ancient custom.

CHAPTER VI

War with Castruccio--Castruccio marches against Prato and retires without making any attempt--The emigrants not being allowed to return, endeavor to enter the city by force, and are repulsed--Change in the mode of electing the great officers of state--The Squittini established--The Florentines under Raymond of Cardona are routed by Castruccio at Altopascio--Treacherous designs of Raymond--The Florentines give the sovereignty of the city to Charles duke of Cambria, who appoints the duke of Athens for his vicar--The duke of Calabria comes to Florence--The Emperor Louis of Bavaria visits Italy--The excitement he produces--Death of Castruccio and of Charles duke of Calabria--Reform of government.

About the same time, Uguccione lost the sovereignty of Lucca and of Pisa, and Castruccio Castracani, a citizen of Lucca, became lord of them, who, being a young man, bold and fierce, and fortunate in his enterprises, in a short time became the head of the Ghibellines in Tuscany. On this account the discords among the Florentines were laid aside for some years, at first to abate the increasing power of Castruccio, and afterward to unite their means for mutual defense against him. And in order to give increased strength and efficacy to their counsels, the Signory appointed twelve citizens whom they called Buonomini, or good men, without whose advice and consent nothing of any importance could be carried into effect. The conclusion of the sovereignty of King Robert being come, the citizens took the government into their own hands, reappointed the usual rectors and magistracies, and were kept united by the dread of Castruccio, who, after many efforts against the lords of Lunigiano, attacked Prato, to the relief of which the Florentines having resolved to go, shut up their shops and houses, and proceeded thither in a body, amounting to twenty thousand foot and one thousand five hundred horse. And in order to reduce the number of Castruccio's friends and augment their own, the Signory declared that every rebel of the Guelphic party who should come to the relief of Prato would be restored to his country; they thus increased their army with an addition of four thousand men. This great force being quickly brought to Prato, alarmed Castruccio so much, that without trying the fortune of battle, he retired toward Lucca. Upon this, disturbances arose in the Florentine camp between the nobility and the people, the latter of whom wished to pursue the foe and destroy him; the former were for returning home, saying they had done enough for Prato in hazarding the safety of Florence on its account, which they did not regret under the circumstances, but now, that necessity no longer existing, the propriety of further risk ceased also, as there was little to be gained and much to lose. Not being able to agree, the question was referred to the Signory, among whom the difference of opinion was equally great; and as the matter spread throughout the city, the people drew together, and used such threatening language against the nobility that they, being apprehensive for their safety, yielded; but the resolution being adopted too late, and by many unwillingly, gave the enemy time to withdraw in safety to Lucca.

This unfortunate circumstance made the people so indignant against the great that the Signory refused to perform the promise made to the exiles, and the latter, anticipating the fact, determined to be beforehand, and were at the gates of Florence to gain admittance into the city before the rest of the forces; but their design did not take effect, for their purpose being foreseen, they were repulsed by those who had remained at home. They then endeavored to acquire by entreaty what they had failed to obtain by force; and sent eight men as ambassadors to the Signory, to remind them of the promise given, and of the dangers they had undergone, in hope of the reward which had been held out to them. And although the nobility, who felt the obligation on account of their having particularly undertaken to fulfill the promise for which the Signory had bound themselves, used their utmost exertion in favor of the exiles, so great was the anger of the multitude on account of their only partial success against Castruccio, that they could not obtain their admission. This occasioned cost and dishonor to the city; for many of the nobility, taking offense at this proceeding, endeavored to obtain by arms that which had been refused to their prayers, and agreed with the exiles that they should come armed to the city, and that those within would arm themselves in their defense. But the affair was discovered before the appointed day arrived, so that those without found the city in arms, and prepared to resist them. So completely subdued were those within, that none dared to take arms; and thus the undertaking was abandoned, without any advantage having been obtained by the party. After the departure of the exiles it was determined to punish those who had been instrumental in bringing them to the city; but, although everyone knew who were the delinquents, none ventured to name and still less to accuse them. It was, therefore, resolved that in order to come at the truth, everyone should write the names of those he believed to be guilty, and present the writing secretly to the Capitano. By this means, Amerigo Donati, Teghiajo, Frescobaldi, and Lotteringo Gherardini were accused; but, the judges being more favorably disposed to them than, perhaps, their misdeeds deserved, each escaped by paying a fine.

The tumults which arose in Florence from the coming of the rebels to the gates, showed that one leader was insufficient for the companies of the people; they, therefore, determined that in future each should have three or four; and to every Gonfalonier two or three Pennonieri (pennon bearers) were added, so that if the whole body were not drawn out, a part might operate under one of them. And as happens in republics, after any disturbance, some old laws are annulled and others renewed, so on this occasion, as it had been previously customary to appoint the Signory for a time only, the then existing Signors and the Colleagues, feeling themselves possessed of sufficient power, assumed the authority to fix upon the Signors that would have to sit during the next forty months, by putting their names into a bag or purse, and drawing them every two months. But, before the expiration of the forty months, many citizens were jealous that their names had not been deposited among the rest, and a new emborsation was made. From this beginning arose the custom of emborsing or enclosing the names of all who should take office in any of the magistracies for a long time to come, as well those whose offices employed them within the city as those abroad, though previously the councils of the retiring magistrates had elected those who were to succeed them. These emborsations were afterward called Squittini, or pollings,--and it was thought they would prevent much trouble to the city, and remove the cause of those tumults which every three, or at most five, years, took place upon the creation of magistrates, from the number of candidates for office. And not being able to adopt a better expedient, they made use of this, but did not observe the defects which lay concealed under such a trivial accommodation.

In 1325, Castruccio, having taken possession of Pistoia, became so powerful that the Florentines, fearing his greatness, resolved, before he should get himself firmly seated in his new conquest, to attack him and withdraw it from his authority. Of their citizens and friends they mustered an army amounting to 20,000 foot and 3,000 horse, and with this body encamped before Altopascio, with the intention of taking the place and thus preventing it from relieving Pistoia. Being successful in the first part of their design, they marched toward Lucca, and laid the country waste in their progress; but from the little prudence and less integrity of their leader, Ramondo di Cardona, they made but small progress; for he, having observed them upon former occasions very prodigal of their liberty, placing it sometimes in the hands of a king, at others in those of a legate, or persons of even inferior quality, thought, if he could bring them into some difficulty, it might easily happen that they would make him their prince. Nor did he fail frequently to mention these matters, and required to have that authority in the city which had been given him over the army, endeavoring to show that otherwise he could not enforce the obedience requisite to a leader. As the Florentines did not consent to this, he wasted time, and allowed Castruccio to obtain the assistance which the Visconti and other tyrants of Lombardy had promised him, and thus become very strong. Ramondo, having willfully let the opportunity of victory pass away, now found himself unable to escape; for Castruccio coming up with him at Altopascio, a great battle ensued in which many citizens were slain and taken prisoners, and among the former fell Ramondo, who received from fortune that reward of bad faith and mischievous counsels which he had richly deserved from the Florentines. The injury they suffered from Castruccio, after the battle, in plunder, prisoners, destruction, and burning of property, is quite indescribable; for, without any opposition, during many months, he led his predatory forces wherever he thought proper, and it seemed sufficient to the Florentines if, after such a terrible event, they could save their city.

Still they were not so absolutely cast down as to prevent them from raising great sums of money, hiring troops, and sending to their friends for assistance; but all they could do was insufficient to restrain such a powerful enemy; so that they were obliged to offer the sovereignty to Charles duke of Calabria, son of King Robert, if they could induce him to come to their defense; for these princes, being accustomed to rule Florence, preferred her obedience to her friendship. But Charles, being engaged in the wars of Sicily, and therefore unable to undertake the sovereignty of the city, sent in his stead Walter, by birth a Frenchman, and duke of Athens. He, as viceroy, took possession of the city, and appointed the magistracies according to his own pleasure; but his mode of proceeding was quite correct, and so completely contrary to his real nature, that everyone respected him.

The affairs of Sicily being composed, Charles came to Florence with a thousand horse. He made his entry into the city in July, 1326, and his coming prevented further pillage of the Florentine territory by Castruccio. However, the influence which they acquired without the city was lost within her walls, and the evils which they did not suffer from their enemies were brought upon them by their friends; for the Signory could not do anything without the consent of the duke of Calabria, who, in the course of one year, drew from the people 400,000 florins, although by the agreement entered into with him, the sum was not to exceed 200,000; so great were the burdens with which either himself or his father constantly oppressed them.

To these troubles were added new jealousies and new enemies; for the Ghibellines of Lombardy became so alarmed upon the arrival of Charles in Tuscany, that Galeazzo Visconti and the other Lombard tyrants, by money and promises, induced Louis of Bavaria, who had lately been elected emperor contrary to the wish of the pope, to come into Italy. After passing through Lombardy he entered Tuscany, and with the assistance of Castruccio, made himself master of Pisa, from whence, having been pacified with sums of money, he directed his course towards Rome. This caused the duke of Calabria to be apprehensive for the safety of Naples; he therefore left Florence, and appointed as his viceroy Filippo da Saggineto.

After the departure of the emperor, Castruccio made himself master of Pisa, but the Florentines, by a treaty with Pistoia, withdrew her from obedience to him. Castruccio then besieged Pistoia, and persevered with so much vigor and resolution, that although the Florentines often attempted to relieve her, by attacking first his army and then his country, they were unable either by force or policy to remove him; so anxious was he to punish the Pistolesi and subdue the Florentines. At length the people of Pistoia were compelled to receive him for their sovereign; but this event, although greatly to his glory, proved but little to his advantage, for upon his return to Lucca he died. And as one event either of good or evil seldom comes alone, at Naples also died Charles duke of Calabria and lord of Florence, so that in a short time, beyond the expectation of their most sanguine hopes, the Florentines found themselves delivered from the domination of the one and the fear of the other. Being again free, they set about the reformation of the city, annulled all the old councils, and created two new ones, the one composed of 300 citizens from the class of the people, the other of 250 from the nobility and the people.

The first was called the Council of the People, the other the Council of the Commune.

CHAPTER VII

The Emperor at Rome--The Florentines refuse to purchase Lucca, and repent of it--Enterprises of the Florentines--Conspiracy of the Bardi and the Frescobaldi--The conspiracy discovered and checked--Maffeo da Marradi appeases the tumult--Lucca is purchased by the Florentines and taken by the Pisans--The duke of Athens at Florence--The nobility determine to make him prince of the city.

The emperor, being arrived at Rome, created an anti-pope, did many things in opposition to the church, and attempted many others, but without effect, so that at last he retired with disgrace, and went to Pisa, where, either because they were not paid, or from disaffection, about 800 German horse mutinied, and fortified themselves at Montechiaro upon the Ceruglio; and when the emperor had left Pisa to go into Lombardy, they took possession of Lucca and drove out Francesco Castracani, whom he had left there. Designing to turn their conquest to account, they offered it to the Florentines for 80,000 florins, which, by the advice of Simone della Tosa, was refused. This resolution, if they had remained in it, would have been of the greatest utility to the Florentines; but as they shortly afterward changed their minds, it became most pernicious; for although at the time they might have obtained peaceful possession of her for a small sum and would not, they afterward wished to have her and could not, even for a much larger amount; which caused many and most hurtful changes to take place in Florence. Lucca, being refused by the Florentines, was purchased by Gherardino Spinoli, a Genoese, for 30,000 florins. And as men are often less anxious to take what is in their power than desirous of that which they cannot attain, as soon as the purchase of Gherardino became known, and for how small a sum it had been bought, the people of Florence were seized with an extreme desire to have it, blaming themselves and those by whose advice they had been induced to reject the offer made to them. And in order to obtain by force what they had refused to purchase, they sent troops to plunder and overrun the country of the Lucchese.

About this time the emperor left Italy. The anti-pope, by means of the Pisans, became a prisoner in France; and the Florentines from the death of Castruccio, which occurred in 1328, remained in domestic peace till 1340, and gave their undivided attention to external affairs, while many wars were carried on in Lombardy, occasioned by the coming of John king of Bohemia, and in Tuscany, on account of Lucca. During this period Florence was ornamented with many new buildings, and by the advice of Giotto, the most distinguished painter of his time, they built the tower of Santa Reparata. Besides this, the waters of the Arno having, in 1333, risen twelve feet above their ordinary level, destroyed some of the bridges and many buildings, all which were restored with great care and expense.

In the year 1340, new sources of disagreement arose. The great had two ways of increasing or preserving their power; the one, so to restrain the emborsation of magistrates, that the lot always fell upon themselves or their friends; the other, that having the election of the rectors, they were always favorable to their party. This second mode they considered of so great importance, that the ordinary rectors not being sufficient for them, they on some occasions elected a third, and at this time they had made an extraordinary appointment, under the title of captain of the guard, of Jacopo Gabrielli of Agobbio, and endowed him with unlimited authority over the citizens. This man, under the sanction of those who governed, committed constant outrages; and among those whom he injured were Piero de' Bardi and Bardo Frescobaldi. These being of the nobility, and naturally proud, could not endure that a stranger, supported by a few powerful men, should without cause injure them with impunity, and consequently entered into a conspiracy against him and those by whom he was supported. They were joined by many noble families, and some of the people, who were offended with the tyranny of those in power. Their plan was, that each should bring into his house a number of armed men, and on the morning after the day of All Saints, when almost all would be in the temples praying for their dead, they should take arms, kill the Capitano and those who were at the head of affairs, and then, with a new Signory and new ordinances, reform the government.

But, as the more a dangerous business is considered, the less willingly it is undertaken, it commonly happens, when there is any time allowed between the determining upon a perilous enterprise and its execution, that the conspiracy by one means or another becomes known. Andrea de' Bardi was one of the conspirators, and upon reconsideration of the matter, the fear of the punishment operated more powerfully upon him than the desire of revenge, and he disclosed the affair to Jacopo Alberti, his brother-in-law. Jacopo acquainted the Priors, and they informed the government. And as the danger was near, All Saints' day being just at hand, many citizens met together in the palace; and thinking their peril increased by delay, they insisted that the Signory should order the alarm to be rung, and called the people together in arms. Taldo Valori was at this time Gonfalonier, and Francesco Salviati one of the Signory, who, being relatives of the Bardi, were unwilling to summon the people with the bell, alleging as a reason that it is by no means well to assemble them in arms upon every slight occasion, for power put into the hands of an unrestrained multitude was never beneficial; that it is an easy matter to excite them to violence, but a difficult thing to restrain them; and that, therefore, it would be taking a more prudent course if they were to inquire into the truth of the affair, and punish the delinquents by the civil authority, than to attempt, upon a simple information, to correct it by such a tumultuous means, and thus hazard the safety of the city. None would listen to these remarks; the Signory were assailed with insolent behavior and indecent expressions, and compelled to sound the alarm, upon which the people presently assembled in arms. On the other hand, the Bardi and the Frescobaldi, finding themselves discovered, that they might conquer with glory or die without shame, armed themselves, in the hope that they would be able to defend that part of the city beyond the river, where their houses were situated; and they fortified the bridge in expectation of assistance, which they expected from the nobles and their friends in the country. Their design was frustrated by the people who, in common with themselves, occupied this part of the city; for these took arms in favor of the Signory, so that, seeing themselves thus circumstanced, they abandoned the bridges, and betook themselves to the street in which the Bardi resided, as being a stronger situation than any other; and this they defended with great bravery.

Jacopo d'Agobbio, knowing the whole conspiracy was directed against himself, in fear of death, terrified and vanquished, kept himself surrounded with forces near the palace of the Signory; but the other rectors, who were much less blamable, discovered greater courage, and especially the podesta or provost, whose name was Maffeo da Marradi. He presented himself among the combatants without any fear, and passing the bridge of the Rubaconte amid the swords of the Bardi, made a sign that he wished to speak to them. Upon this, their reverence for the man, his noble demeanor, and the excellent qualities he was known to possess, caused an immediate cessation of the combat, and induced them to listen to him patiently. He very gravely, but without the use of any bitter or aggravating expressions, blamed their conspiracy, showed the danger they would incur if they still contended against the popular feeling, gave them reason to hope their complaints would be heard and mercifully considered, and promised that he himself would use his endeavors in their behalf. He then returned to the Signory, and implored them to spare the blood of the citizens, showing the impropriety of judging them unheard, and at length induced them to consent that the Bardi and the Frescobaldi, with their friends, should leave the city, and without impediment be allowed to retire to their castles. Upon their departure the people being again disarmed, the Signory proceeded against those only of the Bardi and Frescobaldi families who had taken arms. To lessen their power, they bought of the Bardi the castle of Mangona and that of Vernia; and enacted a law which provided that no citizen should be allowed to possess a castle or fortified place within twenty miles of Florence.

After a few months, Stiatta Frescobaldi was beheaded, and many of his family banished. Those who governed, not satisfied with having subdued the Bardi and the Frescobaldi, as is most commonly the case, the more authority they possessed the worse use they made of it and the more insolent they became. As they had hitherto had one captain of the guard who afflicted the city, they now appointed another for the country, with unlimited authority, to the end that those whom they suspected might abide neither within nor without. And they excited them to such excesses against the whole of the nobility, that these were driven to desperation, and ready to sell both themselves and the city to obtain revenge. The occasion at length came, and they did not fail to use it.

The troubles of Tuscany and Lombardy had brought the city of Lucca under the rule of Mastino della Scala, lord of Verona, who, though bound by contract to assign her to the Florentines, had refused to do so; for, being lord of Parma, he thought he should be able to retain her, and did not trouble himself about his breach of faith. Upon this the Florentines joined the Venetians, and with their assistance brought Mastino to the brink of ruin. They did not, however, derive any benefit from this beyond the slight satisfaction of having conquered him; for the Venetians, like all who enter into league with less powerful states than themselves, having acquired Trevigi and Vicenza, made peace with Mastino without the least regard for the Florentines. Shortly after this, the Visconti, lords of Milan, having taken Parma from Mastino, he found himself unable to retain Lucca, and therefore determined to sell it. The competitors for the purchase were the Florentines and the Pisans; and in the course of the treaty the Pisans, finding that the Florentines, being the richer people, were about to obtain it, had recourse to arms, and, with the assistance of the Visconti, marched against Lucca. The Florentines did not, on that account, withdraw from the purchase, but having agreed upon the terms with Mastino, paid part of the money, gave security for the remainder, and sent Naddo Rucellai, Giovanni di Bernadino de' Medici, and Rosso di Ricciardo de' Ricci, to take possession, who entered Lucca by force, and Mastino's people delivered the city to them. Nevertheless, the Pisans continued the siege, and the Florentines used their utmost endeavors to relieve her; but after a long war, loss of money, and accumulation of disgrace, they were compelled to retire, and the Pisans became lords of Lucca.

The loss of this city, as in like cases commonly happens, exasperated the people of Florence against the members of the government; at every street corner and public place they were openly censured, and the entire misfortune was laid to the charge of their greediness and mismanagement. At the beginning of the war, twenty citizens had been appointed to undertake the direction of it, who appointed Malatesta da Rimini to the command of the forces. He having exhibited little zeal and less prudence, they requested assistance from Robert king of Naples, and he sent them Walter duke of Athens, who, as Providence would have it, to bring about the approaching evils, arrived at Florence just at the moment when the undertaking against Lucca had entirely failed. Upon this the Twenty, seeing the anger of the people, thought to inspire them with fresh hopes by the appointment of a new leader, and thus remove, or at least abate, the causes of calumny against themselves. As there was much to be feared, and that the duke of Athens might have greater authority to defend them, they first chose him for their coadjutor, and then appointed him to the command of the army. The nobility, who were discontented from the causes above mentioned, having many of them been acquainted with Walter, when upon a former occasion he had governed Florence for the duke of Calabria, thought they had now an opportunity, though with the ruin of the city, of subduing their enemies; for there was no means of prevailing against those who had oppressed them but of submitting to the authority of a prince who, being acquainted with the worth of one party and the insolence of the other, would restrain the latter and reward the former. To this they added a hope of the benefits they might derive from him when he had acquired the principality by their means. They, therefore, took several occasions of being with him secretly, and entreated he would take the command wholly upon himself, offering him the utmost assistance in their power. To their influence and entreaty were also added those of some families of the people; these were the Peruzzi, Acciajuoli, Antellesi, and Buonaccorsi, who, being overwhelmed with debts, and without means of their own, wished for those of others to liquidate them, and, by the slavery of their country, to deliver themselves from their servitude to their creditors. These demonstrations excited the ambitious mind of the duke to greater desire of dominion, and in order to gain himself the reputation of strict equity and justice, and thus increase his favor with the plebeians, he prosecuted those who had conducted the war against Lucca, condemned many to pay fines, others to exile, and put to death Giovanni de' Medici, Naddo Rucellai, and Guglielmo Altoviti.

CHAPTER VIII

The Duke of Athens requires to be made prince of Florence--The Signory address the duke upon the subject--The plebeians proclaim him prince of Florence for life--Tyrannical proceedings of the duke--The city disgusted with him--Conspiracies against the duke--The duke discovers the conspiracies, and becomes terrified--The city rises against him--He is besieged in the palace--Measures adopted by the citizens for reform of the government--The duke is compelled to withdraw from the city--Miserable deaths of Guglielmo da Scesi and his son--Departure of the duke of Athens--His character.

These executions greatly terrified the middle class of citizens, but gave satisfaction to the great and to the plebeians;--to the latter, because it is their nature to delight in evil; and to the former, by thus seeing themselves avenged of the many wrongs they had suffered from the people. When the duke passed along the streets he was hailed with loud cheers, the boldness of his proceedings was praised, and both parties joined in open entreaties that he would search out the faults of the citizens, and punish them.

The office of the Twenty began to fall into disuse, while the power of the duke became great, and the influence of fear excessive; so that everyone, in order to appear friendly to him, caused his arms to be painted over their houses, and the name alone was all he needed to be absolutely prince. Thinking himself upon such a footing that he might safely attempt anything, he gave the Signory to understand that he judged it necessary for the good of the city, that the sovereignty should be freely given to him, and that as the rest of the citizens were willing that it should be so, he desired they would also consent. The Signory, notwithstanding many had foreseen the ruin of their country, were much disturbed at this demand; and although they were aware of the dangerous position in which they stood, that they might not be wanting in their duty, resolutely refused to comply. The duke had, in order to assume a greater appearance of religion and humanity, chosen for his residence the convent of the Minor Canons of St. Croce, and in order to carry his evil designs into effect, proclaimed that all the people should, on the following morning, present themselves before him in the piazza of the convent. This command alarmed the Signory much more than his discourse to them had done, and they consulted with those citizens whom they thought most attached to their country and to liberty; but they could not devise any better plan, knowing the power of which the duke was possessed, than to endeavor by entreaty to induce him either to forego his design or to make his government less intolerable. A party of them was, therefore, appointed to wait upon him, one of whom addressed him in the following manner:--

"We appear before you, my lord, induced first by the demand which you have made, and then by the orders you have given for a meeting of the people; for it appears to us very clearly, that it is your intention to effect by extraordinary means the design from which we have hitherto withheld our consent. It is not, however, our intention to oppose you with force, but only to show what a heavy charge you take upon yourself, and the dangerous course you adopt; to the end that you may remember our advice and that of those who, not by consideration of what is beneficial for you, but for the gratification of their own unreasonable wishes, have advised you differently. You are endeavoring to reduce to slavery a city that has always existed in freedom; for the authority which we have at times conceded to the kings of Naples was companionship and not servitude. Have you considered the mighty things which the name of liberty implies to such a city as this, and how delightful it is to those who hear it? It has a power which nothing can subdue, time cannot wear away, nor can any degree of merit in a prince countervail the loss of it. Consider, my lord, how great the force must be that can keep a city like this in subjection, no foreign aid would enable you to do it; neither can you confide in those at home; for they who are at present your friends, and advise you to adopt the course you now pursue, as soon as with your assistance they have overcome their enemies, will at once turn their thoughts toward effecting your destruction, and then take the government upon themselves. The plebeians, in whom you confide, will change upon any accident, however trivial; so that in a very short time you may expect to see the whole city opposed to you, which will produce both their ruin and your own. Nor will you be able to find any remedy for this; for princes who have but few enemies may make their government very secure by the death or banishment of those who are opposed to them; but when the hatred is universal, no security whatever can be found, for you cannot tell from what direction the evil may commence; and he who has to apprehend every man his enemy cannot make himself assured of anyone. And if you should attempt to secure a friend or two, you would only increase the dangers of your situation; for the hatred of the rest would be increased by your success, and they would become more resolutely disposed to vengeance.

"That time can neither destroy nor abate the desire for freedom is most certain; for it has been often observed, that those have reassumed their liberty who in their own persons had never tasted of its charms, and love it only from remembrance of what they have heard their fathers relate; and, therefore, when recovered, have preserved it with indomitable resolution and at every hazard. And even when their fathers could not remember it, the public buildings, the halls of the magistracy, and the insignia of free institutions, remind them of it; and these things cannot fail to be known and greatly desired by every class of citizens.

"What is it you imagine you can do, that would be an equivalent for the sweets of liberty, or make men lose the desire of their present conditions? No; if you were to join the whole of Tuscany to the Florentine rule, if you were to return to the city daily in triumph over her enemies, what could it avail? The glory would not be ours, but yours. We should not acquire fellow-citizens, but partakers of our bondage, who would serve to sink us still deeper in ignominy. And if your conduct were in every respect upright, your demeanor amiable, and your judgments equitable, all these would be insufficient to make you beloved. If you imagine otherwise, you deceive yourself; for, to one accustomed to the enjoyment of liberty, the slightest chains feel heavy, and every tie upon his free soul oppresses him. Besides, it is impossible to find a violent people associated with a good prince, for of necessity they must soon become alike, or their difference produce the ruin of one of them. You may, therefore, be assured, that you will either have to hold this city by force, to effect which, guards, castles, and external aid have oft been found insufficient, or be content with the authority we have conferred; and this we would advise, reminding you that no dominion can be durable to which the governed do not consent; and we have no wish to lead you, blinded by ambition, to such a point that, unable either to stand or advance, you must, to the great injury of both, of necessity fall."

This discourse did not in the slightest degree soften the obdurate mind of the duke, who replied that it was not his intention to rob the city of her liberty, but to restore it to her; for those cities alone are in slavery that are disunited, while the united are free. As Florence, by her factions and ambition, had deprived herself of liberty, he should restore, not take it from her; and as he had been induced to take this charge upon himself, not from his own ambition, but at the entreaty of a great number of citizens, they would do well to be satisfied with that which produced contentment among the rest. With regard to the danger he might incur, he thought nothing of it; for it was not the part of a good man to avoid doing good from his apprehension of evil, and it was the part of a coward to shun a glorious undertaking because some uncertainty attended the success of the attempt; and he knew he should so conduct himself, that they would soon see they had entertained great apprehensions and been in little danger.

The Signory then agreed, finding they could not do better, that on the following morning the people should be assembled in their accustomed place of meeting, and with their consent the Signory should confer upon the duke the sovereignty of the city for one year, on the same conditions as it had been intrusted to the duke of Calabria. It was upon the 8th of November, 1342, when the duke, accompanied by Giovanni della Tosa and all his confederates, with many other citizens, came to the piazza or court of the palace, and having, with the Signory mounted upon the ringhiera, or rostrum (as the Florentines call those steps which lead to the palace), the agreement which had been entered into between the Signory and himself was read. When they had come to the passage which gave the government to him for one year, the people shouted, "FOR LIFE." Upon this, Francesco Rustichelli, one of the Signory, arose to speak, and endeavored to abate the tumult and procure a hearing; but the mob, with their hootings, prevented him from being heard by anyone; so that with the consent of the people the duke was elected, not for one year merely, but for life. He was then borne through the piazza by the crowd, shouting his name as they proceeded.

It is the custom that he who is appointed to the guard of the palace shall, in the absence of the Signory, remain locked within. This office was at that time held by

Rinieri di Giotto, who, bribed by the friends of the duke, without waiting for any force, admitted him immediately. The Signory, terrified and dishonored, retired to their own houses; the palace was plundered by the followers of the duke, the Gonfalon of the people torn to pieces, and the arms of the duke placed over the palace. All this happened to the indescribable sorrow of good men, though to the satisfaction of those who, either from ignorance or malignity, were consenting parties.

The duke, having acquired the sovereignty of the city, in order to strip those of all authority who had been defenders of her liberty, forbade the Signory to assemble in the palace, and appointed a private dwelling for their use. He took their colors from the Gonfaloniers of the companies of the people; abolished the ordinances made for the restraint of the great; set at liberty those who were imprisoned; recalled the Bardi and the Frescobaldi from exile, and forbade everyone from carrying arms about his person. In order the better to defend himself against those within the city, he made friends of all he could around it, and therefore conferred great benefits upon the Aretini and other subjects of the Florentines. He made peace with the Pisans, although raised to power in order that he might carry on war against them; ceased paying interest to those merchants who, during the war against Lucca, had lent money to the republic; increased the old taxes, levied new ones, and took from the Signory all authority. His rectors were Baglione da Perugia and Guglielmo da Scesi, who, with Cerrettieri Bisdomini, were the persons with whom he consulted on public affairs. He imposed burdensome taxes upon the citizens; his decisions between contending parties were unjust; and that precision and humanity which he had at first assumed, became cruelty and pride; so that many of the greatest citizens and noblest people were, either by fines, death, or some new invention, grievously oppressed. And in completing the same bad system, both without the city and within, he appointed six rectors for the country, who beat and plundered the inhabitants. He suspected the great, although he had been benefited by them, and had restored many to their country; for he felt assured that the generous minds of the nobility would not allow them, from any motives, to submit contentedly to his authority. He also began to confer benefits and advantages upon the lowest orders, thinking that with their assistance, and the arms of foreigners, he would be able to preserve the tyranny. The month of May, during which feasts are held, being come, he caused many companies to be formed of the plebeians and very lowest of the people, and to these, dignified with splendid titles, he gave colors and money; and while one party went in bacchanalian procession through the city, others were stationed in different parts of it, to receive them as guests. As the report of the duke's authority spread abroad, many of French origin came to him, for all of whom he found offices and emoluments, as if they had been the most trustworthy of men; so that in a short time Florence became not only subject to French dominion, but adopted their dress and manners; for men and women, without regard to propriety or sense of shame, imitated them. But that which disgusted the people most completely was the violence which, without any distinction of quality or rank, he and his followers committed upon the women.

The people were filled with indignation, seeing the majesty of the state overturned, its ordinances annihilated, its laws annulled, and every decent regulation set at naught; for men unaccustomed to royal pomp could not endure to see this man surrounded with his armed satellites on foot and on horseback; and having now a closer view of their disgrace, they were compelled to honor him whom they in the highest degree hated. To this hatred, was added the terror occasioned by the continual imposition of new taxes and frequent shedding of blood, with which he impoverished and consumed the city.

The duke was not unaware of these impressions existing strongly in the people's minds, nor was he without fear of the consequences; but still pretended to think himself beloved; and when Matteo di Morozzo, either to acquire his favor or to free himself from danger, gave information that the family of the Medici and some others had entered into a conspiracy against him he not only did not inquire into the matter, but caused the informer to be put to a cruel death. This mode of proceeding restrained those who were disposed to acquaint him of his danger and gave additional courage to such as sought his ruin. Bertone Cini, having ventured to speak against the taxes with which the people were loaded, had his tongue cut out with such barbarous cruelty as to cause his death. This shocking act increased the people's rage, and their hatred of the duke; for those who were accustomed to discourse and to act upon every occasion with the greatest boldness, could not endure to live with their hands tied and forbidden to speak.

This oppression increased to such a degree, that not merely the Florentines, who though unable to preserve their liberty cannot endure slavery, but the most servile people on earth would have been roused to attempt the recovery of freedom; and consequently many citizens of all ranks resolved either to deliver themselves from this odious tyranny or die in the attempt. Three distinct conspiracies were formed; one of the great; another of the people, and the third of the working classes; each of which, besides the general causes which operated upon the whole, were excited by some other particular grievance. The great found themselves deprived of all participation in the government; the people had lost the power they possessed, and the artificers saw themselves deficient in the usual remuneration of their labor.

Agnolo Acciajuoli was at this time archbishop of Florence, and by his discourses had formerly greatly favored the duke, and procured him many followers among the higher class of the people. But when he found him lord of the city, and became acquainted with his tyrannical mode of proceeding, it appeared to him that he had misled his countrymen; and to correct the evil he had done, he saw no other course, but to attempt the cure by the means which had caused it. He therefore became the leader of the first and most powerful conspiracy, and was joined by the Bardi, Rossi, Frescobaldi, Scali Altoviti, Magalotti, Strozzi, and Mancini. Of the second, the principals were Manno and Corso Donati, and with them the Pazzi, Cavicciulli, Cerchi, and Albizzi. Of the third the first was Antonio Adimari, and with him the Medici, Bordini, Rucellai, and Aldobrandini. It was the intention of these last, to slay him in the house of the Albizzi, whither he was expected to go on St. John's day, to see the horses run, but he not having gone, their design did not succeed. They then resolved to attack him as he rode through the city; but they found this would be very difficult; for he was always accompanied with a considerable armed force, and never took the same road twice together, so that they had no certainty of where to find him. They had a design of slaying him in the council, although they knew that if he were dead, they would be at the mercy of his followers.

While these matters were being considered by the conspirators, Antonio Adimari, in expectation of getting assistance from them, disclosed the affair to some Siennese, his friends, naming certain of the conspirators, and assuring them that the whole city was ready to rise at once. One of them communicated the matter to Francesco Brunelleschi, not with a design to injure the plot, but in the hope that he would join them. Francesco, either from personal fear, or private hatred of some one, revealed the whole to the duke; whereupon, Pagolo del Mazecha and Simon da Monterappoli were taken, who acquainted him with the number and quality of the conspirators. This terrified him, and he was advised to request their presence rather than to take them prisoners, for if they fled, he might without disgrace, secure himself by banishment of the rest. He therefore sent for Antonio Adimari, who, confiding in his companions, appeared immediately, and was detained. Francesco Brunelleschi and Uguccione Buondelmonti advised the duke to take as many of the conspirators prisoners as he could, and put them to death; but he, thinking his strength unequal to his foes, did not adopt this course, but took another, which, had it succeeded, would have freed him from his enemies and increased his power. It was the custom of the duke to call the citizens together upon some occasions and advise with them. He therefore having first sent to collect forces from without, made a list of three hundred citizens, and gave it to his messengers, with orders to assemble them under the pretense of public business; and having drawn them together, it was his intention either to put them to death or imprison them.

The capture of Antonio Adimari and the sending for forces, which could not be kept secret, alarmed the citizens, and more particularly those who were in the plot, so that the boldest of them refused to attend, and as each had read the list, they sought each other, and resolved to rise at once and die like men, with arms in their hands, rather than be led like calves to the slaughter. In a very short time the chief conspirators became known to each other, and resolved that the next day, which was the 26th July, 1343, they would raise a disturbance in the Old Market place, then arm themselves and call the people to freedom.

The next morning being come, at nine o'clock, according to agreement, they took arms, and at the call of liberty assembled, each party in its own district, under the ensigns and with the arms of the people, which had been secretly provided by the conspirators. All the heads of families, as well of the nobility as of the people, met together, and swore to stand in each other's defense, and effect the death of the duke; except some of the Buondelmonti and of the Cavalcanti, with those four families of the people which had taken so conspicuous a part in making him sovereign, and the butchers, with others, the lowest of the plebeians, who met armed in the piazza in his favor.

The duke immediately fortified the place, and ordered those of his people who were lodged in different parts of the city to mount upon horseback and join those in the court; but, on their way thither, many were attacked and slain. However, about three hundred horse assembled, and the duke was in doubt whether he should come forth and meet the enemy, or defend himself within. On the other hand, the Medici, Cavicciulli, Rucellai, and other families who had been most injured by him, fearful that if he came forth, many of those who had taken arms against him would discover themselves his partisans, in order to deprive him of the occasion of attacking them and increasing the number of his friends, took the lead and assailed the palace. Upon this, those families of the people who had declared for the duke, seeing themselves boldly attacked, changed their minds, and all took part with the citizens, except Uguccione Buondelmonti, who retired into the palace, and Giannozzo Cavalcanti, who having withdrawn with some of his followers to the new market, mounted upon a bench, and begged that those who were going in arms to the piazza, would take the part of the duke. In order to terrify them, he exaggerated the number of his people and threatened all with death who should obstinately persevere in their undertaking against their sovereign. But not finding any one either to follow him, or to chastise his insolence, and seeing his labor fruitless, he withdrew to his own house.

In the meantime, the contest in the piazza between the people and the forces of the duke was very great; but although the place served them for defense, they were overcome, some yielding to the enemy, and others, quitting their horses, fled within the walls. While this was going on, Corso and Amerigo Donati, with a part of the people, broke open the stinche, or prisons; burnt the papers of the provost and of the public chamber; pillaged the houses of the rectors, and slew all who had held offices under the duke whom they could find. The duke, finding the piazza in possession of his enemies, the city opposed to him, and without any hope of assistance, endeavored by an act of clemency to recover the favor of the people. Having caused those whom he had made prisoners to be brought before him, with amiable and kindly expressions he set them at liberty, and made Antonio Adimari a knight, although quite against his will. He caused his own arms to be taken down, and those of the people to be replaced over the palace; but these things coming out of season, and forced by his necessities, did him little good. He remained, notwithstanding all he did, besieged in the palace, and saw that having aimed at too much he had lost all, and would most likely, after a few days, die either of hunger, or by the weapons of his enemies. The citizens assembled in the church of Santa Reparata, to form the new government, and appointed fourteen citizens, half from the nobility and half from the people, who, with the archbishop, were invested with full authority to re-model the state of Florence. They also elected six others to take upon them the duties of provost, till he who should be finally chosen took office, the duties of which were usually performed by a subject of some neighboring state.

Many had come to Florence in defense of the people; among whom were a party from Sienna, with six ambassadors, men of high consideration in their own country. These endeavored to bring the people and the duke to terms; but the former refused to listen to any whatever, unless Guglielmo da Scesi and his son, with Cerrettieri Bisdomini, were first given up to them. The duke would not consent to this; but being threatened by those who were shut up with him, he was forced to comply. The rage of men is certainly always found greater, and their revenge more furious upon the recovery of liberty, than when it has only been defended. Guglielmo and his son were placed among the thousands of their enemies, and the latter was not yet eighteen years old; neither his beauty, his innocence, nor his youth, could save him from the fury of the multitude; but both were instantly slain. Those who could not wound them while alive, wounded them after they were dead; and not satisfied with tearing them to pieces, they hewed their bodies with swords, tore them with their hands, and even with their teeth. And that every sense might be satiated with vengeance, having first heard their moans, seen their wounds, and touched their lacerated bodies, they wished even the stomach to be satisfied, that having glutted the external senses, the one within might also have its share. This rabid fury, however hurtful to the father and son, was favorable to Cerrettieri; for the multitude, wearied with their cruelty toward the former, quite forgot him, so that he, not being asked for, remained in the palace, and during night was conveyed safely away by his friends.

The rage of the multitude being appeased by their blood, an agreement was made that the duke and his people, with whatever belonged to him, should quit the city in safety; that he should renounce all claim, of whatever kind, upon Florence, and that upon his arrival in the Casentino he should ratify his renunciation. On the sixth of August he set out, accompanied by many citizens, and having arrived at the Casentino he ratified the agreement, although unwillingly, and would not have kept his word if Count Simon had not threatened to take him back to Florence. This duke, as his proceedings testified, was cruel and avaricious, difficult to speak with, and haughty in reply. He desired the service of men, not the cultivation of their better feelings, and strove rather to inspire them with fear than love. Nor was his person less despicable than his manners; he was short, his complexion was black, and he had a long, thin beard. He was thus in every respect contemptible; and at the end of ten months, his misconduct deprived him of the sovereignty which the evil counsel of others had given him.

CHAPTER IX

Many cities and territories, subject to the Florentines, rebel--Prudent conduct adopted upon this occasion--The city is divided into quarters--Disputes between the nobility and the people--The bishop endeavors to reconcile them, but does not succeed--The government reformed by the people--Riot of Andrea Strozzi--Serious disagreements between the nobility and the people--They come to arms, and the nobility are subdued--The plague in Florence of which Boccaccio speaks.

These events taking place in the city, induced all the dependencies of the Florentine state to throw off their yoke; so that Arezzo, Castiglione, Pistoia, Volterra, Colle, and San Gemigniano rebelled. Thus Florence found herself deprived of both her tyrant and her dominions at the same moment, and in recovering her liberty, taught her subjects how they might become free. The duke being expelled and the territories lost, the fourteen citizens and the bishop thought it would be better to act kindly toward their subjects in peace, than to make them enemies by war, and to show a desire that their subjects should be free as well as themselves. They therefore sent ambassadors to the people of Arezzo, to renounce all dominion over that city, and to enter into a treaty with them; to the end that as they could not retain them as subjects, they might make use of them as friends. They also, in the best manner they were able, agreed with the other places that they should retain their freedom, and that, being free, they might mutually assist each other in the preservation of their liberties. This prudent course was attended with a most favorable result; for Arezzo, not many years afterward, returned to the Florentine rule, and the other places, in the course of a few months, returned to their former obedience. Thus it frequently occurs that we sooner attain our ends by a seeming indifferent to them, than by more obstinate pursuit.

Having settled external affairs, they now turned to the consideration of those within the city; and after some altercation between the nobility and the people, it was arranged that the nobility should form one-third of the Signory and fill one-half of the other offices. The city was, as we have before shown, divided into sixths; and hence there would be six signors, one for each sixth, except when, from some more than ordinary cause, there had been twelve or thirteen created; but when this had occurred they were again soon reduced to six. It now seemed desirable to make an alteration in this respect, as well because the sixths were not properly divided, as that, wishing to give their proportion to the great, it became desirable to increase the number. They therefore divided the city into quarters, and for each created three signors. They abolished the office of Gonfalonier of Justice, and also the Gonfaloniers of the companies of the people; and instead of the twelve Buonuomini, or good men, created eight counsellors, four from each party. The government having been established in this manner, the city might have been in repose if the great had been content to live in that moderation which civil society requires. But they produced a contrary result, for those out of office would not conduct themselves as citizens, and those who were in government wished to be lords, so that every day furnished some new instance of their insolence and pride. These things were very grievous to the people, and they began to regret that for one tyrant put down, there had sprung up a thousand. The arrogance of one party and the anger of the other rose to such a degree, that the heads of the people complained to the bishop of the improper conduct of the nobility, and what unfit associates they had become for the people; and begged he would endeavor to induce them to be content with their share of administration in the other offices, and leave the magistracy of the Signory wholly to themselves.

The bishop was naturally a well-meaning man, but his want of firmness rendered him easily influenced. Hence, at the instance of his associates, he at first favored the duke of Athens, and afterward, by the advice of other citizens, conspired against him. At the reformation of the government, he had favored the nobility, and now he appeared to incline toward the people, moved by the reasons which they had advanced. Thinking to find in others the same instability of purpose, he endeavored to effect an amicable arrangement. With this design he called together the fourteen who were yet in office, and in the best terms he could imagine advised them to give up the Signory to the people, in order to secure the peace of the city; and assured them that if they refused, ruin would most probably be the result.

This discourse excited the anger of the nobility to the highest pitch, and Ridolfo de' Bardi reproved him in unmeasured terms as a man of little faith; reminding him of his friendship for the duke, to prove the duplicity of his present conduct, and saying, that in driving him away he had acted the part of a traitor. He concluded by telling him, that the honors they had acquired at their own peril, they would at their own peril defend. They then left the bishop, and in great wrath, informed their associates in the government, and all the families of the nobility, of what had been done. The people also expressed their thoughts to each other, and as the nobility made preparations for the defense of their signors, they determined not to wait till they had perfected their arrangements; and therefore, being armed, hastened to the palace, shouting, as they went along, that the nobility must give up their share in the government.

The uproar and excitement were astonishing. The Signors of the nobility found themselves abandoned; for their friends, seeing all the people in arms, did not dare to rise in their defense, but each kept within his own house. The Signors of the people endeavored to abate the excitement of the multitude, by affirming their associates to be good and moderate men; but, not succeeding in their attempt, to avoid a greater evil, sent them home to their houses, whither they were with difficulty conducted. The nobility having left the palace, the office of the four councillors was taken from their party, and conferred upon twelve of the people. To the eight signors who remained, a Gonfalonier of Justice was added, and sixteen Gonfaloniers of the companies of the people; and the council was so reformed, that the government remained wholly in the hands of the popular party.

At the time these events took place there was a great scarcity in the city, and discontent prevailed both among the highest and the lowest classes; in the latter for want of food, and in the former from having lost their power in the state. This circumstance induced Andrea Strozzi to think of making himself sovereign of the city. Selling his corn at a lower price than others did, a great many people flocked to his house; emboldened by the sight of these, he one morning mounted his horse, and, followed by a considerable number, called the people to arms, and in a short time drew together about 4,000 men, with whom he proceeded to the Signory, and demanded that the gates of the palace should be opened. But the signors, by threats and the force which they retained in the palace, drove them from the court; and then by proclamation so terrified them, that they gradually dropped off and returned to their homes, and Andrea, finding himself alone, with some difficulty escaped falling into the hands of the magistrates.

This event, although an act of great temerity, and attended with the result that usually follows such attempts, raised a hope in the minds of the nobility of overcoming the people, seeing that the lowest of the plebeians were at enmity with them. And to profit by this circumstance, they resolved to arm themselves, and with justifiable force recover those rights of which they had been unjustly deprived. Their minds acquired such an assurance of success, that they openly provided themselves with arms, fortified their houses, and even sent to their friends in Lombardy for assistance. The people and the Signory made preparation for their defense, and requested aid from Perugia and Sienna, so that the city was filled with the armed followers of either party. The nobility on this side of the Arno divided themselves into three parts; the one occupied the houses of the Cavicciulli, near the church of St. John; another, the houses of the Pazzi and the Donati, near the great church of St. Peter; and the third those of the Cavalcanti in the New Market. Those beyond the river fortified the bridges and the streets in which their houses stood; the Nerli defended the bridge of the Carraja; the Frescobaldi and the Manelli, the church of the Holy Trinity; and the Rossi and the Bardi, the bridge of the Rubaconte and the Old Bridge. The people were drawn together under the Gonfalon of justice and the ensigns of the companies of the artisans.

Both sides being thus arranged in order of battle, the people thought it imprudent to defer the contest, and the attack was commenced by the Medici and the Rondinelli, who assailed the Cavicciulli, where the houses of the latter open upon the piazza of St. John. Here both parties contended with great obstinacy, and were mutually wounded, from the towers by stones and other missiles, and from below by arrows. They fought for three hours; but the forces of the people continuing to increase, and the Cavicciulli finding themselves overcome by numbers, and hopeless of other assistance, submitted themselves to the people, who saved their houses and property; and having disarmed them, ordered them to disperse among their relatives and friends, and remain unarmed. Being victorious in the first attack, they easily overpowered the Pazzi and the Donati, whose numbers were less than those they had subdued; so that there only remained on this side of the Arno, the Cavalcanti, who were strong both in respect of the post they had chosen and in their followers. Nevertheless, seeing all the Gonfalons against them, and that the others had been overcome by three Gonfalons alone, they yielded without offering much resistance. Three parts of the city were now in the hands of the people, and only one in possession of the nobility; but this was the strongest, as well on account of those who held it, as from its situation, being defended by the Arno; hence it was first necessary to force the bridges. The Old Bridge was first assailed and offered a brave resistance; for the towers were armed, the streets barricaded, and the barricades defended by the most resolute men; so that the people were repulsed with great loss. Finding their labor at this point fruitless, they endeavored to force the Rubaconte Bridge, but no better success resulting, they left four Gonfalons in charge of the two bridges, and with the others attacked the bridge of the Carraja. Here, although the Nerli defended themselves like brave men, they could not resist the fury of the people; for this bridge, having no towers, was weaker than the others, and was attacked by the Capponi, and many families of the people who lived in that vicinity. Being thus assailed on all sides, they abandoned the barricades and gave way to the people, who then overcame the Rossi and the Frescobaldi; for all those beyond the Arno took part with the conquerors.

There was now no resistance made except by the Bardi, who remained undaunted, notwithstanding the failure of their friends, the union of the people against them, and the little chance of success which they seemed to have. They resolved to die fighting, and rather see their houses burned and plundered, than submit to the power of their enemies. They defended themselves with such obstinacy, that many fruitless attempts were made to overcome them, both at the Old Bridge and the Rubaconte; but their foes were always repulsed with loss. There had in former times been a street which led between the houses of the Pitti, from the Roman road to the walls upon Mount St. George. By this way the people sent six Gonfalons, with orders to assail their houses from behind. This attack overcame the resolution of the Bardi, and decided the day in favor of the people; for when those who defended the barricades in the street learned that their houses were being plundered, they left the principal fight and hastened to their defense. This caused the Old Bridge to be lost;

the Bardi fled in all directions and were received into the houses of the Quaratesi, Panzanesi, and Mozzi. The people, especially the lower classes, greedy for spoil, sacked and destroyed their houses, and pulled down and burned their towers and palaces with such outrageous fury, that the most cruel enemy of the Florentine name would have been ashamed of taking part in such wanton destruction.

The nobility being thus overcome, the people reformed the government; and as they were of three kinds, the higher, the middle, and the lower class, it was ordered that the first should appoint two signors; the two latter three each, and that the Gonfalonier should be chosen alternately from either party. Besides this, all the regulations for the restraint of the nobility were renewed; and in order to weaken them still more, many were reduced to the grade of the people. The ruin of the nobility was so complete, and depressed them so much, that they never afterward ventured to take arms for the recovery of their power, but soon became humbled and abject in the extreme. And thus Florence lost the generosity of her character and her distinction in arms.

After these events the city remained in peace till the year 1353. In the course of this period occurred the memorable plague, described with so much eloquence by Giovanni Boccaccio, and by which Florence lost 96,000 souls. In 1348, began the first war with the Visconti, occasioned by the archbishop, then prince of Milan; and when this was concluded, dissensions again arose in the city; for although the nobility were destroyed, fortune did not fail to cause new divisions and new troubles.

BOOK III

CHAPTER I

Reflections upon the domestic discords of republics--A parallel between the discords of Rome and those of Florence--Enmities between the families of the Ricci and the Albizzi--Uguccione de' Ricci causes the laws against the Ghibellines to be renewed in order to injure the Albizzi--Piero degli Albizzi derives advantage from it--Origin of admonitions and the troubles which result from them--Uguccione de' Ricci moderates their injustice--Difficulties increase--A meeting of the citizens--They address the Signory--The Signory attempt to remedy the evils.

Those serious, though natural enmities, which occur between the popular classes and the nobility, arising from the desire of the latter to command, and the disinclination of the former to obey, are the causes of most of the troubles which take place in cities; and from this diversity of purpose, all the other evils which disturb republics derive their origin. This kept Rome disunited; and this, if it be allowable to compare small things with great, held Florence in disunion; although in each city it produced a different result; for animosities were only beginning with the people and nobility of Rome contended, while ours were brought to a conclusion by the contentions of our citizens. A new law settled the disputes of Rome; those of Florence were only terminated by the death and banishment of many of her best people. Those of Rome increased her military virtue, while that of Florence was quite extinguished by her divisions. The quarrels of Rome established different ranks of society, those of Florence abolished the distinctions which had previously existed. This diversity of effects must have been occasioned by the different purposes which the two people had in view. While the people of Rome endeavored to associate with the nobility in the supreme honors, those of Florence strove to exclude the nobility from all participation in them: as the desire of the Roman people was more reasonable, no particular offense was given to the nobility; they therefore consented to it without having recourse to arms; so that, after some disputes concerning particular points, both parties agreed to the enactment of a law which, while it satisfied the people, preserved the nobility in the enjoyment of their dignity.

On the other hand, the demands of the people of Florence being insolent and unjust, the nobility, became desperate, prepared for their defense with their utmost energy, and thus bloodshed and the exile of citizens followed. The laws which were afterward made, did not provide for the common good, but were framed wholly in favor of the conquerors. This too, must be observed, that from the acquisition of power, made by the people of Rome, their minds were very much improved; for all the offices of state being attainable as well by the people as the nobility, the peculiar excellencies of the latter exercised a most beneficial influence upon the former; and as the city increased in virtue she attained a more exalted greatness.

But in Florence, the people being conquerors, the nobility were deprived of all participation in the government; and in order to regain a portion of it, it became necessary for them not only to seem like the people, but to be like them in behavior, mind, and mode of living. Hence arose those changes in armorial bearings, and in the titles of families, which the nobility adopted, in order that they might seem to be of the people; military virtue and generosity of feeling became extinguished in them; the people not possessing these qualities, they could not appreciate them, and Florence became by degrees more and more depressed and humiliated. The virtue of the Roman nobility degenerating into pride, the citizens soon found that the business of the state could not be carried on without a prince. Florence had now come to such a point, that with a comprehensive mind at the head of affairs she would easily have been made to take any form that he might have been disposed to give her; as may be partly observed by a perusal of the preceding book.

Having given an account of the origin of Florence, the commencement of her liberty, with the causes of her divisions, and shown how the factions of the nobility and the people ceased with the tyranny of the duke of Athens, and the ruin of the former, we have now to speak of the animosities between the citizens and the plebeians and the various circumstances which they produced.

The nobility being overcome, and the war with the archbishop of Milan concluded, there did not appear any cause of dissension in Florence. But the evil fortune of the city, and the defective nature of her laws, gave rise to enmities between the family of the Albizzi and that of the Ricci, which divided her citizens as completely as those of the Buondelmonti and the Uberti, or the Donati and the Cerchi had formerly done. The pontiffs, who at this time resided in France, and the emperors, who abode in Germany, in order to maintain their influence in Italy, sent among us multitudes of soldiers of many countries, as English, Dutch, and Bretons. As these, upon the conclusion of a war, were thrown out of pay, though still in the country, they, under the standard of some soldier of fortune, plundered such people as were least prepared to defend themselves. In the year 1353 one of these companies came into Tuscany under the command of Monsignor Reale, of Provence, and his approach terrified all the cities of Italy. The Florentines not only provided themselves forces, but many citizens, among whom were the Albizzi and the Ricci, armed themselves in their own defense. These families were at the time full of hatred against each other, and each thought to obtain the sovereignty of the republic by overcoming his enemy. They had not yet proceeded to open violence, but only contended in the magistracies and councils. The city being all in arms, a quarrel arose in the Old Market place, and, as it frequently happens in similar cases, a great number of people were drawn together. The disturbance spreading, it was told the Ricci that the Albizzi had assailed their partisans, and to the Albizzi that the Ricci were in quest of them. Upon this the whole city arose, and it was all the magistrates could do to restrain these families, and prevent the actual occurrence of a disaster which, without being the fault of either of them, had been willfully though falsely reported as having already taken place. This apparently trifling circumstance served to inflame the minds of the parties, and make each the more resolved to increase the number of their followers. And as the citizens, since the ruin of the nobility, were on such an equality that the magistrates were more respected now than they had previously been, they designed to proceed toward the suppression of this disorder with civil authority alone.

We have before related, that after the victory of Charles I. the government was formed of the Guelphic party, and that it thus acquired great authority over the Ghibellines. But time, a variety of circumstances, and new divisions had so contributed to sink this party feeling into oblivion, that many of Ghibelline descent now filled the highest offices. Observing this, Uguccione, the head of the family of the Ricci, contrived that the law against the Ghibellines should be again brought into operation; many imagining the Albizzi to be of that faction, they having arisen in Arezzo, and come long ago to Florence. Uguccione by this means hoped to deprive the Albizzi of participation in the government, for all of Ghibelline blood who were found to hold offices, would be condemned in the penalties which this law provided. The design of Uguccione was discovered to Piero son of Filippo degli Albizzi, and he resolved to favor it: for he saw that to oppose it would at once declare him a Ghibelline; and thus the law which was renewed by the ambition of the Ricci for his destruction, instead of robbing Piero degli Albizzi of reputation, contributed to increase his influence, although it laid the foundation of many evils. Nor is it possible for a republic to enact a law more pernicious than one relating to matters which have long transpired. Piero having favored this law, which had been contrived by his enemies for his stumbling-block, it became the stepping-stone to his greatness; for, making himself the leader of this new order of things, his authority went on increasing, and he was in greater favor with the Guelphs than any other man.

As there could not be found a magistrate willing to search out who were Ghibellines, and as this renewed enactment against them was therefore of small value, it was provided that authority should be given to the Capitani to find out who were of this faction; and, having discovered, to signify and ADMONISH them that they were not to take upon themselves any office of government; to which ADMONITIONS, if they were disobedient, they became condemned in the penalties. Hence, all those who in Florence are deprived of the power to hold offices are called ammoniti, or ADMONISHED.

The Capitani in time acquiring greater audacity, admonished not only those to whom the admonition was applicable, but any others at the suggestion of their own avarice or ambition; and from 1356, when this law was made, to 1366, there had been admonished above 200 citizens. The Captains of the Parts and the sect of the Guelphs were thus become powerful; for every one honored them for fear of being admonished; and most particularly the leaders, who were Piero degli Albizzi, Lapo da Castiglionchio, and Carlo Strozzi. This insolent mode of proceeding was offensive to many; but none felt so particularly injured with it as the Ricci; for they knew themselves to have occasioned it, they saw it involved the ruin of the republic, and their enemies, the Albizzi, contrary to their intention, became great in consequence.

On this account Uguccione de' Ricci, being one of the Signory, resolved to put an end to the evil which he and his friends had originated, and with a new law provided that to the six Captains of Parts an additional three should be appointed, of whom two should be chosen from the companies of minor artificers, and that before any party could be declared Ghibelline, the declaration of the Capitani must be confirmed by twenty-four Guelphic citizens, appointed for the purpose. This provision tempered for a time the power of the Capitani, so that the admonitions were greatly diminished, if not wholly laid aside. Still the parties of the Albizzi and the Ricci were continually on the alert to oppose each other's laws, deliberations, and enterprises, not from a conviction of their inexpediency, but from a hatred of their promoters.

In such distractions the time passed from 1366 to 1371, when the Guelphs again regained the ascendant. There was in the family of the Buondelmonti a gentleman named Benchi, who, as an acknowledgment of his merit in a war against the Pisans, though one of the nobility, had been admitted among the people, and thus became eligible to office among the Signory; but when about to take his seat with them, a law was made that no nobleman who had become of the popular class should be allowed to assume that office. This gave great offense to Benchi, who, in union with Piero degli Albizzi, determined to depress the less powerful of the popular party with ADMONITIONS, and obtain the government for themselves. By the interest which Benchi possessed with the ancient nobility, and that of Piero with most of the influential citizens, the Guelphic party resumed their ascendancy, and by new reforms among the PARTS, so remodeled the administration as to be able to dispose of the offices of the captains and the twenty-four citizens at pleasure. They then returned to the ADMONITIONS with greater audacity than ever, and the house of the Albizzi became powerful as the head of this faction.

On the other hand, the Ricci made the most strenuous exertions against their designs; so that anxiety universally prevailed, and ruin was apprehended alike from both parties. In consequence of this a great number of citizens, out of love to their country, assembled in the church of St. Piero Scarraggio, and after a long consideration of the existing disorders, presented themselves before the Signors, whom one of the principal among them addressed in the following terms:--

"Many of us, magnificent Signors! were afraid of meeting even for consideration of public business, without being publicly called together, lest we should be noted as presumptuous or condemned as ambitious. But seeing that so many citizens daily assemble in the lodges and halls of the palace, not for any public utility, but only for the gratification of their own ambition, we have thought that as those who assemble for the ruin of the republic are fearless, so still less ought they to be apprehensive who meet together only for its advantage; nor ought we to be anxious respecting the opinion they may form of our assembling, since they are so utterly indifferent to the opinion of others. Our affection for our country, magnificent Signors! caused us to assemble first, and now brings us before you, to speak of grievances already great and daily increasing in our republic, and to offer our assistance for their removal: and we doubt not that, though a difficult undertaking, it will still be attended with success, if you will lay aside all private regards, and authoritatively use the public force.

"The common corruption of all the cities of Italy, magnificent Signors! has infested and still vitiates your own; for when this province had shaken off the imperial yoke, her cities not being subject to any powerful influence that might restrain them, administered affairs, not as free men do, but as a factious populace; and hence have arisen all the other evils and disorders that have appeared. In the first place, there cannot be found among the citizens either unity or friendship, except with those whose common guilt, either against their country or against private individuals, is a bond of union. And as the knowledge of religion and the fear of God seem to be alike extinct, oaths and promises have lost their validity, and are kept as long as it is found expedient; they are adopted only as a means of deception, and he is most applauded and respected whose cunning is most efficient and secure. On this account bad men are received with the approbation due to virtue, and good ones are regarded only in the light of fools.

"And certainly in the cities of Italy all that is corruptible and corrupting is assembled. The young are idle, the old lascivious, and each sex and every age abounds with debasing habits, which the good laws, by misapplication, have lost the power to correct. Hence arises the avarice so observable among the citizens, and that greediness, not for true glory, but for unworthy honors; from which follow hatred, animosities, quarrels, and factions; resulting in deaths, banishments, affliction to all good men, and the advancement of the most unprincipled; for the good, confiding in their innocence, seek neither safety nor advancement by illegal methods as the wicked do, and thus unhonored and undefended they sink into oblivion.

"From proceedings such as these, arise at once the attachment for and influence of parties; bad men follow them through ambition and avarice, and necessity compels the good to pursue the same course. And most lamentable is it to observe how the leaders and movers of parties sanctify their base designs with words that are all piety and virtue; they have the name of liberty constantly in their mouths, though their actions prove them her greatest enemies. The reward which they desire from victory is not the glory of having given liberty to the city, but the satisfaction of having vanquished others, and of making themselves rulers; and to attain their end, there is nothing too unjust, too cruel, too avaricious for them to attempt. Thus laws and ordinances, peace, wars, and treaties are adopted and pursued, not for the public good, not for the common glory of the state, but for the convenience or advantage of a few individuals.

"And if other cities abound in these disorders, ours is more than any infected with them; for her laws, statutes, and civil ordinances are not, nor have they ever been, established for the benefit of men in a state of freedom, but according to the wish of the faction that has been uppermost at the time. Hence it follows that, when one party is expelled, or faction extinguished, another immediately arises; for, in a city that is governed by parties rather than by laws, as soon as one becomes dominant and unopposed, it must of necessity soon divide against itself; for the private methods at first adapted for its defense will now no longer keep it united. The truth of this, both the ancient and modern dissensions of our city prove. Everyone thought that when the Ghibellines were destroyed, the Guelphs would long continue happy and honored; yet after a short time they divided into the Bianchi and Neri, the black faction and the white. When the Bianchi were overcome, the city was not long free from factions; for either, in favor of the emigrants, or on account of the animosity between the nobility and the people, we were still constantly at war. And as if resolved to give up to others, what in mutual harmony we either would not or were unable to retain, we confided the care of our precious liberty first to King Robert, then to his brother, next to his son, and at last to the duke of Athens. Still we have never in any condition found repose, but seem like men who can neither agree to live in freedom nor be content with slavery. Nor did we hesitate (so greatly does the nature of our ordinances dispose us to division), while yet under allegiance to the king, to substitute for his majesty, one of the vilest of men born at Agobbio.

"For the credit of the city, the name of the duke of Athens ought to be consigned to oblivion. His cruel and tyrannical disposition, however, might have taught us wisdom and instructed us how to live; but no sooner was he expelled than we handled our arms, and fought with more hatred, and greater fury than we had ever done on any former occasion; so that the ancient nobility were vanquished the city was left at the disposal of the people. It was generally supposed that no further occasion of quarrel or of party animosity could arise, since those whose pride and insupportable ambition had been regarded as the causes of them were depressed; however, experience proves how liable human judgment is to error, and what false impressions men imbibe, even in regard to the things that most intimately concern them; for we find the pride and ambition of the nobility are not extinct, but only transferred from them to the people who at this moment, according to the usual practice of ambitious men, are endeavoring to render themselves masters of the republic; and knowing they have no chance of success but what is offered by discord, they have again divided the city, and the names of Guelph and Ghibelline, which were beginning to be forgotten (and it would have been well if they had never been heard among us), are repeated anew in our ears.

"It seems almost necessarily ordained, in order that in human affairs there may be nothing either settled or permanent, that in all republics there are what may be called fatal families, born for the ruin of their country. Of this kind of pest our city has produced a more copious brood than any other; for not one but many have disturbed and harassed her: first the Buondelmonti and the Uberti; then the Donati and the Cerchi; and now, oh ridiculous! oh disgraceful thought! the Ricci and the Albizzi have caused a division of her citizens.

"We have not dwelt upon our corrupt habits or our old and continual dissensions to occasion you alarm, but to remind you of their causes; to show that as you doubtless are aware of them, we also keep them in view, and to remind you that their results ought not to make you diffident of your power to repress the disorders of the present time. The ancient families possessed so much influence, and were held in such high esteem, that civil force was insufficient to restrain them; but now, when the empire has lost its ascendancy, the pope is no longer formidable, and the whole of Italy is reduced to a state of the most complete equality, there can be no difficulty. Our republic might more especially than any other (although at first our former practices seem to present a reason to the contrary), not only keep itself united but be improved by good laws and civil regulations, if you, the Signory, would once resolve to undertake the matter; and to this we, induced by no other motive than the love of our country, would most strongly urge you. It is true the corruption of the country is great, and much discretion will be requisite to correct it; but do not impute the past disorders to the nature of the men, but to the times, which, being changed, give reasonable ground to hope that, with better government, our city will be attended with better fortune; for the malignity of the people will be overcome by restraining the ambition and annulling the ordinances of those who have encouraged faction, and adopting in their stead only such principles as are conformable to true civil liberty. And be assured, that these desirable ends will be more certainly attained by the benign influence of the laws, than by a delay which will compel the people to effect them by force and arms."

The Signory, induced by the necessity of the case, of which they were previously aware, and further encouraged by the advice of those who now addressed them, gave authority to fifty-six citizens to provide for the safety of the republic. It is usually found that most men are better adapted to pursue a good course already begun, than to discover one applicable to immediate circumstances. These citizens thought rather of extinguishing existing factions than of preventing the formation of new ones, and effected neither of these objects. The facilities for the establishment of new parties were not removed; and out of those which they guarded against, another more powerful arose, which brought the republic into still greater danger. They, however, deprived three of the family of the Albizzi, and three of that of the Ricci, of all the offices of government, except those of the Guelphic party, for three years; and among the deprived were Piero degli Albizzi and Uguccione de' Ricci. They forbade the citizens to assemble in the palace, except during the sittings of the

Signory. They provided that if any one were beaten, or possession of his property detained from him, he might bring his case before the council and denounce the offender, even if he were one of the nobility; and that if it were proved, the accused should be subject to the usual penalties. This provision abated the boldness of the Ricci, and increased that of the Albizzi; since, although it applied equally to both, the Ricci suffered from it by far the most; for if Piero was excluded from the palace of the Signory, the chamber of the Guelphs, in which he possessed the greatest authority, remained open to him; and if he and his followers had previously been ready to ADMONISH, they became after this injury, doubly so. To this pre-disposition for evil, new excitements were added.

CHAPTER II

The war of the Florentines against the pope's legate, and the causes of it--League against the pope--The censures of the pope disregarded in Florence--The city is divided into two factions, the one the Capitani di Parte, the other of the eight commissioners of the war--Measures adopted by the Guelphic party against their adversaries--The Guelphs endeavor to prevent Salvestro de Medici from being chosen Gonfalonier--Salvestro de Medici Gonfalonier--His law against the nobility, and in favor of the Ammoniti--The Collegi disapprove of the law--Salvestro addresses the council in its favor--The law is passed--Disturbances in Florence.

The papal chair was occupied by Gregory XI. He, like his predecessors, residing at Avignon, governed Italy by legates, who, proud and avaricious, oppressed many of the cities. One of these legates, then at Bologna, taking advantage of a great scarcity of food at Florence, endeavored to render himself master of Tuscany, and not only withheld provisions from the Florentines, but in order to frustrate their hopes of the future harvest, upon the approach of spring, attacked them with a large army, trusting that being famished and unarmed, he should find them an easy conquest. He might perhaps have been successful, had not his forces been mercenary and faithless, and, therefore, induced to abandon the enterprise for the sum of 130,000 florins, which the Florentines paid them. People may go to war when they will, but cannot always withdraw when they like. This contest, commenced by the ambition of the legate, was sustained by the resentment of the Florentines, who, entering into a league with Bernabo of Milan, and with the cities hostile to the church, appointed eight citizens for the administration of it, giving them authority to act without appeal, and to expend whatever sums they might judge expedient, without rendering an account of the outlay.

This war against the pontiff, although Uguccione was now dead, reanimated those who had followed the party of the Ricci, who, in opposition to the Albizzi, had always favored Bernabo and opposed the church, and this, the rather, because the eight commissioners of war were all enemies of the Guelphs. This occasioned Piero degli Albizzi, Lapo da Castiglionchio, Carlo Strozzi, and others, to unite themselves more closely in opposition to their adversaries. The eight carried on the war, and the others admonished during three years, when the death of the pontiff put an end to the hostilities, which had been carried on which so much ability, and with such entire satisfaction to the people, that at the end of each year the eight were continued in office, and were called Santi, or holy, although they had set ecclesiastical censures at defiance, plundered the churches of their property, and compelled the priests to perform divine service. So much did citizens at that time prefer the good of their country to their ghostly consolations, and thus showed the church, that if as her friends they had defended, they could as enemies depress her; for the whole of Romagna, the Marches, and Perugia were excited to rebellion.

Yet while this war was carried on against the pope, they were unable to defend themselves against the captains of the parts and their faction; for the insolence of the Guelphs against the eight attained such a pitch, that they could not restrain themselves from abusive behavior, not merely against some of the most distinguished citizens, but even against the eight themselves; and the captains of the parts conducted themselves with such arrogance, that they were feared more than the Signory. Those who had business with them treated them with greater reverence, and their court was held in higher estimation: so that no ambassador came to Florence, without commission to the captains.

Pope Gregory being dead, and the city freed from external war; there still prevailed great confusion within; for the audacity of the Guelphs was insupportable, and as no available mode of subduing them presented itself, it was thought that recourse must be had to arms, to determine which party was the strongest. With the Guelphs were all the ancient nobility, and the greater part of the most popular leaders, of which number, as already remarked, were Lapo, Piero, and Carlo. On the other side, were all the lower orders, the leaders of whom were the eight commissioners of war, Giorgio Scali and Tommaso Strozzi, and with them the Ricci, Alberti, and Medici. The rest of the multitude, as most commonly happens, joined the discontented party.

It appeared to the heads of the Guelphic faction that their enemies would be greatly strengthened, and themselves in considerable danger in case a hostile Signory should resolve on their subjugation. Desirous, therefore, of being prepared against this calamity, the leaders of the party assembled to take into consideration the state of the city and that of their own friends in particular, and found the ammoniti so numerous and so great a difficulty, that the whole city was excited against them on this account. They could not devise any other remedy than, that as their enemies had deprived them of all the offices of honor, they should banish their opponents from the city, take possession of the palace of the Signory, and bring over the whole state to their own party; in imitation of the Guelphs of former times, who found no safety in the city, till they had driven all their adversaries out of it. They were unanimous upon the main point, but did not agree upon the time of carrying it into execution. It was in the month of April, in the year 1378, when Lapo, thinking delay inadvisable, expressed his opinion, that procrastination was in the highest degree perilous to themselves; as in the next Signory, Salvestro de' Medici would very probably be elected Gonfalonier, and they all knew he was opposed to their party. Piero degli Albizzi, on the other hand, thought it better to defer, since they would require forces, which could not be assembled without exciting observation, and if they were discovered, they would incur great risk. He thereupon judged it preferable to wait till the approaching feast of St. John on which, being the most solemn festival of the city, vast multitudes would be assembled, among whom they might conceal whatever numbers they pleased. To obviate their fears of Salvestro, he was to be ADMONISHED, and if this did not appear likely to be effectual, they would "ADMONISH" one of the Colleague of his quarter, and upon redrawing, as the ballot-boxes would be nearly empty, chance would very likely occasion that either he or some associate of his would be drawn, and he would thus be rendered incapable of sitting as Gonfalonier. They therefore came to the conclusion proposed by Piero, though Lapo consented reluctantly, considering the delay dangerous, and that, as no opportunity can be in all respects suitable, he who waits for the concurrence of every advantage, either never makes an attempt, or, if induced to do so, is most frequently foiled. They "admonished" the Colleague, but did not prevent the appointment of Salvestro, for the design was discovered by the Eight, who took care to render all attempts upon the drawing futile.

Salvestro Alammano de' Medici was therefore drawn Gonfalonier, and, being one of the noblest popular families, he could not endure that the people should be oppressed by a few powerful persons. Having resolved to put an end to their insolence, and perceiving the middle classes favorably disposed, and many of the highest of the people on his side, he communicated his design to Benedetto Alberti, Tommaso Strozzi, and Georgio Scali, who all promised their assistance. They, therefore, secretly draw up a law which had for its object to revive the restrictions upon the nobility, to retrench the authority of the Capitani di Parte, and recall the ammoniti to their dignity. In order to attempt and obtain their ends, at one and the same time, having to consult, first the Colleagues and then the Councils, Salvestro being Provost (which office for the time makes its possessor almost prince of the city), he called together the Colleagues and the Council on the same morning, and the Colleagues being apart, he proposed the law prepared by himself and his friends, which, being a novelty, encountered in their small number so much opposition, that he was unable to have it passed.

Salvestro, seeing his first attempt likely to fail, pretended to leave the room for a private reason, and, without being perceived, went immediately to the Council, and taking a lofty position from which he could be both seen and heard, said:-- "That considering himself invested with the office of Gonfalonier, not so much to preside in private cases (for which proper judges were appointed, who have their regular sittings), as to guard the state, correct the insolence of the powerful, and ameliorate those laws by the influence of which the republic was being ruined, he had carefully attended to both these duties, and to his utmost ability provided for them, but found the perversity of some so much opposed to his just designs as to deprive him of all opportunity of doing good, and them not only of the means of assisting him with their counsel, but even hearing him. Therefore finding he no longer contributed either to the benefit of the republic or of the people generally, he could not perceive any reason for his longer holding the magistracy, of which he was either undeserving, or others thought him so, and would therefore retire to his house, that the people might appoint another in his stead, who would either have greater virtue or better fortune than himself." And having said this, he left the room as if to return home.

Those of the council who were in the secret, and others desirous of novelty, raised a tumult, at which the Signory and the Colleagues came together, and finding the Gonfalonier leaving them, entreatingly and authoritatively detained him, and obliged him to return to the council room, which was now full of confusion. Many of the noble citizens were threatened in opprobrious language; and an artificer seized Carlo Strozzi by the throat, and would undoubtedly have murdered him, but was with difficulty prevented by those around. He who made the greatest disturbance, and incited the city to violence, was Benedetto degli Alberti, who, from a window of the palace, loudly called the people to arms; and presently the courtyards were filled with armed men, and the Colleagues granted to threats, what they had refused to entreaty. The Capitani di Parte had at the same time drawn together a great number of citizens to their hall to consult upon the means of defending themselves against the orders of the Signors, but when they heard the tumult that was raised, and were informed of the course the Councils had adopted, each took refuge in his own house.

Let no one, when raising popular commotions, imagine he can afterward control them at his pleasure, or restrain them from proceeding to the commission of violence. Salvestro intended to enact his law, and compose the city; but it happened otherwise; for the feelings of all had become so excited, that they shut up the shops; the citizens fortified themselves in their houses; many conveyed their valuable property into the churches and monasteries, and everyone seemed to apprehend something terrible at hand. The companies of the Arts met, and each appointed an additional officer or Syndic; upon which the Priors summoned their Colleagues and these Syndics, and consulted a whole day how the city might be appeased with satisfaction to the different parties; but much difference of opinion prevailed, and no conclusion was come to. On the following day the Arts brought forth their banners, which the Signory understanding, and being apprehensive of evil, called the Council together to consider what course to adopt. But scarcely were they met, when the uproar recommenced, and soon the ensigns of the Arts, surrounded by vast numbers of armed men, occupied the courts. Upon this the Council, to give the Arts and the people hope of redress, and free themselves as much as possible from the charge of causing the mischief, gave a general power, which in Florence is called Balia, to the Signors, the Colleagues, the Eight, the Capitani di Parte, and to the Syndics of the Arts, to reform the government of the city, for the common benefit of all. While this was being arranged, a few of the ensigns of the Arts and some of the mob, desirous of avenging themselves for the recent injuries they had received from the Guelphs, separated themselves from the rest, and sacked and burnt the house of Lapo da Castiglionchio, who, when he learned the proceedings of the Signory against the Guelphs, and saw the people in arms, having no other resource but concealment or flight, first took refuge in Santa Croce, and afterward, being disguised as a monk, fled into the Casentino, where he was often heard to blame himself for having consented to wait till St. John's day, before they had made themselves sure of the government. Piero degli Albizzi and Carlo Strozzi hid themselves upon the first outbreak of the tumult, trusting that when it was over, by the interest of their numerous friends and relations, they might remain safely in Florence.

The house of Lapo being burnt, as mischief begins with difficulty but easily increases, many other houses, either through public hatred, or private malice, shared the same fate; and the rioters, that they might have companions more eager than themselves to assist them in their work of plunder, broke open the public prisons, and then sacked the monastery of the Agnoli and the convent of S. Spirito, whither many citizens had taken their most valuable goods for safety. Nor would the public chambers have escaped these destroyers' hands, except out of reverence for one of the Signors, who on horseback, and followed by many citizens in arms, opposed the rage of the mob.

CHAPTER III

Contrary measures adopted by the magistrates to effect a pacification--Luigi Guicciardini the Gonfalonier entreats the magistrates of the Arts to endeavor to pacify the people--Serious riot caused by the plebeians--The woolen Art--The plebeians assemble--The speech of a seditious plebeian--Their resolution thereupon--The Signory discover the designs of the plebeians--Measures adopted to counteract them.

This popular fury being abated by the authority of the Signors and the approach of night, on the following day, the Balia relieved the admonished, on condition that they should not for three years be capable of holding any magistracy. They annulled the laws made by the Guelphs to the prejudice of the citizens; declared Lapo da Castiglionchio and his companions, rebels, and with them many others, who were the objects of universal detestation. After these resolutions, the new Signory were drawn for, and Luigi Guicciardini appointed Gonfalonier, which gave hope that the tumults would soon be appeased; for everyone thought them to be peaceable men and lovers of order. Still the shops were not opened, nor did the citizens lay down their arms, but continued to patrol the city in great numbers; so that the Signory did not assume the magistracy with the usual pomp, but merely assembled within the palace, omitting all ceremony.

This Signory, considering nothing more advisable in the beginning of their magistracy than to restore peace, caused a relinquishment of arms; ordered the shops to be opened, and the strangers who had been called to their aid, to return to their homes. They appointed guards in many parts of the city, so that if the admonished would only have remained quiet, order would soon have been re-established. But they were not satisfied to wait three years for the recovery of their honours; so that to gratify them the Arts again met, and demanded of the Signory, that for the benefit and quiet of the city, they would ordain that no citizens should at any time, whether Signor, Colleague, Capitano di Parte, or Consul of any art whatever, be admonished as a Ghibelline; and further, that new ballots of the Guelphic party should be made, and the old ones burned. These demands were at once acceded to, not only by the Signors, but by all the Councils; and thus it was hoped the tumults newly excited would be settled.

But since men are not satisfied with recovering what is their own, but wish to possess the property of others and to revenge themselves, those who were in hopes of benefiting by these disorders persuaded the artificers that they would never be safe, if several of their enemies were not expelled from the city or destroyed. This terrible doctrine coming to the knowledge of the Signory, they caused the magistrates of the Arts and their Syndics to be brought before them, and Luigi Guicciardini, the Gonfalonier, addressed them in the following words: "If these Signors, and I with them, had not long been acquainted with the fate of this city, that as soon as external wars have ceased the internal commence, we should have been more surprised, and our displeasure would have been greater. But as evils to which we are accustomed are less annoying, we have endured past disturbances patiently, they having arisen for the most part without our fault; and we hoped that, like former troubles, they would soon have an end, after the many and great concessions we had made at your suggestion. But finding that you are yet unsettled, that you contemplate the commission of new crimes against your fellow-citizens, and are desirous of making new exiles, our displeasure increases in proportion to your misconduct. And certainly, could we have believed that during our magistracy the city was to be ruined, whether with or without your concurrence, we should certainly, either by flight or exile, have avoided these horrors. But trusting that we had to do with those who possessed some feelings of humanity and some love of their country, we willingly accepted the magistracy, thinking that by our gentleness we should overcome your ambition. But we perceive from experience that the more humble our behavior, the more concessions we make, the prouder you become, and the more exorbitant are your demands. And though we speak thus, it is not in order to offend, but to amend you. Let others tell you pleasing tales, our design is to communicate only what is for your good. Now we would ask you, and have you answer on your honor, What is there yet ungranted, that you can, with any appearance of propriety, require? You wished to have authority taken from the Capitani di Parte; and it is done. You wished that the ballotings should be burned, and a reformation of them take place; and we consent. You desired that the admonished should be restored to their honours; and it is permitted. At your entreaty we have pardoned those who have burned down houses and plundered churches; many honorable citizens have been exiled to please you; and at your suggestion new restraints have been laid upon the Great. When will there be an end of your demands? and how long will you continue to abuse our liberality? Do you not observe with how much more moderation we bear defeat than you your victory? To what end will your divisions bring our city? Have you forgotten that when disunited Castruccio, a low citizen of Lucca, subdued her? or that a duke of Athens, your hired captain did so too? But when the citizens were united in her defense, an archbishop of Milan and a pope were unable to subdue it, and, after many years of war, were compelled to retire with disgrace.

"Then why would you, by your discords, reduce to slavery in a time of peace, that city, which so many powerful enemies have left free, even in war? What can you expect from your disunion but subjugation? or from the property of which you already have plundered, or may yet plunder us, but poverty? for this property is the means by which we furnish occupation for the whole city, and if you take it from us, our means of finding that occupation is withdrawn. Besides, those who take it will have difficulty in preserving what is dishonestly acquired, and thus poverty and destitution are brought upon the city. Now, I, and these Signors command, and if it were consistent with propriety, we would entreat that you allow your minds to be calmed; be content, rest satisfied with the provisions that have been made for you; and if you should be found to need anything further, make your request with decency and order, and not with tumult; for when your demands are reasonable they will always be complied with, and you will not give occasion to evil designing men to ruin your country and cast the blame upon yourselves." These words conveying nothing but the truth, produced a suitable effect upon the minds of the citizens, who thanking the Gonfalonier for having acted toward them the part of a king Signor, and toward the city that of a good citizen, offered their obedience in whatever might be committed to them. And the Signors, to prove the sincerity of their intentions, appointed two citizens for each of the superior magistracies, who, with Syndics of the arts, were to consider what could be done to restore quite, and report their resolutions to the Signors.

While these things were in progress, a disturbance arose, much more injurious to the republic than anything that had hitherto occurred. The greatest part of the fires and robberies which took place on the previous days were perpetrated by the very lowest of the people; and those who had been the most audacious, were afraid that when the greater differences were composed, they would be punished for the crimes they had committed; and that as usual, they would be abandoned by those who had instigated them to the commission of crime. To this may be added, the hatred of the lower orders toward the rich citizens and the principals of the arts, because they did not think themselves remunerated for their labor in a manner equal to their merits. For in the time of Charles I., when the city was divided into arts, a head or governor was appointed to each, and it was provided that the individuals of each art, should be judged in civil matters by their own superiors. These arts, as we have before observed, were at first twelve; in the course of time they were increased to twenty-one, and attained so much power, that in a few years they grasped the entire government of the city; and as some were in greater esteem than others, they were divided into MAJOR and MINOR; seven were called "major," and fourteen, the "minor arts." From this division, and from other causes which we have narrated above, arose the arrogance of the Capitani di Parte; for those citizens who had formerly been Guelphs, and had the constant disposal of that magistracy, favored the followers of the major and persecuted the minor arts and their patrons; and hence arose the many commotions already mentioned. When the companies of the arts were first organized, many of those trades, followed by the lowest of the people and the plebeians, were not incorporated, but were ranged under those arts most nearly allied to them; and, hence, when they were not properly remunerated for their labor, or their masters oppressed them, they had no one of whom to seek redress, except the magistrate of the art to which theirs was subject; and of him they did not think justice always attainable. Of the arts, that which had always had, and now has, the greatest number of these subordinates, is the woolen; which being both then, and still, the most powerful body, and first in authority, supports the greater part of the plebeians and lowest of the people.

The lower classes, then, the subordinates not only of the woolen, but also of the other arts, were discontented, from the causes just mentioned; and their apprehension of punishment for the burnings and robberies they had committed, did not tend to compose them. Meetings took place in different parts during the night, to talk over the past, and to communicate the danger in which they were, when one of the most daring and experienced, in order to animate the rest, spoke thus:

"If the question now were, whether we should take up arms, rob and burn the houses of the citizens, and plunder churches, I am one of those who would think it worthy of further consideration, and should, perhaps, prefer poverty and safety to the dangerous pursuit of an uncertain good. But as we have already armed, and many offenses have been committed, it appears to me that we have to consider how to lay them aside, and secure ourselves from the consequences of what is already done. I certainly think, that if nothing else could teach us, necessity might. You see the whole city full of complaint and indignation against us; the citizens are closely united, and the signors are constantly with the magistrates. You may be sure they are contriving something against us; they are arranging some new plan to subdue us. We ought therefore to keep two things in view, and have two points to consider; the one is, to escape with impunity for what has been done during the last few days, and the other, to live in greater comfort and security for the time to come. We must, therefore, I think, in order to be pardoned for our faults, commit new ones; redoubling the mischief, and multiplying fires and robberies; and in doing this, endeavor to have as many companions as we can; for when many are in fault, few are punished; small crimes are chastised, but great and serious ones rewarded. When many suffer, few seek vengeance; for general evils are endured more patiently than private ones. To increase the number of misdeeds will, therefore, make forgiveness more easily attainable, and will open the way to secure what we require for our own liberty. And it appears evident that the gain is certain; for our opponents are disunited and rich; their disunion will give us the victory, and their riches, when they have become ours, will support us. Be not deceived about that antiquity of blood by which they exalt themselves above us; for all men having had one common origin, are all equally ancient, and nature has made us all after one fashion. Strip us naked, and we shall all be found alike. Dress us in their clothing, and they in ours, we shall appear noble, they ignoble--for poverty and riches make all the difference. It grieves me much to think that some of you are sorry inwardly for what is done, and resolve to abstain from anything more of the kind. Certainly, if it be so, you are not the men I took you for; because neither shame nor conscience ought to have any influence with you. Conquerors, by what means soever, are never considered aught but glorious. We have no business to think about conscience; for when, like us, men have to fear hunger, and imprisonment, or death, the fear of hell neither can nor ought to have any influence upon them. If you only notice human proceedings, you may observe that all who attain great power and riches, make use of either force or fraud; and what they have acquired either by deceit or violence, in order to conceal the disgraceful methods of attainment, they endeavor to sanctify with the false title of honest gains. Those who either from imprudence or want of sagacity avoid doing so, are always overwhelmed with servitude and poverty; for faithful servants are always servants, and honest men are always poor; nor do any ever escape from servitude but the bold and faithless, or from poverty, but the rapacious and fraudulent. God and nature have thrown all human fortunes into the midst of mankind; and they are thus attainable rather by rapine than by industry, by wicked actions rather than by good. Hence it is that men feed upon each other, and those who cannot defend themselves must be worried. Therefore we must use force when the opportunity offers; and fortune cannot present us one more favorable than the present, when the citizens are still disunited, the Signory doubtful, and the magistrates terrified; for we may easily conquer them before they can come to any settled arrangement. By this means we shall either obtain the entire government of the city, or so large a share of it, as to be forgiven past errors, and have sufficient authority to threaten the city with a renewal of them at some future time. I confess this course is bold and dangerous, but when necessity presses, audacity becomes prudence, and in great affairs the brave never think of dangers. The enterprises that are begun with hazard always have a reward at last; and no one ever escaped from embarrassment without some peril. Besides, it is easy to see from all their preparations of prisons, racks, and instruments of death, that there is more danger in inaction than in endeavoring to secure ourselves; for in the first case the evils are certain, in the latter doubtful. How often have I heard you complain of the avarice of your superiors and the injustice of your magistrates. Now then is the time, not only to liberate yourself from them, but to become so much superior, that they will have more causes of grief and fear from you, than you from them.

The opportunity presented by circumstances passes away, and when gone, it will be vain to think it can be recalled. You see the preparations of our enemies; let us anticipate them; and those who are first in arms will certainly be victors, to the ruin of their enemies and their own exaltation; and thus honors will accrue to many of us and security to all." These arguments greatly inflamed minds already disposed to mischief, so that they determined to take up arms as soon as they had acquired a sufficient number of associates, and bound themselves by oath to mutual defense, in case any of them were subdued by the civil power.

While they were arranging to take possession of the republic, their design became known to the Signory, who, having taken a man named Simone, learned from him the particulars of the conspiracy, and that the outbreak was to take place on the following day. Finding the danger so pressing, they called together the colleagues and those citizens who with the syndics of the arts were endeavoring to effect the union of the city. It was then evening, and they advised the signors to assemble the consuls of the trades, who proposed that whatever armed force was in Florence should be collected, and with the Gonfaloniers of the people and their companies, meet under arms in the piazza next morning. It happened that while Simone was being tortured, a man named Niccolo da San Friano was regulating the palace clock, and becoming acquainted with what was going on, returned home and spread the report of it in his neighborhood, so that presently the piazza of St. Spirito was occupied by above a thousand men. This soon became known to the other conspirators, and San Pietro Maggiore and St. Lorenzo, their places of assembly, were presently full of them, all under arms.

CHAPTER IV

Proceedings of the plebeians--The demand they make of the Signory--They insist that the Signory leave the palace--The Signory leave the palace--Michael di Lando Gonfalonier--Complaints and movements of the plebeians against Michael di Lando--Michael di Lando proceeds against the plebeians and reduces them to order--Character of Michael di Lando.

At daybreak on the 21st of July, there did not appear in the piazza above eighty men in arms friendly to the Signory, and not one of the Gonfaloniers; for knowing the whole city to be in a state of insurrection they were afraid to leave their homes. The first body of plebeians that made its appearance was that which had assembled at San Pietro Maggiore; but the armed force did not venture to attack them. Then came the other multitudes, and finding no opposition, they loudly demanded their prisoners from the Signory; and being resolved to have them by force if they were not yielded to their threats, they burned the house of Luigi Guicciardini; and the Signory, for fear of greater mischief, set them at liberty. With this addition to their strength they took the Gonfalon of Justice from the bearer, and under the shadow of authority which it gave them, burned the houses of many citizens, selecting those whose owners had publicly or privately excited their hatred. Many citizens, to avenge themselves for private injuries, conducted them to the houses of their enemies; for it was quite sufficient to insure its destruction, if a single voice from the mob called out, "To the house of such a one," or if he who bore the Gonfalon took the road toward it. All the documents belonging to the woolen trade were burned, and after the commission of much violence, by way of associating it with something laudable, Salvestro de Medici and sixty-three other citizens were made knights, among whom were Benedetto and Antonio degli Alberti, Tommaso Strozzi and others similarly their friends; though many received the honor against their wills. It was a remarkable peculiarity of the riots, that many who had their houses burned, were on the same day, and by the same party made knights; so close were the kindness and the injury together. This circumstance occurred to Luigi Guicciardini, Gonfalonier of Justice.

In this tremendous uproar, the Signory, finding themselves abandoned by their armed force, by the leaders of the arts, and by the Gonfaloniers, became dismayed; for none had come to their assistance in obedience to orders; and of the sixteen Gonfalons, the ensign of the Golden Lion and of the Vaio, under Giovenco della Stufa and Giovanni Cambi alone appeared; and these, not being joined by any other, soon withdrew. Of the citizens, on the other hand, some, seeing the fury of this unreasonable multitude and the palace abandoned, remained within doors; others followed the armed mob, in the hope that by being among them, they might more easily protect their own houses or those of their friends. The power of the plebeians was thus increased and that of the Signory weakened. The tumult continued all day, and at night the rioters halted near the palace of Stefano, behind the church of St. Barnabas. Their number exceeded six thousand, and before daybreak they obtained by threats the ensigns of the trades, with which and the Gonfalon of Justice, when morning came, they proceeded to the palace of the provost, who refusing to surrender it to them, they took possession of it by force.

The Signory, desirous of a compromise, since they could not restrain them by force, appointed four of the Colleagues to proceed to the palace of the provost, and endeavor to learn what was their intention. They found that the leaders of the plebeians, with the Syndics of the trades and some citizens, had resolved to signify their wishes to the Signory. They therefore returned with four deputies of the plebeians, who demanded that the woolen trade should not be allowed to have a foreign judge; that there should be formed three new companies of the arts; namely, one for the wool combers and dyers, one for the barbers, doublet-makers, tailors, and such like, and the third for the lowest class of people. They required that the three new arts should furnish two Signors; the fourteen minor arts, three; and that the Signory should provide a suitable place of assembly for them. They also made it a condition that no member of these companies should be expected during two years to pay any debt that amounted to less than fifty ducats; that the bank should take no interest on loans already contracted, and that only the principal sum should be demanded; that the condemned and the banished should be forgiven, and the admonished should be restored to participation in the honors of government. Besides these, many other articles were stipulated in favor of their friends, and a requisition made that many of their enemies should be exiled and admonished. These demands, though grievous and dishonorable to the republic, were for fear of further violence granted, by the joint deliberation of the Signors, Colleagues, and Council of the people. But in order to give it full effect, it was requisite that the Council of the Commune should also give its consent; and, as they could not assemble two councils during the same day it was necessary to defer it till the morrow. However the trades appeared content, the plebeians satisfied; and both promised, that these laws being confirmed, every disturbance should cease.

On the following morning, while the Council of the Commune were in consultation, the impatient and volatile multitude entered the piazza, under their respective ensigns, with loud and fearful shouts, which struck terror into all the Council and Signory; and Guerrente Marignolli, one of the latter, influenced more by fear than anything else, under pretense of guarding the lower doors, left the chamber and fled to his house. He was unable to conceal himself from the multitude, who, however, took no notice, except that, upon seeing him, they insisted that all the Signors should quit the palace, and declared that if they refused to comply, their houses should be burned and their families put to death.

The law had now been passed; the Signors were in their own apartments; the Council had descended from the chamber, and without leaving the palace, hopeless of saving the city, they remained in the lodges and courts below, overwhelmed with grief at seeing such depravity in the multitude, and such perversity or fear in those who might either have restrained or suppressed them. The Signory, too, were dismayed and fearful for the safety of their country, finding themselves abandoned by one of their associates, and without any aid or even advice; when, at this moment of uncertainty as to what was about to happen, or what would be best to be done, Tommaso Strozzi and Benedetto Alberti, either from motives of ambition (being desirous of remaining masters of the palace), or because they thought it the most advisable step, persuaded them to give way to the popular impulse, and withdraw privately to their homes. This advice, given by those who had been the leaders of the tumult, although the others yielded, filled Alamanno Acciajuoli and Niccolo del

Bene, two of the Signors, with anger; and, reassuming a little vigor, they said, that if the others would withdraw they could not help it, but they would remain as long as they continued in office, if they did not in the meantime lose their lives. These dissensions redoubled the fears of the Signory and the rage of the people, so that the Gonfalonier, disposed rather to conclude his magistracy in dishonor than in danger, recommended himself to the care of Tommaso Strozzi, who withdrew him from the palace and conducted him to his house. The other Signors were, one after another, conveyed in the same manner, so that Alamanno and Niccolo, not to appear more valiant than wise, seeing themselves left alone, also retired, and the palace fell into the hands of the plebeians and the Eight Commissioners of War, who had not yet laid down their authority.

When the plebeians entered the palace, the standard of the Gonfalonier of Justice was in the hands of Michael di Lando, a wool comber. This man, barefoot, with scarcely anything upon him, and the rabble at his heels, ascended the staircase, and, having entered the audience chamber of the Signory, he stopped, and turning to the multitude said, "You see this palace is now yours, and the city is in your power; what do you think ought to be done?" To which they replied, they would have him for their Gonfalonier and lord; and that he should govern them and the city as he thought best. Michael accepted the command; and, as he was a cool and sagacious man, more favored by nature than by fortune, he resolved to compose the tumult, and restore peace to the city. To occupy the minds of the people, and give himself time to make some arrangement, he ordered that one Nuto, who had been appointed bargello, or sheriff, by Lapo da Castiglionchio, should be sought. The greater part of his followers went to execute this commission; and, to commence with justice the government he had acquired by favor, he commanded that no one should either burn or steal anything; while, to strike terror into all, he caused a gallows to be erected in the court of the palace. He began the reform of government by deposing the Syndics of the trades, and appointing new ones; he deprived the Signory and the Colleagues of their magistracy, and burned the balloting purses containing the names of those eligible to office under the former government.

In the meantime, Ser Nuto, being brought by the mob into the court, was suspended from the gallows by one foot; and those around having torn him to pieces, in little more than a moment nothing remained of him but the foot by which he had been tied.

The Eight Commissioners of War, on the other hand, thinking themselves, after the departure of the Signors, left sole masters of the city, had already formed a new Signory; but Michael, on hearing this, sent them an order to quit the palace immediately; for he wished to show that he could govern Florence without their assistance. He then assembled the Syndics of the trades, and created as a Signory, four from the lowest plebeians; two from the major, and two from the minor trades. Besides this, he made a new selection of names for the balloting purses, and divided the state into three parts; one composed of the new trades, another of the minor, and the third of the major trades. He gave to Salvestro de' Medici the revenue of the shops upon the Old Bridge; for himself he took the provostry of Empoli, and conferred benefits upon many other citizens, friends of the plebeians; not so much for the purpose of rewarding their labors, as that they might serve to screen him from envy.

It seemed to the plebeians that Michael, in his reformation of the state, had too much favored the higher ranks of the people, and that themselves had not a sufficient share in the government to enable them to preserve it; and hence, prompted by their usual audacity, they again took arms, and coming tumultuously into the court of the palace, each body under their particular ensigns, insisted that the Signory should immediately descend and consider new means for advancing their well-being and security. Michael, observing their arrogance, was unwilling to provoke them, but without further yielding to their request, blamed the manner in which it was made, advised them to lay down their arms, and promised that then would be conceded to them, what otherwise, for the dignity of the state, must of necessity be withheld. The multitude, enraged at this reply, withdrew to Santa Maria Novella, where they appointed eight leaders for their party, with officers, and other regulations to ensure influence and respect; so that the city possessed two governments, and was under the direction of two distinct powers. These new leaders determined that Eight, elected from their trades, should constantly reside in the palace with the Signory, and that whatever the Signory should determine must be confirmed by them before it became law. They took from Salvestro de' Medici and Michael di Lando the whole of what their former decrees had granted them, and distributed to many of their party offices and emoluments to enable them to support their dignity. These resolutions being passed, to render them valid they sent two of their body to the Signory, to insist on their being confirmed by the Council, with an intimation, that if not granted they would be vindicated by force. This deputation, with amazing audacity and surpassing presumption, explained their commission to the Signory, upbraided the Gonfalonier with the dignity they had conferred upon him, the honor they had done him, and with the ingratitude and want of respect he had shown toward them. Coming to threats toward the end of their discourse, Michael could not endure their arrogance, and sensible rather of the dignity of the office he held than of the meanness of his origin, determined by extraordinary means to punish such extraordinary insolence, and drawing the sword with which he was girt, seriously wounded, and cause them to be seized and imprisoned.

When the fact became known, the multitude were filled with rage, and thinking that by their arms they might ensure what without them they had failed to effect, they seized their weapons and with the utmost fury resolved to force the Signory to consent to their wishes. Michael, suspecting what would happen, determined to be prepared, for he knew his credit rather required him to be first to the attack than to wait the approach of the enemy, or, like his predecessors, dishonor both the palace and himself by flight. He therefore drew together a good number of citizens (for many began to see their error), mounted on horseback, and followed by crowds of armed men, proceeded to Santa Maria Novella, to encounter his adversaries. The plebeians, who as before observed were influenced by a similar desire, had set out about the same time as Michael, and it happened that as each took a different route, they did not meet in their way, and Michael, upon his return, found the piazza in their possession. The contest was now for the palace, and joining in the fight, he soon vanquished them, drove part of them out of the city, and compelled the rest to throw down their arms and escape or conceal themselves, as well as they could. Having thus gained the victory, the tumults were composed, solely by the talents of the Gonfalonier, who in courage, prudence, and generosity surpassed every other citizen of his time, and deserves to be enumerated among the glorious few who have greatly benefited their country; for had he possessed either malice or ambition, the republic would have been completely ruined, and the city must have fallen under greater tyranny than that of the duke of Athens. But his goodness never allowed a thought to enter his mind opposed to the universal welfare: his prudence enabled him to conduct affairs in such a manner, that a great majority of his own faction reposed the most entire confidence in him; and he kept the rest in awe by the influence of his authority. These qualities subdued the plebeians, and opened the eyes of the superior artificers, who considered how great must be the folly of those, who having overcome the pride of the nobility, could endure to submit to the nauseous rule of the rabble.

CHAPTER V

New regulations for the elections of the Signory--Confusion in the City--Piero degli Albizzi and other citizens condemned to death--The Florentines alarmed by the approach of Charles of Durazzo--The measures adopted in consequence thereof--Insolent Conduct of Giorgio Scali--Benedetto Alberti--Giorgio Scali beheaded.

By the time Michael di Lando had subdued the plebeians, the new Signory was drawn, and among those who composed it, were two persons of such base and mean condition, that the desire increased in the minds of the people to be freed from the ignominy into which they had fallen; and when, upon the first of September, the new Signory entered office and the retiring members were still in the palace, the piazza being full of armed men, a tumultuous cry arose from the midst of them, that none of the lowest of the people should hold office among the Signory. The obnoxious two were withdrawn accordingly. The name of one was Il Tira, of the other Baroccio, and in their stead were elected Giorgio Scali and Francesco di Michele. The company of the lowest trade was also dissolved, and its members deprived of office, except Michael di Lando, Lorenzo di Puccio and a few others of better quality. The honors of government were divided into two parts, one of which was assigned to the superior trades, the other to the inferior; except that the latter were to furnish five Signors, and the former only four. The Gonfalonier was to be chosen alternately from each.

The government thus composed, restored peace to the city for the time; but though the republic was rescued from the power of the lowest plebeians, the inferior trades were still more influential than the nobles of the people, who, however, were obliged to submit for the gratification of the trades, of whose favor they wished to deprive the plebeians. The new establishment was supported by all who wished the continued subjugation of those who, under the name of the Guelphic party, had practiced such excessive violence against the citizens. And as among others, thus disposed, were Giorgio Scali, Benedetto Alberti, Salvestro di Medici, and Tommaso Strozzi, these four almost became princes of the city. This state of the public mind strengthened the divisions already commenced between the nobles of the people, and the minor artificers, by the ambition of the Ricci and the Albizzi; from which, as at different times very serious effects arose, and as they will hereafter be frequently mentioned, we shall call the former the popular party, the latter the plebeian. This condition of things continued three years, during which many were exiled and put to death; for the government lived in constant apprehension, knowing that both within and without the city many were dissatisfied with them. Those within, either attempted or were suspected of attempting every day some new project against them; and those without, being under no restraint, were continually, by means of some prince or republic, spreading reports tending to increase the disaffection.

Gianozzo da Salerno was at this time in Bologna. He held a command under Charles of Durazzo, a descendant of the kings of Naples, who, designing to undertake the conquest of the dominions of Queen Giovanna, retained his captain in that city, with the concurrence of Pope Urban, who was at enmity with the queen. Many Florentine emigrants were also at Bologna, in close correspondence with him and Charles. This caused the rulers in Florence to live in continual alarm, and induced them to lend a willing ear to any calumnies against the suspected. While in this disturbed state of feeling, it was disclosed to the government that Gianozzo da Salerno was about to march to Florence with the emigrants, and that great numbers of those within were to rise in arms, and deliver the city to him. Upon this information many were accused, the principal of whom were Piero degli Albizzi and Carlo Strozzi: and after these Cipriano Mangione, Jacopo Sacchetti, Donato Barbadori, Filippo Strozzi, and Giovanni Anselmi, the whole of whom, except Carlo Strozzi who fled, were made prisoners; and the Signory, to prevent any one from taking arms in their favor, appointed Tommaso Strozzi and Benedetto Alberti with a strong armed force, to guard the city. The arrested citizens were examined, and although nothing was elicited against them sufficient to induce the Capitano to find them guilty, their enemies excited the minds of the populace to such a degree of outrageous and overwhelming fury against them, that they were condemned to death, as it were, by force. Nor was the greatness of his family, or his former reputation of any service to Piero degli Albizzi, who had once been, of all the citizens, the man most feared and honored. Some one, either as a friend to render him wise in his prosperity, or an enemy to threaten him with the fickleness of fortune, had upon the occasion of his making a feast for many citizens, sent him a silver bowl full of sweetmeats, among which a large nail was found, and being seen by many present, was taken for a hint to him to fix the wheel of fortune, which, having conveyed him to the top, must if the rotation continued, also bring him to the bottom. This interpretation was verified, first by his ruin, and afterward by his death.

After this execution the city was full of consternation, for both victors and vanquished were alike in fear; but the worst effects arose from the apprehensions of those possessing the management of affairs; for every accident, however trivial, caused them to commit fresh outrages, either by condemnations, admonitions, or banishment of citizens; to which must be added, as scarcely less pernicious, the frequent new laws and regulations which were made for defense of the government, all of which were put in execution to the injury of those opposed to their faction. They appointed forty-six persons, who, with the Signory, were to purge the republic of all suspected by the government. They admonished thirty-nine citizens, ennobled many of the people, and degraded many nobles to the popular rank. To strengthen themselves against external foes, they took into their pay John Hawkwood, an Englishman of great military reputation, who had long served the pope and others in Italy. Their fears from without were increased by a report that several bodies of men were being assembled by Charles of Durazzo for the conquest of Naples, and many Florentine emigrants were said to have joined him. Against these dangers, in addition to the forces which had been raised, large sums of money were provided; and Charles, having arrived at Arezzo, obtained from the Florentines 40,000 ducats, and promised he would not molest them. His enterprise was immediately prosecuted, and having occupied the kingdom of Naples, he sent Queen Giovanna a prisoner into Hungary. This victory renewed the fears of those who managed the affairs of Florence, for they could not persuade themselves that their money would have a greater influence on the king's mind than the friendship which his house had long retained for the Guelphs, whom they so grievously oppressed.

This suspicion increasing, multiplied oppressions; which again, instead of diminishing the suspicion, augmented it; so that most men lived in the utmost discontent. To this the insolence of Giorgio Scali and Tommaso Strozzi (who by their popular influence overawed the magistrates) also contributed, for the rulers were apprehensive that by the power these men possessed with the plebeians they could set them at defiance; and hence it is evident that not only to good men, but even to the seditious, this government appeared tyrannical and violent. To put a period to the outrageous conduct of Giorgio, it happened that a servant of his accused Giovanni di Cambio of practices against the state, but the Capitano declared him innocent. Upon this, the judge determined to punish the accuser with the same penalties that the accused would have incurred had he been guilty, but Giorgio Scali, unable to save him either by his authority or entreaties, obtained the assistance of Tommaso Strozzi, and with a multitude of armed men, set the informer at liberty and plundered the palace of the Capitano, who was obliged to save himself by flight. This act excited such great and universal animosity against him, that his enemies began to hope they would be able to effect his ruin, and also to rescue the city from the power of the plebeians, who for three years had held her under their arrogant control.

To the realization of this design the Capitano greatly contributed, for the tumult having subsided, he presented himself before the signors, and said "He had cheerfully undertaken the office to which they had appointed him, for he thought he should serve upright men who would take arms for the defense of justice, and not impede its progress. But now that he had seen and had experience of the proceedings of the city, and the manner in which affairs were conducted, that dignity which he had voluntarily assumed with the hope of acquiring honor and emolument, he now more willingly resigned, to escape from the losses and danger to which he found himself exposed." The complaint of the Capitano was heard with the utmost attention by the Signory, who promising to remunerate him for the injury he had suffered and provide for his future security, he was satisfied. Some of them then obtained an interview with certain citizens who were thought to be lovers of the common good, and least suspected by the state; and in conjunction with these, it was concluded that the present was a favorable opportunity for rescuing the city from Giorgio and the plebeians, the last outrage he had committed having completely alienated the great body of the people from him. They judged it best to profit by the occasion before the excitement had abated, for they knew that the favor of the mob is often gained or lost by the most trifling circumstance; and more certainly to insure success, they determined, if possible, to obtain the concurrence of Benedetto Alberti, for without it they considered their enterprise to be dangerous.

Benedetto was one of the richest citizens, a man of unassuming manners, an ardent lover of the liberties of his country, and one to whom tyrannical measures were in the highest degree offensive; so that he was easily induced to concur in their views and consent to Giorgio's ruin. His enmity against the nobles of the people and the Guelphs, and his friendship for the plebeians, were caused by the insolence and tyrannical proceedings of the former; but finding that the plebeians had soon become quite as insolent, he quickly separated himself from them; and the injuries committed by them against the citizens were done wholly without his consent. So that the same motives which made him join the plebeians induced him to leave them.

Having gained Benedetto and the leaders of the trades to their side, they provided themselves with arms and made Giorgio prisoner. Tommaso fled. The next day Giorgio was beheaded; which struck so great a terror into his party, that none ventured to express the slightest disapprobation, but each seemed anxious to be foremost in defense of the measure. On being led to execution, in the presence of that people who only a short time before had idolized him, Giorgio complained of his hard fortune, and the malignity of those citizens who, having done him an undeserved injury, had compelled him to honor and support a mob, possessing neither faith nor gratitude. Observing Benedetto Alberti among those who had armed themselves for the preservation of order, he said, "Do you, too, consent, Benedetto, that this injury shall be done to me? Were I in your place and you in mine, I would take care that no one should injure you. I tell you, however, this day is the end of my troubles and the beginning of yours." He then blamed himself for having confided too much in a people who may be excited and inflamed by every word, motion, and breath of suspicion. With these complaints he died in the midst of his armed enemies, delighted at his fall. Some of his most intimate associates were also put to death, and their bodies dragged about by the mob.

CHAPTER VI

Confusion and riots in the city--Reform of government in opposition to the plebeians--Injuries done to those who favored the plebeians--Michael di Lando banished--Benedetto Alberti hated by the Signory--Fears excited by the coming of Louis of Anjou--The Florentines purchase Arezzo--Benedetto Alberti becomes suspected and is banished--His discourse upon leaving the city--Other citizens banished and admonished--War with Giovanni Galeazzo, duke of Milan.

The death of Giorgio caused very great excitement; many took arms at the execution in favor of the Signory and the Capitano; and many others, either for ambition or as a means for their own safety, did the same. The city was full of conflicting parties, who each had a particular end in view, and wished to carry it into effect before they disarmed. The ancient nobility, called the GREAT, could not bear to be deprived of public honors; for the recovery of which they used their utmost exertions, and earnestly desired that authority might be restored to the Capitani di Parte. The nobles of the people and the major trades were discontented at the share the minor trades and lowest of the people possessed in the government; while the minor trades were desirous of increasing their influence, and the lowest people were apprehensive of losing the companies of their trades and the authority which these conferred.

Such opposing views occasioned Florence, during a year, to be disturbed by many riots. Sometimes the nobles of the people took arms; sometimes the major and sometimes the minor trades and the lowest of the people; and it often happened that, though in different parts, all were at once in insurrection. Hence many conflicts took place between the different parties or with the forces of the palace; for the Signory sometimes yielding, and at other times resisting, adopted such remedies as they could for these numerous evils. At length, after two assemblies of the people, and many Balias appointed for the reformation of the city; after much toil, labor, and imminent danger, a government was appointed, by which all who had been banished since Salvestro de' Medici was Gonfalonier were restored. They who had acquired distinctions or emoluments by the Balia of 1378 were deprived of them. The honors of government were restored to the Guelphic party; the two new Companies of the Trades were dissolved, and all who had been subject to them assigned to their former companies. The minor trades were not allowed to elect the Gonfalonier of Justice, their share of honors was reduced from a half to a third; and those of the highest rank were withdrawn from them altogether. Thus the nobles of the people and the Guelphs repossessed themselves of the government, which was lost by the plebeians after it had been in their possession from 1378 to 1381, when these changes took place.

The new establishment was not less injurious to the citizens, or less troublesome at its commencement than that of the plebeians had been; for many of the nobles of the people, who had distinguished themselves as defenders of the plebeians, were banished, with a great number of the leaders of the latter, among whom was Michael di Lando; nor could all the benefits conferred upon the city by his authority, when in danger from the lawless mob, save him from the rabid fury of the party that was now in power. His good offices evidently excited little gratitude in his countrymen. The neglect of their benefactors is an error into which princes and republics frequently fall; and hence mankind, alarmed by such examples, as soon as they begin to perceive the ingratitude of their rulers, set themselves against them.

As these banishments and executions had always been offensive to Benedetto Alberti, they continued to disgust him, and he censured them both publicly and privately. The leaders of the government began to fear him, for they considered him one of the most earnest friends of the plebeians, and thought he had not consented to the death of Giorgio Scali from disapprobation of his proceeding, but that he might be left himself without a rival in the government. His discourse and his conduct alike served to increase their suspicions, so that all the ruling party had their eyes upon him, and eagerly sought an opportunity of crushing him.

During this state of things, external affairs were not of serious importance, for some which ensued were productive of apprehension rather than of injury. At this time Louis of Anjou came into Italy, to recover the kingdom of Naples for Queen Giovanna, and drive out Charles of Durazzo. His coming terrified the Florentines; for Charles, according to the custom of old friends, demanded their assistance, and Louis, like those who seek new alliances, required their neutrality. The Florentines, that they might seem to comply with the request of Louis, and at the same time assist Charles, discharged from their service Sir John Hawkwood, and transferred him to that of Pope Urban, who was friendly to Charles; but this deceit was at once detected, and Louis considered himself greatly injured by the Florentines. While the war was carried on between Louis and Charles in Puglia, new forces were sent from France in aid of Louis, and on arriving in Tuscany, were by the emigrants of Arezzo conducted to that city, and took it from those who held possession for Charles. And when they were about to change the government of Florence, as they had already done that of Arezzo, Louis died, and the order of things in Puglia and in Tuscany was changed accordingly; for Charles secured the kingdom, which had been all but lost, and the Florentines, who were apprehensive for their own city, purchased Arezzo from those who held it for Louis. Charles, having secured Puglia, went to take possession of Hungary, to which he was heir, leaving, with his wife, his children Ladislaus and Giovanna, who were yet infants. He took possession of Hungary, but was soon after slain there.

As great rejoicings were made in Florence on account of this acquisition as ever took place in any city for a real victory, which served to exhibit the public and private wealth of the people, many families endeavoring to vie with the state itself in displays of magnificence. The Alberti surpassed all others; the tournaments and exhibitions made by them were rather suitable for a sovereign prince than for any private individuals. These things increased the envy with which the family was regarded, and being joined with suspicions which the state entertained of Benedetto, were the causes of his ruin. The rulers could not endure him, for it appeared as if, at any moment, something might occur, which, with the favor of his friends, would enable him to recover his authority, and drive them out of the city. While in this state of suspicion and jealousy, it happened that while he was Gonfalonier of the Companies, his son-in-law, Filippo Magalotti, was drawn Gonfalonier of Justice; and this circumstance increased the fears of the government, for they thought it would strengthen Benedetto's influence, and place the state in the greater peril.

Anxious to provide a remedy, without creating much disturbance, they induced Bese Magalotti, his relative and enemy, to signify to the Signory that Filippo, not having attained the age required for the exercise of that office, neither could nor ought to hold it.

    The question was examined by the signors, and part of them out of hatred, others in order to avoid disunion among themselves, declared Filippo ineligible to the dignity, and in his stead was drawn Bardo Mancini, who was quite opposed to the plebeian interests, and an inveterate foe of Benedetto. This man, having entered upon the duties of his office, created a Balia for the reformation of the state, which banished Benedetto Alberti and admonished all the rest of his family except Antonio. Before his departure, Benedetto called them together, and observing their melancholy demeanor, said, "You see, my fathers, and you the elders of our house, how fortune has ruined me and threatened you. I am not surprised at this, neither ought you to be so, for it always happens thus to those who among a multitude of the wicked, wish to act rightly, and endeavor to sustain, what the many seek to destroy. The love of my country made me take part with Salvestro de Medici and afterward separated me from Giorgio Scali. The same cause compelled me to detest those who now govern, who having none to punish them, will allow no one to reprove their misdeeds. I am content that my banishment should deliver them from the fears they entertain, not of me only, but of all who they think perceives or is acquainted wit their tyrannical and wicked proceedings; and they have aimed their first blow at me, in order the more easily to oppress you. I do not grieve on my own account; for those honors which my country bestowed upon me while free, she cannot in her slavery take from me; and the recollection of my past life will always give me greater pleasure than the pain imparted by the sorrows of exile. I deeply regret that my country is left a prey to the greediness and pride of the few who keep her in subjection. I grieve for you; for I fear that the evils which this day cease to affect me, and commence with you, will pursue you with even greater malevolence than they have me. Comfort, then, each other; resolve to bear up against every misfortune, and conduct yourselves in such a manner, that when disasters befall you (and there will be many), every one may know they have come upon you undeservedly." Not to give a worse impression of his virtue abroad than he had done at home, he made a journey to the sepulcher of Christ, and while upon his return, died at Rhodes. His remains were brought to Florence, and interred with all possible honors, by those who had persecuted him, when alive, with every species of calumny and injustice.

The family of the Alberti was not the only injured party during these troubles of the city; for many others were banished and admonished. Of the former were Piero Benini, Matteo Alderotti, Giovanni and Francesco del Bene, Giovanni Benci, Andrea Adimari, and with them many members of the minor trades. Of the admonished were the Covini, Benini, Rinucci, Formiconi, Corbizzi, Manelli, and Alderotti. It was customary to create the Balia for a limited time; and when the citizens elected had effected the purpose of their appointment, they resigned the office from motives of good feeling and decency, although the time allowed might not have expired. In conformity with this laudable practice, the Balia of that period, supposing they had accomplished all that was expected of them, wished to retire; but when the multitude were acquainted with their intention, they ran armed to the palace, and insisted, that before resigning their power, many other persons should be banished and admonished. This greatly displeased the signors; but without disclosing the extent of their displeasure, they contrived to amuse the multitude with promises, till they had assembled a sufficient body of armed men, and then took such measures, that fear induced the people to lay aside the weapons which madness had led them to take up. Nevertheless, in some degree to gratify the fury of the mob, and to reduce the authority of the plebeian trades, it was provided, that as the latter had previously possessed a third of the honors, they should in future have only a fourth. That there might always be two of the signors particularly devoted to the government, they gave authority to the Gonfalonier of Justice, and four others, to form a ballot-purse of select citizens, from which, in every Signory, two should be drawn.

This government from its establishment in 1381, till the alterations now made, had continued six years; and the internal peace of the city remained undisturbed until 1393. During this time, Giovanni Galeazzo Visconti, usually called the Count of Virtu, imprisoned his uncle Bernabo, and thus became sovereign of the whole of Lombardy. As he had become duke of Milan by fraud, he designed to make himself king of Italy by force. In 1391 he commenced a spirited attack upon the Florentines; but such various changes occurred in the course of the war, that he was frequently in greater danger than the Florentines themselves, who, though they made a brave and admirable defense, for a republic, must have been ruined, if he had survived. As it was, the result was attended with infinitely less evil than their fears of so powerful an enemy had led them to apprehend; for the duke having taken Bologna, Pisa, Perugia, and Sienna, and prepared a diadem with which to be crowned king of Italy at Florence, died before he had tasted the fruit of his victories, or the Florentines began to feel the effect of their disasters.

CHAPTER VII

Maso degli Albizzi--His violence excites the anger of the people--They have recourse to Veri de' Medici--The modesty of Veri--He refuses to assume the dignity of prince, and appeases the people--Discourse of Veri to the Signory--The banished Florentines endeavor to return--They secretly enter the city and raise a tumult--Some of them slain, others taken to the church of St. Reparata--A conspiracy of exiles supported by the duke of Milan--The conspiracy discovered and the parties punished--Various enterprises of the Florentines--Taking of Pisa--War with the king of Naples--Acquisition of Cortona.

During the war with the duke of Milan the office of Gonfalonier of Justice fell to Maso degli Albizzi, who by the death of Piero in 1379, had become the inveterate enemy of the Alberti: and as party feeling is incapable either of repose or abatement, he determined, notwithstanding Benedetto had died in exile, that before the expiration of his magistracy, he would revenge himself on the remainder of that family. He seized the opportunity afforded by a person, who on being examined respecting correspondence maintained with the rebels, accused Andrea and Alberto degli Alberti of such practices. They were immediately arrested, which so greatly excited the people, that the Signory, having provided themselves with an armed force, called the citizens to a general assembly or parliament, and appointed a Balia, by whose authority many were banished, and a new ballot for the offices of government was made. Among the banished were nearly all the Alberti; many members of the trades were admonished, and some put to death. Stung by these numerous injuries, the trades and the lowest of the people rose in arms, considering themselves despoiled both of honor and life. One body of them assembled in the piazza; another ran to the house of Veri de' Medici, who, after the death of Salvestro, was head of the family. The Signory, in order to appease those who came to the piazza or court of the palace, gave them for leaders, with the ensigns of the Guelphs and of the people in their hands, Rinaldo Gianfigliazzi, and Donato Acciajuoli, both men of the popular class, and more attached to the interests of the plebeians than any other. Those who went to the house of Veri de' Medici, begged that he would be pleased to undertake the government, and free them from the tyranny of those citizens who were destroying the peace and safety of the commonwealth.

It is agreed by all who have written concerning the events of this period, that if Veri had had more ambition than integrity he might without any impediment have become prince of the city; for the unfeeling treatment which, whether right or wrong, had been inflicted upon the trades and their friends, had so excited the minds of men to vengeance, that all they required was some one to be their leader. Nor were there wanting those who could inform him of the state of public feeling; for Antonio de' Medici with whom he had for some time been upon terms of most intimate friendship, endeavored to persuade him to undertake the government of the republic. To this Veri replied: "Thy menaces when thou wert my enemy, never alarmed me; nor shall thy counsel, now when thou art my friend, do me any harm." Then, turning toward the multitude, he bade them be of good cheer; for he would be their defender, if they would allow themselves to be advised by him. He then went, accompanied by a great number of citizens, to the piazza, and proceeded directly to the audience chamber of the Signory, whom he addressed to this effect: That he could not regret having lived so as to gain the love of the Florentines; but he was sorry they had formed an opinion of him which his past life had not warranted; for never having done anything that could be construed as either factious or ambitious, he could not imagine how it had happened, that they should think him willing to stir up strife as a discontented person, or usurp the government of his country like an ambitious one. He therefore begged that the infatuation of the multitude might not injure him in their estimation; for, to the utmost of his power, their authority should be restored. He then recommended them to use good fortune with moderation; for it would be much better to enjoy an imperfect victory with safety to the city, than a complete one at her ruin. The Signory applauded Veri's conduct; begged he would endeavor to prevent recourse to arms, and promised that what he and the other citizens might deem most advisable should be done. Veri then returned to the piazza, where the people who had followed him were joined by those led by Donato and Rinaldo, and informed the united companies that he had found the Signory most kindly disposed toward them; that many things had been taken into consideration, which the shortness of time, and the absence of the magistrates, rendered incapable of being finished. He therefore begged they would lay down their arms and obey the Signory; assuring them that humility would prevail rather than pride, entreaties rather than threats; and if they would take his advice, their privileges and security would remain unimpaired. He thus induced them to return peaceably to their homes.

The disturbance having subsided, the Signory armed the piazza, enrolled 2,000 of the most trusty citizens, who were divided equally by Gonfalons, and ordered to be in readiness to give their assistance whenever required; and they forbade the use of arms to all who were not thus enrolled. Having adopted these precautionary measures, they banished and put to death many of those members of the trades who had shown the greatest audacity in the late riots; and to invest the office of Gonfalonier of Justice with more authoritative majesty, they ordered that no one should be eligible to it, under forty-five years of age. Many other provisions for the defense of the state were made, which appeared intolerable to those against whom they were directed, and were odious even to the friends of the Signory themselves, for they could not believe a government to be either good or secure, which needed so much violence for its defense, a violence excessively offensive, not only to those of the Alberti who remained in the city, and to the Medici, who felt themselves injured by these proceedings, but also to many others. The first who attempted resistance was Donato, the son of Jacopo Acciajuoli, who thought of great authority, and the superior rather than the equal of Maso degli Albizzi (who on account of the events which took place while he was Gonfalonier of Justice, was almost at the head of the republic), could not enjoy repose amid such general discontent, or, like many others, convert social evils to his own private advantage, and therefore resolved to attempt the restoration of the exiles to their country, or at least their offices to the admonished. He went from one to another, disseminating his views, showing that the people would not be satisfied, or the ferment of parties subside, without the changes he proposed; and declared that if he were in the Signory, he would soon carry them into effect. In human affairs, delay causes tedium, and haste danger. To avoid what was tedious, Donato Acciajuoli resolved to attempt what involved danger. Michele Acciajuoli his relative, and Niccolo Ricoveri his friend, were of the Signory. This seemed to Donato a conjuncture of circumstances too favorable to be lost, and he requested they would propose a law to the councils, which would include the restoration of the citizens. They, at his entreaty, spoke about the matter to their associates, who replied, that it was improper to attempt any innovation in which the advantage was doubtful and the danger certain. Upon this, Donato, having in vain tried all other means he could think of, excited with anger, gave them to understand that since they would not allow the city to be governed with peaceful measures, he would try what could be done with arms. These words gave so great offense, that being communicated to the heads of the government, Donato was summoned, and having appeared, the truth was proven by those to whom he had intrusted the message, and he was banished to Barletta. Alamanno and Antonio de' Medici were also banished, and all those of that family, who were descended from Alamanno, with many who, although of the inferior artificers, possessed influence with the plebeians. These events took place two years after the reform of government effected by Maso degli Albizzi.

At this time many discontented citizens were at home, and others banished in the adjoining states. Of the latter there lived at Bologna Picchio Cavicciulli, Tommaso de' Ricci, Antonio de' Medici, Benedetto degli Spini, Antonio Girolami, Cristofano di Carlone, and two others of the lowest order, all bold young men, and resolved upon returning to their country at any hazard. These were secretly told by Piggiello and Baroccio Cavicciulli, who, being admonished, lived in Florence, that if they came to the city they should be concealed in their house; from which they might afterward issue, slay Maso degli Albizzi, and call the people to arms, who, full of discontent, would willingly arise, particularly as they would be supported by the Ricci, Adimari, Medici, Manelli, and many other families. Excited with these hopes, on the fourth of August, 1397, they came to Florence, and having entered unobserved according to their arrangement, they sent one of their party to watch Maso, designing with his death to raise the people. Maso was observed to leave his house and proceed to that of an apothecary, near the church of San Pietro Maggiore, which he entered. The man who went to watch him ran to give information to the other conspirators, who took their arms and hastened to the house of the apothecary, but found that Maso had gone. However, undaunted with the failure of their first attempt, they proceeded to the Old Market, where they slew one of the adverse party, and with loud cries of "people, arms, liberty, and death to the tyrants," directed their course toward the New Market, and at the end of the Calimala slew another. Pursuing their course with the same cries, and finding no one join them in arms, they stopped at the Loggia Nighittosa, where, from an elevated situation, being surrounded with a great multitude, assembled to look on rather than assist them, they exhorted the men to take arms and deliver themselves from the slavery which weighed so heavily upon them; declaring that the complaints of the discontented in the city, rather than their own grievances, had induced them to attempt their deliverance. They had heard that many prayed to God for an opportunity of avenging themselves, and vowed they would use it whenever they found anyone to conduct them; but now, when the favorable circumstances occurred, and they found those who were ready to lead them, they stared at each other like men stupefied, and would wait till those who were endeavoring to recover for them their liberty were slain, and their own chains more strongly riveted upon them; they wondered that those who were wont to take arms upon slight occasions, remained unmoved under the pressure of so many and so great evils; and that they could willingly suffer such numbers of their fellow-citizens to be banished, so many admonished, when it was in their power to restore the banished to their country, and the admonished to the honors of the state. These words, although full of truth, produced no effect upon those to whom they were addressed; for they were either restrained by their fears, or, on account of the two murders which had been committed, disgusted with the parties. Thus the movers of the tumult, finding that neither words or deeds had force sufficient to stir anyone, saw, when too late, how dangerous a thing it is to attempt to set a people free who are resolved to be slaves; and, despairing of success, they withdrew to the temple of Santa Reparata, where, not to save their lives, but to defer the moment of their deaths, they shut themselves up. Upon the first rumor of the affair, the Signory being in fear, armed and secured the palace; but when the facts of the case were understood, the parties known, and whither they had betaken themselves, their fears subsided, and they sent the Capitano with a sufficient body of armed men to secure them. The gates of the temple were forced without much trouble; part of the conspirators were slain defending themselves; the remainder were made prisoners and examined, but none were found implicated in the affair except Baroccio and Piggiello Cavicciulli, who were put to death with them.

Shortly after this event, another occurred of greater importance. The Florentines were, as we have before remarked, at war with the duke of Milan, who, finding that with merely open force he could not overcome them, had recourse to secret practices, and with the assistance of the exiles of whom Lombardy was full, he formed a plot to which many in the city were accessory. It was resolved by the conspirators that most of the emigrants, capable of bearing arms, should set out from the places nearest Florence, enter the city by the river Arno, and with their friends hasten to the residences of the chiefs of the government; and having slain them, reform the republic according to their own will. Of the conspirators within the city, was one of the Ricci named Samminiato; and as it often happens in treacherous practices, few are insufficient to effect the purpose of the plot, and among many secrecy cannot be preserved, so while Samminiato was in quest of associates, he found an accuser. He confided the affair to Salvestro Cavicciulli, whose wrongs and those of his friends were thought sufficient to make him faithful; but he, more influenced by immediate fear than the hope of future vengeance, discovered the whole affair to the Signory, who, having caused Samminiato to be taken, compelled him to tell all the particulars of the matter. However, none of the conspirators were taken, except Tommaso Davizi, who, coming from Bologna, and unaware of what had occurred at Florence, was seized immediately upon his arrival. All the others had fled immediately upon the apprehension of Samminiato.

Samminiato and Tommaso having been punished according to their deserts, a Balia was formed of many citizens, which sought the delinquents, and took measures for the security of the state. They declared six of the family of the Ricci rebels; also, six of the Alberti; two of the Medici; three of the Scali; two of the Strozzi; Bindo Altoviti, Bernado Adimari, and many others of inferior quality. They admonished all the family of the Alberti, the Ricci, and the Medici for ten years, except a few individuals. Among the Alberti, not admonished, was Antonio, who was thought to be quiet and peaceable. It happened, however, before all suspicion of the conspiracy had ceased, a monk was taken who had been observed during its progress to pass frequently between Bologna and Florence. He confessed that he had often carried letters to Antonio, who was immediately seized, and, though he denied all knowledge of the matter from the first, the monk's accusation prevailed, and he was fined in a considerable sum of money, and banished a distance of three hundred miles from Florence. That the Alberti might not constantly place the city in jeopardy, every member of the family was banished whose age exceeded fifteen years.

These events took place in the year 1400, and two years afterward, died Giovanni Galeazzo, duke of Milan, whose death as we have said above, put an end to the war, which had then continued twelve years. At this time, the government having gained greater strength, and being without enemies external or internal, undertook the conquest of Pisa, and having gloriously completed it, the peace of the city remained undisturbed from 1400 to 1433, except that in 1412, the Alberti, having crossed the boundary they were forbidden to pass, a Balia was formed which with new provisions fortified the state and punished the offenders with heavy fines. During this period also, the Florentines made war with Ladislaus, king of Naples, who finding himself in great danger ceded to them the city of Cortona of which he was master; but soon afterward, recovering his power, he renewed the war, which became far more disastrous to the Florentines than before; and had it not, in 1414, been terminated by his death, as that of Lombardy had been by the death of the duke of Milan, he, like the duke, would have brought Florence into great danger of losing her liberty. Nor was the war with the king concluded with less good fortune than the former; for when he had taken Rome, Sienna, the whole of La Marca and Romagna, and had only Florence itself to vanquish, he died. Thus death has always been more favorable to the Florentines than any other friend, and more potent to save them than their own valor. From the time of the king's decease, peace was preserved both at home and abroad for eight years, at the end of which, with the wars of Filippo, duke of Milan, the spirit of faction again broke out, and was only appeased by the ruin of that government which continued from 1381 to 1434, had conducted with great glory so many enterprises; acquired Arezzo, Pisa, Cortona, Leghorn, and Monte Pulciano; and would have accomplished more if the citizens had lived in unity, and had not revived former factions; as in the following book will be particularly shown.

BOOK IV

CHAPTER I

License and Slavery peculiar defects in republican governments--Application of this reflection to the state of Florence--Giovanni di Bicci di' Medici re-establishes the authority of his family--Filippo Visconti, duke of Milan, endeavors to make amicable arrangements with the Florentines--Their jealousy of him--Precautionary measures against him--War declared--The Florentines are routed by the ducal forces.

Republican governments, more especially those imperfectly organized, frequently change their rulers and the form of their institutions; not by the influence of liberty or subjection, as many suppose, but by that of slavery and license; for with the nobility or the people, the ministers respectively of slavery or licentiousness, only the name of liberty is in any estimation, neither of them choosing to be subject either to magistrates or laws. When, however, a good, wise, and powerful citizen appears (which is but seldom), who establishes ordinances capable of appeasing or restraining these contending dispositions, so as to prevent them from doing mischief, then the government may be called free, and its institutions firm and secure; for having good laws for its basis, and good regulations for carrying them into effect, it needs not, like others, the virtue of one man for its maintenance. With such excellent laws and institutions, many of those ancient republics, which were of long duration, were endowed. But these advantages are, and always have been, denied to those which frequently change from tyranny to license, or the reverse; because, from the powerful enemies which each condition creates itself, they neither have, nor can possess any stability; for tyranny cannot please the good, and license is offensive to the wise: the former may easily be productive of mischief, while the latter can scarcely be beneficial; in the former, the insolent have too much authority, and in the latter, the foolish; so that each requires for their welfare the virtue and the good fortune of some individual who may be removed by death, or become unserviceable by misfortune.

Hence, it appears, that the government which commenced in Florence at the death of Giorgio Scali, in 1381, was first sustained by the talents of Maso degli Albizzi, and then by those of Niccolo da Uzzano. The city remained tranquil from 1414 to 1422; for King Ladislaus was dead, and Lombardy divided into several parts; so that there was nothing either internal or external to occasion uneasiness. Next to Niccolo da Uzzano in authority, were Bartolomeo Valori, Neroni di Nigi, Rinaldo degli Albizzi, Neri di Gino, and Lapo Niccolini. The factions that arose from the quarrels of the Albizzi and the Ricci, and which were afterward so unhappily revived by Salvestro de' Medici, were never extinguished; for though the party most favored by the rabble only continued three years, and in 1381 was put down, still, as it comprehended the greatest numerical proportion, it was never entirely extinct, though the frequent Balias and persecutions of its leaders from 1381 to 1400, reduced it almost to nothing. The first families that suffered in this way were the Alberti, the Ricci, and the Medici, which were frequently deprived both of men and money; and if any of them remained in the city, they were deprived of the honors of government. These oft-repeated acts of oppression humiliated the faction, and almost annihilated it. Still, many retained the remembrance of the injuries they had received, and a desire of vengeance remained pent in their bosoms, ungratified and unquenched. Those nobles of the people, or new nobility, who peaceably governed the city, committed two errors, which eventually caused the ruin of their party; the first was, that by long continuance in power they became insolent; the second, that the envy they entertained toward each other, and their uninterrupted possession of power, destroyed that vigilance over those who might injure them, which they ought to have exercised. Thus daily renewing the hatred of a mass of the people by their sinister proceedings, and either negligent of the threatened dangers, because rendered fearless by prosperity, or encouraging them through mutual envy, they gave an opportunity to the family of the Medici to recover their influence. The first to do so was Giovanni di Bicci de' Medici, who having become one of the richest men, and being of a humane and benevolent disposition, obtained the supreme magistracy by the consent of those in power. This circumstance gave so much gratification to the mass of the people (the multitude thinking they had now found a defender), that not without occasion the judicious of the party observed it with jealousy, for they perceived all the former feelings of the city revived. Niccolo da Uzzano did not fail to acquaint the other citizens with the matter, explaining to them how dangerous it was to aggrandize one who possessed so much influence; that it was easy to remedy an evil at its commencement, but exceedingly difficult after having allowed it to gather strength; and that Giovanni possessed several qualities far surpassing those of Salvestro. The associates of Niccolo were uninfluenced by his remarks; for they were jealous of his reputation, and desired to exalt some person, by means of whom he might be humbled.

This was the state of Florence, in which opposing feelings began to be observable, when Filippo Visconti, second son of Giovanni Galeazzo, having, by the death of his brother, become master of all Lombardy, and thinking he might undertake almost anything, greatly desired to recover Genoa, which enjoyed freedom under the Dogiate of Tommaso da Campo Fregoso. He did not think it advisable to attempt this, or any other enterprise, till he had renewed amicable relations with the Florentines, and made his good understanding with them known; but with the aid of their reputation he trusted he should attain his wishes. He therefore sent ambassadors to Florence to signify his desires. Many citizens were opposed to his design, but did not wish to interrupt the peace with Milan, which had now continued for many years. They were fully aware of the advantages he would derive from a war with Genoa, and the little use it would be to Florence. Many others were inclined to accede to it, but would set a limit to his proceedings, which, if he were to exceed, all would perceive his base design, and thus they might, when the treaty was broken, more justifiably make war against him. The question having been strongly debated, an amicable arrangement was at length effected, by which Filippo engaged not to interfere with anything on the Florentine side of the rivers Magra and Panaro.

Soon after the treaty was concluded, the duke took possession of Brescia, and shortly afterward of Genoa, contrary to the expectation of those who had advocated peace; for they thought Brescia would be defended by the Venetians, and Genoa would be able to defend herself. And as in the treaty which Filippo made with the Doge of Genoa, he had acquired Serezana and other places situated on this side the Magra, upon condition that, if he wished to alienate them, they should be given to the Genoese, it was quite palpable that he had broken the treaty; and he had, besides, entered into another treaty with the legate of Bologna, in opposition to his engagement respecting the Panaro. These things disturbed the minds of the citizens, and made them, apprehensive of new troubles, consider the means to be adopted for their defense.

The dissatisfaction of the Florentines coming to the knowledge of Filippo, he, either to justify himself, or to become acquainted with their prevailing feelings, or to lull them to repose, sent ambassadors to the city, to intimate that he was greatly surprised at the suspicions they entertained, and offered to revoke whatever he had done that could be thought a ground of jealousy. This embassy produced no other effect than that of dividing the citizens; one party, that in greatest reputation, judged it best to arm, and prepare to frustrate the enemy's designs; and if he were to remain quiet, it would not be necessary to go to war with him, but an endeavor might be made to preserve peace. Many others, whether envious of those in power, or fearing a rupture with the duke, considered it unadvisable so lightly to entertain suspicions of an ally, and thought his proceedings need not have excited so much distrust; that appointing the ten and hiring forces was in itself a manifest declaration of war, which, if undertaken against so great a prince, would bring certain ruin upon the city without the hope of any advantage; for possession could never be retained of the conquests that might be made, because Romagna lay between, and the vicinity of the church ought to prevent any attempt against Romagna itself. However the views of those who were in favor of war prevailed, the Council of Ten were appointed, forces were hired, and new taxes levied, which, as they were more burdensome upon the lower than the upper ranks, filled the city with complaints, and all condemned the ambition and avarice of the great, declaring that, to gratify themselves and oppress the people, they would go to war without any justifiable motive.

They had not yet come to an open rupture with the duke, but everything tended to excite suspicion; for Filippo had, at the request of the legate of Bologna (who was in fear of Antonio Bentivogli, an emigrant of Bologna at Castel Bolognese), sent forces to that city, which, being close upon the Florentine territory, filled the citizens with apprehension; but what gave every one greater alarm, and offered sufficient occasion for the declaration of war, was the expedition made by the duke against Furli. Giorgio Ordelaffi was lord of Furli, who dying, left Tibaldo, his son, under the guardianship of Filippo. The boy's mother, suspicious of his guardian, sent him to Lodovico Alidossi, her father, who was lord of Imola, but she was compelled by the people of Furli to obey the will of her deceased husband, to withdraw him from the natural guardian, and place him in the hands of the duke. Upon this Filippo, the better to conceal his purpose, caused the Marquis of Ferrara to send Guido Torello as his agent, with forces, to seize the government of Furli, and thus the territory fell into the duke's hands. When this was known at Florence, together with the arrival of forces at Bologna, the arguments in favor of war were greatly strengthened, but there were still many opposed to it, and among the rest Giovanni de' Medici, who publicly endeavored to show, that even if the ill designs of the duke were perfectly manifest, it would still be better to wait and let him commence the attack, than to assail him; for in the former case they would be justified in the view of the princes of Italy as well as in their own; but if they were to strike the first blow at the duke, public opinion would be as favorable to him as to themselves; and besides, they could not so confidently demand assistance as assailants, as they might do if assailed; and that men always defend themselves more vigorously when they attack others. The advocates of war considered it improper to await the enemy in their houses, and better to go and seek him; that fortune is always more favorable to assailants than to such as merely act on the defensive, and that it is less injurious, even when attended with greater immediate expense, to make war at another's door than at our own. These views prevailed, and it was resolved that the ten should provide all the means in their power for rescuing Furli from the hands of the duke.

Filippo, finding the Florentines resolved to occupy the places he had undertaken to defend, postponed all personal considerations, and sent Agnolo della Pergola with a strong force against Imola, that Ludovico, having to provide for the defense of his own possessions, might be unable to protect the interests of his grandson. Agnolo approached Imola while the forces of the Florentines were at Modigliana, and an intense frost having rendered the ditches of the city passable, he crossed them during the night, captured the place, and sent Lodovico a prisoner to Milan. The Florentines finding Imola in the hands of the enemy, and the war publicly known, sent their forces to Furli and besieged it on all sides. That the duke's people might not relieve it, they hired Count Alberigo, who from Zagonara, his own domain, overran the country daily, up to the gates of Imola. Agnolo della Pergola, finding the strong position which the Florentines had taken prevented him from relieving Furli, determined to attempt the capture of Zagonara, thinking they would not allow that place to be lost, and that in the endeavor to relieve it they would be compelled to give up their design against Furli, and come to an engagement under great disadvantage. Thus the duke's people compelled Alberigo to sue for terms, which he obtained on condition of giving up Zagonara, if the Florentines did not relieve him within fifteen days. This misfortune being known in the Florentine camp and in the city, and all being anxious that the enemy should not obtain the expected advantage, they enabled him to secure a greater; for having abandoned the siege of Furli to go to the relief of Zagonara, on encountering the enemy they were soon routed, not so much by the bravery of their adversaries as by the severity of the season; for, having marched many hours through deep mud and heavy rain, they found the enemy quite fresh, and were therefore easily vanquished. Nevertheless, in this great defeat, famous throughout all Italy, no death occurred except those of Lodovico degli Obizi and two of his people, who having fallen from their horses were drowned in the morass.

CHAPTER II

The Florentines murmur against those who had been advocates of the war--Rinaldo degli Albizzi encourages the citizens--Measures for the prosecution of the war--Attempt of the higher classes to deprive the plebeians of their share in the government--Rinaldo degli Albizzi addresses an assembly of citizens and advises the restoration of the Grandi--Niccolo da Uzzano wishes to have Giovanni de' Medici on their side--Giovanni disapproves of the advice of Rinaldo degli Albizzi.

The defeat at Zagonara spread consternation throughout Florence; but none felt it so severely as the nobility, who had been in favor of the war; for they perceived their enemies to be inspirited and themselves disarmed, without friends, and opposed by the people, who at the corners of streets insulted them with sarcastic expressions, complaining of the heavy taxes, and the unnecessary war, and saying, "Oh! they appointed the ten to frighten the enemy. Have they relieved Furli, and rescued her from the hands of the duke? No! but their designs have been discovered; and what had they in view? not the defense of liberty; for they do not love her; but to aggrandize their own power, which God has very justly abated. This is not the only enterprise by many a one with which they have oppressed the city; for the war against King Ladislaus was of a similar kind. To whom will they flee for assistance now? to Pope Martin, whom they ridiculed before the face of Braccio; or to Queen Giovanna, whom they abandoned, and compelled to throw herself under the protection of the king of Aragon?" To these reproaches was added all that might be expected from an enraged multitude.

Seeing the discontent so prevalent, the Signory resolved to assemble a few citizens, and with soft words endeavor to soothe the popular irritation. On this occasion, Rinaldo degli Albizzi, the eldest son of Maso, who, by his own talents and the respect he derived from the memory of his father, aspired to the first offices in the government, spoke at great length; showing that it is not right to judge of actions merely by their effects; for it often happens that what has been very maturely considered is attended with unfavorable results: that if we are to applaud evil counsels because they are sometimes followed by fortunate events, we should only encourage men in error which would bring great mischief upon the republic; because evil counsel is not always attended with happy consequences. In the same way, it would be wrong to blame a wise resolution, because if its being attended with an unfavorable issue; for by so doing, we should destroy the inclination of citizens to offer advice and speak the truth. He then showed the propriety of undertaking the war; and that if it had not been commenced by the Florentines in Romagna the duke would have assailed them in Tuscany. But since it had pleased God, that the Florentine people should be overcome, their loss would be still greater if they allowed themselves to be dejected; but if they set a bold front against adversity, and made good use of the means within their power, they would not be sensible of their loss or the duke of his victory. He assured them they ought not to be alarmed by impending expenses and consequent taxation; because the latter might be reduced, and the future expense would not be so great as the former had been; for less preparation is necessary for those engaged in self-defense than for those who design to attack others. He advised them to imitate the conduct of their forefathers, who, by courageous conduct in adverse circumstances, had defended themselves against all their enemies.

Thus encouraged, the citizens engaged Count Oddo the son of Braccio, and united with him, for directing the operations of the war, Niccolo Piccinino, a pupil of his father's, and one of the most celebrated of all who had served under him. To these they added other leaders, and remounted some of those who had lost their horses in the late defeat. They also appointed twenty citizens to levy new taxes, who finding the great quite subdued by the recent loss, took courage and drained them without mercy.

These burdens were very grievous to the nobility, who at first, in order to conciliate, did not complain of their own particular hardships, but censured the tax generally as unjust, and advised that something should be done in the way of relief; but their advice was rejected in the Councils. Therefore, to render the law as offensive as possible, and to make all sensible of its injustice, they contrived that the taxes should be levied with the utmost rigor, and made it lawful to kill any that might resist the officers employed to collect them. Hence followed many lamentable collisions, attended with the blood and death of citizens. It began to be the impression of all, that arms would be resorted to, and all prudent persons apprehended some approaching evil; for the higher ranks, accustomed to be treated with respect, could not endure to be used like dogs; and the rest were desirous that the taxation should be equalized. In consequence of this state of things, many of the first citizens met together, and it was resolved that it had become necessary for their safety, that some attempt should be made to recover the government; since their want of vigilance had encouraged men to censure public actions, and allowed those to interfere in affairs who had hitherto been merely the leaders of the rabble. Having repeatedly discussed the subject, they resolved to meet again at an appointed hour, when upwards of seventy citizens assembled in the church of St. Stephen, with the permission of Lorenzo Ridolfi and Francesco Gianfigliazzi, both members of the Signory. Giovanni de' Medici was not among them either because being under suspicion he was not invited or that entertaining different views he was unwilling to interfere.

Rinaldo degli Albizzi addressed the assembly, describing the condition of the city, and showing how by their own negligence it had again fallen under the power of the plebeians, from whom it had been wrested by their fathers in 1381. He reminded them of the iniquity of the government which was in power from 1378 to 1381, and that all who were then present had to lament, some a father, others a grandfather, put to death by its tyranny. He assured them they were now in the same danger, and that the city was sinking under the same disorders. The multitude had already imposed a tax of its own authority; and would soon, if not restrained by greater force or better regulations, appoint the magistrates, who, in this case, would occupy their places, and overturn the government which for forty-two years had ruled the city with so much glory; the citizens would then be subject to the will of the multitude, and live disorderly and dangerous, or be under the command of some individual who might make himself prince. For these reasons he was of opinion, that whoever loved his country and his honor must arouse himself, and call to mind the virtue of Bardo Mancini, who, by the ruin of the Alberti, rescued the city from the dangers then impending; and that the cause of the audacity now assumed by the multitude was the extensive Squittini or Pollings, which, by their negligence, were allowed to be made; for thus the palace had become filled with low men. He therefore concluded, that the only means of remedying the evil was to restore the government to the nobility, and diminish the authority of the minor trades by reducing the companies from fourteen to seven, which would give the plebeians less authority in the Councils, both by the reduction in their number and by increasing the authority of the great; who, on account of former enmities, would be disinclined to favor them. He added, that it is a good thing to know how to avail themselves of men according to the times; and that as their fathers had used the plebeians to reduce the influence of the great, that now, the great having been humbled, and the plebeians become insolent, it was well to restrain the insolence of the latter by the assistance of the former. To effect this they might proceed either openly or otherwise, for some of them belonging to the Council of Ten, forces might be led into the city without exciting observation.

Rinaldo was much applauded, and his advice was approved of by the whole assembly. Niccolo da Uzzano who, among others, replied to it, said, "All that Rinaldo had advanced was correct, and the remedies he proposed good and certain, if they could be adopted without an absolute division of the city; and this he had no doubt would be effected if they could induce Giovanni de' Medici to join them; for with him on their side, the multitude being deprived of their chief and stay, would be unable to oppose them; but that if he did not concur with them they could do nothing without arms, and that with them they would incur the risk of being vanquished, or of not being able to reap the fruit of victory." He then modestly reminded them of what he had said upon a former occasion, and of their reluctance to remedy the evil when it might easily have been done; that now the same remedy could not be attempted without incurring the danger of greater evils, and therefore there was nothing left for them to do but to gain him over to their side, if practicable. Rinaldo was then commissioned to wait upon Giovanni and try if he could induce him to join them.

He undertook this commission, and in the most prevailing words he could make use of endeavored to induce him to coincide with their views; and begged that he would not by favoring an audacious mob, enable them to complete the ruin both of the government and the city. To this Giovanni replied, that he considered it the duty of a good and wise citizen to avoid altering the institutions to which a city is accustomed; there being nothing so injurious to the people as such a change; for many are necessarily offended, and where there are several discontented, some unpropitious event may be constantly apprehended. He said it appeared to him that their resolution would have two exceedingly pernicious effects; the one conferring honors on those who, having never possessed them, esteemed them the less, and therefore had the less occasion to grieve for their absence; the other taking them from those who being accustomed to their possession would never be at rest till they were restored to them. It would thus be evident that the injury done to one party, was greater than the benefit they had conferred upon the other; so that whoever was the author of the proposition, he would gain few friends and make many enemies, and that the latter would be more resolutely bent on injuring him than the former would be zealous for his defense, for mankind are naturally more disposed to revenge than to gratitude, as if the latter could only be exercised with some inconvenience to themselves, while the former brings alike gratification and profit. Then, directing his discourse more particularly to Rinaldo, he said, "And you, if you could call to mind past events, and knew how craftily affairs are conducted in this city, would not be so eager in this pursuit; for he who advises it, when by your aid he has wrested the power from the people, will, with the people's assistance, who will have become your enemies, deprive you of it. And it will happen to you as to Benedetto Alberti, who, at the persuasion of those who were not his friends, consented to the ruin of Giorgio Scali and Tommaso Strozzi, and shortly afterward was himself sent into exile by the very same men." He therefore advised Rinaldo to think more maturely of these things, and endeavor to imitate his father, who, to obtain the benevolence of all, reduced the price of salt, provided that whoever owed taxes under half a florin should be at liberty to pay them or not, as he thought proper, and that at the meeting of the Councils every one should be free from the importunities of his creditors. He concluded by saying, that as regarded himself, he was disposed to let the government of the city remain as it was.

CHAPTER III

Giovanni de' Medici acquires the favor of the people--Bravery of Biaggio del Melano--Baseness of Zanobi del Pino--The Florentines obtain the friendship of the lord of Faenza--League of the Florentines with the Venetians--Origin of the Catasto--The rich citizens discontented with it--Peace with the duke of Milan--New disturbances on account of the Catasto.

These events, and the circumstances attending them, becoming known to the people, contributed greatly to increase the reputation of Giovanni, and brought odium on those who had made the proposals; but he assumed an appearance of indifference, in order to give less encouragement to those who by his influence were desirous of change. In his discourse he intimated to every one that it is not desirable to promote factions, but rather to extinguish them; and that whatever might be expected of him, he only sought the union of the city. This, however, gave offense to many of his party; for they would have rather seen him exhibit greater activity. Among others so disposed, was Alamanno de' Medici, who being of a restless disposition, never ceased exciting him to persecute enemies and favor friends; condemning his coldness and slow method of proceeding, which he said was the cause of his enemies' practicing against him, and that these practices would one day effect the ruin of himself and his friends. He endeavored to excite Cosmo, his son, with similar discourses; but Giovanni, for all that was either disclosed or foretold him, remained unmoved, although parties were now declared, and the city in manifest disunion.

There were at the palace, in the service of the Signory, two chancellors, Ser Martino and Ser Pagolo. The latter favored the party of Niccolo da Uzzano, the former that of Giovanni; and Rinaldo, seeing Giovanni unwilling to join them, thought it would be advisable to deprive Ser Martino of his office, that he might have the palace more completely under his control. The design becoming known to his adversaries, Ser Martino was retained and Ser Pagolo discharged, to the great injury and displeasure of Rinaldo and his party. This circumstance would soon have produced most mischievous effects, but for the war with which the city was threatened, and the recent defeat suffered at Zagonara, which served to check the audacity of the people; for while these events were in progress at Florence, Agnolo della Pergola, with the forces of the duke, had taken all the towns and cities possessed by the Florentines in Romagna, except Castracaro and Modigliano; partly from the weakness of the places themselves, and partly by the misconduct of those who had the command of them. In the course of the campaign, two instances occurred which served to show how greatly courage is admired even in enemies, and how much cowardice and pusillanimity are despised.

Biaggio del Melano was castellan in the fortress of Monte Petroso. Being surrounded by enemies, and seeing no chance of saving the place, which was already in flames, he cast clothes and straw from a part which was not yet on fire, and upon these he threw his two little children, saying to the enemy, "Take to yourselves those goods which fortune has bestowed upon me, and of which you may deprive me; but those of the mind, in which my honor and glory consist, I will not give up, neither can you wrest them from me." The besiegers ran to save the children, and placed for their father ropes and ladders, by which to save himself, but he would not use them, and rather chose to die in the flames than owe his safety to the enemies of his country: an example worthy of that much lauded antiquity, which offers nothing to surpass it, and which we admire the more from the rarity of any similar occurrence. Whatever could be recovered from the ruins, was restored for the use of the children, and carefully conveyed to their friends; nor was the republic less grateful; for as long as they lived, they were supported at her charge.

An example of an opposite character occurred at Galeata, where Zanobi del Pino was governor; he, without offering the least resistance, gave up the fortress to the enemy; and besides this, advised Agnolo della Pergola to leave the Alps of Romagna, and come among the smaller hills of Tuscany, where he might carry on the war with less danger and greater advantage. Agnolo could not endure the mean and base spirit of this man, and delivered him to his own attendants, who, after many reproaches, gave him nothing to eat but paper painted with snakes, saying, that of a Guelph they would make him a Ghibelline; and thus fasting, he died in a few days.

At this time Count Oddo and Niccolo Piccinino entered the Val di Lamona, with the design of bringing the lord of Faenza over to the Florentines, or at least inducing him to restrain the incursions of Agnolo della Pergola into Romagna; but as this valley is naturally strong, and its inhabitants warlike, Count Oddo was slain there, and Niccolo Piccinino sent a prisoner to Faenza. Fortune, however, caused the Florentines to obtain by their loss, what, perhaps, they would have failed to acquire by victory; for Niccolo so prevailed with the lord of Faenza and his mother, that they became friends of the Florentines. By this treaty, Niccolo Piccinino was set at liberty, but did not take the advice he had given others; for while in treaty with the city, concerning the terms of his engagement, either the conditions proposed were insufficient, or he found better elsewhere; for quite suddenly he left Arezzo, where he had been staying, passed into Lombardy, and entered the service of the duke.

The Florentines, alarmed by this circumstance, and reduced to despondency by their frequent losses, thought themselves unable to sustain the war alone, and sent ambassadors to the Venetians, to beg they would lend their aid to oppose the greatness of one who, if allowed to aggrandize himself, would soon become as dangerous to them as to the Florentines themselves. The Venetians were advised to adopt the same course by Francesco Carmignuola, one of the most distinguished warriors of those times, who had been in the service of the duke, and had afterward quitted it; but they hesitated, not knowing how far to trust him; for they thought his enmity with the duke was only feigned. While in this suspense, it was found that the duke, by means of a servant of Carmignuola, had caused poison to be given him in his food, which, although it was not fatal, reduced him to extremity. The truth being discovered, the Venetians laid aside their suspicion; and as the Florentines still solicited their assistance, a treaty was formed between the two powers, by which they agreed to carry on the war at the common expense of both: the conquests in Lombardy to be assigned to the Venetians; those in Romagna and Tuscany to the Florentines; and Carmignuola was appointed Captain General of the League. By this treaty the war was commenced in Lombardy, where it was admirably conducted; for in a few months many places were taken from the duke, together with the city of Brescia, the capture of which was in those days considered a most brilliant exploit.

The war had continued from 1422 to 1427, and the citizens of Florence were so wearied of the taxes that had been imposed during that time, that it was resolved to revise them, preparatory to their amelioration. That they might be equalized according to the means of each citizen, it was proposed that whoever possessed property of the value of one hundred florins should pay half a florin of taxes. Individual contribution would thus be determined by an invariable rule, and not left to the discretion of parties; and as it was found that the new method would press heavily upon the powerful classes, they used their utmost endeavors to prevent it from becoming law. Giovanni de' Medici alone declared himself in favor of it, and by his means it was passed. In order to determine the amount each had to pay, it was necessary to consider his property in the aggregate, which the Florentines call accatastare, in which in this application of it would signify TO RATE or VALUE, and hence this tax received the name of catasto. The new method of rating formed a powerful check to the tyranny of the great, who could no longer oppress the lower classes, or silence them with threats in the council as they had formerly done, and it therefore gave general satisfaction, though to the wealthy classes it was in the highest degree offensive. But as it is found men are never satisfied, but that the possession of one advantage only makes them desire more, the people, not content with the equality of taxation which the new law produced, demanded that the same rule should be applied to past years; that in investigation should be made to determine how much, according to the Catasto, the rich had paid less than their share, and that they should now pay up to an equality with those who, in order to meet the demand unjustly made, had been compelled to sell their possessions. This proposal alarmed the great more than the Catasto had done; and in self-defense they unceasingly decried it, declaring it in the highest degree unjust in being laid not only on immovable but movable property, which people possess to-day and lose to-morrow; that many persons have hidden wealth which the Catasto cannot reach; that those who leave their own affairs to manage those of the republic should be less burdened by her, it being enough for them to give their labour, and that it was unjust of the city to take both their property and their time, while of others she only took money. The advocates of the Catasto replied, that if movable property varies, the taxes would also vary, and frequently rating it would remedy the evil to which it was subject; that it was unnecessary to mention those who possessed hidden property; for it would be unreasonable to take taxes for that which produced no interest, and that if it paid anything, it could not fail to be discovered: that those who did not like to labor for the republic might cease to do so; for no doubt she would find plenty of loving citizens who would take pleasure in assisting her with both money and counsel: that the advantages and honors of a participation in the government are so great, that of themselves they are a sufficient remuneration to those who thus employ themselves, without wishing to be excused from paying their share of taxes. But, they added, the real grievance had not been mentioned: for those who were offended with the Catasto, regretted they could no longer involve the city in all the difficulties of war without injury to themselves, now that they had to contribute like the rest; and that if this law had then been in force they would not have gone to war with King Ladislaus, or the Duke Filippo, both which enterprises had been not through necessity, but to impoverish the citizens. The excitement was appeased by Giovanni de' Medici, who said, "It is not well to go into things so long past, unless to learn something for our present guidance; and if in former times the taxation has been unjust, we ought to be thankful, that we have now discovered a method of making it equitable, and hope that this will be the means of uniting the citizens, not of dividing them; which would certainly be the case were they to attempt the recovery of taxes for the past, and make them equal to the present; and that he who is content with a moderate victory is always most successful; for those who would more than conquer, commonly lose." With such words as these he calmed the disturbance, and this retrospective equalization was no longer contemplated.

The war with the duke still continued; but peace was at length restored by means of a legate of the pope. The duke, however, from the first disregarded the conditions, so that the league again took arms, and meeting the enemy's forces at Maclovio routed them. After this defeat the duke again made proposals for peace, to which the Florentines and Venetians both agreed; the former from jealousy of the Venetians, thinking they had spent quite enough money in the aggrandizement of others; the latter, because they found Carmignuola, after the defeat of the duke, proceed but coldly in their cause; so that they thought it no longer safe to trust him. A treaty was therefore concluded in 1428, by which the Florentines recovered the places they had lost in Romagna; and the Venetians kept Brescia, to which the duke added Bergamo and the country around it. In this war the Florentines expended three millions and a half of ducats, extended the territory and power of the Venetians, and brought poverty and disunion upon themselves.

Being at peace with their neighbors, domestic troubles recommenced. The great citizens could not endure the Catasto, and not knowing how to set it aside, they endeavored to raise up more numerous enemies to the measure, and thus provide themselves with allies to assist them in annulling it. They therefore instructed the officers appointed to levy the tax, that the law required them to extend the Catasto over the property of their nearest neighbors, to see if Florentine wealth was concealed among it. The dependent states were therefore ordered to present a schedule of their property against a certain time. This was extremely offensive to the people of Volterra, who sent to the Signory to complain of it; but the officers, in great wrath, committed eighteen of the complainants to prison. The Volterrani, however, out of regard for their fellow-countrymen who were arrested, did not proceed to any violence.

CHAPTER IV

Death of Giovanni de' Medici--His character--Insurrection of Volterra--Volterra returns to her allegiance--Niccolo Fortebraccio attacks the Lucchese--Diversity of opinion about the Lucchese war--War with Lucca--Astore Gianni and Rinaldo degli Albizzi appointed commissaries--Violence of Astorre Gianni.

About this time Giovanni de' Medici was taken ill, and finding his end approach, called his sons Cosmo and Lorenzo to him, to give them his last advice, and said, "I find I have nearly reached the term which God and nature appointed at my birth, and I die content, knowing that I leave you rich, healthy, and of such standing in society, that if you pursue the same course that I have, you will live respected in Florence, and in favor with everyone. Nothing cheers me so much at this moment, as the recollection that I have never willfully offended anyone; but have always used my utmost endeavors to confer benefits upon all. I would have you do so too. With regard to state affairs, if you would live in security, take just such a share as the laws and your countrymen think proper to bestow, thus you will escape both danger and envy; for it is not what is given to any individual, but what he has determined to possess, that occasions odium. You will thus have a larger share than those who endeavor to engross more than belongs to them; for they thus usually lose their own, and before they lose it, live in constant disquiet. By adopting this method, although among so many enemies, and surrounded by so many conflicting interests, I have not only maintained my reputation but increased my influence. If you pursue the same course, you will be attended by the same good fortune; if otherwise, you may be assured, your end will resemble that of those who in our own times have brought ruin both upon themselves and their families." Soon after this interview with his sons, Giovanni died, regretted by everyone, as his many excellencies deserved. He was compassionate; not only bestowing alms on those who asked them, but very frequently relieving the necessities of the poor, without having been solicited so to do. He loved all; praised the good, and pitied the infirmities of the wicked. He never sought the honors of government; yet enjoyed them all; and never went to the palace unless by request. He loved peace and shunned war; relieved mankind in adversity, and assisted them in prosperity; never applied the public money to his own uses, but contributed to the public wealth. He was courteous in office; not a man of great eloquence, but possessed of extraordinary prudence. His demeanor expressed melancholy; but after a short time his conversation became pleasant and facetious. He died exceedingly rich in money, but still more in good fame and the best wishes of mankind; and the wealth and respect he left behind him were not only preserved but increased by his son Cosmo.

The Volterran ambassadors grew weary of lying in prison, and to obtain their liberty promised to comply with the commands of the Florentines. Being set free and returned to their city, the time arrived for the new Priors to enter upon office, and among those who were drawn, was one named Giusto, a plebeian, but possessing great influence with his class, and one of those who had been imprisoned at Florence. He, being inflamed with hatred against the Florentines on account of his public as well as personal injuries, was further stimulated by Giovanni di Contugi, a man of noble family, and his colleague in office, to induce the people, by the authority of the Priors and his own influence, to withdraw their country from the power of the Florentines, and make himself prince. Prompted by these motives, Giusto took arms, rode through the city, seized the Capitano, who resided in it, on behalf of the Florentines, and with the consent of the people, became lord of Volterra. This circumstance greatly displeased the Florentines; but having just made peace with the duke, and the treaty being yet uninfringed on either side, they bethought themselves in a condition to recover the place; and that the opportunity might not be lost, they immediately appointed Rinaldo degli Albizzi and Palla Strozzi commissaries, and sent them upon the expedition. In the meantime, Giusto, who expected the Florentines would attack him, requested assistance of Lucca and Sienna. The latter refused, alleging her alliance with Florence; and Pagolo Guinigi, to regain the favor of the Florentines, which he imagined he had lost in the war with the duke and by his friendship for Filippo, not only refused assistance to Giusto, but sent his messenger prisoner to Florence.

The commissaries, to come upon the Volterrani unawares, assembled their cavalry, and having raised a good body of infantry in the Val d'Arno Inferiore, and the country about Pisa, proceeded to Volterra. Although attacked by the Florentines and abandoned by his neighbors, Giusto did not yield to fear; but, trusting to the strength of the city and the ruggedness of the country around it, prepared for his defense.

There lived at Volterra one Arcolano, brother of that Giovanni Contugi who had persuaded Giusto to assume the command. He possessed influence among the nobility, and having assembled a few of his most confidential friends, he assured them that by this event, God had come to the relief of their necessities; for if they would only take arms, deprive Giusto of the Signory, and give up the city to the Florentines, they might be sure of obtaining the principal offices, and the place would retain all its ancient privileges. Having gained them over, they went to the palace in which Giusto resided; and while part of them remained below, Arcolano, with three others, proceeded to the chamber above, where finding him with some citizens, they drew him aside, as if desirous to communicate something of importance, and conversing on different subjects, let him to the lower apartment, and fell upon him with their swords. They, however, were not so quick as to prevent Giusto from making use of his own weapon; for with it he seriously wounded two of them; but being unable to resist so many, he was at last slain, and his body thrown into the street. Arcolano and his party gave up the city to the Florentine commissaries, who, being at hand with their forces, immediately took possession; but the condition of Volterra was worse than before; for among other things which operated to her disadvantage, most of the adjoining countryside was separated from her, and she was reduced to the rank of a vicariate.

Volterra having been lost and recovered almost at the same time, present circumstances afforded nothing of sufficient importance to occasion a new war, if ambition had not again provoked one. Niccolo Fortebraccio, the son of a sister of Braccio da Perugia, had been in the service of the Florentines during most of their wars with the duke. Upon the restoration of peace he was discharged; but when the affair of Volterra took place, being encamped with his people at Fucecchio, the commissaries availed themselves both of himself and his forces. Some thought that while Rinaldo conducted the expedition along with him, he persuaded him, under one pretext or another, to attack the Lucchese, assuring him, that if he did so, the Florentines would consent to undertake an expedition against them, and would appoint him to the command. When Volterra was recovered, and Niccolo returned to his quarters at Fucecchio, he, either at the persuasion of Rinaldo, or of his own accord, in November, 1429, took possession of Ruoti and Compito, castles belonging to the Lucchese, with three hundred cavalry and as many infantry, and then descending into the plain, plundered the inhabitants to a vast amount. The news of this incursion having reached Florence, persons of all classes were seen gathered in parties throughout the city discussing the matter, and nearly all were in favor of an expedition against Lucca. Of the Grandees thus disposed, were the Medici and their party, and with them also Rinaldo, either because he thought the enterprise beneficial to the republic, or induced by his own ambition and the expectation of being appointed to the command. Niccolo da Uzzano and his party were opposed to the war. It seems hardly credible that such contrary opinions should prevail, though at different times, in the same men and the same city, upon the subject of war; for the same citizens and people that, during the ten years of peace had incessantly blamed the war undertaken against Duke Filippo, in defense of liberty, now, after so much expense and trouble, with their utmost energy, insisted on hostilities against Lucca, which, if successful, would deprive that city of her liberty; while those who had been in favor of a war with the duke, were opposed to the present; so much more ready are the multitude to covet the possessions of others than to preserve their own, and so much more easily are they led by the hope of acquisition than by the fear of loss. The suggestions of the latter appear incredible till they are verified; and the pleasing anticipations of the former are cherished as facts, even while the advantages are very problematical, or at best, remote. The people of Florence were inspired with hope, by the acquisitions which Niccolo Fortebraccio had made, and by letters received from their rectors in the vicinity of Lucca; for their deputies at Vico and Pescia had written, that if permission were given to them to receive the castles that offered to surrender, the whole country of Lucca would very soon be obtained. It must, however, be added, that an ambassador was sent by the governor of Lucca to Florence, to complain of the attack made by Niccolo, and to entreat that the Signory would not make war against a neighbor, and a city that had always been friendly to them. The ambassador was Jacopo Viviani, who, a short time previously, had been imprisoned by Pagolo Guinigi, governor of Lucca, for having conspired against him. Although he had been found guilty, his life was spared, and as Pagolo thought the forgiveness mutual, he reposed confidence in him. Jacopo, more mindful of the danger he had incurred than of the lenity exercised toward him, on his arrival in Florence secretly instigated the citizens to hostilities; and these instigations, added to other hopes, induced the Signory to call the Council together, at which 498 citizens assembled, before whom the principal men of the city discussed the question.

Among the first who addressed the assembly in favor of the expedition, was Rinaldo. He pointed out the advantage that would accrue from the acquisition, and justified the enterprise from its being left open to them by the Venetians and the duke, and that as the pope was engaged in the affairs of Naples, he could not interfere. He then remarked upon the facility of the expedition, showing that Lucca, being now in bondage to one of her own citizens, had lost her natural vigor and former anxiety for the preservation of her liberty, and would either be surrendered to them by the people in order to expel the tyrant, or by the tyrant for fear of the people. He recalled the remembrance of the injuries done to the republic by the governor of Lucca; his malevolent disposition toward them; and their embarrassing situation with regard to him, if the pope or the duke were to make war upon them; and concluded that no enterprise was ever undertaken by the people of Florence with such perfect facility, more positive advantage, or greater justice in its favor.

In a reply to this, Niccolo da Uzzano stated that the city of Florence never entered on a more unjust or more dangerous project, or one more pregnant with evil, than this. In the first place they were going to attack a Guelphic city, that had always been friendly to the Florentine people, and had frequently, at great hazard, received the Guelphs into her bosom when they were expelled from their own country. That in the history of the past there was not an instance, while Lucca was free, of her having done an injury to the Florentines; and that if they had been injured by her enslavers, as formerly by Castruccio, and now by the present governor, the fault was not in the city, but in her tyrant. That if they could assail the latter without detriment to the people, he should have less scruple, but as this was impossible, he could not consent that a city which had been friendly to Florence should be plundered of her wealth. However, as it was usual at present to pay little or no regard either to equity or injustice, he would consider the matter solely with reference to the advantage of Florence. He thought that what could not easily be attended by pernicious consequences might be esteemed useful, but he could not imagine how an enterprise should be called advantageous in which the evils were certain and the utility doubtful. The certain evils were the expenses with which it would be attended; and these, he foresaw, would be sufficiently great to alarm even a people that had long been in repose, much more one wearied, as they were, by a tedious and expensive war. The advantage that might be gained was the acquisition of Lucca, which he acknowledged to be great; but the hazards were so enormous and immeasurable, as in his opinion to render the conquest quite impossible. He could not induce himself to believe that the Venetians, or Filippo, would willingly allow them to make the acquisition; for the former only consented in appearance, in order to avoid the semblance of ingratitude, having so lately, with Florentine money, acquired such an extent of dominion. That as regarded the duke, it would greatly gratify him to see them involved in new wars and expenses; for, being exhausted and defeated on all sides, he might again assail them; and that if, after having undertaken it, their enterprise against Lucca were to prove successful, and offer them the fullest hope of victory, the duke would not want an opportunity of frustrating their labors, either by assisting the Lucchese secretly with money, or by apparently disbanding his own troops, and then sending them, as if they were soldiers of fortune, to their relief. He therefore advised that they should give up the idea, and behave toward the tyrant in such a way as to create him as many enemies as possible; for there was no better method of reducing Lucca than to let them live under the tyrant, oppressed and exhausted by him; for, if prudently managed, that city would soon get into such a condition that he could not retain it, and being ignorant or unable to govern itself, it must of necessity fall into their power. But he saw that his discourse did not please them, and that his words were unheeded; he would, however, predict this to them, that they were about to commence a war in which they would expend vast sums, incur great domestic dangers, and instead of becoming masters of Lucca, they would deliver her from her tyrant, and of a friendly city, feeble and oppressed, they would make one free and hostile, and that in time she would become an obstacle to the greatness of their own republic.

The question having been debated on both sides, they proceeded to vote, as usual, and of the citizens present only ninety-eight were against the enterprise. Thus determined in favor of war, they appointed a Council of Ten for its management, and hired forces, both horse and foot. Astorre Gianni and Rinaldo degli Albizzi were appointed commissaries, and Niccolo Fortebraccio, on agreeing to give up to the Florentines the places he had taken, was engaged to conduct the enterprise as their captain. The commissaries having arrived with the army in the country of the Lucchese, divided their forces; one part of which, under Astorre, extended itself along the plain, toward Camaiore and Pietrasanta, while Rinaldo, with the other division, took the direction of the hills, presuming that when the citizens found themselves deprived of the surrounding country, they would easily submit. The proceedings of the commissaries were unfortunate, not that they failed to occupy many places, but from the complaints made against them of mismanaging the operations of the war; and Astorre Gianni had certainly given very sufficient cause for the charges against him.

There is a fertile and populous valley near Pietrasanta, called Seravezza, whose inhabitants, on learning the arrival of the commissary, presented themselves before him and begged he would receive them as faithful subjects of the Florentine republic. Astorre pretended to accept their proposal, but immediately ordered his forces to take possession of all the passes and strong positions of the valley, assembled the men in the principal church, took them all prisoners, and then caused his people to plunder and destroy the whole country, with the greatest avarice and cruelty, making no distinction in favor of consecrated places, and violating the women, both married and single. These things being known in Florence, displeased not only the magistracy, but the whole city.

CHAPTER V

The inhabitants of Seravezza appeal to the Signory--Complaints against Rinaldo degli Albizzi--The commissaries changed--Filippo Brunelleschi proposes to submerge the country about Lucca--Pagolo Guinigi asks assistance of the duke of Milan--The duke sends Francesco Sforza--Pagolo Guinigi expelled--The Florentines routed by the forces of the duke--The acquisitions of the Lucchese after the victory--Conclusion of the war.

A few of the inhabitants of the valley of Seravezza, having escaped the hands of the commissary, came to Florence and acquainted every one in the streets with their miserable situation; and by the advice of those who, either through indignation at his wickedness or from being of the opposite party, wished to punish the commissary, they went to the Council of Ten, and requested an audience. This being granted, one of them spoke to the following effect: "We feel assured, magnificent lords, that we shall find credit and compassion from the Signory, when you learn how your commissary has taken possession of our country, and in what manner he has treated us. Our valley, as the memorials of your ancient houses abundantly testify, was always Guelphic, and has often proved a secure retreat to your citizens when persecuted by the Ghibellines. Our forefathers, and ourselves too, have always revered the name of this noble republic as the leader and head of their party. While the Lucchese were Guelphs we willingly submitted to their government; but when enslaved by the tyrant, who forsook his old friends to join the Ghibelline faction, we have obeyed him more through force than good will. And God knows how often we have prayed, that we might have an opportunity of showing our attachment to our ancient party. But how blind are mankind in their wishes! That which we desired for our safety has proved our destruction. As soon as we learned that your ensigns were approaching, we hastened to meet your commissary, not as an enemy, but as the representative of our ancient lords; placed our valley, our persons, and our fortunes in his hands, and commended them to his good faith, believing him to possess the soul, if not of a Florentine, at least of a man. Your lordships will forgive us; for, unable to support his cruelties, we are compelled to speak. Your commissary has nothing of the man but the shape, nor of a Florentine but the name; a more deadly pest, a more savage beast, a more horrid monster never was imagined in the human mind; for, having assembled us in our church under pretense of wishing to speak with us, he made us prisoners. He then burned and destroyed the whole valley, carried off our property, ravaged every place, destroyed everything, violated the women, dishonored the virgins, and dragging them from the arms of their mothers, gave them up to the brutality of his soldiery. If by any injury to the Florentine people we merited such treatment, or if he had vanquished us armed in our defense, we should have less reason for complaint; we should have accused ourselves, and thought that either our mismanagement or our arrogance had deservedly brought the calamity upon us; but after having freely presented ourselves to him unarmed, to be robbed and plundered with such unfeeling barbarity, is more than we can bear. And though we might have filled Lombardy with complaints and charges against this city, and spread the story of our misfortunes over the whole of Italy, we did not wish to slander so just and pious a republic, with the baseness and perfidy of one wicked citizen, whose cruelty and avarice, had we known them before our ruin was complete, we should have endeavored to satiate (though indeed they are insatiable), and with one-half of our property have saved the rest. But the opportunity is past; we are compelled to have recourse to you, and beg that you will succor the distresses of your subjects, that others may not be deterred by our example from submitting themselves to your authority. And if our extreme distress cannot prevail with you to assist us, be induced, by your fear of the wrath of God, who has seen his temple plundered and burned, and his people betrayed in his bosom." Having said this they threw themselves on the ground, crying aloud, and praying that their property and their country might be restored to them; and that if the Signory could not give them back their honor, they would, at least, restore husbands to their wives, and children to their fathers. The atrocity of the affair having already been made known, and now by the living words of the sufferers presented before them, excited the compassion of the magistracy. They ordered the immediate return of Astorre, who being tried, was found guilty, and admonished. They sought the goods of the inhabitants of Seravezza; all that could be recovered was restored to them, and as time and circumstance gave opportunity, they were compensated for the rest.

Complaints were made against Rinaldo degli Albizzi, that he carried on the war, not for the advantage of the Florentine people, but his own private emolument; that as soon as he was appointed commissary, he lost all desire to take Lucca, for it was sufficient for him to plunder the country, fill his estates with cattle, and his house with booty; and, not content with what his own satellites took, he purchased that of the soldiery, so that instead of a commissary he became a merchant. These calumnies coming to his ears, disturbed the temper of this proud but upright man, more than quite became his dignity. He was so exasperated against the citizens and magistracy, that without waiting for or asking permission, he returned to Florence, and, presenting himself before the Council of Ten, he said that he well knew how difficult and dangerous a thing it was to serve an unruly people and a divided city, for the one listens to every report, the other pursues improper measures; they neglect to reward good conduct, and heap censure upon whatever appears doubtful; so that victory wins no applause, error is accused by all, and if vanquished, universal condemnation is incurred; from one's own party through envy, and from enemies through hatred, persecution results. He confessed that the baseness of the present calumnies had conquered his patience and changed the temper of his mind; but he would say, he had never, for fear of a false accusation, avoided doing what appeared to him beneficial to the city. However, he trusted the magistrates would in future be more ready to defend their fellow-citizens, so that the latter might continue anxious to effect the prosperity of their country; that as it was not customary at Florence to award triumphs for success, they ought at least to be protected from calumny; and that being citizens themselves, and at any moment liable to false accusations, they might easily conceive how painful it is to an upright mind to be oppressed with slander. The Ten endeavored, as well as circumstances would admit, to soothe the acerbity of his feelings, and confided the care of the expedition to Neri di Gino and Alamanno Salviati, who, instead of overrunning the country, advanced near to Lucca. As the weather had become extremely cold, the forces established themselves at Campannole, which seemed to the commissaries waste of time; and wishing to draw nearer the place, the soldiery refused to comply, although the Ten had insisted they should pitch their camp before the city, and would not hear of any excuse.

At that time there lived at Florence, a very distinguished architect, named Filippo di Ser Brunelleschi, of whose works our city is full, and whose merit was so extraordinary, that after his death his statue in marble was erected in the principal church, with an inscription underneath, which still bears testimony to those who read it, of his great talents. This man pointed out, that in consequence of the relative positions of the river Serchio and the city of Lucca, the wastes of the river might be made to inundate the surrounding country, and place the city in a kind of lake. His reasoning on this point appeared so clear, and the advantage to the besiegers so obvious and inevitable, that the Ten were induced to make the experiment. The result, however, was quite contrary to their expectation, and produced the utmost disorder in the Florentine camp; for the Lucchese raised high embankments in the direction of the ditch made by our people to conduct the waters of the Serchio, and one night cut through the embankment of the ditch itself, so that having first prevented the water from taking the course designed by the architect, they now caused it to overflow the plain, and compelled the Florentines, instead of approaching the city as they wished, to take a more remote position.

The design having failed, the Council of Ten, who had been re-elected, sent as commissary, Giovanni Guicciardini, who encamped before Lucca, with all possible expedition. Pagolo Guinigi finding himself thus closely pressed, by the advice of Antonio del Rosso, then representative of the Siennese at Lucca, sent Salvestro Trento and Leonardo Bonvisi to Milan, to request assistance from the duke; but finding him indisposed to comply, they secretly engaged, on the part of the people, to deliver their governor up to him and give him possession of the place; at the same time intimating, that if he did not immediately follow this advice, he would not long have the opportunity, since it was the intention of Pagolo to surrender the city to the Florentines, who were very anxious to obtain it. The duke was so much alarmed with this idea, that, setting aside all other considerations, he caused Count Francesco Sforza, who was engaged in his service, to make a public request for permission to go to Naples; and having obtained it, he proceeded with his forces directly to Lucca, though the Florentines, aware of the deception, and apprehensive of the consequences, had sent to the count, Boccacino Alamanni, his friend, to frustrate this arrangement. Upon the arrival of the count at Lucca, the Florentines removed their camp to Librafatta, and the count proceeded immediately to Pescia, where Pagolo Diacceto was lieutenant governor, who, promoted by fear rather than any better motive, fled to Pistoia, and if the place had not been defended by Giovanni Malavolti, to whom the command was intrusted, it would have been lost. The count failing in his attempt went to Borgo a Buggiano which he took, and burned the castle of Stigliano, in the same neighborhood.

The Florentines being informed of these disasters, found they must have recourse to those remedies which upon former occasions had often proved useful. Knowing that with mercenary soldiers, when force is insufficient, corruption commonly prevails, they offered the count a large sum of money on condition that he should quit the city, and give it up to them. The count finding that no more money was to be had from Lucca, resolved to take it of those who had it to dispense, and agreed with the Florentines, not to give them Lucca, which for decency he could not consent to, but to withdraw his troops, and abandon it, on condition of receiving fifty thousand ducats; and having made this agreement, to induce the Lucchese to excuse him to the duke, he consented that they should expel their tyrant.

Antonio del Rosso, as we remarked above, was Siennese ambassador at Lucca, and with the authority of the count he contrived the ruin of Pagolo Guinigi. The heads of the conspiracy were Pierro Cennami and Giovanni da Chivizzano. The count resided upon the Serchio, at a short distance from the city, and with him was Lanzilao, the son of Pagolo. The conspirators, about forty in number, went armed at night in search of Pagolo, who, on hearing the noise they made, came toward them quite astonished, and demanded the cause of their visit; to which Piero Cennami replied, that they had long been governed by him, and led about against the enemy, to die either by hunger or the sword, but were resolved to govern themselves for the future, and demanded the keys of the city and the treasure. Pagolo said the treasure was consumed, but the keys and himself were in their power; he only begged that as his command had begun and continued without bloodshed, it might conclude in the same manner. Count Francesco conducted Pagolo and his son to the duke, and they afterward died in prison.

The departure of the count having delivered Lucca from her tyrant, and the

Florentines from their fear of his soldiery, the former prepared for her defense, and the latter resumed the siege. They appointed the count of Urbino to conduct their forces, and he pressed the Lucchese so closely, that they were again compelled to ask the assistance of the duke, who dispatched Niccolo Piccinino, under the same pretense as he previously sent Count Francesco. The Florentine forces met him on his approach to Lucca, and at the passage of the Serchio a battle ensued, in which they were routed, the commissary with a few of his men escaping to Pisa. This defeat filled the Florentines with dismay, and as the enterprise had been undertaken with the entire approbation of the great body of the people, they did not know whom to find fault with, and therefore railed against those who had been appointed to the management of the war, reviving the charges made against Rinaldo. They were, however, more severe against Giovanni Guicciardini than any other, declaring that if he had wished, he might have put a period to the war at the departure of Count Francesco, but that he had been bribed with money, for he had sent home a large sum, naming the party who had been intrusted to bring it, and the persons to whom it had been delivered. These complaints and accusations were carried to so great a length that the captain of the people, induced by the public voice, and pressed by the party opposed to the war, summoned him to trial. Giovanni appeared, though full of indignation. However his friends, from regard to their own character, adopted such a course with the Capitano as induced him to abandon the inquiry.

After this victory, the Lucchese not only recovered the places that had belonged to them, but occupied all the country of Pisa except Beintina, Calcinaja, Livorno, and Librafatta; and, had not a conspiracy been discovered that was formed in Pisa, they would have secured that city also. The Florentines again prepared for battle, and appointed Micheletto, a pupil of Sforza, to be their leader. The duke, on the other hand, followed up this victory, and that he might bring a greater power against the Florentines, induced the Genoese, the Siennese, and the governor of Piombino, to enter into a league for the defense of Lucca, and to engage Niccolo Piccinino to conduct their forces. Having by this step declared his design, the Venetians and the Florentines renewed their league, and the war was carried on openly in Tuscany and Lombardy, in each of which several battles were fought with variety of fortune. At length, both sides being wearied out, they came to terms for the cessation of hostilities, in May, 1433. By this arrangement the Florentines, Lucchese, and Siennese, who had each occupied many fortresses belonging to the others, gave them all up, and each party resumed its original possessions.

CHAPTER VI

Cosmo de' Medici, his character and mode of proceedings--The greatness of Cosmo excites the jealousy of the citizens--The opinion of Niccolo da Uzzano--Scandalous divisions of the Florentines--Death of Niccolo da Uzzano--Bernardo Guadagni, Gonfalonier, adopts measures against Cosmo--Cosmo arrested in the palace--He is apprehensive of attempts against his life.

During the war the malignant humors of the city were in constant activity. Cosmo de' Medici, after the death of Giovanni, engaged more earnestly in public affairs, and conducted himself with more zeal and boldness in regard to his friends than his father had done, so that those who rejoiced at Giovanni's death, finding what the son was likely to become, perceived they had no cause for exultation. Cosmo was one of the most prudent of men; of grave and courteous demeanor, extremely liberal and humane. He never attempted anything against parties, or against rulers, but was bountiful to all; and by the unwearied generosity of his disposition, made himself partisans of all ranks of the citizens. This mode of proceeding increased the difficulties of those who were in the government, and Cosmo himself hoped that by its pursuit he might be able to live in Florence as much respected and as secure as any other citizen; or if the ambition of his adversaries compelled him to adopt a different course, arms and the favor of his friends would enable him to become more so. Averardo de' Medici and Puccio Pucci were greatly instrumental in the establishment of his power; the former by his boldness, the latter by unusual prudence and sagacity, contributed to his aggrandizement. Indeed the advice of wisdom of Puccio were so highly esteemed, that Cosmo's party was rather distinguished by the name of Puccio than by his own.

By this divided city the enterprise against Lucca was undertaken; and the bitterness of party spirit, instead of being abated, increased. Although the friends of

Cosmo had been in favor of it, many of the adverse faction were sent to assist in the management, as being men of greater influence in the state. Averardo de' Medici and the rest being unable to prevent this, endeavored with all their might to calumniate them; and when any unfavorable circumstance occurred (and there were many), fortune and the exertions of the enemy were never supposed to be the causes, but solely the want of capacity in the commissary. This disposition aggravated the offenses of Astorre Gianni; this excited the indignation of Rinaldo degli Albizzi, and made him resign his commission without leave; this, too, compelled the captain of the people to require the appearance of Giovanni Guicciardini, and from this arose all the other charges which were made against the magistrates and the commissaries. Real evils were magnified, unreal ones feigned, and the true and the false were equally believed by the people, who were almost universally their foes. All these events and extraordinary modes of proceeding were perfectly known to Niccolo da Uzzano and the other leaders of the party; and they had often consulted together for the purpose of finding a remedy, but without effect; though they were aware of the danger of allowing them to increase, and the great difficulty that would attend any attempt to remove or abate them. Niccolo da Uzzano was the earliest to take offense; and while the war was proceeding without, and these troubles within, Niccolo Barbadoro desirous of inducing him to consent to the ruin of Cosmo, waited upon him at his house; and finding him alone in his study, and very pensive, endeavored, with the best reasons he could advance, to persuade him to agree with Rinaldo on Cosmo's expulsion. Niccolo da Uzzano replied as follows: "It would be better for thee and thy house, as well as for our republic, if thou and those who follow thee in this opinion had beards of silver instead of gold, as is said of thee; for advice proceeding from the hoary head of long experience would be wiser and of greater service to all. It appears to me, that those who talk of driving Cosmo out of Florence would do well to consider what is their strength, and what that of Cosmo. You have named one party, that of the nobility, the other that of the plebeians. If the fact corresponded with the name, the victory would still be most uncertain, and the example of the ancient nobility of this city, who were destroyed by the plebeians, ought rather to impress us with fear than with hope. We have, however, still further cause for apprehension from the division of our party, and the union of our adversaries. In the first place, Neri di Gino and Nerone di Nigi, two of our principal citizens, have never so fully declared their sentiments as to enable us to determine whether they are most our friends our those of our opponents. There are many families, even many houses, divided; many are opposed to us through envy of brothers or relatives. I will recall to your recollection two or three of the most important; you may think of the others at your leisure. Of the sons of Maso degli Albizzi, Luca, from envy of Rinaldo, has thrown himself into their hands. In the house of Guicciardini, of the sons of Luigi, Piero is the enemy of Giovanni and in favor of our adversaries. Tommaso and Niccolo Soderini openly oppose us on account of their hatred of their uncle Francesco. So that if we consider well what we are, and what our enemies, I cannot see why we should be called NOBLE any more than they. If it is because they are followed by the plebeians, we are in a worse condition on that account, and they in a better; for were it to come either to arms or to votes, we should not be able to resist them. True it is, we still preserve our dignity, our precedence, the priority of our position, but this arises from the former reputation of the government, which has now continued fifty years; and whenever we come to the proof, or they discover our weakness we shall lose it. If you were to say, the justice of our cause ought to augment our influence and diminish theirs I answer, that this justice requires to be perceived and believed by others as well as by ourselves, but this is not the case; for the justice of our cause is wholly founded upon our suspicion that Cosmo designs to make himself prince of the city. And although we entertain this suspicion and suppose it to be correct, others have it not; but what is worse, they charge us with the very design of which we accuse him. Those actions of Cosmo which lead us to suspect him are, that he lends money indiscriminately, and not to private persons only, but to the public; and not to Florentines only, but to the condottieri, the soldiers of fortune. Besides, he assists any citizen who requires magisterial aid; and, by the universal interest he possesses in the city, raises first one friend and then another to higher grades of honor. Therefore, to adduce our reasons for expelling him, would be to say that he is kind, generous, liberal, and beloved by all. Now tell me, what law is there which forbids, disapproves, or condemns men for being pious, liberal, and benevolent? And though they are all modes adopted by those who aim at sovereignty, they are not believed to be such, nor have we sufficient power to make them to be so esteemed; for our conduct has robbed us of confidence, and the city, naturally partial and (having always lived in faction) corrupt, cannot lend its attention to such charges. But even if we were successful in an attempt to expel him (which might easily happen under a favorable Signory), how could we (being surrounded by his innumerable friends, who would constantly reproach us, and ardently desire to see him again in the city) prevent his return? It would be impossible for they being so numerous, and having the good will of all upon their side, we should never be secure from them. And as many of his first discovered friends as you might expel, so many enemies would you make, so that in a short time he would return, and the result would be simply this, that we had driven him out a good man and he had returned to us a bad one; for his nature would be corrupted by those who recalled him, and he, being under obligation, could not oppose them. Or should you design to put him to death, you could not attain your purpose with the magistrates, for his wealth, and the corruption of your minds, will always save him. But let us suppose him put to death, or that being banished, he did not return, I cannot see how the condition of our republic would be ameliorated; for if we relieve her from Cosmo, we at once make her subject to Rinaldo, and it is my most earnest desire that no citizen may ever, in power and authority, surpass the rest. But if one of these must prevail, I know of no reason that should make me prefer Rinaldo to Cosmo. I shall only say, may God preserve the city from any of her citizens usurping the sovereignty, but if our sins have deserved this, in mercy save us from Rinaldo. I pray thee, therefore, do not advise the adoption of a course on every account pernicious, nor imagine that, in union with a few, you would be able to oppose the will of the many; for the citizens, some from ignorance and others from malice, are ready to sell the republic at any time, and fortune has so much favored them, that they have found a purchaser. Take my advice then; endeavor to live moderately; and with regard to liberty, you will find as much cause for suspicion in our party as in that of our adversaries. And when troubles arise, being of neither side, you will be agreeable to both, and you will thus provide for your own comfort and do no injury to any." These words somewhat abated the eagerness of Barbadoro, so that tranquillity prevailed during the war with Lucca. But this being ended, and Niccolo da Uzzano dead, the city being at peace and under no restraint, unhealthy humors increased with fearful rapidity. Rinaldo, considering himself now the leader of the party, constantly entreated and urged every citizen whom he thought likely to be Gonfalonier, to take up arms and deliver the country from him who, from the malevolence of a few and the ignorance of the multitude, was inevitably reducing it to slavery. These practices of Rinaldo, and those of the contrary side, kept the city full of apprehension, so that whenever a magistracy was created, the numbers of each party composing it were made publicly known, and upon drawing for the Signory the whole city was aroused. Every case brought before the magistrates, however trivial, was made a subject of contention among them. Secrets were divulged, good and evil alike became objects of favor and opposition, the benevolent and the wicked were alike assailed, and no magistrate fulfilled the duties of his office with integrity. In this state of confusion, Rinaldo, anxious to abate the power of Cosmo, and knowing that Bernardo Guadagni was likely to become Gonfalonier, paid his arrears of taxes, that he might not, by being indebted to the public, be incapacitated for holding the office. The drawing soon after took place, and fortune, opposed to our welfare, caused Bernardo to be appointed for the months of September and October. Rinaldo immediately waited upon him, and intimated how much the party of the nobility, and all who wished for repose, rejoiced to find he had attained that dignity; that it now rested with him to act in such a manner as to realize their pleasing expectations. He then enlarged upon the danger of disunion, and endeavored to show that there was no means of attaining the blessing of unity but by the destruction of Cosmo, for he alone, by the popularity acquired with his enormous wealth, kept them depressed; that he was already so powerful, that if not hindered, he would soon become prince, and that it was the part of a good citizen, in order to prevent such a calamity, to assemble the people in the piazza, and restore liberty to his country. Rinaldo then reminded the new Gonfalonier how Salvestro de' Medici was able, though unjustly, to restrain the power of the Guelphs, to whom, by the blood of their ancestors, shed in its cause, the government rightly belonged; and argued that what he was able unjustly to accomplish against so many, might surely be easily performed with justice in its favor against one! He encouraged him with the assurance that their friends would be ready in arms to support him; that he need not regard the plebeians, who adored Cosmo, since their assistance would be of no greater avail than Giorgio Scali had found it on a similar occasion; and that with regard to his wealth, no apprehension was necessary, for when he was under the power of the Signory, his riches would be so too. In conclusion, he averred that this course would unite and secure the republic, and crown the Gonfalonier with glory. Bernardo briefly replied, that he thought it necessary to act exactly as Rinaldo had advised, and that as the time was suitable for action, he should provide himself with forces, being assured from what Rinaldo had said, he would be supported by his colleagues. Bernardo entered upon the duties of his office, prepared his followers, and having concerted with Rinaldo, summoned Cosmo, who, though many friends dissuaded him from it, obeyed the call, trusting more to his own innocence than to the mercy of the Signory. As soon as he had entered the palace he was arrested. Rinaldo, with a great number of armed men, and accompanied by nearly the whole of his party, proceeded to the piazza, when the Signory assembled the people, and created a Balia of two hundred persons for the reformation of the city. With the least possible delay they entered upon the consideration of reform, and of the life or death of Cosmo. Many wished him to be banished, others to be put to death, and several were silent, either from compassion toward him or for fear of the rest, so that these differences prevented them from coming to any conclusion. There is an apartment in the tower of the palace which occupies the whole of one floor, and is called the Alberghettino, in which Cosmo was confined, under the charge of Federigo Malavolti. In this place, hearing the assembly of the Councils, the noise of arms which proceeded from the piazza, and the frequent ringing of the bell to assemble the Balia, he was greatly apprehensive for his safety, but still more less his private enemies should cause him to be put to death in some unusual manner. He scarcely took any food, so that in four days he ate only a small quantity of bread, Federigo, observing his anxiety, said to him, "Cosmo, you are afraid of being poisoned, and are evidently hastening your end with hunger. You wrong me if you think I would be a party to such an atrocious act. I do not imagine your life to be in much danger, since you have so many friends both within the palace and without; but if you should eventually lose it, be assured they will use some other medium than myself for that purpose, for I will never imbue my hands in the blood of any, still less in yours, who never injured me; therefore cheer up, take some food, and preserve your life for your friends and your country. And that you may do so with greater assurance, I will partake of your meals with you." These words were of great relief to Cosmo, who, with tears in his eyes, embraced and kissed Federigo, earnestly thanking him for so kind and affectionate conduct, and promising, if ever the opportunity were given him, he would not be ungrateful.

CHAPTER VII

Cosmo is banished to Padua--Rinaldo degli Albizzi attempts to restore the nobility--New disturbances occasioned by Rinaldo degli Albizzi--Rinaldo takes arms against the Signory--His designs are disconcerted--Pope Eugenius in Florence--He endeavors to reconcile the parties--Cosmo is recalled--Rinaldo and his party banished--Glorious return of Cosmo.

Cosmo in some degree recovered his spirits, and while the citizens were disputing about him, Federigo, by way of recreation, brought an acquaintance of the Gonfalonier to take supper with him, an amusing and facetious person, whose name was Il Farnagaccio. The repast being nearly over, Cosmo, who thought he might turn this visit to advantage, for he knew the man very intimately, gave a sign to Federigo to leave the apartment, and he, guessing the cause, under pretense of going for something that was wanted on the table, left them together. Cosmo, after a few friendly expressions addressed to Il Farnagaccio, gave him a small slip of paper, and desired him to go to the director of the hospital of Santa Maria Nuova, for one thousand one hundred ducats; he was to take the hundred for himself, and carry the thousand to the Gonfalonier, and beg that he would take some suitable occasion of coming to see him. Farnagaccio undertook the commission, the money was paid, Bernardo became more humane, and Cosmo was banished to Padua, contrary to the wish of Rinaldo, who earnestly desired his death. Averardo and many others of the house of Medici were also banished, and with them Puccio and Giovanni Pucci. To silence those who were dissatisfied with the banishment of Cosmo, they endowed with the power of a Balia, the Eight of War and the Capitano of the People. After his sentence, Cosmo on the third of October, 1433, came before the Signory, by whom the boundary to which he was restricted was specified; and they advised him to avoid passing it, unless he wished them to proceed with greater severity both against himself and his property. Cosmo received his sentence with a cheerful look, assuring the Signory that wherever they determined to send him, he would willingly remain. He earnestly begged, that as they had preserved his life they would protect it, for he knew there were many in the piazza who were desirous to take it; and assured them, that wherever he might be, himself and his means were entirely at the service of the city, the people, and the Signory. He was respectfully attended by the Gonfalonier, who retained him in the palace till night, then conducted him to his own house to supper, and caused him to be escorted by a strong armed force to his place of banishment. Wherever the cavalcade passed, Cosmo was honorably received, and was publicly visited by the Venetians, not as an exile, but with all the respect due to one in the highest station.

Florence, widowed of so great a citizen, one so generally beloved, seemed to be universally sunk in despondency; victors and the vanquished were alike in fear. Rinaldo, as if inspired with a presage of his future calamities, in order not to appear deficient to himself or his party, assembled many citizens, his friends, and informed them that he foresaw their approaching ruin for having allowed themselves to be overcome by the prayers, the tears, and the money of their enemies; and that they did not seem aware they would soon themselves have to entreat and weep, when their prayers would not be listened to, or their tears excite compassion; and that of the money received, they would have to restore the principal, and pay the interest in tortures, exile, and death; that it would have been much better for them to have done nothing than to have left Cosmo alive, and his friends in Florence; for great offenders ought either to remain untouched, or be destroyed; that there was now no remedy but to strengthen themselves in the city, so that upon the renewed attempts of their enemies, which would soon take place, they might drive them out with arms, since they had not sufficient civil authority to expel them. The remedy to be adopted, he said, was one that he had long before advocated, which was to regain the friendship of the grandees, restoring and conceding to them all the honors of the city, and thus make themselves strong with that party, since their adversaries had joined the plebeians. That by this means they would become the more powerful side, for they would possess greater energy, more comprehensive talent and an augmented share of influence; and that if this last and only remedy were not adopted, he knew not what other means could be made use of to preserve the government among so many enemies, or prevent their own ruin and that of the city.

Mariotto Baldovinetti, one of the assembly, was opposed to this plan, on account of the pride and insupportable nature of the nobility; and said, that it would be folly to place themselves again under such inevitable tyranny for the sake of avoiding imaginary dangers from the plebeians. Rinaldo, finding his advice unfavorably received, vexed at his own misfortune and that of his party, imputed the whole to heaven itself, which had resolved upon it, rather than to human ignorance and blunders. In this juncture of affairs, no remedial measure being attempted, a letter was found written by Agnolo Acciajuoli to Cosmo, acquainting him with the disposition of the city in his favor, and advising him, if possible, to excite a war, and gain the friendship of Neri di Gino; for he imagined the city to be in want of money, and as she would not find anyone to serve her, the remembrance of him would be revived in the minds of the citizens, and they would desire his return; and that if Neri were detached from Rinaldo, the party of the latter would be so weakened, as to be unable to defend themselves. This letter coming to the hands of the magistrates, Agnolo was taken, put to the torture, and sent into exile. This example, however, did not at all deter Cosmo's party.

It was now almost a year since Cosmo had been banished, and the end of August, 1434, being come, Niccolo di Cocco was drawn Gonfalonier for the two succeeding months, and with him eight signors, all partisans of Cosmo. This struck terror into Rinaldo and his party; and as it is usual for three days to elapse before the new Signory assume the magistracy and the old resign their authority, Rinaldo again called together the heads of his party. He endeavored to show them their certain and immediate danger, and that their only remedy was to take arms, and cause Donato Velluti, who was yet Gonfalonier, to assemble the people in the piazza and create a Balia. He would then deprive the new Signory of the magistracy, appoint another, burn the present balloting purses, and by means of a new Squittini, provide themselves with friends. Many thought this course safe and requisite; others, that it was too violent, and likely to be attended with great evil. Among those who disliked it was Palla Strozzi, a peaceable, gentle, and humane person, better adapted for literary pursuits than for restraining a party, or opposing civil strife. He said that bold and crafty resolutions seem promising at their commencement, but are afterward found difficult to execute, and generally pernicious at their conclusion; that he thought the fear of external wars (the duke's forces being upon the confines of Romagna), would occupy the minds of the Signory more than internal dissensions; but, still, if any attempt should be made, and it could not take place unnoticed, they would have sufficient time to take arms, and adopt whatever measures might be found necessary for the common good, which being done upon necessity, would occasion less excitement among the people and less danger to themselves. It was therefore concluded, that the new Signory should come in; that their proceedings should be watched, and if they were found attempting anything against the party, each should take arms, and meet in the piazza of San Pulinari, situated near the palace, and whence they might proceed wherever it was found necessary. Having come to this conclusion, Rinaldo's friends separated.

The new Signory entered upon their office, and the Gonfalonier, in order to acquire reputation, and deter those who might intend to oppose him, sent Donato Velluti, his predecessor, to prison, upon the charge of having applied the public money to his own use. He then endeavored to sound his colleagues with respect to Cosmo: seeing them desirous of his return, he communicated with the leaders of the Medici party, and, by their advice, summoned the hostile chiefs, Rinaldo degli Albizzi, Ridolfo Peruzzi, and Niccolo Barbadoro. After this citation, Rinaldo thought further delay would be dangerous: he therefore left his house with a great number of armed men, and was soon joined by Ridolfo Peruzzi and Niccolo Barbadoro. The force accompanying them was composed of several citizens and a great number of disbanded soldiers then in Florence: and all assembled according to appointment in the piazza of San Pulinari. Palla Strozzi and Giovanni Guicciardini, though each had assembled a large number of men, kept in their houses; and therefore Rinaldo sent a messenger to request their attendance and to reprove their delay. Giovanni replied, that he should lend sufficient aid against their enemies, if by remaining at home he could prevent his brother Piero from going to the defense of the palace. After many messages Palla came to San Pulinari on horseback, accompanied by two of his people on foot, and unarmed. Rinaldo, on meeting him, sharply reproved him for his negligence, declaring that his refusal to come with the others arose either from defect of principle or want of courage; both of which charges should be avoided by all who wished to preserve such a character as he had hitherto possessed; and that if he thought this abominable conduct to his party would induce their enemies when victorious to spare him from death or exile, he deceived himself; but for himself (Rinaldo) whatever might happen, he had the consolation of knowing, that previously to the crisis he had never neglected his duty in council, and that when it occurred he had used every possible exertion to repel it with arms; but that Palla and the others would experience aggravated remorse when they considered they had upon three occasions betrayed their country; first when they saved Cosmo; next when they disregarded his advice; and now the third time by not coming armed in her defense according to their engagement. To these reproaches Palla made no reply audible to those around, but, muttering something as he left them, returned to his house.

The Signory, knowing Rinaldo and his party had taken arms, finding themselves abandoned, caused the palace to be shut up, and having no one to consult they knew not what course to adopt. However, Rinaldo, by delaying his coming to the piazza, having waited in expectation of forces which did not join him, lost the opportunity of victory, gave them courage to provide for their defense, and allowed many others to join them, who advised that means should be used to induce their adversaries to lay down their arms. Thereupon, some of the least suspected, went on the part of the Signory to Rinaldo, and said, they did not know what occasion they had given his friends for thus assembling in arms; that they never had any intention of offending him, and if they had spoken of Cosmo, they had no design of recalling him; so if their fears were thus occasioned they might at once be dispelled, for that if they came to the palace they would be graciously received, and all their complaints attended to. These words produced no change in Rinaldo's purpose; he bade them provide for their safety by resigning their offices, and said that then the government of the city would be reorganized, for the mutual benefit of all.

It rarely happens, where authorities are equal and opinions contrary, that any good resolution is adopted. Ridolfo Peruzzi, moved by the discourse of the citizens, said, that all he desired was to prevent the return of Cosmo, and this being granted to them seemed a sufficient victory; nor would he, to obtain a greater, fill the city with blood; he would therefore obey the Signory; and accordingly went with his people to the palace, where he was received with a hearty welcome. Thus Rinaldo's delay at San Pulinari, Palla's want of courage, and Ridolfo's desertion, deprived their party of all chance of success; while the ardor of the citizens abated, and the pope's authority did not contribute to its revival.

Pope Eugenius was at this time at Florence, having been driven from Rome by the people. These disturbances coming to his knowledge, he thought it a duty suitable to his pastoral office to appease them, and sent the patriarch Giovanni Vitelleschi, Rinaldo's most intimate friend, to entreat the latter to come to an interview with him, as he trusted he had sufficient influence with the Signory to insure his safety and satisfaction, without injury or bloodshed to the citizens. By his friend's persuasion, Rinaldo proceeded with all his followers to Santa Maria Nuova, where the pope resided. Eugenius gave him to understand, that the Signory had empowered him to settle the differences between them, and that all would be arranged to his satisfaction, if he laid down his arms. Rinaldo, having witnessed Palla's want of zeal, and the fickleness of Ridolfo Peruzzi, and no better course being open to him, placed himself in the pope's hands, thinking that at all events the authority of his holiness would insure his safety. Eugenius then sent word to Niccolo Barbadoro, and the rest who remained without, that they were to lay down their arms, for Rinaldo was remaining with the pontiff, to arrange terms of agreement with the signors; upon which they immediately dispersed, and laid aside their weapons.

The Signory, seeing their adversaries disarmed, continued to negotiate an arrangement by means of the pope; but at the same time sent secretly to the mountains of Pistoia for infantry, which, with what other forces they could collect, were brought into Florence by night. Having taken possession of all the strong positions in the city, they assembled the people in the piazza and created a new balia, which, without delay, restored Cosmo and those who had been exiled with him to their country; and banished, of the opposite party, Rinaldo degli Albizzi, Ridolfo Peruzzi, Niccolo Barbadoro, and Palla Strozzi, with so many other citizens, that there were few places in Italy which did not contain some, and many others beyond her limits were full of them. By this and similar occurrences, Florence was deprived of men of worth, and of much wealth and industry.

The pope, seeing such misfortunes befall those who by his entreaties were induced to lay down their arms, was greatly dissatisfied, and condoled with Rinaldo on the injuries he had received through his confidence in him, but advised him to be patient, and hope for some favorable turn of fortune. Rinaldo replied, "The want of confidence in those who ought to have trusted me, and the great trust I have reposed in you, have ruined both me and my party. But I blame myself principally for having thought that you, who were expelled from your own country, could preserve me in mine. I have had sufficient experience of the freaks of fortune; and as I have never trusted greatly to prosperity, I shall suffer less inconvenience from adversity; and I know that when she pleases she can become more favorable. But if she should never change, I shall not be very desirous of living in a city in which individuals are more powerful than the laws; for that country alone is desirable in which property and friends may be safely enjoyed, not one where they may easily be taken from us, and where friends, from fear of losing their property, are compelled to abandon each other in their greatest need. Besides, it has always been less painful to good men to hear of the misfortunes of their country than to witness them; and an honorable exile is always held in greater esteem than slavery at home." He then left the pope, and, full of indignation, blaming himself, his own measures, and the coldness of his friends, went into exile.

Cosmo, on the other hand, being informed of his recall, returned to Florence; and it has seldom occurred that any citizen, coming home triumphant from victory, was received by so vast a concourse of people, or such unqualified demonstrations of regard as he was upon his return from banishment; for by universal consent he was hailed as the benefactor of the people, and the FATHER OF HIS COUNTRY.

BOOK V

CHAPTER I

The vicissitudes of empires--The state of Italy--The military factions of Sforza and Braccio--The Bracceschi and the Sforzeschi attack the pope, who is expelled by the Romans--War between the pope and the duke of Milan--The Florentines and the Venetians assist the pope--Peace between the pope and the duke of Milan--Tyranny practiced by the party favorable to the Medici.

It may be observed, that provinces amid the vicissitudes to which they are subject, pass from order into confusion, and afterward recur to a state of order again; for the nature of mundane affairs not allowing them to continue in an even course, when they have arrived at their greatest perfection, they soon begin to decline. In the same manner, having been reduced by disorder, and sunk to their utmost state of depression, unable to descend lower, they, of necessity, reascend; and thus from good they gradually decline to evil, and from evil again return to good. The reason is, that valor produces peace; peace, repose; repose, disorder; disorder, ruin; so from disorder order springs; from order virtue, and from this, glory and good fortune. Hence, wise men have observed, that the age of literary excellence is subsequent to that of distinction in arms; and that in cities and provinces, great warriors are produced before philosophers. Arms having secured victory, and victory peace, the buoyant vigor of the martial mind cannot be enfeebled by a more excusable indulgence than that of letters; nor can indolence, with any greater or more dangerous deceit, enter a well regulated community. Cato was aware of this when the philosophers, Diogenes and Carneades, were sent ambassadors to the senate by the Athenians; for perceiving with what earnest admiration the Roman youth began to follow them, and knowing the evils that might result to his country from this specious idleness, he enacted that no philosopher should be allowed to enter Rome. Provinces by this means sink to ruin, from which, men's sufferings having made them wiser, they again recur to order, if they be not overwhelmed by some extraordinary force. These causes made Italy, first under the ancient Tuscans, and afterward under the Romans, by turns happy and unhappy; and although nothing has subsequently arisen from the ruins of Rome at all corresponding to her ancient greatness (which under a well-organized monarchy might have been gloriously effected), still there was so much bravery and intelligence in some of the new cities and governments that afterward sprang up, that although none ever acquired dominion over the rest, they were, nevertheless, so balanced and regulated among themselves, as to enable them to live in freedom, and defend their country from the barbarians.

Among these governments, the Florentines, although they possessed a smaller extent of territory, were not inferior to any in power and authority; for being situated in the middle of Italy, wealthy, and prepared for action, they either defended themselves against such as thought proper to assail them, or decided victory in favor of those to whom they became allies. From the valor, therefore, of these new governments, if no seasons occurred of long-continued peace, neither were any exposed to the calamities of war; for that cannot be called peace in which states frequently assail each other with arms, nor can those be considered wars in which no men are slain, cities plundered, or sovereignties overthrown; for the practice of arms fell into such a state of decay, that wars were commenced without fear, continued without danger, and concluded without loss. Thus the military energy which is in other countries exhausted by a long peace, was wasted in Italy by the contemptible manner in which hostilities were carried on, as will be clearly seen in the events to be described from 1434 to 1494, from which it will appear how the barbarians were again admitted into Italy, and she again sunk under subjection to them. Although the transactions of our princes at home and abroad will not be viewed with admiration of their virtue and greatness like those of the ancients, perhaps they may on other accounts be regarded with no less interest, seeing what masses of high spirited people were kept in restraint by such weak and disorderly forces. And if, in detailing the events which took place in this wasted world, we shall not have to record the bravery of the soldier, the prudence of the general, or the patriotism of the citizen, it will be seen with what artifice, deceit, and cunning, princes, warriors, and leaders of republics conducted themselves, to support a reputation they never deserved. This, perhaps, will not be less useful than a knowledge of ancient history; for, if the latter excites the liberal mind to imitation, the former will show what ought to be avoided and decried.

Italy was reduced to such a condition by her rulers, that when, by consent of her princes, peace was restored, it was soon disturbed by those who retained their armies, so that glory was not gained by war nor repose by peace. Thus when the league and the duke of Milan agreed to lay aside their arms in 1433, the soldiers, resolved upon war, directed their efforts against the church. There were at this time two factions or armed parties in Italy, the Sforzesca and the Braccesca. The leader of the former was the Count Francesco, the son of Sforza, and of the latter, Niccolo Piccinino and Niccolo Fortebraccio. Under the banner of one or other of these parties almost all the forces of Italy were assembled. Of the two, the Sforzesca was in greatest repute, as well from the bravery of the count himself, as from the promise which the duke of Milan had made him of his natural daughter, Madonna Bianca, the prospect of which alliance greatly strengthened his influence. After the peace of Lombardy, these forces, from various causes attacked Pope Eugenius. Niccolo Fortebraccio was instigated by the ancient enmity which Braccio had always entertained against the church; the count was induced by ambition: so that Niccolo assailed Rome, and the count took possession of La Marca.

The Romans, in order to avoid the war, drove Pope Eugenius from their city: and he, having with difficulty escaped, came to Florence, where seeing the imminent danger of his situation, being abandoned by the princes (for they were unwilling again to take up arms in his cause, after having been so anxious to lay them aside), he came to terms with the count, and ceded to him the sovereignty of La Marca, although, to the injury of having occupied it, he had added insult; for in signing the place, from which he addressed letters to his agents, he said in Latin, according to the Latin custom, *Ex Girfalco nostro Firmiano, invito Petro et Paulo*. Neither was he satisfied with this concession, but insisted upon being appointed Gonfalonier of the church, which was also granted; so much more was Eugenius alarmed at the prospect of a dangerous war than of an ignominious peace. The count, having been thus been reconciled to the pontiff, attacked Niccolo Fortebraccio, and during many months various encounters took place between them, from all which greater injury resulted to the pope and his subjects, than to either of the belligerents. At length, by the intervention of the duke of Milan, an arrangement, by way of a truce, was made, by which both became princes in the territories of the church.

The war thus extinguished at Rome was rekindled in Romagna by Batista da Canneto, who at Bologna slew some of the family of the Grifoni, and expelled from the city the governor who resided there for the pope, along with others who were opposed to him. To enable himself to retain the government, he applied for assistance to Filippo; and the pope, to avenge himself for the injury, sought the aid of the Venetians and Florentines. Both parties obtained assistance, so that very soon two large armies were on foot in Romagna. Niccolo Piccinino commanded for the duke, Gattamelata and Niccolo da Tolentino for the Venetians and Florentines. They met near Imola, where a battle ensued, in which the Florentines and Venetians were routed, and Niccolo da Tolentino was sent prisoner to Milan where, either through grief for his loss or by some unfair means, he died in a few days.

The duke, on this victory, either being exhausted by the late wars, or thinking the League after their defeat would not be in haste to resume hostilities, did not pursue his good fortune, and thus gave the pope and his colleagues time to recover themselves. They therefore appointed the Count Francesco for their leader, and undertook to drive Niccolo Fortebraccio from the territories of the church, and thus terminate the war which had been commenced in favor of the pontiff. The Romans, finding the pope supported by so large an army, sought a reconciliation with him, and being successful, admitted his commissary into the city. Among the places possessed by Niccolo Fortebraccio, were Tivoli, Montefiascone, Citta di Castello, and Ascesi, to the last of which, not being able to keep the field, he fled, and the count besieged him there. Niccolo's brave defense making it probable that the war would be of considerable duration, the duke deemed to necessary to prevent the League from obtaining the victory, and said that if this were not effected he would very soon have to look at the defense of his own territories. Resolving to divert the count from the siege, he commanded Niccolo Piccinino to pass into Tuscany by way of Romagna; and the League, thinking it more important to defend Tuscany than to occupy Ascesi, ordered the count to prevent the passage of Niccolo, who was already, with his army, at Furli. The count accordingly moved with his forces, and came to Cesena, having left the war of La Marca and the care of his own territories to his brother Lione; and while Niccolo Piccinino was endeavoring to pass by, and the count to prevent him, Fortebraccio attacked Lione with great bravery, made him prisoner, routed his forces, and pursuing the advantage of his victory, at once possessed himself of many places in La Marca. This circumstance greatly perplexed the count, who thought he had lost all his territories; so, leaving part of his force to check Piccinino, with the remainder he pursued Fortebraccio, whom he attacked and conquered. Fortebraccio was taken prisoner in the battle, and soon after died of his wounds. This victory restored to the pontiff all the places that had been taken from him by Fortebraccio, and compelled the duke of Milan to sue for peace, which was concluded by the intercession of Niccolo da Esta, marquis of Ferrara; the duke restoring to the church the places he had taken from her, and his forces retiring into Lombardy. Batista da Canneto, as in the case with all who retain authority only by the consent and forces of another, when the duke's people had quitted Romagna, unable with his own power to keep possession of Bologna, fled, and Antonio Bentivogli, the head of the opposite party, returned to his country.

All this took place during the exile of Cosmo, after whose return, those who had restored him, and a great number of persons injured by the opposite party, resolved at all events to make themselves sure of the government; and the Signory for the months of November and December, not content with what their predecessors had done in favor of their party extended the term and changed the residences of several who were banished, and increased the number of exiles. In addition to these evils, it was observed that citizens were more annoyed on account of their wealth, their family connections or private animosities, than for the sake of the party to which they adhered, so that if these prescriptions had been accompanied with bloodshed, they would have resembled those of Octavius and Sylla, though in reality they were not without some stains; for Antonio di Bernardo Guadagni was beheaded, and four other citizens, among whom were Zanobi dei Belfratelli and Cosmo Barbadori, passing the confines to which they were limited, proceeded to Venice, where the Venetians, valuing the friendship of Cosmo de' Medici more than their own honor, sent them prisoners to him, and they were basely put to death. This circumstance greatly increased the influence of that party, and struck their enemies with terror, finding that such a powerful republic would so humble itself to the Florentines. This, however, was supposed to have been done, not so much out of kindness to Cosmo, as to excite dissensions in Florence, and by means of bloodshed make greater certainty of division among the citizens, for the Venetians knew there was no other obstacle to their ambition so great as the union of her people.

The city being cleared of the enemies, or suspected enemies of the state, those in possession of the government now began to strengthen their party by conferring benefits upon such as were in a condition to serve them, and the family of the Alberti, with all who had been banished by the former government, were recalled. All the nobility, with few exceptions, were reduced to the ranks of the people, and the possessions of the exiles were divided among themselves, upon each paying a small acknowledgment. They then fortified themselves with new laws and provisos, made new Squittini, withdrawing the names of their adversaries from the purses, and filling them with those of their friends. Taking advice from the ruin of their enemies, they considered that to allow the great offices to be filled by mere chance of drawing, did not afford the government sufficient security, they therefore resolved that the magistrates possessing the power of life and death should always be chosen from among the leaders of their own party, and therefore that the Accoppiatori, or persons selected for the imborsation of the new Squittini, with the Signory who had to retire from office, should make the new appointments. They gave to eight of the guard authority to proceed capitally, and provided that the exiles, when their term of banishment was complete, should not be allowed to return, unless from the Signory and Colleagues, which were thirty-seven in number, the consent of thirty-four was obtained. It was made unlawful to write to or to receive letters from them; every word, sign, or action that gave offense to the ruling party was punished with the utmost rigor; and if there was still in Florence any suspected person whom these regulations did not reach, he was oppressed with taxes imposed for the occasion. Thus in a short time, having expelled or impoverished the whole of the adverse party, they established themselves firmly in the government. Not to be destitute of external assistance, and to deprive others of it, who might use it against themselves, they entered into a league, offensive and defensive, with the pope, the Venetians, and the duke of Milan.

CHAPTER II

Death of Giovanni II.--Rene of Anjou and Alfonso of Aragon aspire to the kingdom--Alfonso is routed and taken by the Genoese--Alfonso being a prisoner of the duke of Milan, obtains his friendship--The Genoese disgusted with the duke of Milan--Divisions among the Genoese--The Genoese, by means of Francesco Spinola, expel the duke's governor--League against the duke of Milan--Rinaldo degli Albizzi advises the duke to make war against the Florentines--His discourse to the duke--The duke adopts measures injurious to the Florentines--Niccolo Piccinino appointed to command the duke's forces--Preparations of the Florentines--Piccinino routed before Barga.

The affairs of Florence being in this condition, Giovanna, queen of Naples, died, and by her will appointed Rene of Anjou to be her successor. Alfonso, king of Aragon, was at this time in Sicily, and having obtained the concurrence of many barons, prepared to take possession of the kingdom. The Neapolitans, with whom a greater number of barons were also associated, favored Rene. The pope was unwilling that either of them should obtain it; but desired the affairs of Naples to be administered by a governor of his own appointing.

In the meantime Alfonso entered the kingdom, and was received by the duke of Sessa; he brought with him some princes, whom he had engaged in his service, with the design (already possessing Capua, which the prince of Taranto held in his name) of subduing the Neapolitans, and sent his fleet to attack Gaeta, which had declared itself in their favor. They therefore demanded assistance of the duke of Milan, who persuaded the Genoese to undertake their defense; and they, to satisfy the duke their sovereign, and protect the merchandise they possessed, both at Naples and Gaeta, armed a powerful fleet. Alfonso hearing of this, augmented his own naval force, went in person to meet the Genoese, and coming up with them near the island of Ponzio, an engagement ensued, in which the Aragonese were defeated, and Alfonso, with many of the princes of his suite, made prisoners, and sent by the Genoese to the Filippo.

This victory terrified the princes of Italy, who, being jealous of the duke's power, thought it would give him a great opportunity of being sovereign of the whole country. But so contrary are the views of men, that he took a directly opposite course. Alfonso was a man of great sagacity, and as soon as an opportunity presented itself of communicating with Filippo, he proved to him how completely he contravened his own interests, by favoring Rene and opposing himself; for it would be the business of the former, on becoming king of Naples, to introduce the French into Milan; that in an emergency he might have assistance at hand, without the necessity of having to solicit a passage for his friends. But he could not possibly secure this advantage without effecting the ruin of the duke, and making his dominions a French province; and that the contrary of all this would result from himself becoming lord of Naples; for having only the French to fear, he would be compelled to love and caress, nay even to obey those who had it in their power to open a passage for his enemies. That thus the title of king of king of Naples would be with himself (Alfonso), but the power and authority with Filippo; so that it was much more the duke's business than his own to consider the danger of one course and the advantage of the other; unless he rather wished to gratify his private prejudices than to give security to his dominions. In the one case he would be a free prince, in the other, placed between two powerful sovereigns, he would either be robbed of his territories or live in constant fear, and have to obey them like a slave. These arguments so greatly influenced the duke, that, changing his design, he set Alfonso at liberty, sent him honorably to Genoa and then to Naples. From thence the king went to Gaeta, which as soon as his liberation had become known, was taken possession of by some nobles of his party.

The Genoese, seeing that the duke, without the least regard for them, had liberated the king, and gained credit to himself through the dangers and expense which they had incurred; that he enjoyed all the honor of the liberation, and they were themselves exposed to the odium of the capture, and the injuries consequent upon the king's defeat, were greatly exasperated. In the city of Genoa, while in the enjoyment of her liberty, a magistrate is created with the consent of the people, whom they call the Doge; not that he is absolutely a prince, or that he alone has the power of determining matters of government; but that, as the head of the state, he proposes those questions or subjects which have to be considered and determined by the magistrates and the councils. In that city are many noble families so powerful, that they are with great difficulty induced to submit to the authority of the law. Of these, the most powerful are the Fregosa and the Adorna, from whom arise the dissensions of the city, and the impotence of her civil regulations; for the possession of this high office being contested by means inadmissible in well-regulated communities, and most commonly with arms in their hands, it always occurs that one party is oppressed and the other triumphant; and sometimes those who fail in the pursuit have recourse to the arms of strangers, and the country they are not allowed to rule they subject to foreign authority. Hence it happens, that those who govern in Lombardy most commonly command in Genoa, as occurred at the time Alfonso of Aragon was made prisoner. Among the leading Genoese who had been instrumental in subjecting the republic to Filippo, was Francesco Spinola, who, soon after he had reduced his country to bondage, as always happens in such cases, became suspected by the duke. Indignant at this, he withdrew to a sort of voluntary exile at Gaeta, and being there when the naval expedition was in preparation, and having conducted himself with great bravery in the action, he thought he had again merited so much of the duke's confidence as would obtain for him permission to remain undisturbed at Genoa. But the duke still retained his suspicions; for he could not believe that a vacillating defender of his own country's liberty would be faithful to himself; and Francesco Spinola resolved again to try his fortune, and if possible restore freedom to his country, and honorable safety for himself; for he was there was no probability of regaining the forfeited affection of his fellow-citizens, but by resolving at his own peril to remedy the misfortunes which he had been so instrumental in producing. Finding the indignation against the duke universal, on account of the liberation of the king, he thought the moment propitious for the execution of his design. He communicated his ideas to some whom he knew to be similarly inclined, and his arguments ensured their co-operation.

The great festival of St. John the Baptist being come, when Arismeno, the new governor sent by the duke, was to enter Genoa, and he being already arrived, accompanied by Opicino, the former governor, and many Genoese citizens, Francesco Spinola thought further delay improper; and, issuing from his house with those acquainted with his design, all armed, they raised the cry of liberty. It was wonderful to see how eagerly the citizens and people assembled at the word; so that those who for any reason might be favorable to Filippo, not only had no time to arm, but scarcely to consider the means of escape. Arismeno, with some Genoese, fled to the fortress which was held for the duke, Opicino, thinking that if he could reach the palace, where two thousand men were in arms, and at his command, he might be able either to effect his own safety, or induce his friends to defend themselves, took that direction; but before he arrived at the piazza he was slain, his body divided into many pieces and scattered about the city. The Genoese having placed the government in the hands of free magistrates, in a few days recovered the castle, and the other strongholds possessed by the duke, and delivered themselves entirely from his yoke.

These transactions, though at first they had alarmed the princes of Italy with the apprehension that the duke would become too powerful, now gave them hope, seeing the turn they had taken, of being able to restrain him; and, notwithstanding the recent league, the Florentines and Venetians entered into alliance with the Genoese. Rinaldo degli Albizzi and the other leading Florentine exiles, observing the altered aspect of affairs, conceived hopes of being able to induce the duke to make war against Florence, and having arrived at Milan, Rinaldo addressed him in the following manner: "If we, who were once your enemies, come now confidently to supplicate your assistance to enable us to return to our country, neither you, nor anyone, who considers the course and vicissitudes of human affairs, can be at all surprised; for of our past conduct toward yourself and our present intentions toward our country, we can adduce palpable and abundant reasons. No good man will ever reproach another who endeavors to defend his country, whatever be his mode of doing so; neither have we had any design of injuring you, but only to preserve our country from detriment; and we appeal to yourself, whether, during the greatest victories of our league, when you were really desirous of peace, we were not even more anxious for it than yourself; so that we do not think we have done aught to make us despair altogether of favor from you. Nor can our country itself complain that we now exhort you to use those arms against her, from which we have so pertinaciously defended her; for that state alone merits the love of all her citizens, which cares with equal affection for all; not one that favors a few, and casts from her the great mass of her children. Nor are the arms that men use against their country to be universally condemned; for communities, although composed of many, resemble individual bodies; and as in these, many infirmities arise which cannot be cured without the application of fire or of steel, so in the former, there often occur such numerous and great evils, that a good and merciful citizen, when there is a necessity for the sword, would be much more to blame in leaving her uncured, than by using this remedy for her preservation. What greater disease can afflict a republic than slavery? and what remedy is more desirable for adoption than the one by which alone it can be effectually removed? No wars are just but those that are necessary; and force is merciful when it presents the only hope of relief. I know not what necessity can be greater than ours, or what compassion can exceed that which rescues our country from slavery. Our cause is therefore just, and our purpose merciful, as both yourself and we may be easily convinced. The amplest justice is on your side; for the Florentines have not hesitated, after a peace concluded with so much solemnity, to enter into league with those who have rebelled against you; so that if our cause is insufficient to excite you against them, let your own just indignation do so; and the more so, seeing the facility of the undertaking. You need be under no apprehension from the memory of the past, in which you may have observed the power of that people and their pertinency in self-defense; though these might reasonably excite fear, if they were still animated by the valor of former times. But now, all is entirely the reverse; for what power can be expected in a city that has recently expelled the greatest part of her wealth and industry? What indomitable resolution need be apprehended from the people whom so many and such recent enmities have disunited? The disunion which still prevails will prevent wealthy citizens advancing money as they used to do on former occasions; for though men willingly contribute according to their means, when they see their own credit, glory, and private advantage dependent upon it, or when there is a hope of regaining in peace what has been spent in war, but not when equally oppressed under all circumstances, when in war they suffer the injuries of the enemy, and in peace, the insolence of those who govern them. Besides this, the people feel more deeply the avarice of their rulers, than the rapacity of the enemy; for there is hope of being ultimately relieved from the latter evil, but none from the former. Thus, in the last war, you had to contend with the whole city; but now with only a small portion. You attempted to take the government from many good citizens; but now you oppose only a few bad ones. You then endeavored to deprive a city of her liberty, now you come to restore it. As it is unreasonable to suppose that under such disparity of circumstances, the result should be the same, you have now every reason to anticipate an easy victory; and how much it will strengthen your own government, you may easily judge; having Tuscany friendly, and bound by so powerful an obligation, in your enterprises, she will be even of more service to you than Milan. And, although, on former occasions, such an acquisition might be looked upon as ambitious and unwarrantable, it will now be considered merciful and just. Then do not let this opportunity escape, and be assured, that although your attempts against the city have been attended with difficulty, expense, and disgrace, this will with facility procure you incalculable advantage and an honorable renown."

Many words were not requisite to induce the duke to hostilities against the Florentines, for he was incited to it by hereditary hatred and blind ambition, and still more, by the fresh injuries which the league with the Genoese involved; yet his past expenses, the dangerous measures necessary, the remembrance of his recent losses, and the vain hopes of the exiles, alarmed him. As soon as he had learned the revolt of Genoa, he ordered Niccolo Piccinino to proceed thither with all his cavalry and whatever infantry he could raise, for the purpose of recovering her, before the citizens had time to become settled and establish a government; for he trusted greatly in the fortress within the city, which was held for him. And although Niccolo drove the Genoese from the mountains, took from them the valley of Pozeveri, where they had entrenched themselves, and obliged them to seek refuge within the walls of the city, he still found such an insurmountable obstacle in the resolute defense of the citizens, that he was compelled to withdraw. On this, at the suggestion of the Florentine exiles, he commanded Niccolo to attack them on the eastern side, upon the confines of Pisa in the Genoese territory, and to push the war with his utmost vigor, thinking this plan would manifest and develop the course best to be adopted. Niccolo therefore besieged and took Serezana, and having committed great ravages, by way of further alarming the Florentines he proceeded to Lucca, spreading a report that it was his intention to go to Naples to render assistance to the king of

Aragon. Upon these new events Pope Eugenius left Florence and proceeded to Bologna, where he endeavored to effect an amicable arrangement between the league and the duke, intimating to the latter, that if he would not consent to some treaty, the pontiff must send Francesco Sforza to assist the league, for the latter was now his confederate, and served in his pay. Although the pope greatly exerted himself in this affair, his endeavors were unavailing; for the duke would not listen to any proposal that did not leave him the possession of Genoa, and the league had resolved that she should remain free; and, therefore, each party, having no other resource, prepared to continue the war.

In the meantime Niccolo Piccinino arrived at Lucca, and the Florentines, being doubtful what course to adopt, ordered Neri di Gino to lead their forces into the Pisan territory, induced the pontiff to allow Count Francesco to join him, and with their forces they halted at San Gonda. Piccinino then demanded admission into the kingdom of Naples, and this being refused, he threatened to force a passage. The armies were equal, both in regard of numbers and the capacity of their leaders, and unwilling to tempt fortune during the bad weather, it being the month of December, they remained several days without attacking each other. The first movement was made by Niccolo Piccinino, who being informed that if he attacked Vico Pisano by night, he could easily take possession of the place, made the attempt, and having failed, ravaged the surrounding country, and then burned and plundered the town of San Giovanni alla Vena. This enterprise, though of little consequence, excited him to make further attempts, the more so from being assured that the count and Neri were yet in their quarters, and he attacked Santa Maria in Castello and Filetto, both which places he took. Still the Florentine forces would not stir; not that the count entertained any fear, but because, out of regard to the pope, who still labored to effect an accommodation, the government of Florence had deferred giving their final consent to the war. This course, which the Florentines adopted from prudence, was considered by the enemy to be only the result of timidity, and with increased boldness they led their forces up to Barga, which they resolved to besiege. This new attack made the Florentines set aside all other considerations, and resolve not only to relieve Barga, but to invade the Lucchese territory. Accordingly the count proceeded in pursuit of Niccolo, and coming up with him before Barga, an engagement took place, in which Piccinino was overcome, and compelled to raise the siege.

The Venetians considering the duke to have broken the peace, send Giovan Francesco da Gonzaga, their captain, to Ghiaradadda, who, by severely wasting the duke's territories, induced him to recall Niccolo Piccinino from Tuscany. This circumstance, together with the victory obtained over Niccolo, emboldened the Florentines to attempt the recovery of Lucca, since the duke, whom alone they feared, was engaged with the Venetians, and the Lucchese having received the enemy into their city, and allowed him to attack them, would have no ground of complaint.

CHAPTER III

The Florentines go to war with Lucca--Discourse of a citizen of Lucca to animate the plebeians against the Florentines--The Lucchese resolve to defend themselves--They are assisted by the duke of Milan--Treaty between the Florentines and the Venetians--Francesco Sforza, captain of the league, refuses to cross the Po in the service of the Venetians and returns to Tuscany--The bad faith of the Venetians toward the Florentines--Cosmo de' Medici at Venice--Peace between the Florentines and the Lucchese--The Florentines effect a reconciliation between the pope and the Count di Poppi--The pope consecrates the church of Santa Reparata--Council of Florence.

The count commenced operations against Lucca in April, 1437, and the Florentines, desirous of recovering what they had themselves lost before they attacked others, retook Santa Maria in Castello, and all the places which Piccinino had occupied. Then, entering the Lucchese territory, they besieged Camaiore, the inhabitants of which, although faithful to their rulers, being influenced more by immediate danger than by attachment to their distant friends, surrendered. In the same manner, they obtained Massa and Serezana. Toward the end of May they proceeded in the direction of Lucca, burning the towns, destroying the growing crops, grain, trees, and vines, driving away the cattle, and leaving nothing undone to injure the enemy. The Lucchese, finding themselves abandoned by the duke, and hopeless of defending the open country, forsook it; entrenched and fortified the city, which they doubted not, being well garrisoned, they would be able to defend for a time, and that, in the interim, some event would occur for their relief, as had been the case during the former wars which the Florentines had carried on against them. Their only apprehension arose from the fickle minds of the plebeians, who, becoming weary of the siege, would have more consideration of their own danger than of other's liberty, and would thus compel them to submit to some disgraceful and ruinous capitulation. In order to animate them to defense, they were assembled in the public piazza, and some of the eldest and most esteemed of the citizens addressed them in the following terms: "You are doubtless aware that what is done from necessity involves neither censure nor applause; therefore, if you should accuse us of having caused the present war, by receiving the ducal forces into the city, and allowing them to commit hostilities against the Florentines, you are greatly mistaken. You are well acquainted with the ancient enmity of the Florentines against you, which is not occasioned by any injuries you have done them, or by fear on their part, but by our weakness and their own ambition; for the one gives them hope of being able to oppress us, and the other incites them to attempt it. It is then vain to imagine that any merit of yours can extinguish that desire in them, or that any offense you can commit, can provoke them to greater animosity. They endeavor to deprive you of your liberty; you must resolve to defend it; and whatever they may undertake against us for that purpose, although we may lament, we need not wonder. We may well grieve, therefore, that they attack us, take possession of our towns, burn our houses, and waste our country. But who is so simple as to be surprised at it? for were it in our power, we should do just the same to them, or even worse. They declare war against us now, they say, for having received Niccolo; but if we had not received him, they would have done the same and assigned some other ground for it; and if the evil had been delayed, it would most probably have been greater. Therefore, you must not imagine it to be occasioned by his arrival, but rather by your own ill fortune and their ambition; for we could not have refused admission to the duke's forces, and, being come, we could not prevent their aggressions. You know, that without the aid of some powerful ally we are incapable of self-defense, and that none can render us this service more powerfully or faithfully than the duke. He restored our liberty; it is reasonable to expect he will defend it. He has always been the greatest foe of our inveterate enemies; if, therefore, to avoid incensing the Florentines we had excited his anger, we should have lost our best friend, and rendered our enemy more powerful and more disposed to oppress us; so that it is far preferable to have this war upon our hands, and enjoy the favor of the duke, than to be in peace without it. Besides, we are justified in expecting that he will rescue us from the dangers into which we are brought on his account, if we only do not abandon our own cause. You all know how fiercely the Florentines have frequently assailed us, and with what glory we have maintained our defense. We have often been deprived of every hope, except in God and the casualties which time might produce, and both have proved our friends. And as they have delivered us formerly, why should they not continue to do so. Then we were forsaken by the whole of Italy; now we have the duke in our favor; besides we have a right to suppose that the Venetians will not hastily attack us; for they will not willingly see the power of Florence increased. On a former occasion the Florentines were more at liberty; they had greater hope of assistance, and were more powerful in themselves, while we were in every respect weaker; for then a tyrant governed us, now we defend ourselves; then the glory of our defense was another's, now it is our own; then they were in harmony, now they are disunited, all Italy being filled with their banished citizens. But were we without the hope which these favorable circumstances present, our extreme necessity should make us firmly resolved on our defense. It is reasonable to fear every enemy, for all seek their own glory and your ruin; above all others, you have to dread the Florentines, for they would not be satisfied by submission and tribute, or the dominion of our city, but they would possess our entire substance and persons, that they might satiate their cruelty with our blood, and their avarice with our property, so that all ranks ought to dread them. Therefore do not be troubled at seeing our crops destroyed, our towns burned, our fortresses occupied; for if we preserve the city, the rest will be saved as a matter of course; if we lose her, all else would be of no advantage to us; for while retaining our liberty, the enemy can hold them only with the greatest difficulty, while losing it they would be preserved in vain. Arm, therefore; and when in the fight, remember that the reward of victory will be safety, not only to your country, but to your homes, your wives, and your children." The speaker's last words were received with the utmost enthusiasm by the people, who promised one and all to die rather than abandon their cause, or submit to any terms that could violate their liberty. They then made arrangements for the defense of the city.

In the meantime, the Florentine forces were not idle; and after innumerable mischiefs done to the country took Monte Carlo by capitulation. They then besieged Uzzano, in order that the Lucchese, being pressed on all sides, might despair of assistance, and be compelled to submission by famine. The fortress was very strong, and defended by a numerous garrison, so that its capture would be by no means an easy undertaking. The Lucchese, as might be expected, seeing the imminent peril of their situation, had recourse to the duke, and employed prayers and remonstrances to induce him to render them aid. They enlarged upon their own merits and the offenses of the Florentines; and showed how greatly it would attach the duke's friends to him to find they were defended, and how much disaffection it would spread among them, if they were left to be overwhelmed by the enemy; that if they lost their liberties and their lives, he would lose his honor and his friends, and forfeit the confidence of all who from affection might be induced to incur dangers in his behalf; and added tears to entreaties, so that if he were unmoved by gratitude to them, he might be induced to their defense by motives of compassion. The duke, influenced by his inveterate hostility against the Florentines, his new obligation to the Lucchese, and, above all, by his desire to prevent so great an acquisition from falling into the hands of his ancient enemies, determined either to send a strong force into Tuscany, or vigorously to assail the Venetians, so as to compel the Florentines to give up their enterprise and go to their relief.

It was soon known in Florence that the duke was preparing to send forces into Tuscany. This made the Florentines apprehensive for the success of their enterprise; and in order to retain the duke in Lombardy, they requested the Venetians to press him with their utmost strength. But they also were alarmed, the marquis of Mantua having abandoned them and gone over to the duke; and thus, finding themselves almost defenseless, they replied, "that instead of increasing their responsibilities, they should be unable to perform their part in the war, unless the Count Francesco were sent to them to take the command of the army, and with the special understanding that he should engage to cross the Po in person. They declined to fulfil their former engagements unless he were bound to do so; for they could not carry on the war without a leader, or repose confidence in any except the count; and he himself would be useless to them, unless he came under an obligation to carry on the war whenever they might think needful." The Florentines thought the war ought to be pushed vigorously in Lombardy; but they saw that if they lost the count their enterprise against Lucca was ruined; and they knew well that the demand of the Venetians arose less from any need they had of the count, than from their desire to frustrate this expedition. The count, on the other hand, was ready to pass into Lombardy whenever the league might require him, but would not alter the tenor of his engagement; for he was unwilling to sacrifice the hope of the alliance promised to him by the duke.

The Florentines were thus embarrassed by two contrary impulses, the wish to possess Lucca, and the dread of a war with Milan. As commonly happens, fear was the most powerful, and they consented, after the capture of Uzzano, that the count should go into Lombardy. There still remained another difficulty, which, depending on circumstances beyond the reach of their influence, created more doubts and uneasiness than the former; the count would not consent to pass the Po, and the Venetians refused to accept him on any other condition. Seeing no other method of arrangement, than that each should make liberal concessions, the Florentines induced the count to cross the river by a letter addressed to the Signory of Florence, intimating that this private promise did not invalidate any public engagement, and that he might still refrain from crossing; hence it resulted that the Venetians, having commenced the war, would be compelled to proceed, and that the evil apprehended by the Florentines would be averted. To the Venetians, on the other hand, they averred that this private letter was sufficiently binding, and therefore they ought to be content; for if they could save the count from breaking with his father-in-law, it was well to do so, and that it could be of no advantage either to themselves or the Venetians to publish it without some manifest necessity. It was thus determined that the count should pass into Lombardy; and having taken Uzzano, and raised bastions about Lucca to restrain in her inhabitants, placed the management of the siege in the hands of the commissaries, crossed the Apennines, and proceeded to Reggio, when the Venetians, alarmed at his progress, and in order to discover his intentions, insisted upon his immediately crossing the Po, and joining the other forces. The count refused compliance, and many mutual recriminations took place between him and Andrea Mauroceno, their messenger on this occasion, each charging the other with arrogance and treachery: after many protestations, the one of being under no obligation to perform that service, and the other of not being bound to any payment, they parted, the count to return to Tuscany, the other to Venice.

The Florentines had sent the count to encamp in the Pisan territory, and were in hopes of inducing him to renew the war against the Lucchese, but found him indisposed to do so, for the duke, having been informed that out of regard to him he had refused to cross the Po, thought that by this means he might also save the Lucchese, and begged the count to endeavor to effect an accommodation between the Florentines and the Lucchese, including himself in it, if he were able, declaring, at the same time, the promised marriage should be solemnized whenever he thought proper. The prospect of this connection had great influence with the count, for, as the duke had no sons, it gave him hope of becoming sovereign of Milan. For this reason he gradually abated his exertions in the war, declared he would not proceed unless the Venetians fulfilled their engagement as to the payment, and also retained him in the command; that the discharge of the debt would not alone be sufficient, for desiring to live peaceably in his own dominions, he needed some alliance other than that of the Florentines, and that he must regard his own interests, shrewdly hinting that if abandoned by the Venetians, he would come to terms with the duke.

These indirect and crafty methods of procedure were highly offensive to the Florentines, for they found their expedition against Lucca frustrated, and trembled for the safety of their own territories if ever the count and the duke should enter into a mutual alliance. To induce the Venetians to retain the count in the command, Cosmo de' Medici went to Venice, hoping his influence would prevail with them, and discussed the subject at great length before the senate, pointing out the condition of the Italian states, the disposition of their armies, and the great preponderance possessed by the duke. He concluded by saying, that if the count and the duke were to unite their forces, they (the Venetians) might return to the sea, and the Florentines would have to fight for their liberty. To this the Venetians replied, that they were acquainted with their own strength and that of the Italians, and thought themselves able at all events to provide for their own defense; that it was not their custom to pay soldiers for serving others; that as the Florentines had used the count's services, they must pay him themselves; with respect to the security of their own states, it was rather desirable to check the count's pride than to pay him, for the ambition of men is boundless, and if he were now paid without serving, he would soon make some other demand, still more unreasonable and dangerous. It therefore seemed necessary to curb his insolence, and not allow it to increase till it became incorrigible; and that if the Florentines, from fear or any other motive, wished to preserve his friendship, they must pay him themselves. Cosmo returned without having effected any part of his object.

The Florentines used the weightiest arguments they could adopt to prevent the count from quitting the service of the League, a course he was himself reluctant to follow, but his desire to conclude the marriage so embarrassed him, that any trivial accident would have been sufficient to determine his course, as indeed shortly happened. The count had left his territories in La Marca to the care of Il Furlano, one of his principal condottieri, who was so far influenced by the duke as to take command under him, and quit the count's service. This circumstance caused the latter to lay aside every idea but that of his own safety, and to come to agreement with the duke; among the terms of which compact was one that he should not be expected to interfere in the affairs of Romagna and Tuscany. The count then urged the Florentines to come to terms with the Lucchese, and so convinced them of the necessity of this, that seeing no better course to adopt, they complied in April, 1438, by which treaty the Lucchese retained their liberty, and the Florentines Monte Carlo and a few other fortresses. After this, being full of exasperation, they despatched letters to every part of Italy, overcharged with complaints, affecting to show that since God and men were averse to the Lucchese coming under their dominion, they had made peace with them. And it seldom happens that any suffer so much for the loss of their own lawful property as they did because they could not obtain the possessions of others.

Though the Florentines had now so many affairs in hand, they did not allow the proceedings of their neighbors to pass unnoticed, or neglect the decoration of their city. As before observed, Niccolo Fortebraccio was dead. He had married a daughter of the Count di Poppi, who, at the decease of his son-in-law, held the Borgo San Sepolcro, and other fortresses of that district, and while Niccolo lived, governed them in his name. Claiming them as his daughter's portion, he refused to give them up to the pope, who demanded them as property held of the church, and who, upon his refusal, sent the patriarch with forces to take possession of them. The count, finding himself unable to sustain the attack, offered them to the Florentines, who declined them; but the pope having returned to Florence, they interceded with him in the count's behalf. Difficulties arising, the patriarch attacked the Casentino, took Prato Vecchio, and Romena, and offered them also to the Florentines, who refused them likewise, unless the pope would consent they should restore them to the count, to which, after much hesitation, he acceded, on condition that the Florentines should prevail with the Count di Poppi to restore the Borgo to him. The pope was thus satisfied, and the Florentines having so far completed the building of their cathedral church of Santa Reparata, which had been commenced long ago, as to enable them to perform divine service in it, requested his holiness to consecrate it. To this the pontiff willingly agreed, and the Florentines, to exhibit the wealth of the city and the splendor of the edifice, and do greater honor to the pope, erected a platform from Santa Maria Novella, where he resided, to the cathedral he was about to consecrate, six feet in height and twelve feet wide, covered with rich drapery, for the accommodation of the pontiff and his court, upon which they proceeded to the building, accompanied by those civic magistrates, and other officers who were appointed to take part in the procession. The usual ceremonies of consecration having been completed, the pope, to show his affection for the city, conferred the honor of knighthood upon Giuliano Davanzati, their Gonfalonier of Justice, and a citizen of the highest reputation; and the Signory, not to appear less gracious than the pope, granted to the new created knight the government of Pisa for one year.

There were at that time certain differences between the Roman and the Greek churches, which prevented perfect conformity in divine service; and at the last council of Bale, the prelates of the Western church having spoken at great length upon the subject, it was resolved that efforts should be made to bring the emperor and the Greek prelates to the council at Bale, to endeavor to reconcile the Greek church with the Roman. Though this resolution was derogatory to the majesty of the Greek empire, and offensive to its clergy, yet being then oppressed by the Turks, and fearing their inability for defense, in order to have a better ground for requesting assistance, they submitted; and therefore, the emperor, the patriarch, with other prelates and barons of Greece, to comply with the resolution of the council, assembled at Bale, came to Venice; but being terrified by the plague then prevailing, it was resolved to terminate their differences at Florence. The Roman and Greek prelates having held a conference during several days, in which many long discussions took place, the Greeks yielded, and agreed to adopt the ritual of the church of Rome.

CHAPTER IV

New wars in Italy--Niccolo Piccinino, in concert with the duke of Milan, deceives the pope, and takes many places from the church--Niccolo attacks the Venetians--Fears and precautions of the Florentines--The Venetians request assistance of the Florentines and of Sforza--League against the duke of Milan--The Florentines resolve to send the count to assist the Venetians--Neri di Gino Capponi at Venice--His discourse to the senate--Extreme joy of the Venetians.

Peace being restored between the Lucchese and Florentines, and the duke and the count having become friends, hopes were entertained that the arms of Italy would be laid aside, although those in the kingdom of Naples, between Rene of Anjou and Alfonso of Aragon, could find repose only by the ruin of one party or the other. And though the pope was dissatisfied with the loss of so large a portion of his territories, and the ambition of the duke and the Venetians was obvious, still it was thought that the pontiff, from necessity, and the others from weariness, would be advocates of peace. However, a different state of feeling prevailed, for neither the duke nor the Venetians were satisfied with their condition; so that hostilities were resumed, and Lombardy and Tuscany were again harassed by the horrors of war. The proud mind of the duke could not endure that the Venetians should possess Bergamo and Brescia, and he was still further annoyed, by hearing, that they were constantly in arms, and in the daily practice of annoying some portion of his territories. He thought, however, that he should not only be able to restrain them, but to recover the places he had lost, if the pope, the Florentines, and the count could be induced to forego the Venetian alliance. He therefore resolved to take Romagna from the pontiff, imagining that his holiness could not injure him, and that the Florentines, finding the conflagration so near, either for their own sake would refrain from interference, or if they did not, could not conveniently attack him. The duke was also aware of the resentment of the Florentines against the Venetians, on account of the affair of Lucca, and he therefore judged they would be the less eager to take arms against him on their behalf. With regard to the Count Francesco, he trusted that their new friendship, and the hope of his alliance would keep him quiet. To give as little color as possible for complaint, and to lull suspicion, particularly, because in consequence of his treaty with the count, the latter could not attack Romagna, he ordered Niccolo Piccinino, as if instigated by his own ambition to do so.

When the agreement between the duke and the count was concluded, Niccolo was in Romagna, and in pursuance of his instructions from the duke, affected to be highly incensed, that a connection had been established between him and the count, his inveterate enemy. He therefore withdrew himself and his forces to Camurata, a place between Furli and Ravenna, which he fortified, as if designing to remain there some time, or till a new enterprise should present itself. The report of his resentment being diffused, Niccolo gave the pope to understand how much the duke was under obligation to him, and how ungrateful he proved; and he was persuaded that, possessing nearly all the arms of Italy, under the two principal generals, he could render himself sole ruler: but if his holiness pleased, of the two principal generals whom he fancied he possessed, one would become his enemy, and the other be rendered useless; for, if money were provided him, and he were kept in pay, he would attack the territories held of the church by the count, who being compelled to look to his own interests, could not subserve the ambition of Filippo. The pope giving entire credence to this representation, on account of its apparent reasonableness, sent Niccolo five thousand ducats and loaded him with promises of states for himself and his children. And though many informed him of the deception, he could not give credit to them, nor would he endure the conversation of any who seemed to doubt the integrity of Niccolo's professions. The city of Ravenna was held for the church by Ostasio da Polenta. Niccolo finding further delay would be detrimental, since his son Francesco had, to the pope's great dishonor, pillaged Spoleto, determined to attack Ravenna, either because he judged the enterprise easy, or because he had a secret understanding with Ostasio, for in a few days after the attack, the place capitulated. He then took Bologna, Imola, and Furli; and (what is worthy of remark) of twenty fortresses held in that country for the pope, not one escaped falling into his hands. Not satisfied with these injuries inflicted on the pontiff, he resolved to banter him by his words as well as ridicule him by his deeds, and wrote, that he had only done as his holiness deserved, for having unblushingly attempted to divide two such attached friends as the duke and himself, and for having dispersed over Italy letters intimating that he had quitted the duke to take part with the Venetians. Having taken possession of Romagna, Niccolo left it under the charge of his son, Francesco, and with the greater part of his troops, went into Lombardy, where joining the remainder of the duke's forces, he attacked the country about Brescia, and having soon completely conquered it, besieged the city itself.

The duke, who desired the Venetians to be left defenseless, excused himself to the pope, the Florentines, and the count, saying, that if the doings of Niccolo were contrary to the terms of the treaty, they were equally contrary to his wishes, and by secret messengers, assured them that when an occasion presented itself, he would give them a convincing proof that they had been performed in disobedience to his instructions. Neither the count nor the Florentines believed him, but thought, with reason, that these enterprises had been carried on to keep them at bay, till he had subdued the Venetians, who, being full of pride, and thinking themselves able alone to resist the duke, had not deigned to ask for any assistance, but carried on the war under their captain, Gattamelata.

Count Francesco would have wished, with the consent of the Florentines, to go to the assistance of king Rene, if the events of Romagna and Lombardy had not hindered him; and the Florentines would willingly have consented, from their ancient friendship to the French dynasty, but the duke was entirely in favor of Alfonso. Each being engaged in wars near home, refrained from distant undertakings. The Florentines, finding Romagna occupied with the duke's forces, and the Venetians defeated, as if foreseeing their own ruin in that of others, entreated the count to come to Tuscany, where they might consider what should be done to resist Filippo's power, which was now greater than it had ever before been; assuring him that if his insolence were not in some way curbed, all the powers of Italy would soon have to submit to him. The count felt the force of the fears entertained by the Florentines, but his desire to secure the duke's alliance kept him in suspense; and the duke, aware of this desire, gave him the greatest assurance that his hopes would be realized as shortly as possible, if he abstained from hostilities against him. As the lady was now of marriageable age, the duke had frequently made all suitable preparations for the celebration of the ceremony, but on one pretext or another they had always been wholly set aside. He now, to give the count greater confidence, added deeds to his words, and sent him thirty thousand florins, which, by the terms of the marriage contract, he had engaged to pay.

Still the war in Lombardy proceeded with greater vehemence than ever; the Venetians constantly suffered fresh losses of territory, and the fleets they equipped upon the rivers were taken by the duke's forces; the country around Verona and Brescia was entirely occupied, and the two cities themselves so pressed, that their speedy fall was generally anticipated. The marquis of Mantua, who for many years had led the forces of their republic, quite unexpectedly resigned his command, and went over to the duke's service. Thus the course which pride prevented them from adopting at the commencement of the war, fear compelled them to take during its progress; for knowing there was no help for them but in the friendship of the Florentines and the count, they began to make overtures to obtain it, though with shame and apprehension; for they were afraid of receiving a reply similar to that which they had given the Florentines, when the latter applied for assistance in the enterprise against Lucca and the count's affairs. However, they found the Florentines more easily induced to render aid than they expected, or their conduct deserved; so much more were the former swayed by hatred of their ancient enemy, than by resentment of the ingratitude of their old and habitual friends. Having foreseen the necessity into which the Venetians must come, they had informed the count that their ruin must involve his own; that he was deceived if he thought the duke, while fortune, would esteem him more than if he were in adversity; that the duke was induced to promise him his daughter by the fear he entertained of him; that what necessity occasions to be promised, it also causes to be performed; and it was therefore desirable to keep the duke in that necessity, which could be done without supporting the power of the Venetians. Therefore he might perceive, that if the Venetians were compelled to abandon their inland territories, he would not only lose the advantages derivable from them, but also those to be obtained from such as feared them; and that if he considered well the powers of Italy, he would see that some were poor, and others hostile; that the Florentines alone were not, as he had often said, sufficient for his support; so that on every account it was best to keep the Venetians powerful by land. These arguments, conjoined with the hatred which the count had conceived against Filippo, by supposing himself duped with regard to the promised alliance, induced him to consent to a new treaty; but still he would not consent to cross the Po. The agreement was concluded in February, 1438; the Venetians agreeing to pay two-thirds of the expense of the war, the Florentines one-third, and each engaging to defend the states which the count possessed in La Marca. Nor were these the only forces of the league, for the lord of Faenza, the sons of Pandolfo Malatesti da Rimino and Pietro Giampagolo Orsini also joined them. They endeavored, by very liberal offers, to gain over the marquis of Mantua, but could not prevail against the friendship and stipend of the duke; and the lord of Faenza, after having entered into compact with the league, being tempted by more advantageous terms, went over to him. This made them despair of being able to effect an early settlement of the troubles of Romagna.

The affairs of Lombardy were in this condition: Brescia was so closely besieged by the duke's forces, that constant apprehensions were entertained of her being compelled by famine to a surrender; while Verona was so pressed, that a similar fate was expected to await her, and if one of these cities were lost, all the other preparations for the war might be considered useless, and the expenses already incurred as completely wasted. For this there was no remedy, but to send the count into Lombardy; and to this measure three obstacles presented themselves. The first was, to induce him to cross the Po, and prosecute the war in whatever locality might be found most advisable; the second, that the count being at a distance, the Florentines would be left almost at the mercy of the duke, who, issuing from any of his fortresses, might with part of his troops keep the count at bay, and with the rest introduce into Tuscany the Florentine exiles, whom the existing government already dreaded; the third was, to determine what route the count should take to arrive safely in the Paduan territory, and join the Venetian forces. Of these three difficulties, the second, which particularly regarded the Florentines, was the most serious; but, knowing the necessity of the case, and wearied out by the Venetians, who with unceasing importunity demanded the count, intimating that without him they should abandon all hope, they resolved to relieve their allies rather than listen to the suggestions of their own fears. There still remained the question about the route to be taken, for the safety of which they determined the Venetians should provide; and as they had sent Neri Capponi to treat with the count and induce him to cross the Po, they determined that the same person should also proceed to Venice, in order to make the benefit the more acceptable to the Signory, and see that all possible security were given to the passage of the forces.

Neri embarked at Cesena and went to Venice; nor was any prince ever received with so much honor as he was; for upon his arrival, and the matters which his intervention was to decide and determine, the safety of the republic seemed to depend. Being introduced to the senate, and in presence of the Doge, he said, "The Signory of Florence, most serene prince, has always perceived in the duke's greatness the source of ruin both to this republic and our own, and that the safety of both states depends upon their separate strength and mutual confidence. If such had been the opinion of this illustrious Signory, we should ourselves have been in better condition, and your republic would have been free from the dangers that now threaten it. But as at the proper crisis you withheld from us confidence and aid, we could not come to the relief of your distress, nor could you, being conscious of this, freely ask us; for neither in your prosperity nor adversity have you clearly perceived our motives. You have not observed, that those whose deeds have once incurred our hatred, can never become entitled to our regard; nor can those who have once merited our affection ever after absolutely cancel their claim. Our attachment to your most serene Signory is well known to you all, for you have often seen Lombardy filled with our forces and our money for your assistance. Our hereditary enmity to Filippo and his house is universally known, and it is impossible that love or hatred, strengthened by the growth of years, can be eradicated from our minds by any recent act either of kindness or neglect. We have always thought, and are still of the same opinion, that we might now remain neutral, greatly to the duke's satisfaction, and with little hazard to ourselves; for if by your ruin he were to become lord of Lombardy, we should still have sufficient influence in Italy in free us from any apprehension on our own account; for every increase of power and territory augments that animosity and envy, from which arise wars and the dismemberment of states. We are also aware what heavy expenses and imminent perils we should avoid, by declining to involve ourselves in these disputes; and how easily the field of battle may be transferred from Lombardy to Tuscany, by our interference in your behalf. Yet all these apprehensions are at once overborne by our ancient affection for the senate and people of Venice, and we have resolved to come to your relief with the same zeal with which we should have armed in our own defense, had we been attacked. Therefore, the senate of Florence, judging it primarily necessary to relieve Verona and Brescia, and thinking this impossible without the count, have sent me, in the first instance, to persuade him to pass into Lombardy, and carry on the war wherever it may be most needful; for you are aware he is under no obligation to cross the Po. To induce him to do so, I have advanced such arguments as are suggested by the circumstances themselves, and which would prevail with us. He, being invincible in arms, cannot be surpassed in courtesy, and the liberality he sees the Florentines exercise toward you, he has resolved to outdo; for he is well aware to what dangers Tuscany will be exposed after his departure, and since we have made your affairs our primary consideration, he has also resolved to make his own subservient to yours. I come, therefore, to tender his services, with seven thousand cavalry and two thousand infantry, ready at once to march against the enemy, wherever he may be. And I beg of you, so do my lords at Florence and the count, that as his forces exceed the number he has engaged to furnish you, out of your liberality, would remunerate him, that he may not repent of having come to your assistance, nor we, who have prevailed with him to do so." This discourse of Neri to the senate was listened to with that profound attention which an oracle might be imagined to command; and his audience were so moved by it, that they could not restrain themselves, till the prince had replied, as strict decorum on such occasions required, but rising from their seats, with uplifted hands, and most of them with tears in their eyes, they thanked the Florentines for their generous conduct, and the ambassador for his unusual dispatch; and promised that time should never cancel the remembrance of such goodness, either in their own hearts, or their children's; and that their country, thenceforth, should be common to the Florentines with themselves.

CHAPTER V

Francesco Sforza marches to assist the Venetians, and relieves Verona--He attempts to relieve Brescia but fails--The Venetians routed by Piccinino upon the Lake of Garda--Piccinino routed by Sforza; the method of his escape--Piccinino surprises Verona--Description of Verona--Recovered by Sforza--The duke of Milan makes war against the Florentines--Apprehensions of the Florentines--Cardinal Vitelleschi their enemy.

When their demonstrations of gratitude had subsided, the Venetian senate, by the aid of Neri di Gino, began to consider the route the count ought to take, and how to provide him with necessaries. There were four several roads; one by Ravenna, along the beach, which on account of its being in many places interrupted by the sea and by marshes, was not approved. The next was the most direct, but rendered inconvenient by a tower called the Uccellino, which being held for the duke, it would be necessary to capture; and to do this, would occupy more time than could be spared with safety to Verona and Brescia. The third was by the brink of the lake; but as the Po had overflowed its banks, to pass in this direction was impossible. The fourth was by the way of Bologna to Ponte Puledrano, Cento, and Pieve; then between the Bondeno and the Finale to Ferrara, and thence they might by land or water enter the Paduan territory, and join the Venetian forces. This route, though attended with many difficulties, and in some parts liable to be disputed by the enemy, was chosen as the least objectionable. The count having received his instructions, commenced his march, and by exerting the utmost celerity, reached the Paduan territory on the twentieth of June. The arrival of this distinguished commander in Lombardy filled Venice and all her dependencies with hope; for the Venetians, who only an instant before had been in fear for their very existence, began to contemplate new conquests.

The count, before he made any other attempt, hastened to the relief of Verona; and to counteract his design, Niccolo led his forces to Soave, a castle situated between the Vincentino and the Veronese, and entrenched himself by a ditch that extended from Soave to the marshes of the Adige. The count, finding his passage by the plain cut off, resolved to proceed by the mountains, and thus reach Verona, thinking Niccolo would imagine this way to be so rugged and elevated as to be impracticable, or if he thought otherwise, he would not be in time to prevent him; so, with provisions for eight days, he took the mountain path, and with his forces, arrived in the plain, below Soave. Niccolo had, even upon this route, erected some bastions for the purpose of preventing him, but they were insufficient for the purpose; and finding the enemy had, contrary to his expectations, effected a passage, to avoid a disadvantageous engagement he crossed to the opposite side of the Adige, and the count entered Verona without opposition.

Having happily succeeded in his first project, that of relieving Verona, the count now endeavored to render a similar service to Brescia. This city is situated so close to the Lake of Garda, that although besieged by land, provisions may always be sent into it by water. On this account the duke had assembled a large force in the immediate vicinity of the lake, and at the commencement of his victories occupied all the places which by its means might relieve Brescia. The Venetians also had galleys upon the lake, but they were unequal to a contest with those of the duke. The count therefore deemed it advisable to aid the Venetian fleet with his land forces, by which means he hoped to obtain without much difficulty those places which kept Brescia in blockade. He therefore encamped before Bardolino, a fortress situated upon the lake, trusting that after it was taken the others would surrender. But fortune opposed this design, for a great part of his troops fell sick; so, giving up the enterprise, he went to Zevio, a Veronese castle, in a healthy and plentiful situation. Niccolo, upon the count's retreat, not to let slip an opportunity of making himself master of the lake, left his camp at Vegasio, and with a body of picked men took the way thither, attacked the Venetian fleet with the utmost impetuosity, and took nearly the whole of it. By this victory almost all the fortresses upon the lake fell into his hands.

The Venetians, alarmed at this loss, and fearing that in consequence of it Brescia would surrender, solicited the count, by letters and messengers, to go to its relief; and he, perceiving that all hope of rendering assistance from the lake was cut off, and that to attempt an approach by land, on account of the ditches, bastions, and other defenses erected by Niccolo, was marching to certain destruction, determined that as the passage by the mountains had enabled him to relieve Verona, it should also contribute to the preservation of Brescia. Having taken this resolution, the count left Zevio, and by way of the Val d'Acri went to the Lake of St. Andrea, and thence to Torboli and Peneda, upon the Lake of Garda. He then proceeded to Tenna, and besieged the fortress, which it was necessary to occupy before he could reach Brescia.

Niccolo, on being acquainted with the count's design, led his army to Peschiera. He then, with the marquis of Mantua and a chosen body of men, went to meet him, and coming to an engagement, was routed, his people dispersed, and many of them taken, while others fled to the fleet, and some to the main body of his army. It was now nightfall, and Niccolo had escaped to Tenna, but he knew that if he were to remain there till morning, he must inevitably fall into the enemy's hands; therefore, to avoid a catastrophe which might be regarded as almost fatal, he resolved to make a dangerous experiment. Of all his attendants he had only with him a single servant, a Dutchman, of great personal strength, and who had always been devotedly attached to him. Niccolo induced this man to take him upon his shoulders in a sack, as if he had been carrying property of his master's, and to bear him to a place of security. The enemy's lines surrounded Tenna, but on account of the previous day's victory, all was in disorder, and no guard was kept, so that the Dutchman, disguised as a trooper, passed through them without any opposition, and brought his master in safety to his own troops.

Had this victory been as carefully improved as it was fortunately obtained, Brescia would have derived from it greater relief and the Venetians more permanent advantage; but they, having thoughtlessly let it slip, the rejoicings were soon over, and Brescia remained in her former difficulties. Niccolo, having returned to his forces, resolved by some extraordinary exertion to cancel the impression of his death, and deprive the Venetians of the change of relieving Brescia. He was acquainted with the topography of the citadel of Verona, and had learned from prisoners whom he had taken, that it was badly guarded, and might be very easily recovered. He perceived at once that fortune presented him with an opportunity of regaining the laurels he had lately lost, and of changing the joy of the enemy for their recent victory into sorrow for a succeeding disaster. The city of Verona is situated in Lombardy, at the foot of the mountains which divide Italy from Germany, so that it occupies part both of hill and plain. The river Adige rises in the valley of Trento, and entering Italy, does not immediately traverse the country, but winding to the left, along the base of the hills, enters Verona, and crosses the city, which it divides unequally, giving much the larger portion to the plain. On the mountain side of the river are two fortresses, formidable rather from their situation than from their actual strength, for being very elevated they command the whole place. One is called San Piero, the other San Felice. On the opposite side of the Adige, upon the plain, with their backs against the city walls, are two other fortresses, about a mile distant from each other, one called the Old the other the New Citadel, and a wall extends between them that may be compared to a bowstring, of which the city wall is the arc. The space comprehended within this segment is very populous, and is called the Borgo of St. Zeno. Niccolo Piccinino designed to capture these fortresses and the Borgo, and he hoped to succeed without much difficulty, as well on account of the ordinary negligence of the guard, which their recent successes would probably increase, as because in war no enterprise is more likely to be successful than one which by the enemy is deemed impossible. With a body of picked men, and accompanied by the marquis of Mantua, he proceeded by night to Verona, silently scaled the walls, and took the New Citadel: then entering the place with his troops, he forced the gate of S. Antonio, and introduced the whole of his cavalry. The Venetian garrison of the Old Citadel hearing an uproar, when the guards of the New were slaughtered, and again when the gate was forced, being now aware of the presence of enemies, raised an alarm, and called the people to arms. The citizens awaking in the utmost confusion, some of the boldest armed and hastened to the rector's piazza. In the meantime, Niccolo's forces had pillaged the Borgo of San Zeno; and proceeding onward were ascertained by the people to be the duke's forces, but being defenseless they advised the Venetian rectors to take refuge in the fortresses, and thus save themselves and the place; as it was more advisable to preserve their lives and so rich a city for better fortune, than by endeavoring to repel the present evil, encounter certain death, and incur universal pillage. Upon this the rectors and all the Venetian party, fled to the fortress of San Felice. Some of the first citizens, anxious to avoid being plundered by the troops, presented themselves before Niccolo and the marquis of Mantua, and begged they would rather take possession of a rich city, with honor to themselves, than of a poor one to their own disgrace; particularly as they had not induced either the favor of its former possessors, or the animosity of its present masters, by self-defense. The marquis and Niccolo encouraged them, and protected their property to the utmost of their power during such a state of military license. As they felt sure the count would endeavor to recover the city, they made every possible exertion to gain possession of the fortresses, and those they could not seize they cut off from the rest of the place by ditches and barricades, so that the enemy might be shut out.

The Count Francesco was with his army at Tenna; and when the report was first brought to him he refused to credit it; but being assured of the fact by parties whom it would have been ridiculous to doubt, he resolved, by the exertion of uncommon celerity, to repair the evil negligence had occasioned; and though all his officers advised the abandonment of Verona and Brescia, and a march to Vicenza, lest he might be besieged by the enemy in his present situation, he refused, but resolved to attempt the recovery of Verona. During the consultation, he turned to the Venetian commissaries and to Bernardo de' Medici, who was there as commissary for the Florentines, and promised them the recovery of the place if one of the fortresses should hold out. Having collected his forces, he proceeded with the utmost speed to Verona. Observing his approach, Niccolo thought he designed, according to the advice he had received, to go to Vicenza, but finding him continue to draw near, and taking the direction of San Felice, he prepared for its defense--though too late; for the barricades were not completed; his men were dispersed in quest of plunder, or extorting money from the inhabitants by way of ransom; and he could not collect them in time to prevent the count's troops from entering the fortress. They then descended into the city, which they happily recovered, to Niccolo's disgrace, and with the loss of great numbers of his men. He himself, with the marquis of Mantua, first took refuge in the citadel, and thence escaping into the country, fled to Mantua, where, having assembled the relics of their army, they hastened to join those who were at the siege of Brescia. Thus in four days Verona was lost and again recovered from the duke. The count, after this victory, it being now winter and the weather very severe, having first with considerable difficulty thrown provisions into Brescia, went into quarters at Verona, and ordered, that during the cold season, galleys should be provided at Torboli, that upon the return of spring, they might be in a condition to proceed vigorously to effect the permanent relief of Brescia.

The duke, finding the war suspended for a time, the hope he had entertained of occupying Brescia and Verona annihilated, and the money and counsels of the Florentines the cause of this, and seeing that neither the injuries they had received from the Venetians could alienate them, nor all the promises he had made attach them to himself, he determined, in order to make them feel more closely the effects of the course they had adopted, to attack Tuscany; to which he was strenuously advised by the Florentine exiles and Niccolo. The latter advocated this from his desire to recover the states of Braccio, and expel the count from La Marca; the former, from their wish to return home, and each by suitable arguments endeavored to induce the duke to follow the plan congenial to their own views. Niccolo argued that he might be sent into Tuscany, and continue the siege of Brescia; for he was master of the lake, the fortresses were well provided, and their officers were qualified to oppose the count should he undertake any fresh enterprise; which it was not likely he would do without first relieving Brescia, a thing impossible; and thus the duke might carry on the war in Tuscany, without giving up his attempts in Lombardy; intimating that the Florentines would be compelled, as soon as he entered Tuscany, to recall the count to avoid complete ruin; and whatever course they took, victory to the duke must be the result. The exiles affirmed, that if Niccolo with his army were to approach Florence, the people oppressed with taxes, and wearied out by the insolence of the great, would most assuredly not oppose him, and pointed out the facility of reaching Florence; for the way by the Casentino would be open to them, through the friendship of Rinaldo and the Count di Poppi; and thus the duke, who was previously inclined to the attempt, was induced by their joint persuasions to make it. The Venetians, on the other hand, though the winter was severe, incessantly urged the count to relieve Brescia with all his forces. The count questioned the possibility of so doing, and advised them to wait the return of spring, in the meantime strengthening their fleet as much as possible, and then assist it both by land and water. This rendered the Venetians dissatisfied; they were dilatory in furnishing provisions, and consequently many deserted from their army.

The Florentines, being informed of these transactions, became alarmed, perceiving the war threatening themselves, and the little progress made in Lombardy.

Nor did the suspicion entertained by them of the troops of the church give them less uneasiness; not that the pope was their enemy, but because they saw those forces more under the sway of the patriarch, who was their greatest foe. Giovanni Vitelleschi of Corneto was at first apostolic notary, then bishop of Recanati, and afterward patriarch of Alexandria; but at last, becoming a cardinal, he was called Cardinal of Florence. He was bold and cunning; and, having obtained great influence, was appointed to command all the forces of the church, and conduct all the enterprises of the pontiff, whether in Tuscany, Romagna, the kingdom of Naples, or in Rome. Hence he acquired so much power over the pontiff, and the papal troops, that the former was afraid of commanding him, and the latter obeyed no one else. The cardinal's presence at Rome, when the report came of Niccolo's design to march into Tuscany, redoubled the fear of the Florentines; for, since Rinaldo was expelled, he had become an enemy of the republic, from finding that the arrangements made by his means were not only disregarded, but converted to Rinaldo's prejudice, and caused the laying down of arms, which had given his enemies an opportunity of banishing him. In consequence of this, the government thought it would be advisable to restore and indemnify Rinaldo, in case Niccolo came into Tuscany and were joined by him. Their apprehensions were increased by their being unable to account for Niccolo's departure from Lombardy, and his leaving one enterprise almost completed, to undertake another so entirely doubtful; which they could not reconcile with their ideas of consistency, except by supposing some new design had been adopted, or some hidden treachery intended. They communicated their fears to the pope, who was now sensible of his error in having endowed the cardinal with too much authority.

CHAPTER VI

The pope imprisons the cardinal and assists the Florentines--Difference of opinion between the count and the Venetians respecting the management of the war. The Florentines reconcile them--The count wishes to go into Tuscany to oppose Piccinino, but is prevented by the Venetians--Niccolo Piccinino in Tuscany--He takes Marradi, and plunders the neighborhood of Florence--Description of Marradi--Cowardice of Bartolomeo Orlandini--Brave resistance of Castel San Niccolo--San Niccolo surrenders--Piccinino attempts to take Cortona, but fails.

While the Florentines were thus anxious, fortune disclosed the means of securing themselves against the patriarch's malevolence. The republic everywhere exercised the very closest espionage over epistolary communication, in order to discover if any persons were plotting against the state. It happened that letters were intercepted at Monte Pulciano, which had been written by the patriarch to Niccolo without the pope's knowledge; and although they were written in an unusual character, and the sense so involved that no distinct idea could be extracted, the obscurity itself, and the whole aspect of the matter so alarmed the pontiff, that he resolved to seize the person of the cardinal, a duty he committed to Antonio Rido, of Padua, who had the command of the castle of St. Angelo, and who, after receiving his instructions, soon found an opportunity of carrying them into effect. The patriarch, having determined to go into Tuscany, prepared to leave Rome on the following day, and ordered the castellan to be upon the drawbridge of the fortress in the morning, for he wished to speak with him as he passed. Antonio perceived this to be the favorable moment, informed his people what they were to do, and awaited the arrival of the patriarch upon the bridge, which adjoined the building, and might for the purpose of security be raised or lowered as occasion required. The appointed time found him punctual; and Antonio, having drawn him, as if for the convenience of conversation, on to the bridge, gave a signal to his men, who immediately raised it, and in a moment the cardinal, from being a commander of armies, found himself a prisoner of the castellan. The patriarch's followers at first began to use threats, but being informed of the pope's directions they were appeased. The castellan comforting him with kind words, he replied, that "the great do not make each other prisoners to let them go again; and that those whom it is proper to take, it is not well to set free." He shortly afterward died in prison. The pope appointed Lodovico, patriarch of Aquileia, to command his troops; and, though previously unwilling to interfere in the wars of the league and the duke, he was now content to take part in them, and engaged to furnish four thousand horse and two thousand foot for the defense of Tuscany.

The Florentines, freed from this cause for anxiety, were still apprehensive of Niccolo, and feared confusion in the affairs of Lombardy, from the differences of opinion that existed between the count and the Venetians. In order the better to become acquainted with the intentions of the parties, they sent Neri di Gini Capponi and Giuliano Davanzati to Venice, with instructions to assist in the arrangement of the approaching campaign; and ordered that Neri, having discovered how the Venetians were disposed, should proceed to the count, learn his designs, and induce him to adopt the course that would be most advantageous to the League. The ambassadors had only reached Ferrara, when they were told that Niccolo Piccinino had crossed the Po with six thousand horse. This made them travel with increased speed; and, having arrived at Venice, they found the Signory fully resolved that Brescia should be relieved without waiting for the return of spring; for they said that "the city would be unable to hold out so long, the fleet could not be in readiness, and that seeing no more immediate relief, she would submit to the enemy; which would render the duke universally victorious, and cause them to lose the whole of their inland possessions." Neri then proceeded to Verona to ascertain the count's opinion, who argued, for many reasons, that to march to Brescia before the return of spring would be quite useless, or even worse; for the situation of Brescia, being considered in conjunction with the season, nothing could be expected to result but disorder and fruitless toil to the troops; so that, when the suitable period should arrive, he would be compelled to return to Verona with his army, to recover from the injuries sustained in the winter, and provide necessaries for the summer; and thus the time available for the war would be wasted in marching and countermarching. Orsatto Justiniani and Giovanni Pisani were deputed on the part of Venice to the count at Verona, having been sent to consider these affairs, and with them it was agreed that the Venetians should pay the count ninety thousand ducats for the coming year, and to each of the soldiers forty ducats; that he should set out immediately with the whole army and attack the duke, in order to compel him, for his own preservation, to recall Niccolo into Lombardy. After this agreement the ambassadors returned to Venice; and the Venetians, having so large an amount of money to raise, were very remiss with their commissariat.

In the meantime, Niccolo Piccinino pursued his route, and arrived in Romagna, where he prevailed upon the sons of Pandolfo Malatesti to desert the Venetians and enter the duke's service. This circumstance occasioned much uneasiness in Venice, and still more at Florence; for they thought that with the aid of the Malatesti they might resist Niccolo; but finding them gone over to the enemy, they were in fear lest their captain, Piero Giampagolo Orsini, who was in the territories of the Malatesti, should be disarmed and rendered powerless. The count also felt alarmed, for, through Niccolo's presence in Tuscany, he was afraid of losing La Marca; and, urged by a desire to look after his own affairs, he hastened to Venice, and being introduced to the Doge, informed him that the interests of the League required his presence in Tuscany; for the war ought to be carried on where the leader and forces of the enemy were, and not where his garrisons and towns were situated; for when the army is vanquished the war is finished; but to take towns and leave the armament entire, usually allowed the war to break out again with greater virulence; that Tuscany and La Marca would be lost if Niccolo were not vigorously resisted, and that, if lost, there would be no possibility of the preservation of Lombardy. But supposing the danger to Lombardy not so imminent, he did not intend to abandon his own subjects and friends, and that having come into Lombardy as a prince, he did not intend to return a mere condottiere. To this the Doge replied, it was quite manifest that, if he left Lombardy, or even recrossed the Po, all their inland territories would be lost; in that case they were unwilling to spend any more money in their defense. For it would be folly to attempt defending a place which must, after all, inevitably be lost; and that it is less disgraceful and less injurious to lose dominions only, then to lose both territory and money. That if the loss of their inland possessions should actually result, it would then be seen how highly important to the preservation of Romagna and Tuscany the reputation of the Venetians had been. On these accounts they were of quite a different opinion from the count; for they saw that whoever was victor in Lombardy would be so everywhere else, that conquest would be easily attainable now, when the territories of the duke were left almost defenseless by the departure of Niccolo, and that he would be ruined before he could order Niccolo's recall, or provide himself with any other remedy; that whoever attentively considered these things would see, that the duke had sent Niccolo into Tuscany for no other reason than to withdraw the count from his enterprise, and cause the war, which was now at his own door, to be removed to a greater distance. That if the count were to follow Niccolo, unless at the instigation of some very pressing necessity, he would find his plan successful, and rejoice in the adoption of it; but if he were to remain in Lombardy, and allow Tuscany to shift for herself, the duke would, when too late, see the imprudence of his conduct, and find that he had lost his territories in Lombardy and gained nothing in Tuscany. Each party having spoken, it was determined to wait a few days to see what would result from the agreement of the Malatesti with Niccolo; whether the Florentines could avail themselves of Piero Giampagolo, and whether the pope intended to join the League with all the earnestness he had promised. Not many days after these resolutions were adopted, it was ascertained that the Malatesti had made the agreement more from fear than any ill-will toward the League; that Piero Giampagolo had proceeded with his force toward Tuscany, and that the pope was more disposed than ever to assist them. This favorable intelligence dissipated the count's fears, and he consented to remain in Lombardy, and that Neri Capponi should return to Florence with a thousand of his own horse, and five hundred from the other parties. It was further agreed, that if the affairs of Tuscany should require the count's presence, Neri should write to him, and he would proceed thither to the exclusion of every other consideration. Neri arrived at Florence with his forces in April, and Giampagolo joined them the same day. In the meantime, Niccolo Piccinino, the affairs of Romagna being settled, purposed making a descent into Tuscany, and designing to go by the mountain passes of San Benedetto and the valley of Montone, found them so well guarded by the contrivance of Niccolo da Pisa, that his utmost exertions would be useless in that direction. As the Florentines, upon this sudden attack, were unprovided with troops and officers, they had sent into the defiles of these hills many of their citizens, with infantry raised upon the emergency to guard them, among whom was Bartolomeo Orlandini, a cavaliere, to whom was intrusted the defense of the castle of Marradi and the adjacent passes. Niccolo Piccinino, finding the route by San Benedetto impracticable, on account of the bravery of its commander, thought the cowardice of the officer who defended that of Marradi would render the passage easy. Marradi is a castle situated at the foot of the mountains which separate Tuscany from Romagna; and, though destitute of walls, the river, the mountains, and the inhabitants, make it a place of great strength; for the peasantry are warlike and faithful, and the rapid current undermining the banks has left them of such tremendous height that it is impossible to approach it from the valley if a small bridge over the stream be defended; while on the mountain side the precipices are so steep and perpendicular as to render it almost impregnable. In spite of these advantages, the pusillanimity of Bartolomeo Orlandini rendered the men cowardly and the fortress untenable; for as soon as he heard of the enemy's approach he abandoned the place, fled with all his forces, and did not stop till he reached the town of San Lorenzo. Niccolo, entering the deserted fortress, wondered it had not been defended, and, rejoicing over his acquisition, descended into the valley of the Mugello, where he took some castles, and halted with his army at Pulicciano. Thence he overran the country as far as the mountains of Fiesole; and his audacity so increased that he crossed the Arno, plundering and destroying everything to within three miles of Florence.

The Florentines, however, were not dismayed. Their first concern was to give security to the government, for which they had no cause for apprehension, so universal was the good will of the people toward Cosmo; and besides this, they had restricted the principal offices to a few citizens of the highest class, who with their vigilance would have kept the populace in order, even if they had been discontented or desirous of change. They also knew by the compact made in Lombardy what forces Neri would bring with him, and expected the troops of the pope. These prospects sustained their courage till the arrival of Neri di Gino, who, on account of the disorders and fears of the city, determined to set out immediately and check Niccolo. With the cavalry he possessed, and a body of infantry raised entirely from the people, he recovered Remole from the hands of the enemy, where having encamped, he put a stop to all further depredations, and gave the inhabitants hopes of repelling the enemy from the neighborhood. Niccolo finding that, although the Florentines were without troops, no disturbance had arisen, and learning what entire composure prevailed in the city, thought he was wasting time, and resolved to undertake some other enterprise to induce them to send forces after him, and give him a chance of coming to an engagement, by means of which, if victorious, he trusted everything would succeed to his wishes.

Francesco, Count di Poppi, was in the army of Niccolo, having deserted the Florentines, with whom he was in league, when the enemy entered the Mugello; and though with the intention of securing him as soon as they had an idea of his design, they increased his appointments, and made him commissary over all the places in his vicinity; still, so powerful is the attachment to party, that no benefit or fear could eradicate the affection he bore toward Rinaldo and the late government; so that as soon as he knew Niccolo was at hand he joined him, and with the utmost solicitude entreated him to leave the city and pass into the Casentino, pointing out to him the strength of the country, and how easily he might thence harass his enemies. Niccolo followed his advice, and arriving in the Casentino, took Romena and Bibbiena, and then pitched his camp before Castel San Niccolo. This fortress is situated at the foot of the mountains which divide the Casentino from the Val d'Arno; and being in an elevated situation, and well garrisoned, it was difficult to take, though Niccolo, with catapults and other engines, assailed it without intermission. The siege had continued more than twenty days, during which the Florentines had collected all their forces, having assembled under several leaders, three thousand horse, at Fegghine, commanded by Piero Giampagolo Orsini, their captain, and Neri Capponi and Bernardo de' Medici, commissaries. Four messengers, from Castel San Niccolo, were sent to them to entreat succor. The commissaries having examined the site, found it could not be relieved, except from the Alpine regions, in the direction of the Val d'Arno, the summit of which was more easily attainable by the enemy than by themselves, on account of their greater proximity, and because the Florentines could not approach without observation; so that it would be making a desperate attempt, and might occasion the destruction of the forces. The commissaries, therefore, commended their fidelity, and ordered that when they could hold out no longer, they should surrender. Niccolo took the fortress after a siege of thirty-two days; and the loss of so much time, for the attainment of so small an advantage, was the principle cause of the failure of his expedition; for had he remained with his forces near Florence, he would have almost deprived the government of all power to compel the citizens to furnish money: nor would they so easily have assembled forces and taken other precautions, if the enemy had been close upon them, as they did while he was at a distance. Besides this, many would have been disposed to quiet their apprehensions of Niccolo, by concluding a peace; particularly, as the contest was likely to be of some duration. The desire of the Count di Poppi to avenge himself on the inhabitants of San Niccolo, long his enemies, occasioned his advice to Piccinino, who adopted it for the purpose of pleasing him; and this caused the ruin of both. It seldom happens, that the gratification of private feelings, fails to be injurious to the general convenience.

Niccolo, pursuing his good fortune, took Rassina and Chiusi. The Count di Poppi advised him to halt in these parts, arguing that he might divide his people between Chiusi, Caprese, and the Pieve, render himself master of this branch of the Apennines, and descend at pleasure into the Casentino, the Val d'Arno, the Val di Chiane, or the Val di Tavere, as well as be prepared for every movement of the enemy. But Niccolo, considering the sterility of these places, told him, "his horses could not eat stones," and went to the Borgo San Sepolcro, where he was amicably received, but found that the people of Citta di Castello, who were friendly to the Florentines, could not be induced to yield to his overtures. Wishing to have Perugia at his disposal, he proceeded thither with forty horse, and being one of her citizens, met with a kind reception. But in a few days he became suspected, and having attempted unsuccessfully to tamper with the legate and people of Perugia, he took eight thousand ducats from them, and returned to his army. He then set on foot secret measures, to seduce Cortona from the Florentines, but the affair being discovered, his attempts were fruitless. Among the principal citizens was Bartolomeo di Senso, who being appointed to the evening watch of one of the gates, a countryman, his friend, told him, that if he went he would be slain. Bartolomeo, requesting to know what was meant, he became acquainted with the whole affair, and revealed it to the governor of the place, who, having secured the leaders of the conspiracy, and doubled the guards at the gates, waited till the time appointed for the coming of Niccolo, who finding his purpose discovered, returned to his encampment.

CHAPTER VII

Brescia relieved by Sforza--His other victories--Piccinino is recalled into Lombardy--He endeavors to bring the Florentines to an engagement--He is routed before Anghiari--Serious disorders in the camp of the Florentines after the victory--Death of Rinaldo degli Albizzi--His character--Neri Capponi goes to recover the Casentino--The Count di Poppi surrenders--His discourse upon quitting his possessions.

While these events were taking place in Tuscany, so little to the advantage of the duke, his affairs in Lombardy were in a still worse condition. The Count Francesco, as soon as the season would permit, took the field with his army, and the Venetians having again covered the lake with their galleys, he determined first of all to drive the duke from the water; judging, that this once effected, his remaining task would be easy. He therefore, with the Venetian fleet, attacked that of the duke, and destroyed it. His land forces took the castles held for Filippo, and the ducal troops who were besieging Brescia, being informed of these transactions, withdrew; and thus, the city, after standing a three years' siege, was at length relieved. The count then went in quest of the enemy, whose forces were encamped before Soncino, a fortress situated upon the River Oglio; these he dislodged and compelled to retreat to Cremona, where the duke again collected his forces, and prepared for his defense. But the count constantly pressing him more closely, he became apprehensive of losing either the whole, or the greater part, of his territories; and perceiving the unfortunate step he had taken, in sending Niccolo into Tuscany, in order to correct his error, he wrote to acquaint him with what had transpired, desiring him, with all possible dispatch, to leave Tuscany and return to Lombardy.

In the meantime, the Florentines, under their commissaries, had drawn together their forces, and being joined by those of the pope, halted at Anghiari, a castle placed at the foot of the mountains that divide the Val di Tavere from the Val di Chiane, distant four miles from the Borgo San Sepolcro, on a level road, and in a country suitable for the evolutions of cavalry or a battlefield. As the Signory had heard of the count's victory and the recall of Niccolo, they imagined that without again drawing a sword or disturbing the dust under their horses' feet, the victory was their own, and the war at an end, they wrote to the commissaries, desiring them to avoid an engagement, as Niccolo could not remain much longer in Tuscany. These instructions coming to the knowledge of Piccinino, and perceiving the necessity of his speedy return, to leave nothing unattempted, he determined to engage the enemy, expecting to find them unprepared, and not disposed for battle. In this determination he was confirmed by Rinaldo, the Count di Poppi, and other Florentine exiles, who saw their inevitable ruin in the departure of Niccolo, and hoped, that if he engaged the enemy, they would either be victorious, or vanquished without dishonor. This resolution being adopted, Niccolo led his army, unperceived by the enemy, from Citta di Castello to the Borgo, where he enlisted two thousand men, who, trusting the general's talents and promises, followed him in hope of plunder. Niccolo then led his forces in battle array toward Anghiari, and had arrived within two miles of the place, when Micheletto Attendulo observed great clouds of dust, and conjecturing at once, that it must be occasioned by the enemy's approach, immediately called the troops to arms. Great confusion prevailed in the Florentine camp, for the ordinary negligence and want of discipline were now increased by their presuming the enemy to be at a distance, and they were more disposed to fight than to battle; so that everyone was unarmed, and some wandering from the camp, either led by their desire to avoid the excessive heat, or in pursuit of amusement. So great was the diligence of the commissaries and of the captain, that before the enemy's arrival, the men were mounted and prepared to resist their attack; and as Micheletto was the first to observe their approach, he was also first armed and ready to meet them, and with his troops hastened to the bridge which crosses the river at a short distance from Anghiari. Pietro Giampagolo having previous to the surprise, filled up the ditches on either side of the road, and leveled the ground between the bridge and Anghiari, and Micheletto having taken his position in front of the former, the legate and Simoncino, who led the troops of the church, took post on the right, and the commissaries of the Florentines, with Pietro Giampagolo, their captain, on the left; the infantry being drawn up along the banks of the river. Thus, the only course the enemy could take, was the direct one over the bridge; nor had the Florentines any other field for their exertions, excepting that their infantry were ordered, in case their cavalry were attacked in flank by the hostile infantry, to assail them with their cross bows, and prevent them from wounding the flanks of the horses crossing the bridge. Micheletto bravely withstood the enemy's charge upon the bridge; but Astorre and Francesco Piccinino coming up, with a picked body of men, attacked him so vigorously, that he was compelled to give way, and was pushed as far as the foot of the hill which rises toward the Borgo d'Anghiari; but they were in turn repulsed and driven over the bridge, by the troops that took them in flank. The battle continued two hours, during which each side had frequent possession of the bridge, and their attempts upon it were attended with equal success; but on both sides of the river, the disadvantage of Niccolo was manifest; for when his people crossed the bridge, they found the enemy unbroken, and the ground being leveled, they could manoeuvre without difficulty, and the weary be relieved by such as were fresh. But when the Florentines crossed, Niccolo could not relieve those that were harassed, on account of the hindrance interposed by the ditches and embankments on each side of the road; thus whenever his troops got possession of the bridge, they were soon repulsed by the fresh forces of the Florentines; but when the bridge was taken by the Florentines, and they passed over and proceeded upon the road, Niccolo having no opportunity to reinforce his troops, being prevented by the impetuosity of the enemy and the inconvenience of the ground, the rear guard became mingled with the van, and occasioned the utmost confusion and disorder; they were forced to flee, and hastened at full speed toward the Borgo. The Florentine troops fell upon the plunder, which was very valuable in horses, prisoners, and military stores, for not more than a thousand of the enemy's cavalry reached the town. The people of the Borgo, who had followed Niccolo in the hope of plunder, became booty themselves, all of them being taken, and obliged to pay a ransom. The colors and carriages were also captured. This victory was much more advantageous to the Florentines than injurious to the duke; for, had they been conquered, Tuscany would have been his own; but he, by his defeat, only lost the horses and accoutrements of his army, which could be replaced without any very serious expense.

Nor was there ever an instance of wars being carried on in an enemy's country with less injury to the assailants than at this; for in so great a defeat, and in a battle which continued four hours, only one man died, and he, not from wounds inflicted by hostile weapons, or any honorable means, but, having fallen from his horse, was trampled to death. Combatants then engaged with little danger; being nearly all mounted, covered with armor, and preserved from death whenever they chose to surrender, there was no necessity for risking their lives; while fighting, their armor defended them, and when they could resist no longer, they yielded and were safe.

This battle, from the circumstances which attended and followed it, presents a striking example of the wretched state of military discipline in those times. The enemy's forces being defeated and driven into the Borgo, the commissaries desired to pursue them, in order to make the victory complete, but not a single condottiere or soldier would obey, alleging, as a sufficient reason for their refusal, that they must take care of the booty and attend to their wounded; and, what is still more surprising, the next day, without permission from the commissaries, or the least regard for their commanders, they went to Arezzo, and, having secured their plunder, returned to Anghiari; a thing so contrary to military order and all subordination, that the merest shadow of a regular army would easily and most justly have wrested from them the victory they had so undeservedly obtained. Added to this, the men-at-arms, or heavy-armed horse, who had been taken prisoners, whom the commissaries wished to be detained that they might not rejoin the enemy, were set at liberty, contrary to their orders. It is astonishing, that an army so constructed should have sufficient energy to obtain the victory, or that any should be found so imbecile as to allow such a disorderly rabble to vanquish them. The time occupied by the Florentine forces in going and returning from Arezzo, gave Niccolo opportunity of escaping from the Borgo, and proceeding toward Romagna. Along with him also fled the Florentine exiles, who, finding no hope of their return home, took up their abodes in various parts of Italy, each according to his own convenience. Rinaldo made choice of Ancona; and, to gain admission to the celestial country, having lost the terrestrial, he performed a pilgrimage to the holy sepulcher; whence having returned, he died suddenly while at table at the celebration of the marriage of one of his daughters; an instance of fortune's favor, in removing him from the troubles of this world upon the least sorrowful day of his exile. Rinaldo d'Albizzi appeared respectable under every change of condition; and would have been more so had he lived in a united city, for many qualities were injurious to him in a factious community, which in an harmonious one would have done him honor.

When the forces returned from Arezzo, Niccolo being then gone, the commissaries presented themselves at the Borgo, the people of which were willing to submit to the Florentines; but their offer was declined, and while negotiations were pending, the pope's legate imagined the commissaries designed to take it from the church. Hard words were exchanged and hostilities might have ensued between the Florentine and ecclesiastical forces, if the misunderstanding had continued much longer; but as it was brought to the conclusion desired by the legate, peace was restored.

While the affair of the Borgo San Sepolcro was in progress, Niccolo Piccinino was supposed to have marched toward Rome; other accounts said La Marca, and hence the legate and the count's forces moved toward Perugia to relieve La Marca or Rome, as the case might be, and Bernardo de Medici accompanied them. Neri led the Florentine forces to recover the Casentino, and pitched his camp before Rassina, which he took, together with Bibbiena, Prato Vecchio, and Romena. From thence he proceeded to Poppi and invested it on two sides with his forces, in one direction toward the plain of Certomondo, in the other upon the hill extending to Fronzole. The count finding himself abandoned to his fate, had shut himself up in Poppi, not with any hope of assistance, but with a view to make the best terms he could. Neri pressing him, he offered to capitulate, and obtained reasonable conditions, namely, security for himself and family, with leave to take whatever he could carry away, on condition of ceding his territories and government to the Florentines. When he perceived the full extent of his misfortune, standing upon the bridge which crosses the Arno, close to Poppi, he turned to Neri in great distress, and said, "Had I well considered my own position and the power of the Florentines, I should now have been a friend of the republic and congratulating you on your victory, not an enemy compelled to supplicate some alleviation of my woe. The recent events which to you bring glory and joy, to me are full of wretchedness and sorrow. Once I possessed horses, arms, subjects, grandeur and wealth: can it be surprising that I part with them reluctantly? But as you possess both the power and the inclination to command the whole of Tuscany, we must of necessity obey you; and had I not committed this error, my misfortune would not have occurred, and your liberality could not have been exercised; so, that if you were to rescue me from entire ruin, you would give the world a lasting proof of your clemency. Therefore, let your pity pass by my fault, and allow me to retain this single house to leave to the descendants of those from whom your fathers have received innumerable benefits." To this Neri replied: "That his having expected great results from men who were capable of doing only very little, had led him to commit so great a fault against the republic of Florence; that, every circumstance considered, he must surrender all those places to the Florentines, as an enemy, which he was unwilling to hold as a friend: that he had set such an example, as it would be most highly impolitic to encourage; for, upon a change of fortune, it might injure the republic, and it was not himself they feared, but his power while lord of the Casentino. If, however, he could live as a prince in Germany, the citizens would be very much gratified; and out of love to those ancestors of whom he had spoken, they would be glad to assist him." To this, the count, in great anger, replied: "He wished the Florentines at a much greater distance." Attempting no longer to preserve the least urbanity of demeanor, he ceded the place and all its dependencies to the Florentines, and with his treasure, wife, and children, took his departure, mourning the loss of a territory which his forefathers had held during four hundred years. When all these victories were known at Florence, the government and people were transported with joy. Benedetto de' Medici, finding the report of Niccolo having proceeded either to Rome or to La Marca, incorrect, returned with his forces to Neri, and they proceeded together to Florence, where the highest honors were decreed to them which it was customary with the city to bestow upon her victorious citizens, and they were received by the Signory, the Capitani di Parte, and the whole city, in triumphal pomp.

BOOK VI

CHAPTER I

Reflections on the object of war and the use of victory--Niccolo reinforces his army--The duke of Milan endeavors to recover the services of Count Francesco Sforza--Suspicions of the Venetians--They acquire Ravenna--The Florentines purchase the Borgo San Sepolcro of the pope--Piccinino makes an excursion during the winter--The count besieged in his camp before Martinengo--The insolence of Niccolo Piccinino--The duke in revenge makes peace with the league--Sforza assisted by the Florentines.

Those who make war have always and very naturally designed to enrich themselves and impoverish the enemy; neither is victory sought or conquest desirable, except to strengthen themselves and weaken the enemy. Hence it follows, that those who are impoverished by victory or debilitated by conquest, must either have gone beyond, or fallen short of, the end for which wars are made. A republic or a prince is enriched by the victories he obtains, when the enemy is crushed and possession is retained of the plunder and ransom. Victory is injurious when the foe escapes, or when the soldiers appropriate the booty and ransom. In such a case, losses are unfortunate, and conquests still more so; for the vanquished suffers the injuries inflicted by the enemy, and the victor those occasioned by his friends, which being less justifiable, must cause the greater pain, particularly from a consideration of his being thus compelled to oppress his people by an increased burden of taxation. A ruler possessing any degree of humanity, cannot rejoice in a victory that afflicts his subjects. The victories of the ancient and well organized republics, enabled them to fill their treasuries with gold and silver won from their enemies, to distribute gratuities to the people, reduce taxation, and by games and solemn festivals, disseminate universal joy. But the victories obtained in the times of which we speak, first emptied the treasury, and then impoverished the people, without giving the victorious party security from the enemy. This arose entirely from the disorders inherent in their mode of warfare; for the vanquished soldiery, divesting themselves of their accoutrements, and being neither slain nor detained prisoners, only deferred a renewed attack on the conqueror, till their leader had furnished them with arms and horses. Besides this, both ransom and booty being appropriated by the troops, the victorious princes could not make use of them for raising fresh forces, but were compelled to draw the necessary means from their subjects' purses, and this was the only result of victory experienced by the people, except that it diminished the ruler's reluctance to such a course, and made him less particular about his mode of oppressing them. To such a state had the practice of war been brought by the sort of soldiery then on foot, that the victor and the vanquished, when desirous of their services, alike needed fresh supplies of money; for the one had to re-equip them, and the other to bribe them; the vanquished could not fight without being remounted, and the conquerors would not take the field without a new gratuity. Hence it followed, that the one derived little advantage from the victory, and the other was the less injured by defeat; for the routed party had to be re-equipped, and the victorious could not pursue his advantage.

From this disorderly and perverse method of procedure, it arose, that before Niccolo's defeat became known throughout Italy, he had again reorganized his forces, and harassed the enemy with greater vigor than before. Hence, also, it happened, that after his disaster at Tenna, he so soon occupied Verona: that being deprived of his army at Verona, he was shortly able to appear with a large force in Tuscany; that being completely defeated at Anghiari, before he reached Tuscany, he was more powerful in the field than ever. He was thus enabled to give the duke of Milan hopes of defending Lombardy, which by his absence appeared to be lost; for while Niccolo spread consternation throughout Tuscany, disasters in the former province so alarmed the duke, that he was afraid his utter ruin would ensue before Niccolo, whom he had recalled, could come to his relief, and check the impetuous progress of the count. Under these impressions, the duke, to insure by policy that success which he could not command by arms, had recourse to remedies, which on similar occasions had frequently served his turn. He sent Niccolo da Esti, prince of Ferrara, to the count who was then at Peschiera, to persuade him, "That this war was not to his advantage; for if the duke became so ruined as to be unable to maintain his position among the states of Italy, the count would be the first to suffer; for he would cease to be of importance either with the Venetians or the Florentines; and to prove the sincerity of his wish for peace, he offered to fulfill the engagement he had entered into with regard to his daughter, and send her to Ferrara; so that as soon as peace was established, the union might take place." The count replied, "That if the duke really wished for peace, he might easily be gratified, as the Florentines and the Venetians were equally anxious for it. True, it was, he could with difficulty credit him, knowing that he had never made peace but from necessity, and when this no longer pressed him, again desired war. Neither could he give credence to what he had said concerning the marriage, having been so repeatedly deceived; yet when peace was concluded, he would take the advice of his friends upon that subject."

The Venetians, who were sometimes needlessly jealous of their soldiery, became greatly alarmed at these proceedings; and not without reason. The count was aware of this, and wishing to remove their apprehensions, pursued the war with unusual vigor; but his mind had become so unsettled by ambition, and the Venetians' by jealousy, that little further progress was made during the remainder of the summer, and upon the return of Niccolo into Lombardy, winter having already commenced, the armies withdrew into quarters, the count to Verona, the Florentine forces to Tuscany, the duke's to Cremona, and those of the pope to Romagna. The latter, after having been victorious at Anghiari, made an unsuccessful attack upon Furli and Bologna, with a view to wrest them from Niccolo Piccinino; but they were gallantly defended by his son Francesco. However, the arrival of the papal forces so alarmed the people of Ravenna with the fear of becoming subject to the church, that, by consent of Ostasio di Polenta their lord, they placed themselves under the power of the Venetians; who, in return for the territory, and that Ostasio might never retake by force what he had imprudently given them, sent him and his son to Candia, where they died. In the course of these affairs, the pope, notwithstanding the victory at Anghiari, became so in want of money, that he sold the fortress of Borgo San Sepolcro to the Florentines for 25,000 ducats.

Affairs being thus situated, each party supposed winter would protect them from the evils of war, and thought no more of peace. This was particularly the case with the duke, who, being rendered doubly secure by the season and by the presence of Niccolo, broke off all attempts to effect a reconciliation with the count, reorganized Niccolo's forces, and made every requisite preparation for the future struggle. The count being informed of this, went to Venice to consult with the senate on the course to be pursued during the next year. Niccolo, on the other hand, being quite prepared, and seeing the enemy unprovided, did not await the return of spring, but crossed the Adda during severe weather, occupied the whole Brescian territory, except Oddula and Acri, and made prisoners two thousand horse belonging to Francesco's forces, who had no apprehension of an attack. But the greatest source of anxiety to the count, and alarm to the Venetians, was the desertion of his service by Ciarpellone, one of his principal officers. Francesco, on learning these matters, immediately left Venice, and, arriving at Brescia, found that Niccolo, after doing all the mischief he could, had retired to his quarters; and therefore, finding the war concluded for the present was not disposed to rekindle it, but rather to use the opportunity afforded by the season and his enemies, of reorganizing his forces, so as to be able, when spring arrived, to avenge himself for his former injuries. To this end he induced the Venetians to recall the forces they had in Tuscany, in the Florentine service, and to order that to succeed Gattamelata, who was dead, Micheletto Attendulo should take the command.

On the approach of spring, Niccolo Piccinino was the first to take the field, and encamped before Cignano, a fortress twelve miles from Brescia; the count marched to its relief, and the war between them was conducted in the usual manner. The count, apprehensive for the city of Bergamo, besieged Martinengo, a castle so situated that the possession of it would enable him to relieve the former, which was closely pressed by Niccolo, who, having foreseen that the enemy could impede him only from the direction of Martinengo, had put the castle into a complete state of defense, so that the count was obliged to lend his whole force to the siege. Upon this, Niccolo placed his troops in a situation calculated to intercept the count's provisions, and fortified himself with trenches and bastions in such a manner that he could not be attacked without the most manifest hazard to his assailant. Hence the besiegers were more distressed than the people of Martinengo whom they besieged.

The count could not hold his position for want of food, nor quit it without imminent danger; so that the duke's victory appeared certain, and defeat equally inevitable to the count and the Venetians.

But fortune, never destitute of means to assist her favorites, or to injure others, caused the hope of victory to operate so powerfully upon Niccolo Piccinino, and made him assume such a tone of unbounded insolence, that, losing all respect for himself and the duke, he sent him word that, having served under his ensign for so long, without obtaining sufficient land to serve him for a grave, he wished to know from himself what was to be the reward of his labors; for it was in his power to make him master of Lombardy, and place all his enemies in his power; and, as a certain victory ought to be attended by a sure remuneration, he desired the duke to concede to him the city of Piacenza, that when weary with his lengthened services he might at last betake himself to repose. Nor did he hesitate, in conclusion, to threaten, if his request were not granted, to abandon the enterprise. This injurious and most insolent mode of proceeding highly offended the duke, and, on further consideration, he determined rather to let the expedition altogether fail, than consent to his general's demand. Thus, what all the dangers he had incurred, and the threats of his enemies, could not draw from him, the insolent behavior of his friends made him willing to propose. He resolved to come to terms with the count, and sent Antonio Guido Buono, of Tortona, to offer his daughter and conditions of peace, which were accepted with great pleasure by the count, and also by the colleagues as far as themselves were concerned. The terms being secretly arranged, the duke sent to command Niccolo to make a truce with the count for one year; intimating, that being exhausted with the expense, he could not forego a certain peace for a doubtful victory. Niccolo was utterly astonished at this resolution, and could not imagine what had induced the duke to lose such a glorious opportunity; nor could he surmise that, to avoid rewarding his friends, he would save his enemies, and therefore to the utmost of his power he opposed this resolution; and the duke was obliged, in order to induce his compliance, to threaten that if he did not obey he would give him up to his soldiers and his enemies. Niccolo submitted, with the feelings of one compelled to leave country and friends, complaining of his hard fate, that fortune and the duke were robbing him of the victory over his enemies. The truce being arranged, the marriage of the duke's daughter, Bianca, to the count was solemnized, the duke giving Cremona for her portion. This being over, peace was concluded in November, 1441, at which Francesco Barbadico and Pagolo Trono were present for the Venetians, and for the Florentines Agnolo Acciajuoli. Peschiera, Asola, and Lonato, castles in the Mantuan territory, were assigned to the Venetians.

The war in Lombardy was concluded; but the dissensions in the kingdom of Naples continued, and the inability to compose them occasioned the resumption of those arms which had been so recently laid aside. Alfonso, of Aragon, had, during these wars, taken from Rene the whole kingdom except Naples; so that, thinking he had the victory in his power, he resolved during the siege of Naples to take Benevento, and his other possessions in that neighborhood, from the count; and thought he might easily accomplish this while the latter was engaged in the wars of Lombardy. Having heard of the conclusion of peace, Alfonso feared the count would not only come for the purpose of recovering his territories, but also to favor Rene; and Rene himself had hope of his assistance for the same reason. The latter, therefore, sent to the count, begging he would come to the relief of a friend, and avenge himself of an enemy. On the other hand, Alfonso entreated Filippo, for the sake of the friendship which subsisted between them, to find the count some other occupation, that, being engaged in greater affairs, he might not have an opportunity of interfering between them. Filippo complied with this request, without seeming to be aware that he violated the peace recently made, so greatly to his disadvantage. He therefore signified to pope Eugenius, that the present was a favorable opportunity for recovering the territories which the count had taken from the church; and, that he might be in a condition to use it, offered him the services of Niccolo Piccinino, and engaged to pay him during the war; who, since the peace of Lombardy, had remained with his forces in Romagna. Eugenius eagerly took the advice, induced by his hatred of the count, and his desire to recover his lost possessions; feeling assured that, although on a former occasion he had been duped by Niccolo, it would be improper, now that the duke interfered, to suspect any deceit; and, joining his forces to those of Niccolo, he assailed La Marca. The count, astonished at such an unexpected attack, assembled his troops, and went to meet the enemy. In the meantime, King Alfonso took possession of Naples, so that the whole kingdom, except Castelnuova, was in his power. Leaving a strong guard at Castelnuova Rene set out and came to Florence, where he was most honorably received; and having remained a few days, finding he could not continue the war, he withdrew to Marseilles.

In the meantime, Alfonso took Castelnuova, and the count found himself assailed in the Marca Inferiore, both by the pope and Niccolo. He applied to the Venetians and the Florentines for assistance, in men and money, assuring them that if they did not determine to restrain the pope and king, during his life, they would soon afterward find their very existence endangered, for both would join Filippo and divide Italy among them. The Florentines and Venetians hesitated for a time, both to consider the propriety of drawing upon themselves the enmity of the pope and the king, and because they were then engaged in the affairs of the Bolognese. Annibale Bentivoglio had driven Francesco Piccinino from Bologna, and for defense against the duke, who favored Francesco, he demanded and received assistance of the Venetians and Florentines; so that, being occupied with these matters they could not resolve to assist the count, but Annibale, having routed Francesco Piccinino, and those affairs seeming to be settled, they resolved to support him. Designing however to make sure of the duke, they offered to renew the league with him, to which he was not averse; for, although he consented that war should be made against the count, while King Rene was in arms, yet finding him now conquered, and deprived of the whole kingdom, he was not willing that the count should be despoiled of his territories; and therefore, not only consented that assistance should be given him, but wrote to Alfonso to be good enough to retire to his kingdom, and discontinue hostilities against the count; and although reluctantly, yet in acknowledgment of his obligations to the duke, Alfonso determined to satisfy him, and withdrew with his forces beyond the Tronto.

CHAPTER II

Discords of Florence--Jealousy excited against Neri di Gino Capponi--Baldaccio d'Anghiari murdered--Reform of government in favor of the Medici--Enterprises of Sforza and Piccinino--Death of Niccolo Piccinino--End of the war--Disturbances in Bologna--Annibale Bentivoglio slain by Battista Canneschi, and the latter by the people--Santi, supposed to be the son of Ercole Bentivoglio, is called to govern the city of Bologna--Discourse of Cosmo de' Medici to him--Perfidious designs of the duke of Milan against Sforza--General war in Italy--Losses of the duke of Milan--The duke has recourse to the count, who makes peace with him--Offers of the duke and the Venetians to the count--The Venetians furtively deprive the count of Cremona.

While the affairs of Romagna proceeded thus, the city of Florence was not tranquil. Among the citizens of highest reputation in the government, was Neri di Gino Capponi, of whose influence Cosmo de' Medici had more apprehension than any other; for to the great authority which he possessed in the city was added his influence with the soldiery. Having been often leader of the Florentine forces he had won their affection by his courage and talents; and the remembrance of his own and his father's victories (the latter having taken Pisa, and he himself having overcome Niccolo Piccinino at Anghiari) caused him to be beloved by many, and feared by those who were averse to having associates in the government. Among the leaders of the Florentine army was Baldaccio d'Anghiari, an excellent soldier, for in those times there was not one in Italy who surpassed him in vigor either of body or mind; and possessing so much influence with the infantry, whose leader he had always been, many thought they would follow him wherever he chose to lead them. Baldaccio was the intimate friend of Neri, who loved him for his talents, of which he had been a constant witness. This excited great suspicion in the other citizens, who, thinking it alike dangerous either to discharge or retain him in their service, determined to destroy him, and fortune seemed to favor their design. Bartolommeo Orlandini was Gonfalonier of Justice; the same person who was sent to the defense of Marradi, when Niccolo Piccinino came into Tuscany, as we have related above, and so basely abandoned the pass, which by its nature was almost impregnable. So flagrant an instance of cowardice was very offensive to Baldaccio, who, on many occasions, both by words and letters, had contributed to make the disgraceful fact known to all. The shame and vexation of Bartolommeo were extreme, so that of all things he wished to avenge himself, thinking, with the death of his accuser, to efface the stain upon his character.

This feeling of Bartolommeo Orlandini was known to other citizens, so that they easily persuaded him to put Baldaccio to death, and at one avenge himself, and deliver his country from a man whom they must either retain at great peril, or discharge to their greater confusion. Bartolommeo having therefore resolved to murder him, concealed in his own apartment at the palace several young men, all armed; and Baldaccio, entering the piazza, whither it was his daily custom to come, to confer with the magistrates concerning his command, the Gonfalonier sent for him, and he, without any suspicion, obeyed. Meeting him in the corridor, which leads to the chambers of the Signory, they took a few turns together discoursing of his office, when being close to the door of the apartments in which the assassins were concealed, Bartolommeo gave them the signal, upon which they rushed out, and finding Baldaccio alone and unarmed, they slew him, and threw the body out of the window which looks from the palace toward the dogano, or customhouse. It was thence carried into the piazza, where the head being severed, it remained the whole day exposed to the gaze of the people. Baldaccio was married, and had only one child, a boy, who survived him but a short time; and his wife, Annalena, thus deprived of both husband and offspring, rejected every proposal for a second union. She converted her house into a monastery, to which she withdrew, and, being joined by many noble ladies, lived in holy seclusion to the end of her days. The convent she founded, and which is named from her, preserves her story in perpetual remembrance.

This circumstance served to weaken Neri's power, and made him lose both influence and friends. Nor did this satisfy the citizens who held the reins of government; for it being ten years since their acquisition of power, and the authority of the Balia expired, many began to exhibit more boldness, both in words and deeds, than seemed consistent with their safety; and the leaders of the party judged, that if they wished to preserve their influence, some means must be adopted to increase it. To this end, in 1444 the councils created a new Balia, which reformed the government, gave authority to a limited number to create the Signory, re-established the Chancery of Reformations, depriving Filippo Peruzzi of his office of president in it, and appointing another wholly under their influence. They prolonged the term of exile to those who were banished; put Giovanni di Simone Vespucci in prison; deprived the Accoppiatori of their enemies of the honors of government, and with them the sons of Piero Baroncelli, the whole of the Seragli, Bartolommeo Fortini, Francesco Castellani, and many others. By these means they strengthened their authority and influence, and humbled their enemies, or those whom they suspected of being so.

Having thus recovered and confirmed their government, they then turned their attention to external affairs. As observed above, Niccolo Piccinino was abandoned by King Alfonso, and the count having been aggrandized by the assistance of the Florentines, attacked and routed him near Fermo, where, after losing nearly the whole of his troops, Niccolo fled to Montecchio, which he fortified in such a manner that in a short time he had again assembled so large an army as enabled him to make head against the count; particularly as the season was now come for them to withdraw into quarters. His principal endeavor during the winter was to collect troops, and in this he was assisted both by the pope and Alfonso; so that, upon the approach of spring, both leaders took the field, and Niccolo, being the strongest, reduced the count to extreme necessity, and would have conquered him if the duke had not contrived to frustrate his designs. Filippo sent to beg he would come to him with all speed, for he wished to have a personal interview, that he might communicate matters of the highest importance. Niccolo, anxious to hear them, abandoned a certain victory for a very doubtful advantage; and leaving his son Francesco to command the army, hastened to Milan. The count being informed of the circumstance, would not let slip the opportunity of fighting in the absence of Niccolo; and, coming to an engagement near the castle of Monte Loro, routed the father's forces and took the son prisoner. Niccolo having arrived at Milan saw that the duke had duped him, and learning the defeat of his army and the capture of his son, he died of grief in 1445, at the age of sixty-four, having been a brave rather than a fortunate leader. He left two sons, Francesco and Jacopo, who, possessing less talent than their father, were still more unfortunate; so that the arms of the family became almost annihilated, while those of Sforza, being favored by fortune, attained augmented glory. The pope, seeing Niccolo's army defeated and himself dead, having little hope of assistance from Aragon, sought peace with the count, and, by the intervention of the Florentines, succeeded. Of La Marca, the pope only retained Osimo, Fabriano, and Recanati; all the rest remained in the count's possession.

Peace being restored to La Marca, the whole of Italy would have obtained repose had it not been disturbed by the Bolognese. There were in Bologna two very powerful families, the Canneschi and the Bentivogli. Of the latter, Annibale was the head; of the former, Battista, who, as a means of confirming their mutual confidence, had contracted family alliances; but among men who have the same objects of ambition in view, it is easy to form connections, but difficult to establish friendship. The Bolognese were in a league with the Venetians and Florentines, which had been effected by the influence of Annibale, after they had driven out Francesco Piccinino; and Battista, knowing how earnestly the duke desired to have the city favorable to him, proposed to assassinate Annibale, and put Bologna into his power. This being agreed upon, on the twenty-fifth of June, 1445, he attacked Annibale with his men, and slew him: and then, with shouts of "the duke, the duke," rode through the city. The Venetian and Florentine commissaries were in Bologna at the time, and at first kept themselves within doors; but finding that the people, instead of favoring the murderers, assembled in the piazza, armed in great numbers, mourning the death of Annibale, they joined them; and, assembling what forces they could, attacked the Canneschi, soon overpowered them, slew part, and drove the remainder out of the city. Battista, unable to effect his escape, or his enemies his capture, took refuge in a vault of his house, used for storing grain. The friends of the Bentivogli, having sought him all day, and knowing he had not left the city, so terrified his servants, that one of them, a groom, disclosed the place of his concealment, and being drawn forth in complete armor he was slain, his body dragged about the streets, and afterward burned. Thus the duke's authority was sufficient to prompt the enterprise, but his force was not at hand to support it.

The tumults being settled by the death of Battista, and the flight of the Canneschi, Bologna still remained in the greatest confusion. There not being one of the house of Bentivogli of age to govern, Annibale having left but one son whose name was Giovanni, only six years old, it was apprehended that disunion would ensue among the Bentivogli, and cause the return of the Cannecshi, and the ruin both of their own country and party. While in this state of apprehension, Francesco, sometime Count di Poppi, being at Bologna, informed the rulers of the city, that if they wished to be governed by one of the blood of Annibale, he could tell them of one; and related that about twenty years ago, Ercole, cousin of Annibale, being at Poppi, became acquainted with a girl of the castle, of whom was born a son named Santi, whom Ercole, on many occasions acknowledged to be his own, nor could he deny it, for whoever knew him and saw the boy, could not fail to observe the strongest resemblance. The citizens gave credit to the tale, and immediately sent to Florence to see the young man, and procure of Cosmo and Neri permission to return with him to Bologna. The reputed father of Santi was dead, and he lived under the protection of his uncle, whose name was Antonio da Cascese. Antonio was rich, childless, and a friend of Neri, to whom the matter becoming known, he thought it ought neither to be despised nor too hastily accepted; and that it would be best for Santi and those who had been sent from Bologna, to confer in the presence of Cosmo. They were accordingly introduced, and Santi was not merely honored but adored by them, so greatly were they influenced by the spirit of party. However, nothing was done at the time, except that Cosmo, taking Santi apart, spoke to him thus: "No one can better advise you in this matter than yourself; for you have to take that course to which your own mind prompts you. If you be the son of Ercole Bentivoglio, you will naturally aspire to those pursuits which are proper to your family and worthy of your father; but if you be the son of Agnolo da Cascese, you will remain in Florence, and basely spend the remainder of your days in some branch of the woolen trade." These words greatly influenced the youth, who, though he had at first almost refused to adopt such a course, said, he would submit himself wholly to what Cosmo and Neri should determine. They, assenting to the request of the Bolognese, provided suitable apparel, horses, and servants; and in a few days he was escorted by a numerous cavalcade to Bologna, where the guardianship of Annibale's son and of the city were placed in his hands. He conducted himself so prudently, that although all his ancestors had been slain by their enemies, he lived in peace and died respected by everyone.

After the death of Niccolo Piccinino and the peace of La Marca, Filippo wishing to procure a leader of his forces, secretly negotiated with Ciarpellone, one of the principal captains of Count Francesco, and arrangements having been made, Ciarpellone asked permission to go to Milan to take possession of certain castles which had been given him by Filippo during the late wars. The count suspecting what was in progress, in order to prevent the duke from accommodating himself at his expense, caused Ciarpellone to be arrested, and soon afterward put to death; alleging that he had been detected plotting against him. Filippo was highly annoyed and indignant, which the Venetians and the Florentines were glad to observe, for their greatest fear was, that the duke and the count should become friends.

The duke's anger caused the renewal of war in La Marca. Gismondo Malatesti, lord of Rimino, being son-in-law of the count, expected to obtain Pesaro; but the count, having obtained possession, gave it to his brother, Alessandro. Gismondo, offended at this, was still further exasperated at finding that Federigo di Montefeltro, his enemy, by the count's assistance, gained possession of Urbino. He therefore joined the duke, and solicited the pope and the king to make war against the count, who, to give Gismondo a taste of the war he so much desired, resolved to take the initiative, and attacked him immediately. Thus Romagna and La Marca were again in complete confusion, for Filippo, the king, and the pope, sent powerful assistance to Gismondo, while the Florentines and Venetians supplied the count with money, though not with men. Nor was Filippo satisfied with the war in Romagna, but also desired to take Cremona and Pontremoli from the count; but Pontremoli was defended by the Florentines, and Cremona by the Venetians. Thus the war was renewed in Lombardy, and after several engagements in the Cremonese, Francesco Piccinino, the leader of the duke's forces, was routed at Casale, by Micheletto and the Venetian troops. This victory gave the Venetians hope of obtaining the duke's dominions. They sent a commissary to Cremona, attacked the Ghiaradadda, and took the whole of it, except Crema. Then crossing the Adda, they overran the country as far as Milan. Upon this the duke had recourse to Alfonso, and entreated his assistance, pointing out the danger his kingdom would incur if Lombardy were to fall into the hands of the Venetians. Alfonso promised to send him troops, but apprised him of the difficulties which would attend their passage, without the permission of the count.

Filippo, driven to extremity, then had recourse to Francesco, and begged he would not abandon his father-in-law, now that he had become old and blind. The count was offended with the duke for making war against him; but he was jealous of the increasing greatness of the Venetians, and he himself began to be in want of money, for the League supplied him sparingly. The Florentines, being no longer in fear of the duke, ceased to stand in need of the count, and the Venetians desired his ruin; for they thought Lombardy could not be taken from him except by this means; yet while Filippo sought to gain him over, and offered him the entire command of his forces, on condition that he should restore La Marca to the pope and quit the Venetian alliance, ambassadors were sent to him by that republic, promising him Milan, if they took it, and the perpetual command of their forces, if he would push the war in La Marca, and prevent Alfonso from sending troops into Lombardy. The offers of the Venetians were great, as also were their claims upon him, having begun the war in order to save him from losing Cremona; while the injuries received from the duke were fresh in his memory, and his promises had lost all influence, still the count hesitated; for on the one hand, were to be considered his obligations to the League, his pledged faith, their recent services, and his hopes of the future, all which had their influence on him; on the other, were the entreaties of his father-in-law, and above all, the bane which he feared would be concealed under the specious offers of the Venetians, for he doubted not, that both with regard to Milan and their other promises, if they were victorious, he would be at their mercy, to which no prudent men would ever submit if he could avoid it. These difficulties in the way of his forming a determination, were obviated by the ambition of the Venetians, who, seeing a chance of occupying Cremona, from secret intelligence with that city, under a different pretext, sent troops into its neighborhood; but the affair was discovered by those who commanded Cremona for the count, and measures were adopted which prevented its success. Thus without obtaining Cremona, they lost the count's friendship, who, now being free from all other considerations, joined the duke.

CHAPTER III

Death of Filippo Visconti, duke of Milan--The Milanese appoint Sforza their captain--Milan becomes a republic--The pope endeavors to restore peace to Italy--The Venetians oppose this design--Alfonso attacks the Florentines--The neighborhood of Piombino becomes the principal theater of war--Scarcity in the Florentine camp--Disorders occur in the Neapolitan and Florentine armies--Alfonso sues for peace and is compelled to retreat--Pavia surrenders to the count--Displeasure of the Milanese--The count besieges Caravaggio--The Venetians endeavor to relieve the place--They are routed by the count before Caravaggio.

Pope Eugenius being dead, was succeeded by Nicholas V. The count had his whole army at Cotignola, ready to pass into Lombardy, when intelligence was brought him of the death of Filippo, which happened on the last day of August, 1447. This event greatly afflicted him, for he doubted whether his troops were in readiness, on account of their arrears of pay; he feared the Venetians, who were his armed enemies, he having recently forsaken them and taken part with the duke; he was in apprehension from Alfonso, his inveterate foe; he had no hope from the pontiff or the Florentines; for the latter were allies of the Venetians, and he had seized the territories of the former. However, he resolved to face his fortune and be guided by circumstances; for it often happens, that when engaged in business valuable ideas are suggested, which in a state of inaction would never have occurred. He had great hopes, that if the Milanese were disposed to defend themselves against the ambition of the Venetians, they could make use of no other power but his. Therefore, he proceeded confidently into the Bolognese territory, thence to Modena and Reggio, halted with his forces upon the Lenza, and sent to offer his services at Milan. On the death of the duke, part of the Milanese were inclined to establish a republic; others wished to choose a prince, and of these, one part favored the count, and another Alfonso. However, the majority being in favor of freedom, they prevailed over the rest, and organized a republic, to which many cities of the Duchy refused obedience; for they, too, desired to live in the enjoyment of their liberty, and even those who did not embrace such views, refused to submit to the sovereignty of the Milanese. Lodi and Piacenza surrendered themselves to the Venetians; Pavia and Parma became free. This confused state of things being known to the count, he proceeded to Cremona, where his ambassadors and those of the Milanese arranged for him to command the forces of the new republic, with the same remuneration he had received from the duke at the time of his decease. To this they added the possession of Brescia, until Verona was recovered, when he should have that city and restore Brescia to the Milanese.

Before the duke's death, Pope Nicholas, after his assumption of the pontificate, sought to restore peace among the princes of Italy, and with this object endeavored, in conjunction with the ambassadors sent by the Florentines to congratulate him on his accession, to appoint a diet at Ferrara to attempt either the arrangement of a long truce, or the establishment of peace. A congress was accordingly held in that city, of the pope's legate and the Venetian, ducal, and Florentine representatives. King Alfonso had no envoy there. He was at Tivoli with a great body of horse and foot, and favorable to the duke; both having resolved, that having gained the count over to their side, they would openly attack the Florentines and Venetians, and till the arrival of the count in Lombardy, take part in the treaty for peace at Ferrara, at which, though the king did not appear, he engaged to concur in whatever course the duke should adopt. The conference lasted several days, and after many debates, resolved on either a truce for five years, or a permanent peace, whichsoever the duke should approve; and the ducal ambassadors, having returned to Milan to learn his decision, found him dead. Notwithstanding this, the Milanese were disposed to adopt the resolutions of the assembly, but the Venetians refused, indulging great hopes of becoming masters of Lombardy, particularly as Lodi and Piacenza, immediately after the duke's death, had submitted to them. They trusted that either by force or by treaty they could strip Milan of her power; and then so press her, as to compel her also to surrender before any assistance could arrive; and they were the more confident of this from seeing the Florentines involved in war with King

Alfonso.

The king being at Tivoli, and designing to pursue his enterprise against Tuscany, as had been arranged between himself and Filippo, judging that the war now commenced in Lombardy would give him both time and opportunity, and wishing to have a footing in the Florentine state before he openly commenced hostilities, opened a secret understanding with the fortress of Cennina, in the Val d'Arno Superiore, and took possession of it. The Florentines, surprised with this unexpected event, perceiving the king already in action, and resolved to do them all the injury in his power, hired forces, created a council of ten for management of the war, and prepared for the conflict in their usual manner. The king was already in the Siennese, and used his utmost endeavors to reduce the city, but the inhabitants of Sienna were firm in their attachment to the Florentines, and refused to receive him within their walls or into any of their territories. They furnished him with provisions, alleging in excuse, the enemy's power and their inability to resist. The king, finding he could not enter by the Val d'Arno, as he had first intended, both because Cennina had been already retaken, and because the Florentines were now in some measure prepared for their defense, turned toward Volterra, and occupied many fortresses in that territory. Thence he proceeded toward Pisa, and with the assistance of Fazio and Arrigo de' Conti, of the Gherardesca, took some castles, and issuing from them, assailed Campiglia, but could not take it, the place being defended by the Florentines, and it being now in the depth of winter. Upon this the king, leaving garrisons in the places he had taken to harass the surrounding country, withdrew with the remainder of his army to quarters in the Siennese. The Florentines, aided by the season, used the most active exertions to provide themselves troops, whose captains were Federigo, lord of Urbino, and Gismondo Malatesti da Rimino, who, though mutual foes, were kept so united by the prudence of the commissaries, Neri di Gino and Bernardetto de' Medici, that they broke up their quarters while the weather was still very severe and recovered not only the places that had been taken in the territory of Pisa, but also the Pomerancie in the neighborhood of Volterra, and so checked the king's troops, which at first had overrun the Maremma, that they could scarcely retain the places they had been left to garrison.

Upon the return of the spring the commissaries halted with their whole force, consisting of five thousand horse and two thousand foot, at the Spedaletto. The king approached with his army, amounting to fifteen thousand men, within three miles of Campiglia, but when it was expected he would attack the place he fell upon Piombino, hoping, as it was insufficiently provided, to take it with very little trouble, and thus acquire a very important position, the loss of which would be severely felt by the Florentines; for from it he would be able to exhaust them with a long war, obtain his own provision by sea, and harass the whole territory of Pisa. They were greatly alarmed at this attack, and, considering that if they could remain with their army among the woods of Campiglia, the king would be compelled to retire either in defeat or disgrace. With this view they equipped four galleys at Livorno, and having succeeded in throwing three hundred infantry into Piombino, took up their own position at the Caldane, a place where it would be difficult to attack them; and they thought it would be dangerous to encamp among the thickets of the plain.

The Florentine army depended for provisions on the surrounding places, which, being poor and thinly inhabited, had difficulty in supplying them. Consequently the troops suffered, particularly from want of wine, for none being produced in that vicinity, and unable to procure it from more distant places, it was impossible to obtain a sufficient quantity. But the king, though closely pressed by the Florentines, was well provided except in forage, for he obtained everything else by sea. The Florentines, desirous to supply themselves in the same manner, loaded four vessels with provisions, but, upon their approach, they were attacked by seven of the king's galleys, which took two of them and put the rest to flight. This disaster made them despair of procuring provisions, so that two hundred men of a foraging party, principally for want of wine, deserted to the king, and the rest complained that they could not live without it, in a situation where the heat was so excessive and the water bad. The commissaries therefore determined to quit the place, and endeavor to recover those castles which still remained in the enemy's power; who, on his part, though not suffering from want of provisions, and greatly superior in numbers, found his enterprise a failure, from the ravages made in his army by those diseases which the hot season produces in marshy localities; and which prevailed to such an extent that many died daily, and nearly all were affected. These circumstances occasioned overtures of peace. The king demanded fifty thousand florins, and the possession of Piombino. When the terms were under consideration, many citizens, desirous of peace, would have accepted them, declaring there was no hope of bringing to a favorable conclusion a war which required so much money to carry it on. But Neri Capponi going to Florence, placed the matter in a more correct light, and it was then unanimously determined to reject the proposal, and take the lord of Piombino under their protection, with an alliance offensive and defensive, provided he did not abandon them, but assist in their defense as hitherto. The king being informed of this resolution, saw that, with his reduced army, he could not gain the place, and withdrew in the same condition as if completely routed, leaving behind him two thousand dead. With the remainder of his sick troops he retired to the Siennese territory, and thence to his kingdom, incensed against the Florentines, and threatening them with new wars upon the return of spring.

While these events were proceeding in Tuscany the Count Sforza, having become leader of the Milanese forces, strenuously endeavored to secure the friendship of Francesco Piccinino, who was also in their service, that he might support him in his enterprises, or be less disposed to do him injury. He then took the field with his army, upon which the people of Pavia, conscious of their inability to resist him, and unwilling to obey the Milanese, offered to submit themselves to his authority, on condition that he should not subject them to the power of Milan. The count desired the possession of Pavia, and considered the circumstance a happy omen, as it would enable him to give a color to his designs. He was not restrained from treachery either by fear or shame; for great men consider failure disgraceful,--a fraudulent success the contrary. But he was apprehensive that his possession of the city would excite the animosity of the Milanese, and perhaps induce them to throw themselves under the power of the Venetians. If he refused to accept the offer, he would have occasion to fear the duke of Savoy, to whom many citizens were inclined to submit themselves; and either alternative would deprive him of the sovereignty of Lombardy. Concluding there was less danger in taking possession of the city than in allowing another to have it, he determined to accept the proposal of the people of Pavia, trusting he would be able to satisfy the Milanese, to whom he pointed out the danger they must have incurred had he not complied with it; for her citizens would have surrendered themselves to the Venetians or to the duke of Savoy; so that in either case they would have been deprived of the government, and therefore they ought to be more willing to have himself as their neighbor and friend, than a hostile power such as either of the others, and their enemy. The Milanese were upon this occasion greatly perplexed, imagining they had discovered the count's ambition, and the end he had in view; but they thought it desirable to conceal their fears, for they did not know, if the count were to desert them, to whom they could have recourse except the Venetians, whose pride and tyranny they naturally dreaded. They therefore resolved not to break with the count, but by his assistance remedy the evils with which they were threatened, hoping that when freed from them they might rescue themselves from him also; for at that time they were assailed not only by the Venetians but by the Genoese and the duke of Savoy, in the name of Charles of Orleans, the son of a sister of Filippo, but whom the count easily vanquished. Thus their only remaining enemies were the Venetians, who, with a powerful army, determined to occupy their territories, and had already taken possession of Lodi and Piacenza, before which latter place the count encamped; and, after a long siege, took and pillaged the city. Winter being set in, he led his forces into quarters, and then withdrew to Cremona, where, during the cold season, he remained in repose with his wife.

In the spring, the Venetian and Milanese armies again took the field. It was the design of the Milanese, first to recover Lodi and then to come to terms with the Venetians; for the expenses of the war had become very great, and they were doubtful of their general's sincerity, so that they were anxious alike for the repose of peace, and for security against the count. They therefore resolved that the army should march to the siege of Carravaggio, hoping that Lodi would surrender, on that fortress being wrested from the enemy's hands. The count obeyed, though he would have preferred crossing the Adda and attacking the Brescian territory. Having encamped before Caravaggio, he so strongly entrenched himself, that if the enemy attempted to relieve the place, they would have to attack him at a great disadvantage. The Venetian army, led by Micheletto, approached within two bowshots of the enemy's camp, and many skirmishes ensued. The count continued to press the fortress, and reduced it to the very last extremity, which greatly distressed the Venetians, since they knew the loss of it would involve the total failure of their expedition. Very different views were entertained by their military officers respecting the best mode of relieving the place, but they saw no course open except to attack the enemy in his trenches, in spite of all obstacles. The castle was, however, considered of such paramount importance, that the Venetian senate, though naturally timid, and averse to all hazardous undertakings, chose rather to risk everything than allow it to fall into the hands of the enemy.

They therefore resolved to attack the count at all events, and early the next morning commenced their assault upon a point which was least defended. At the first charge, as commonly happens in a surprise, Francesco's whole army was thrown into dismay. Order, however, was soon so completely restored by the count, that the enemy, after various efforts to gain the outworks, were repulsed and put to flight; and so entirely routed, that of twelve thousand horse only one thousand escaped the hands of the Milanese, who took possession of all the carriages and military stores; nor had the Venetians ever before suffered such a thorough rout and overthrow. Among the plunder and prisoners, crouching down, as if to escape observation, was found a Venetian commissary, who, in the course of the war and before the fight, had spoken contemptuously of the count, calling him "bastard," and "base-born." Being made prisoner, he remembered his faults, and fearing punishment, being taken before the count, was agonized with terror; and, as is usual with mean minds (in prosperity insolent, in adversity abject and cringing), prostrated himself, weeping and begging pardon for the offenses he had committed. The count, taking him by the arm, raised him up, and encouraged him to hope for the best. He then said he wondered how a man so prudent and respectable as himself, could so far err as to speak disparagingly of those who did not merit it; and as regarded the insinuations which he had made against him, he really did not know how Sforza his father, and Madonna Lucia his mother, had proceeded together, not having been there, and having no opportunity of interfering in the matter, so that he was not liable either to blame or praise. However, he knew very well, that in regard to his own actions he had conducted himself so that no one could blame him; and in proof of this he would refer both the Venetian senate and himself to what had happened that day. He then advised him in future to be more respectful in speaking of others, and more cautious in regard to his own proceedings.

CHAPTER IV

The count's successes--The Venetians come to terms with him--Views of the Venetians--Indignation of the Milanese against the count--Their ambassador's address to him--The count's moderation and reply--The count and the Milanese prepare for war--Milanese ambassadors at Venice--League of the Venetians and Milanese--The count dupes the Venetians and Milanese--He applies for assistance to the Florentines--Diversity of opinions in Florence on the subject--Neri di Gino Capponi averse to assisting the count--Cosmo de' Medici disposed to do so--The Florentines sent ambassadors to the count.

After this victory, the count marched into the Brescian territory, occupied the whole country, and then pitched his camp within two miles of the city. The Venetians, having well-grounded fears that Brescia would be next attacked, provided the best defense in their power. They then collected the relics of their army, and, by virtue of the treaty, demanded assistance of the Florentines; who, being relieved from the war with Alfonso, sent them one thousand foot and two thousand horse, by whose aid the Venetians were in a condition to treat for peace. At one time it seemed the fate of their republic to lose by war and win by negotiation; for what was taken from them in battle was frequently restored twofold on the restoration of peace. They knew the Milanese were jealous of the count, and that he wished to be not their captain merely, but their sovereign; and as it was in their power to make peace with either of the two (the one desiring it from ambition, the other from fear), they determined to make choice of the count, and offer him assistance to effect his design; persuading themselves, that as the Milanese would perceive they had been duped by him, they would in revenge place themselves in the power of any one rather than in his; and that, becoming unable either to defend themselves or trust the count, they would be compelled, having no other resource, to fall into their hands. Having taken this resolution, they sounded the count, and found him quite disposed for peace, evidently desirous that the honor and advantage of the victory at Caravaggio should be his own, and not accrue to the Milanese. The parties therefore entered into an agreement, in which the Venetians undertook to pay the count thirteen thousand florins per month, till he should obtain Milan, and to furnish him, during the continuance of the war, four thousand horse and two thousand foot. The count engaged to restore to the Venetians the towns, prisoners, and whatever else had been taken by him during the late campaigns, and content himself with those territories which the duke possessed at the time of his death.

When this treaty became known at Milan, it grieved the citizens more than the victory at Caravaggio had exhilarated them. The rulers of the city mourned, the people complained, women and children wept, and all exclaimed against the count as false and perfidious. Although they could not hope that either prayers or promises would divert him from his ungrateful design, they sent ambassadors to see with what kind of color he would invest his unprincipled proceedings, and being admitted to his presence, one of them spoke to the following effect;--"It is customary with those who wish to obtain a favor, to make use either of prayers, presents, or threats, that pity, convenience, or fear, may induce a compliance with their requests. But as with cruel, avaricious, or, in their own conceit, powerful men, these arguments have no weight, it is vain to hope, either to soften them by prayers, win them by presents, or alarm them by menaces. We, therefore, being now, though late, aware of thy pride, cruelty, and ambition, come hither, not to ask aught, nor with the hope, even if we were so disposed, of obtaining it, but to remind thee of the benefits thou hast received from the people of Milan, and to prove with what heartless ingratitude thou hast repaid them, that at least, under the many evils oppressing us, we may derive some gratification from telling thee how and by whom they have been produced. Thou canst not have forgotten thy wretched condition at the death of the duke Filippo; the king and the pope were both thine enemies; thou hadst abandoned the Florentines and the Venetians, who, on account of their just indignation, and because they stood in no further need of thee, were almost become thy declared enemies. Thou wert exhausted by thy wars against the church;

with few followers, no friends, or any money; hopeless of being able to preserve either thy territories or thy reputation. From these circumstances thy ruin must have ensued, but for our simplicity; we received thee to our home, actuated by reverence for the happy memory of our duke, with whom, being connected by marriage and renewed alliance, we believed thy affection would descend to those who had inherited his authority, and that, if to the benefits he had conferred on thee, our own were added, the friendship we sought to establish would not only be firm, but inseparable; with this impression, we added Verona or Brescia to thy previous appointments. What more could we either give or promise thee? What else couldst thou, not from us merely, but from any others, have either had or expected? Thou receivedst from us an unhoped-for benefit, and we, in return, an unmerited wrong. Neither hast thou deferred until now the manifestation of thy base designs; for no sooner wert thou appointed to command our armies, than, contrary to every dictate of propriety, thou didst accept Pavia, which plainly showed what was to be the result of thy friendship; but we bore with the injury, in hope that the greatness of the advantage would satisfy thy ambition. Alas! those who grasp at all cannot be satisfied with a part. Thou didst promise that we should possess the conquests which thou might afterward make; for thou wert well aware that what was given at many times might be withdrawn at once, as was the case after the victory at Caravaggio, purchased by our money and blood, and followed by our ruin. Oh! unhappy states, which have to guard against their oppressor; but much more wretched those who have to trust to mercenary and faithless arms like thine! May our example instruct posterity, since that of Thebes and Philip of Macedon, who, after victory over her enemies, from being her captain became her foe and her prince, could not avail us.

"The only fault of which we are conscious is our over-weening confidence in one whom we ought not to have trusted; for thy past life, thy restless mind, incapable of repose, ought to have put us on our guard; neither ought we to have confided in one who betrayed the lord of Lucca, set a fine upon the Florentines and the Venetians, defied the duke, despised the king, and besides all this, persecuted the church of God, and the Divinity himself with innumerable atrocities. We ought not to have fancied that so many potentates possessed less influence over the mind of Francesco Sforza, than the Milanese; or that he would preserve unblemished that faith towards us which he had on so many occasions broken with them. Still this want of caution in us does not excuse the perfidy in thee; nor can it obliterate the infamy with which our just complaints will blacken thy character throughout the world, or prevent the remorse of thy conscience, when our arms are used for our own destruction; for thou wilt see that the sufferings due to parricides are fully deserved by thee. And though ambition should blind thine eyes, the whole world, witness to thine iniquity, will compel thee to open them; God himself will unclose them, if perjuries, if violated faith, if treacheries displease him, and if, as ever, he is still the enemy of the wicked. Do not, therefore, promise thyself any certainty of victory; for the just wrath of the Almighty will weigh heavily upon thee; and we are resolved to lose our liberty only with our lives; but if we found we could not ultimately defend it, we would submit ourselves to anyone rather than to thee. And if our sins be so great that in spite of our utmost resolution, we should still fall into thy hands, be quite assured, that the sovereignty which is commenced in deceit and villainy, will terminate either in thyself or thy children with ignominy and blood."

The count, though not insensible to the just reproaches of the Milanese, did not exhibit either by words or gestures any unusual excitement, and replied, that "He willingly attributed to their angry feelings all the serious charges of their indiscreet harangue; and he would reply to them in detail, were he in the presence of anyone who could decide their differences; for it would be evident that he had not injured the Milanese, but only taken care that they should not injure him. They well knew how they had proceeded after the victory of Caravaggio; for, instead of rewarding him with either Verona or Brescia, they sought peace with the Venetians, that all the blame of the quarrel might rest on him, themselves obtaining the fruit of victory, the credit of peace, and all the advantages that could be derived from the war. It would thus be manifest they had no right to complain, when he had effected the arrangements which they first attempted to make; and that if he had deferred to do so a little longer, he would have had reason to accuse them of the ingratitude with which they were now charging him. Whether the charge were true or false, that God, whom they had invoked to avenge their injuries, would show at the conclusion of the war, and would demonstrate which was most his friend, and who had most justice on their side."

Upon the departure of the ambassadors, the count determined to attack the Milanese, who prepared for their defense, and appointed Francesco and Jacopo Piccinino (attached to their cause, on account of the ancient feud of the families of Braccio and Sforza) to conduct their forces in support of liberty; at least till they could deprive the count of the aid of the Venetians, who they did not think would long be either friendly or faithful to him. On the other hand, the count, perfectly aware of this, thought it not imprudent, supposing the obligation of the treaty insufficient, to bind them by the ties of interest; and, therefore, in assigning to each their portion of the enterprise, he consented that the Venetians should attack Crema, and himself, with the other forces, assail the remainder of the territory. The advantage of this arrangement kept the Venetians so long in alliance with the count, that he was enabled to conquer the whole of the Milanese territory, and to press the city so closely, that the inhabitants could not provide themselves with necessaries; despairing of success, they sent envoys to the Venetians to beg they would compassionate their distress, and, as ought to be the case between republics, assist them in defense of their liberty against a tyrant, whom, if once master of their city, they would be unable to restrain; neither did they think he would be content with the boundaries assigned him by the treaty, but would expect all the dependencies of Milan.

The Venetians had not yet taken Crema, and wishing before they changed sides, to effect this point, they PUBLICLY answered the envoys, that their engagements with the count prevented them from defending the Milanese; but SECRETLY, gave them every assurance of their wish to do so.

The count had approached so near Milan with his forces, that he was disputing the suburbs with the inhabitants, when the Venetians having taken Crema, thought they need no longer hesitate to declare in favor of the Milanese, with whom they made peace and entered into alliance; among the terms of which was the defense of their liberty unimpaired. Having come to this agreement, they ordered their forces to withdraw from the count's camp and to return to the Venetian territory. They informed him of the peace made with the Milanese, and gave him twenty days to consider what course he would adopt. He was not surprised at the step taken by the Venetians, for he had long foreseen it, and expected its occurrence daily; but when it actually took place, he could not avoid feeling regret and displeasure similar to what the Milanese had experienced when he abandoned them. He took two days to consider the reply he would make to the ambassadors whom the Venetians had sent to inform him of the treaty, and during this time he determined to dupe the Venetians, and not abandon his enterprise; therefore, appearing openly to accept the proposal for peace, he sent his ambassadors to Venice with full credentials to effect the ratification, but gave them secret orders not to do so, and with pretexts or caviling to put it off. To give the Venetians greater assurance of his sincerity, he made a truce with the Milanese for a month, withdrew from Milan and divided his forces among the places he had taken. This course was the occasion of his victory and the ruin of the Milanese; for the Venetians, confident of peace, were slow in preparing for war, and the Milanese finding the truce concluded, the enemy withdrawn, and the Venetians their friends, felt assured that the count had determined to abandon his design. This idea injured them in two ways: one, by neglecting to provide for their defense; the next, that, being seed-time, they sowed a large quantity of grain in the country which the enemy had evacuated, and thus brought famine upon themselves. On the other hand, all that was injurious to his enemies favored the count, and the time gave him opportunity to take breath and provide himself with assistance.

The Florentines during the war of Lombardy had not declared in favor of either party, or assisted the count either in defense of the Milanese or since; for he never having been in need had not pressingly requested it; and they only sent assistance to the Venetians after the rout at Caravaggio, in pursuance of the treaty. Count Francesco, standing now alone, and not knowing to whom else he could apply, was compelled to request immediate aid of the Florentines, publicly from the state, and privately from friends, particularly from Cosmo de' Medici, with whom he had always maintained a steady friendship, and by whom he had constantly been faithfully advised and liberally supported. Nor did Cosmo abandon him in his extreme necessity, but supplied him generously from his own resources, and encouraged him to prosecute his design. He also wished the city publicly to assist him, but there were difficulties in the way. Neri di Gino Capponi, one of the most powerful citizens of Florence, thought it not to the advantage of the city, that the count should obtain Milan; and was of opinion that it would be more to the safety of Italy for him to ratify the peace than pursue the war. In the first place, he apprehended that the Milanese, through their anger against the count, would surrender themselves entirely to the Venetians, which would occasion the ruin of all. Supposing he should occupy Milan, it appeared to him that so great military superiority, combined with such an extent of territory, would be dangerous to themselves, and that if as count he was intolerable, he would become doubly so as duke. He therefore considered it better for the republic of Florence and for Italy, that the count should be content with his military reputation, and that Lombardy should be divided into two republics, which could never be united to injure others, and separately are unable to do so. To attain this he saw no better means than to refrain from aiding the count, and continuing in the former league with the Venetians. These reasonings were not satisfactory to Cosmo's friends, for they imagined that Neri had argued thus, not from a conviction of its advantage to the republic, but to prevent the count, as a friend of Cosmo, from becoming duke, apprehending that Cosmo would, in consequence of this, become too powerful.

Cosmo, in reply, pointed out, that to lend assistance to the count would be highly beneficial both to Italy and the republic; for it was unwise to imagine the Milanese could preserve their own liberty; for the nature of their community, their mode of life, and their hereditary feuds were opposed to every kind of civil government, so that it was necessary, either that the count should become duke of Milan, or the Venetians her lords. And surely under such circumstances, no one could doubt which would be most to their advantage, to have for their neighbor a powerful friend or a far more powerful foe. Neither need it be apprehended that the Milanese, while at war with the count, would submit to the Venetians; for the count had a stronger party in the city, and the Venetians had not, so that whenever they were unable to defend themselves as freemen, they would be more inclined to obey the count than the Venetians.

These diverse views kept the city long in suspense; but at length it was resolved to send ambassadors to the count to settle the terms of agreement, with instructions, that if they found him in such a condition as to give hopes of his ultimate success, they were to close with him, but, if otherwise, they were to draw out the time in diplomacy.

CHAPTER V

Prosecution of the war between the count and the Milanese--The Milanese reduced to extremity--The people rise against the magistrates--Milan surrenders to the count--League between the new duke of Milan and the Florentines, and between the king of Naples and the Venetians--Venetian and Neapolitan ambassadors at Florence--Answer of Cosmo de' Medici to the Venetian ambassador--Preparations of the Venetians and the king of Naples for the war--The Venetians excite disturbances in Bologna--Florence prepares for war--The emperor, Frederick III. at Florence--War in Lombardy between the duke of Milan and the Venetians--Ferrando, son of the king of Naples, marches into Tuscany against the Florentines.

The ambassadors were at Reggio when they heard that the count had become lord of Milan; for as soon as the truce had expired, he approached the city with his forces, hoping quickly to get possession of it in spite of the Venetians, who could bring no relief except from the side of the Adda, which route he could easily obstruct, and therefore had no apprehension (being then winter) of their arrival, and he trusted that, before the return of spring, he would be victorious, particularly, as by the death of Francesco Piccinino, there remained only Jacopo his brother, to command the Milanese. The Venetians had sent an ambassador to Milan to confirm the citizens in their resolution of defense, promising them powerful and immediate aid. During the winter a few slight skirmishes had taken place between the count and the Venetians; but on the approach of milder weather, the latter, under Pandolfo Malatesti, halted with their army upon the Adda, and considering whether, in order to succor the Milanese, they ought to risk a battle, Pardolfo, their general, aware of the count's abilities, and the courage of his army, said it would be unadvisable to do so, and that, under the circumstances, it was needless, for the count, being in great want of forage, could not keep the field, and must soon retire. He therefore advised them to remain encamped, to keep the Milanese in hope, and prevent them from surrendering. This advice was approved by the Venetians, both as being safe, and because, by keeping the Milanese in this necessity, they might be the sooner compelled to submit to their dominion; for they felt quite sure that the injuries they had received would always prevent their submission to the count.

In the meantime, the Milanese were reduced to the utmost misery; and as the city usually abounded with poor, many died of hunger in the streets; hence arose complaints and disturbances in several parts, which alarmed the magistrates, and compelled them to use their utmost exertions to prevent popular meetings. The multitude are always slow to resolve on commotion; but the resolution once formed, any trivial circumstance excites it to action. Two men in humble life, talking together near the Porta Nuova of the calamities of the city, their own misery, and the means that might be adopted for their relief, others beginning to congregate, there was soon collected a large crowd; in consequence of it a report was spread that the neighborhood of Porta Nuova had risen against the government. Upon this, all the lower orders, who only waited for an example, assembled in arms, and chose Gasparre da Vicomercato to be their leader. They then proceeded to the place where the magistrates were assembled, and attacked them so impetuously that all who did not escape by flight were slain: among the number, as being considered a principal cause of the famine, and gratified at their distress, fell Lionardo Veniero, the Venetian ambassador. Having thus almost become masters of the city, they considered what course was next to be adopted to escape from the horrors surrounding them, and to procure peace. A feeling universally prevailed, that as they could not preserve their own liberty, they ought to submit to a prince who could defend them. Some proposed King Alfonso, some the duke of Savoy, and others the king of France, but none mentioned the count, so great was the general indignation against him. However, disagreeing with the rest, Gasparre da Vicomercato proposed him, and explained in detail that if they desired relief from war, no other plan was open, since the people of Milan required a certain and immediate peace, and not a distant hope of succor. He apologized for the count's proceedings, accused the Venetians, and all the powers of Italy, of which some from ambition and others from avarice were averse to their possessing freedom. Having to dispose of their liberty, it would be preferable, he said, to obey one who knew and could defend them; so that, by their servitude they might obtain peace, and not bring upon themselves greater evils and more dangerous wars. He was listened to with the most profound attention; and, having concluded his harangue, it was unanimously resolved by the assembly, that the count should be called in, and Gasparre was appointed to wait upon him and signify their desire. By the people's command he conveyed the pleasing and happy intelligence to the count, who heard it with the utmost satisfaction, and entered Milan as prince on the twenty-sixth of February, 1450, where he was received with the greatest possible joy by those who, only a short time previously had heaped on him all the slanders that hatred could inspire.

The news of this event reaching Florence, orders were immediately sent to the envoys who were upon the way to Milan, that instead of treating for his alliance with the count, they should congratulate the duke upon his victory; they, arranging accordingly, had a most honorable reception, and were treated with all possible respect; for the duke well knew that in all Italy he could not find braver or more faithful friends, to defend him against the power of the Venetians, than the Florentines, who, being no longer in fear of the house of Visconti, found themselves opposed by the Aragonese and Venetians; for the Aragonese princes of Naples were jealous of the friendship which the Florentines had always evinced for the family of France; and the Venetians seeing the ancient enmity of the Florentines against the Visconti transferred to themselves, resolved to injure them as much as possible; for they knew how pertinaciously and invariably they had persecuted the Lombard princes. These considerations caused the new duke willingly to join the Florentines, and united the Venetians and King Alfonso against their common enemies; impelling them at the same time to hostilities, the king against the Florentines, and the Venetians against the duke, who, being fresh in the government, would, they imagined, be unable to resist them, even with all the aid he could obtain.

But as the league between the Florentines and the Venetians still continued, and as the king, after the war of Piombino, had made peace with the former, it seemed indecent to commence an open rupture until some plausible reason could be assigned in justification of offensive measures. On this account each sent ambassadors to Florence, who, on the part of their sovereigns, signified that the league formed between them was made not for injury to any, but solely for the mutual defense of their states. The Venetian ambassador then complained that the Florentines had allowed Alessandro, the duke's brother, to pass into Lombardy with his forces; and besides this, had assisted and advised in the treaty made between the duke and the marquis of Mantua, matters which he declared to be injurious to the Venetians, and inconsistent with the friendship hitherto subsisting between the two governments; amicably reminding them, that one who inflicts unmerited injury, gives others just ground of hostility, and that those who break a peace may expect war. The Signory appointed Cosmo de' Medici to reply to what had been said by the Venetian ambassador, and in a long and excellent speech he recounted the numerous advantages conferred by the city on the Venetian republic; showed what an extent of dominion they had acquired by the money, forces, and counsel of the Florentines, and reminded him that, although the friendship had originated with the Florentines, they had never given occasion of enmity; and as they desired peace, they greatly rejoiced when the treaty was made, if it had been entered into for the sake of peace, and not of war. True it was, he wondered much at the remarks which had been made, seeing that such light and trivial matters should give offense to so great a republic; but if they were worthy of notice he must have it universally understood, that the Florentines wished their country to be free and open to all; and that the duke's character was such, that if he desired the friendship of the marquis of Mantua, he had no need of anyone's favor or advice. He therefore feared that these cavils were produced by some latent motive, which it was not thought proper to disclose. Be this as it might, they would freely declare to all, that in the same proportion as the friendship of the Florentines was beneficial their enmity could be destructive.

The matter was hushed up; and the ambassadors, on their departure, appeared perfectly satisfied. But the league between the king and the Venetians made the Florentines and the duke rather apprehend war than hope for a long continuance of peace. They therefore entered into an alliance, and at the same time the enmity of the Venetians transpired by a treaty with the Siennese, and the expulsion of all Florentine subjects from their cities and territories. Shortly after this, Alfonso did the same, without any consideration of the peace made the year previous, and not having even the shadow of an excuse. The Venetians attempted to take Bologna, and having armed the emigrants, and united to them a considerable force, introduced them into the city by night through one of the common sewers. No sooner had they entered, than they raised a cry, by which Santi Bentivogli, being awakened, was told that the whole city was in possession of the rebels. But though many advised him to escape, saying that he could not save the city by his stay, he determined to confront the danger, and taking arms encouraged his followers, assembled a few friends, attacked and routed part of the rebels, slew many more, and drove the remainder out of the city. By this act of bravery all agreed he had fully proved himself a genuine scion of the house of the Bentivogli.

These events and demonstrations gave the Florentines an earnest of approaching war; they consequently followed their usual practice on similar occasions, and created the Council of Ten. They engaged new condottieri, sent ambassadors to Rome, Naples, Venice, Milan, and Sienna, to demand assistance from their friends, gain information about those they suspected, decide such as were wavering, and discover the designs of the foe. From the pope they obtained only general expressions of an amicable disposition and admonitions to peace; from the king, empty excuses for having expelled the Florentines, and offers of safe conduct for whoever should demand it; and although he endeavored, as much as possible, to conceal every indication of his hostile designs, the ambassadors felt convinced of his unfriendly disposition, and observed many preparations tending to the injury of the republic. The League with the duke was strengthened by mutual obligations, and through his means they became friends with the Genoese, the old differences with them respecting reprisals, and other small matters of dispute, being composed, although the Venetians used every possible means to prevent it, and entreated the emperor of Constantinople to expel all Florentines from his dominions; so fierce was the animosity with which they entered on this war, and so powerful their lust of dominion, that without the least hesitation they sought the destruction of those who had been the occasion of their own power. The emperor, however, refused to listen to them. The Venetian senate forbade the Florentine ambassadors to enter their territories, alleging, that being in league with the king, they could not entertain them without his concurrence. The Siennese received the ambassadors with fair words, fearing their own ruin before the League could assist them, and therefore endeavored to appease the powers whose attack they were unable to resist. The Venetians and the king (as was then conjectured) were disposed to send ambassadors to Florence to justify the war. But the Venetian envoy was not allowed to enter the Florentine dominions, and the king's ambassador, being unwilling to perform his office alone, the embassy was not completed; and thus the Venetians learned, that however little they might esteem the Florentines, the latter had still less respect for them.

In the midst of these fears, the emperor, Frederick III., came into Italy to be crowned. On the thirtieth of January, 1451, he entered Florence with fifteen hundred horse, and was most honorably received by the Signory. He remained in the city till the sixth of February, and then proceeded to Rome for his coronation, where, having been solemnly consecrated, and his marriage celebrated with the empress, who had come to Rome by sea, he returned to Germany, and again passed through Florence in May, with the same honors as upon his arrival. On his return, having derived some benefits from the marquis of Mantua, he conceded to him Modena and Reggio. In the meantime, the Florentines did not fail to prepare themselves for immediate war; and to augment their influence, and strike the enemy with terror, they, in conjunction with the duke, entered into alliance with the king of France for the mutual defense of their states. This treaty was published with great pomp throughout all Italy.

The month of May, 1452, having arrived, the Venetians thought it not desirable to defer any longer their attack upon the duke, and with sixteen thousand horse and six thousand foot assailed his territories in the direction of Lodi, while the marquis of Montferrat, instigated either by his own ambition or the entreaties of the Venetians, did the same on the side of Alexandria. The duke assembled a force of eighteen thousand cavalry and three thousand infantry, garrisoned Alexandria and Lodi, and all the other places where the enemy might annoy them. He then attacked the Brescian territory, and greatly harassed the Venetians; while both parties alike plundered the country and ravaged the smaller towns. Having defeated the marquis of Montferrat at Alexandria, the duke was able to unite his whole force against the Venetians and invade their territory.

While the war in Lombardy proceeded thus, giving rise to various trifling incidents unworthy of recital, King Alfonso and the Florentines carried on hostilities in Tuscany, but in a similarly inefficient manner, evincing no greater talent, and incurring no greater danger. Ferrando, the illegitimate son of Alfonso, entered the country with twelve thousand troops, under the command of Federigo, lord of Urbino. Their first attempt was to attack Fojano, in the Val di Chiane; for, having the Siennese in their favor, they entered the Florentine territory in that direction. The walls of the castle were weak, and it was small, and consequently poorly manned, but the garrison were, among the soldiers of that period, considered brave and faithful. Two hundred infantry were also sent by the Signory for its defense. Before this castle, thus provided, Ferrando sat down, and either from the valor of its defenders or his own deficiencies, thirty-six days elapsed before he took it. This interval enabled the city to make better provision for places of greater importance, to collect forces and conclude more effective arrangements than had hitherto been made. The enemy next proceeded into the district of Chiane, where they attacked two small towns, the property of private citizens, but could not capture them. They then encamped before the Castellina, a fortress upon the borders of the Chianti, within ten miles of Sienna, weak from its defective construction, and still more so by its situation; but, notwithstanding these defects, the assailants were compelled to retire in disgrace, after having lain before it forty-four days. So formidable were those armies, and so perilous those wars, that places now abandoned as untenable were then defended as impregnable. While Ferrando was encamped in the Chianti he made many incursions, and took considerable booty from the Florentine territories, extending his depredations within six miles of the city, to the great alarm and injury of the people, who at this time, having sent their forces to the number of eight thousand soldiers under Astorre da Faenza and Gismondo Malatesti toward Castel di Colle, kept them at a distance from the enemy, lest they should be compelled to an engagement; for they considered that so long as they were not beaten in a pitched battle, they could not be vanquished in the war generally; for small castles, when lost, were recovered at the peace, and larger places were in no danger, because the enemy would not venture to attack them. The king had also a fleet of about twenty vessels, comprising galleys and smaller craft, which lay off Pisa, and during the siege of Castellina were moored near the Rocca di Vada, which, from the negligence of the governor, he took, and then harassed the surrounding country. However, this annoyance was easily removed by a few soldiers sent by the Florentines to Campiglia, and who confined the enemy to the coast.

CHAPTER VI

Conspiracy of Stefano Porcari against the papal government--The conspirators discovered and punished--The Florentines recover the places they had lost--Gherardo Gambacorti, lord of Val di Bagno, endeavors to transfer his territories to the king of Naples--Gallant conduct of Antonio Gualandi, who counteracts the design of Gambacorti--Rene of Anjou is called into Italy by the Florentines--Rene returns to France--The pope endeavors to restore peace--Peace proclaimed--Jacopo Piccinino attacks the Siennese.

The pontiff did not interfere in these affairs further than to endeavor to bring the parties to a mutual accommodation; but while he refrained from external wars he incurred the danger of more serious troubles at home. Stefano Porcari was a Roman citizen, equally distinguished for nobility of birth and extent of learning, but still more by the excellence of his character. Like all who are in pursuit of glory, he resolved either to perform or to attempt something worthy of memory, and thought he could not do better than deliver his country from the hands of the prelates, and restore the ancient form of government; hoping, in the event of success, to be considered a new founder or second father of the city. The dissolute manners of the priesthood, and the discontent of the Roman barons and people, encouraged him to look for a happy termination of his enterprise; but he derived his greatest confidence from those verses of Petrarch in the canzone which begins, "Spirto gentil che quelle membra reggi," where he says,--

"Sopra il Monte Tarpejo canzon vedra, Un cavalier, ch' Italia tutta onora, Pensoso piu d'altrui, che di se stesso."

Stefano, believing poets are sometimes endowed with a divine and prophetic spirit, thought the event must take place which Petrarch in this canzone seemed to foretell, and that he was destined to effect the glorious task; considering himself in learning, eloquence, friends, and influence, superior to any other citizen of Rome. Having taken these impressions, he had not sufficient prudence to avoid discovering his design by his discourse, demeanor, and mode of living; so that the pope becoming acquainted with it, in order to prevent the commission of some rash act, banished him to Bologna and charged the governor of the city to compel his appearance before him once every day. Stefano was not daunted by this first check, but with even greater earnestness prosecuted his undertaking, and, by such means as were available, more cautiously corresponded with his friends, and often went and returned from Rome with such celerity as to be in time to present himself before the governor within the limit allowed for his appearance. Having acquired a sufficient number of partisans, he determined to make the attempt without further delay, and arranged with his friends at Rome to provide an evening banquet, to which all the conspirators were invited, with orders that each should bring with him his most trust-worthy friends, and himself promised to be with him before the entertainment was served. Everything was done according to this orders, and Stefano Porcari arrived at the place appointed. Supper being brought in, he entered the apartment dressed in cloth of gold, with rich ornaments about his neck, to give him a dignified appearance and commanding aspect. Having embraced the company, he delivered a long oration to dispose their minds to the glorious undertaking. He then arranged the measures to be adopted, ordering that one part of them should, on the following morning, take possession of the pontiff's palace, and that the other should call the people of Rome to arms. The affair came to the knowledge of the pope the same night, some say by treachery among the conspirators, and others that he knew of Porcari's presence at Rome. Be this as it may, on the night of the supper Stefano, and the greater part of his associates, were arrested, and afterward expiated their crime by death. Thus ended his enterprise; and though some may applaud his intentions, he must stand charged with deficiency of understanding; for such undertakings, though possessing some slight appearance of glory, are almost always attended with ruin.

Gherardo Gambacorti was lord of Val di Bagno, and his ancestors as well as himself had always been in the pay or under the protection of the Florentines. Alfonso endeavored to induce him to exchange his territory for another in the kingdom of Naples. This became known to the Signory, who, in order to ascertain his designs, sent an ambassador to Gambacorti, to remind him of the obligations of his ancestors and himself to their republic, and induce him to continue faithful to them. Gherardo affected the greatest astonishment, assured the ambassador with solemn oaths that no such treacherous thought had ever entered his mind, and that he would gladly go to Florence and pledge himself for the truth of his assertions; but being unable, from indisposition, he would send his son as an hostage. These assurances, and the proposal with which they were accompanied, induced the Florentines to think Gherardo had been slandered, and that his accuser must be alike weak and treacherous. Gherardo, however, hastened his negotiation with redoubled zeal, and having arranged the terms, Alfonso sent Frate Puccio, a knight of Jerusalem, with a strong body of men to the Val di Bagno, to take possession of the fortresses and towns, the people of which, being attached to the Florentine republic, submitted unwillingly.

Frate Puccio had already taken possession of nearly the whole territory, except the fortress of Corzano. Gambacorti was accompanied, while transferring his dominions, by a young Pisan of great courage and address, named Antonio Gualandi, who, considering the whole affair, the strength of the place, the well known bravery of the garrison, their evident reluctance to give it up, and the baseness of Gambacorti, at once resolved to make an effort to prevent the fulfillment of his design; and Gherardo being at the entrance, for the purpose of introducing the Aragonese, he pushed him out with both his hands, and commanded the guards to shut the gate upon such a scoundrel, and hold the fortress for the Florentine republic. When this circumstance became known in Bagno and the neighboring places, the inhabitants took up arms against the king's forces, and, raising the Florentine standard, drove them out. The Florentines learning these events, imprisoned Gherardo's son, and sent troops to Bagno for the defense of the territory, which having hitherto been governed by its own prince, now became a vicariate. The traitor Gherardo escaped with difficulty, leaving his wife, family, and all his property, in the hands of those whom he had endeavored to betray. This affair was considered by the Florentines of great importance; for had the king succeeded in securing the territory, he might have overrun the Val di Tavere and the Casentino at his pleasure, and would have caused so much annoyance, that they could no longer have allowed their whole force to act against the army of the Aragonese at Sienna.

In addition to the preparations made by the Florentines in Italy to resist the hostile League, they sent as ambassador, Agnolo Acciajuoli, to request that the king of France would allow Rene of Anjou to enter Italy in favor of the duke and themselves, and also, that by his presence in the country, he might defend his friends and attempt the recovery of the kingdom of Naples; for which purpose they offered him assistance in men and money. While the war was proceeding in Lombardy and Tuscany, the ambassador effected an arrangement with King Rene, who promised to come into Italy during the month of June, the League engaging to pay him thirty thousand florins upon his arrival at Alexandria, and ten thousand per month during the continuance of the war. In pursuance of this treaty, King Rene commenced his march into Italy, but was stopped by the duke of Savoy and the marquis of Montferrat, who, being in alliance with the Venetians, would not allow him to pass. The Florentine ambassador advised, that in order to uphold the influence of his friends, he should return to Provence, and conduct part of his forces into Italy by sea, and, in the meantime, endeavor, by the authority of the king of France, to obtain a passage for the remainder through the territories of the duke. This plan was completely successful; for Rene came into Italy by sea, and his forces, by the mediation of the king of France, were allowed a passage through Savoy. King Rene was most honorably received by Duke Francesco, and joining his French with the Italian forces, they attacked the Venetians with so much impetuosity, that they shortly recovered all the places which had been taken in the Cremonese. Not content with this, they occupied nearly the whole Brescian territory; so that the Venetians, unable to keep the field, withdrew close to the walls of Brescia.

Winter coming on, the duke deemed it advisable to retire into quarters, and appointed Piacenza for the forces of Rene, where, having passed the whole of the cold season of 1453, without attempting anything, the duke thought of taking the field, on the approach of spring, and stripping the Venetians of the remainder of their possessions by land, but was informed by the king that he was obliged of necessity to return to France. This determination was quite new and unexpected to the duke, and caused him the utmost concern; but though he immediately went to dissuade Rene from carrying it into effect, he was unable either by promises or entreaties to divert him from his purpose. He engaged, however, to leave part of his forces, and send his son for the service of the League. The Florentines were not displeased at this; for having recovered their territories and castles, they were no longer in fear of Alfonso, and on the other hand, they did not wish the duke to obtain any part of Lombardy but what belonged to him. Rene took his departure, and send his son John into Italy, according to his promise, who did not remain in Lombardy, but came direct to Florence, where he was received with the highest respect.

The king's departure made the duke desirous of peace. The Venetians, Alfonso, and the Florentines, being all weary of the war, were similarly disposed; and the pope continued to wish it as much as ever; for during this year the Turkish emperor, Mohammed, had taken Constantinople and subdued the whole of Greece. This conquest alarmed the Christians, more especially the Venetians and the pope, who already began to fancy the Mohammedans at their doors. The pope therefore begged the Italian potentates to send ambassadors to himself, with authority to negotiate a general peace, with which all complied; but when the particular circumstances of each case came to be considered, many difficulties were found in the war of effecting it. King Alfonso required the Florentines to reimburse the expenses he had incurred in the war, and the Florentines demanded some compensation from him. The Venetians thought themselves entitled to Cremona from the duke; while he insisted upon the restoration of Bergamo, Brescia, and Crema; so that it seemed impossible to reconcile such conflicting claims. But what could not be effected by a number at Rome was easily managed at Milan and Venice by two; for while the matter was under discussion at Rome, the duke and the Venetians came to an arrangement on the ninth of April, 1454, by virtue of which, each party resumed what they possessed before the war, the duke being allowed to recover from the princes of Montferrat and Savoy the places they had taken. To the other Italian powers a month was allowed to ratify the treaty. The pope and the Florentines, and with them the Siennese and other minor powers, acceded to it within the time. Besides this, the Florentines, the Venetians, and the duke concluded a treaty of peace for twenty-five years. King Alfonso alone exhibited dissatisfaction at what had taken place, thinking he had not been sufficiently considered, that he stood, not on the footing of a principal, but only ranked as an auxiliary, and therefore kept aloof, and would not disclose his intentions. However, after receiving a legate from the pope, and many solemn embassies from other powers, he allowed himself to be persuaded, principally by means of the pontiff, and with his son joined the League for thirty years. The duke and the king also contracted a twofold relationship and double marriage, each giving a daughter to a son of the other. Notwithstanding this, that Italy might still retain the seeds of war, Alfonso would not consent to the peace, unless the League would allow him, without injury to themselves, to make war upon the Genoese, Gismondo Malatesti, and Astorre, prince of Faenza. This being conceded, his son Ferrando, who was at Sienna, returned to the kingdom, having by his coming into Tuscany acquired no dominion and lost a great number of his men.

Upon the establishment of a general peace, the only apprehension entertained was, that it would be disturbed by the animosity of Alfonso against the Genoese; yet it happened otherwise. The king, indeed, did not openly infringe the peace, but it was frequently broken by the ambition of the mercenary troops. The Venetians, as usual on the conclusion of a war, had discharged Jacopo Piccinino, who with some other unemployed condottieri, marched into Romagna, thence into the Siennese, and halting in the country, took possession of many places. At the commencement of these disturbances, and the beginning of the year 1455, Pope Nicholas died, and was succeeded by Calixtus III., who, to put a stop to the war newly broken out so near home, immediately sent Giovanni Ventimiglia, his general, with what forces he could furnish. These being joined by the troops of the Florentines and the duke of Milan, both of whom furnished assistance, attacked Jacopo, near Bolsena, and though Ventimiglia was taken prisoner, yet Jacopo was worsted, and retreated in disorder to Castiglione della Pescaia, where, had he not been assisted by Alfonso, his force would have been completely annihilated. This made it evident that Jacopo's movement had been made by order of Alfonso, and the latter, as if palpably detected, to conciliate his allies, after having almost alienated them with this unimportant war, ordered Jacopo to restore to the Siennese the places he had taken, and they gave him twenty thousand florins by way of ransom, after which he and his forces were received into the kingdom of Naples.

CHAPTER VII

Christendom alarmed by the progress of the Turks--The Turks routed before Belgrade--Description of a remarkable hurricane--War against the Genoese and Gismondo Malatesti--Genoa submits to the king of France--Death of Alfonso king of Naples--Succeeded by his son Ferrando--The pope designs to give the kingdom of Naples to his nephew Piero Lodovico Borgia--Eulogy of Pius II.--Disturbances in Genoa between John of Anjou and the Fregosi--The Fregosi subdued--John attacks the kingdom of Naples--Ferrando king of Naples routed--Ferrando reinstated--The Genoese cast off the French yoke--John of Anjou routed in the kingdom of Naples.

The pope, though anxious to restrain Jacopo Piccinino, did not neglect to make provision for the defense of Christendom, which seemed in danger from the Turks. He sent ambassadors and preachers into every Christian country, to exhort princes and people to arm in defense of their religion, and with their persons and property to contribute to the enterprise against the common enemy. In Florence, large sums were raised, and many citizens bore the mark of a red cross upon their dress to intimate their readiness to become soldiers of the faith. Solemn processions were made, and nothing was neglected either in public or private, to show their willingness to be among the most forward to assist the enterprise with money, counsel, or men. But the eagerness for this crusade was somewhat abated, by learning that the Turkish army, being at the siege of Belgrade, a strong city and fortress in Hungary, upon the banks of the Danube, had been routed and the emperor wounded; so that the alarm felt by the pope and all Christendom, on the loss of Constantinople, having ceased to operate, they proceeded with deliberately with their preparations for war; and in Hungary their zeal was cooled through the death of Giovanni Corvini the Waiwode, who commanded the

Hungarian forces on that memorable occasion, and fell in the battle.

To return to the affairs of Italy. In the year 1456, the disturbances occasioned by Jacopo Piccinino having subsided, and human weapons laid aside, the heavens seemed to make war against the earth; dreadful tempestuous winds then occurring, which produced effects unprecedented in Tuscany, and which to posterity will appear marvelous and unaccountable. On the twenty-fourth of August, about an hour before daybreak, there arose from the Adriatic near Ancona, a whirlwind, which crossing from east to west, again reached the sea near Pisa, accompanied by thick clouds, and the most intense and impenetrable darkness, covering a breadth of about two miles in the direction of its course. Under some natural or supernatural influence, this vast and overcharged volume of condensed vapor burst; its fragments contended with indescribable fury, and huge bodies sometimes ascending toward heaven, and sometimes precipitated upon the earth, struggled, as it were, in mutual conflict, whirling in circles with intense velocity, and accompanied by winds, impetuous beyond all conception; while flashes of awful brilliancy, and murky, lurid flames incessantly broke forth. From these confused clouds, furious winds, and momentary fires, sounds issued, of which no earthquake or thunder ever heard could afford the least idea; striking such awe into all, that it was thought the end of the world had arrived, that the earth, waters, heavens, and entire universe, mingling together, were being resolved into their ancient chaos. Wherever this awful tempest passed, it produced unprecedented and marvelous effects; but these were more especially experienced near the castle of St. Casciano, about eight miles from Florence, upon the hill which separates the valleys of Pisa and Grieve. Between this castle and the Borgo St. Andrea, upon the same hill, the tempest passed without touching the latter, and in the former, only threw down some of the battlements and the chimneys of a few houses; but in the space between them, it leveled many buildings quite to the ground. The roofs of the churches of St. Martin, at Bagnolo, and Santa Maria della Pace, were carried more than a mile, unbroken as when upon their respective edifices. A muleteer and his beasts were driven from the road into the adjoining valley, and found dead. All the large oaks and lofty trees which could not bend beneath its influence, were not only stripped of their branches but borne to a great distance from the places where they grew, and when the tempest had passed over and daylight made the desolation visible, the inhabitants were transfixed with dismay. The country had lost all its habitable character; churches and dwellings were laid in heaps; nothing was heard but the lamentations of those whose possessions had perished, or whose cattle or friends were buried beneath the ruins; and all who witnessed the scene were filled with anguish or compassion. It was doubtless the design of the Omnipotent, rather to threaten Tuscany than to chastise her; for had the hurricane been directed over the city, filled with houses and inhabitants, instead of proceeding among oaks and elms, or small and thinly scattered dwellings, it would have been such a scourge as the mind, with all its ideas of horror, could not have conceived. But the Almighty desired that this slight example should suffice to recall the minds of men to a knowledge of himself and of his power.

To return to our history. King Alfonso was dissatisfied with the peace, and as the war which he had unnecessarily caused Jacopo Piccinino to make against the Siennese, had produced no important result, he resolved to try what could be done against those whom the conditions of the League permitted him to attack. He therefore, in the year 1456, assailed the Genoese, both by sea and by land, designing to deprive the Fregosi of the government and restore the Adorni. At the same time, he ordered Jacopo Piccinino to cross the Tronto, and attack Gismondo Malatesti, who, having fortified his territories, did not concern himself, and this part of the king's enterprise produced no effect; but his proceedings against Genoa occasioned more wars against himself and his kingdom than he could have wished. Piero Fregoso was then doge of Genoa, and doubting his ability to sustain the attack of the king, he determined to give what he could not hold, to some one who might defend it against his enemies, in hope, that at a future period, he should obtain a return for the benefit conferred. He therefore sent ambassadors to Charles VII. of France, and offered him the government of Genoa. Charles accepted the offer, and sent John of Anjou, the son of King Rene, who had a short time previously left Florence and returned to France, to take possession with the idea, that he, having learned the manners and customs of Italy, would be able to govern the city; and also that this might give him an opportunity of undertaking the conquest of Naples, of which Rene, John's father, had been deprived by Alfonso. John, therefore, proceeded to Genoa, where he was received as prince, and the fortresses, both of the city and the government, given up to him. This annoyed Alfonso, with the fear that he had brought upon himself too powerful an enemy. He was not, however, dismayed; but pursued his enterprise vigorously, and had led his fleet to Porto, below Villamarina, when he died after a sudden illness, and thus John and the Genoese were relieved from the war. Ferrando, who succeeded to the kingdom of his father Alfonso, became alarmed at having so powerful an enemy in Italy, and was doubtful of the disposition of many of his barons, who being desirous of change, he feared would take part with the French. He was also apprehensive of the pope, whose ambition he well knew, and who seeing him new in the government, might design to take it from him. He had no hope except from the duke of Milan, who entertained no less anxiety concerning the affairs of the kingdom than Ferrando; for he feared that if the French were to obtain it, they would endeavor to annex his own dominions; which he knew they considered to be rightfully their own. He, therefore, soon after the death of Alfonso, sent letters and forces to Ferrando; the latter to give him aid and influence, the former to encourage him with an intimation that he would not, under any circumstances, forsake him. The pontiff intended, after the death of Alfonso, to give the kingdom of Naples to his nephew Piero Lodovico Borgia, and, to furnish a decent pretext for his design and obtain the concurrence of the powers of Italy in its favor he signified a wish to restore that realm to the dominion of the church of Rome; and therefore persuaded the duke not to assist Ferrando. But in the midst of these views and opening enterprises, Calixtus died, and Pius II. of Siennese origin, of the family of the Piccolomini, and by name AEneas, succeeded to the pontificate. This pontiff, free from the ties of private interest, having no object but to benefit Christendom and honor the church, at the duke's entreaty crowned Ferrando king of Naples; judging it easier to establish peace if the kingdom remained in the hands which at present held it, than if he were to favor the views of the French, or, as Calixtus purposed, take it for himself. Ferrando, in acknowledgment of the benefit, created Antonio, one of the pope's nephews, prince of Malfi, gave him an illegitimate daughter of his own in marriage, and restored Benevento and Terracina to the church.

It thus appeared that the internal dissensions of Italy might be quelled, and the pontiff prepared to induce the powers of Christendom to unite in an enterprise against the Turks (as Calixtus had previously designed) when differences arose between the Fregosi and John of Anjou, the lord of Genoa, which occasioned greater and more important wars than those recently concluded. Pietrino Fregoso was at his castle of Riviera, and thought he had not been rewarded by John in proportion to his family's merits; for it was by their means the latter had become prince of the city. This impression drove the parties into open enmity; a circumstance gratifying to Ferrando, who saw in it relief from his troubles, and the sole means of procuring his safety: he therefore assisted Pietrino with money and men, trusting to drive John out of the Genoese territory. The latter being aware of his design, sent for aid to France; and, on obtaining it, attacked Pietrino, who, through his numerous friends, entertained the strongest assurance of success; so that John was compelled to keep within the city, into which Pietrino having entered by night, took possession of some parts of it; but upon the return of day, his people were all either slain or made prisoners by John's troops, and he himself was found among the dead.

This victory gave John hopes of recovering the kingdom; and in October, 1459, he sailed thither from Genoa, with a powerful fleet, and landed at Baia; whence he proceeded to Sessa, by the duke of which place he was favorably received. The prince of Taranto, the Aquilani, with several cities and other princes, also joined him; so that a great part of the kingdom fell into his hands. On this Ferrando applied for assistance to the pope and the duke of Milan; and, to diminish the number of his enemies, made peace with Gismondo Malatesti, which gave so much offense to Jacopo Piccinino, the hereditary enemy of Gismondo, that he resigned his command under Ferrando, and joined his rival. Ferrando also sent money to Federigo, lord of Urbino, and collected with all possible speed what was in those times considered a tolerable army; which, meeting the enemy upon the river Sarni, an engagement ensued in which Ferrando was routed, and many of his principal officers taken. After this defeat, the city of Naples alone, with a few smaller places and princes of inferior note, adhered to Ferrando, the greater part having submitted to John. Jacopo Piccinino, after the victory, advised an immediate march upon Naples; but John declined this, saying, he would first reduce the remainder of the kingdom, and then attack the seat of government. This resolution occasioned the failure of his enterprise; for he did not consider how much more easily the members follow the head than the head the members.

After his defeat, Ferrando took refuge in Naples, whither the scattered remnants of his people followed him; and by soliciting his friends, he obtained money and a small force. He sent again for assistance to the pope and the duke, by both of whom he was supplied more liberally and speedily than before; for they began to entertain most serious apprehensions of his losing the kingdom. His hopes were thus revived; and, marching from Naples, he regained his reputation in his dominions, and soon obtained the places of which he had been deprived. While the war was proceeding in the kingdom, a circumstance occurred by which John of Anjou lost his influence, and all chance of success in the enterprise. The Genoese had become so weary of the haughty and avaricious dominion of the French, that they took arms against the viceroy, and compelled him to seek refuge in the castelletto; the Fregosi and the Adorni united in the enterprise against him, and were assisted with money and troops by the duke of Milan, both for the recovery and preservation of the government. At the same time, King Rene coming with a fleet to the assistance of his son, and hoping to recover Genoa by means of the castelletto, upon landing his forces was so completely routed, that he was compelled to return in disgrace to Provence. When the news of his father's defeat reached Naples, John was greatly alarmed, but continued the war for a time by the assistance of those barons who, being rebels, knew they would obtain no terms from Ferrando. At length, after various trifling occurrences, the two royal armies came to an engagement, in which John was routed near Troia, in the year 1463. He was, however, less injured by his defeat than by the desertion of Jacopo Piccinino, who joined Ferrando; and, being abandoned by his troops, he was compelled to take refuge in Istria, and thence withdrew to France. This war continued four years. John's failure was attributable to negligence; for victory was often within his grasp, but he did not take proper means to secure it. The Florentines took no decisive part in this war. John, king of Aragon, who succeeded upon the death of Alfonso, sent ambassadors to request their assistance for his nephew Ferrando, in compliance with the terms of the treaty recently made with his father Alfonso. The Florentines replied, that they were under no obligation; that they did not think proper to assist the son in a war commenced by the father with his own forces; and that as it was begun without either their counsel or knowledge, it must be continued and concluded without their help. The ambassadors affirmed the engagement to be binding on the Florentines, and themselves to be answerable for the event of the war; and then in great anger left the city. Thus with regard to external affairs, the Florentines continued tranquil during this war; but the case was otherwise with their domestic concerns, as will be particularly shown in the following book.

BOOK VII

CHAPTER I

Connection of the other Italian governments with the history of Florence--Republics always disunited--Some differences are injurious; others not so--The kind of dissensions prevailing at Florence--Cosmo de' Medici and Neri Capponi become powerful by dissimilar means--Reform in the election of magistrates favorable to Cosmo--Complaints of the principal citizens against the reform in elections--Luca Pitti, Gonfalonier of Justice, restrains the imborsations by force--Tyranny and pride of Luca Pitti and his party--Palace of the Pitti--Death of Cosmo de' Medici--His liberality and magnificence--His modesty--His prudence--Sayings of Cosmo.

It will perhaps appear to the readers of the preceding book that, professing only to write of the affairs of Florence, I have dilated too much in speaking of those which occurred in Lombardy and Naples. But as I have not already avoided, so it is not my intention in future to forbear, similar digressions. For although we have not engaged to give an account of the affairs of Italy, still it would be improper to neglect noticing the most remarkable of them. If they were wholly omitted, our history would not be so well understood, neither would it be so instructive or agreeable; since from the proceedings of the other princes and states of Italy, have most commonly arisen those wars in which the Florentines were compelled to take part. Thus, from the war between John of Anjou and King Ferrando, originated those serious enmities and hatreds which ensued between Ferrando and the Florentines, particularly the house of Medici. The king complained of a want of assistance during the war, and of the aid afforded to his enemy; and from his anger originated the greatest evils, as will be hereafter seen. Having, in speaking of external affairs, come down to the year 1463, it will be necessary in order to make our narrative of the contemporaneous domestic transactions clearly understood, to revert to a period several years back. But first, according to custom, I would offer a few remarks referring to the events about to be narrated, and observe, that those who think a republic may be kept in perfect unity of purpose are greatly deceived. True it is, that some divisions injure republics, while others are beneficial to them. When accompanied by factions and parties they are injurious; but when maintained without them they contribute to their prosperity. The legislator of a republic, since it is impossible to prevent the existence of dissensions, must at least take care to prevent the growth of faction. It may therefore be observed, that citizens acquire reputation and power in two ways; the one public, the other private. Influence is acquired publicly by winning a battle, taking possession of a territory, fulfilling the duties of an embassy with care and prudence, or by giving wise counsel attended by a happy result. Private methods are conferring benefits upon individuals, defending them against the magistrates, supporting them with money, and raising them to undeserved honors; or with public games and entertainments gaining the affection of the populace. This mode of procedure produces parties and cliques; and in proportion as influence thus acquired is injurious, so is the former beneficial, if quite free from party spirit; because it is founded upon the public good, and not upon private advantage. And though it is impossible to prevent the existence of inveterate feuds, still if they be without partisans to support them for their own individual benefit, they do not injure a republic, but contribute to its welfare; since none can attain distinction, but as he contributes to her good, and each party prevents the other from infringing her liberties. The dissensions of Florence were always accompanied by factions, and were therefore always pernicious; and the dominant party only remained united so long as its enemies held it in check. As soon as the strength of the opposition was annihilated, the government, deprived of the restraining influence of its adversaries, and being subject to no law, fell to pieces. The party of Cosmo de' Medici gained the ascendant in 1434; but the depressed party being very numerous, and composed of several very influential persons, fear kept the former united, and restrained their proceedings within the bounds of moderation, so that no violence was committed by them, nor anything done calculated to excite popular dislike.

Consequently, whenever this government required the citizens' aid to recover or strengthen its influence, the latter were always willing to gratify its wishes; so that from 1434 to 1455, during a period of twenty-one years, the authority of a balia was granted to it six times.

There were in Florence, as we have frequently observed, two principally powerful citizens, Cosmo de' Medici and Neri Capponi. Neri acquired his influence by public services; so that he had many friends but few partisans. Cosmo, being able to avail himself both of public and private means, had many partisans as well as friends. While both lived, having always been united, they obtained from the people whatever they required; for in them popularity and power were united. But in the year 1455, Neri being dead, and the opposition party extinct, the government found a difficulty in resuming its authority; and this was occasioned, remarkably enough, by Cosmo's private friends, and the most influential men in the state; for, not fearing the opposite party, they became anxious to abate his power. This inconsistency was the beginning of the evils which took place in 1456; so that those in power were openly advised in the deliberative councils not to renew the power of the balia, but to close the balloting purses, and appoint the magistrates by drawing from the pollings or squittini previously made. To restrain this disposition, Cosmo had the choice of two alternatives, either forcibly to assume the government, with the partisans he possessed, and drive out the others, or to allow the matter to take its course, and let his friends see they were not depriving him of power, but rather themselves. He chose the latter; for he well knew that at all events the purses being filled with the names of his own friends, he incurred no risk, and could take the government into his own hands whenever he found occasion. The chief offices of state being again filled by lot, the mass of the people began to think they had recovered their liberty, and that the decisions of the magistrates were according to their own judgments, unbiased by the influence of the Great. At the same time, the friends of different grandees were humbled; and many who had commonly seen their houses filled with suitors and presents, found themselves destitute of both. Those who had previously been very powerful were reduced to an equality with men whom they had been accustomed to consider inferior; and those formerly far beneath them were now become their equals. No respect or deference was paid to them; they were often ridiculed and derided, and frequently heard themselves and the republic mentioned in the open streets without the least deference; thus they found it was not Cosmo but themselves that had lost the government. Cosmo appeared not to notice these matters; and whenever any subject was proposed in favor of the people he was the first to support it. But the greatest cause of alarm to the higher classes, and his most favorable opportunity of retaliation, was the revival of the catasto, or property-tax of 1427, so that individual contributions were determined by statute, and not by a set of persons appointed for its regulation.

This law being re-established, and a magistracy created to carry it into effect, the nobility assembled, and went to Cosmo to beg he would rescue them and himself from the power of the plebeians, and restore to the government the reputation which had made himself powerful and them respected. He replied, he was willing to comply with their request, but wished the law to be obtained in the regular manner, by consent of the people, and not by force, of which he would not hear on any account. They then endeavored in the councils to establish a new balia, but did not succeed. On this the grandees again came to Cosmo, and most humbly begged he would assemble the people in a general council or parliament, but this he refused, for he wished to make them sensible of their great mistake; and when Donato Cocchi, being Gonfalonier of Justice, proposed to assemble them without his consent, the Signors who were of Cosmo's party ridiculed the idea so unmercifully, that the man's mind actually became deranged, and he had to retire from office in consequence. However, since it is undesirable to allow matters to proceed beyond recovery, the Gonfalon of Justice being in the hands of Luca Pitti, a bold-spirited man, Cosmo determined to let him adopt what course he thought proper, that if any trouble should arise it might be imputed to Luca and not to himself. Luca, therefore, in the beginning of his magistracy, several times proposed to the people the appointment of a new balia; and, not succeeding, he threatened the members of the councils with injurious and arrogant expressions, which were shortly followed by corresponding conduct; for in the month of August, 1458, on the eve of Saint Lorenzo, having filled the piazza, and compelled them to assent to a measure to which he knew them to be averse. Having recovered power, created a new balia, and filled the principal offices according to the pleasure of a few individuals, in order to commence that government with terror which they had obtained by force, they banished Girolamo Machiavelli, with some others, and deprived many of the honors of government. Girolamo, having transgressed the confines to which he was limited, was declared a rebel. Traveling about Italy, with the design of exciting the princes against his country, he was betrayed while at Lunigiana, and, being brought to Florence, was put to death in prison.

This government, during the eight years it continued, was violent and insupportable; for Cosmo, being now old, and through ill health unable to attend to public affairs as formerly, Florence became a prey to a small number of her own citizens. Luca Pitti, in return for the services he had performed for the republic, as made a knight, and to be no less grateful than those who had conferred the dignity upon him, he ordered that the priors, who had hitherto been called priors of the trades, should also have a name to which they had no kind of claim, and therefore called them priors of liberty. He also ordered, that as it had been customary for the gonfalonier to sit upon the right hand of the rectors, he should in future take his seat in the midst of them. And that the Deity might appear to participate in what had been done, public processions were made and solemn services performed, to thank him for the recovery of the government. The Signory and Cosmo made Luca Pitti rich presents, and all the citizens were emulous in imitation of them; so that the money given amounted to no less a sum than twenty thousand ducats. He thus attained such influence, that not Cosmo but himself now governed the city; and his pride so increased, that he commenced two superb buildings, one in Florence, the other at Ruciano, about a mile distant, both in a style of royal magnificence; that in the city, being larger than any hitherto built by a private person. To complete them, he had recourse to the most extraordinary means; for not only citizens and private individuals made him presents and supplied materials, but the mass of people, of every grade, also contributed. Besides this, any exiles who had committed murders, thefts, or other crimes which made them amenable to the laws, found a safe refuge within their walls, if they were able to contribute toward their decoration or completion. The other citizens, though they did not build like him, were no less violent or rapacious, so that if Florence were not harassed by external wars, she was ruined by the wickedness of her own children. During this period the wars of Naples took place. The pope also commenced hostilities in Romagna against the Malatesti, from whom he wished to take Rimino and Cesena, held by them. In these designs, and his intentions of a crusade against the Turks, was passed the pontificate of Pius II.

Florence continued in disunion and disturbance. The dissensions continued among the party of Cosmo, in 1455, from the causes already related, which by his prudence, as we have also before remarked, he was enabled to tranquilize; but in the year 1464, his illness increased, and he died. Friends and enemies alike grieved for his loss; for his political opponents, perceiving the rapacity of the citizens, even during the life of him who alone restrained them and made their tyranny supportable, were afraid, lest after his decease, nothing but ruin would ensue. Nor had they much hope of his son Piero, who though a very good man, was of infirm health, and new in the government, and they thought he would be compelled to give way; so that, being unrestrained, their rapacity would pass all bounds. On these accounts, the regret was universal. Of all who have left memorials behind them, and who were not of the military profession, Cosmo was the most illustrious and the most renowned. He not only surpassed all his contemporaries in wealth and authority, but also in generosity and prudence; and among the qualities which contributed to make him prince in his own country, was his surpassing all others in magnificence and generosity. His liberality became more obvious after his death, when Piero, his son, wishing to know what he possessed, it appeared there was no citizen of any consequence to whom Cosmo had not lent a large sum of money; and often, when informed of some nobleman being in distress, he relieved him unasked. His magnificence is evident from the number of public edifices he erected; for in Florence are the convents and churches of St. Marco and St. Lorenzo, and the monastery of Santa Verdiana; in the mountains of Fiesole, the church and abbey of St. Girolamo; and in the Mugello, he not only restored, but rebuilt from its foundation, a monastery of the Frati Minori, or Minims. Besides these, in the church of Santa Croce, the Servi, the Agnoli, and in San Miniato, he erected splendid chapels and altars; and besides building the churches and chapels we have mentioned, he provided them with all the ornaments, furniture, and utensils suitable for the performance of divine service. To these sacred edifices are to be added his private dwellings, one in Florence, of extent and elegance adapted to so great a citizen, and four others, situated at Careggi, Fiesole, Craggiulo, and Trebbio, each, for size and grandeur, equal to royal palaces. And, as if it were not sufficient to be distinguished for magnificence of buildings in Italy alone, he erected an hospital at Jerusalem, for the reception of poor and infirm pilgrims. Although his habitations, like all his other works and actions, were quite of a regal character, and he alone was prince in Florence, still everything was so tempered with his prudence, that he never transgressed the decent moderation of civil life; in his conversation, his servants, his traveling, his mode of living, and the relationships he formed, the modest demeanor of the citizen was always evident; for he was aware that a constant exhibition of pomp brings more envy upon its possessor than greater realities borne without ostentation. Thus in selecting consorts for his sons, he did not seek the alliance of princes, but for Giovanni chose Corneglia degli Allesandri, and for Piero, Lucrezia de' Tornabuoni. He gave his granddaughters, the children of Piero, Bianca to Guglielmo de' Pazzi, and Nannina to Bernardo Ruccellai. No one of his time possessed such an intimate knowledge of government and state affairs as himself; and hence amid such a variety of fortune, in a city so given to change, and among a people of such extreme inconstancy, he retained possession of the government thirty-one years; for being endowed with the utmost prudence, he foresaw evils at a distance, and therefore had an opportunity either of averting them, or preventing their injurious results. He thus not only vanquished domestic and civil ambition, but humbled the pride of many princes with so much fidelity and address, that whatever powers were in league with himself and his country, either overcame their adversaries, or remained uninjured by his alliance; and whoever were opposed to him, lost either their time, money, or territory. Of this the Venetians afford a sufficient proof, who, while in league with him against Duke Filippo were always victorious, but apart from him were always conquered; first by Filippo and then by Francesco. When they joined Alfonso against the Florentine republic, Cosmo, by his commercial credit, so drained Naples and Venice of money, that they were glad to obtain peace upon any terms it was thought proper to grant. Whatever difficulties he had to contend with, whether within the city or without, he brought to a happy issue, at once glorious to himself and destructive to his enemies; so that civil discord strengthened his government in Florence, and war increased his power and reputation abroad. He added to the Florentine dominions, the Borgo of St. Sepolcro, Montedoglio, the Casentino and Val di Bagno. His virtue and good fortune overcame all his enemies and exalted his friends. He was born in the year 1389, on the day of the saints Cosmo and Damiano. His earlier years were full of trouble, as his exile, captivity, and personal danger fully testify; and having gone to the council of Constance, with Pope John, in order to save his life, after the ruin of the latter, he was obliged to escape in disguise. But after the age of forty, he enjoyed the greatest felicity; and not only those who assisted him in public business, but his agents who conducted his commercial speculations throughout Europe, participated in his prosperity. Hence many enormous fortunes took their origin in different families of Florence, as in that of the Tornabuoni, the Benci, the Portinari, and the Sassetti. Besides these, all who depended upon his advice and patronage became rich; and, though he was constantly expending money in building churches, and in charitable purposes, he sometimes complained to his friends that he had never been able to lay out so much in the service of God as to find the balance in his own favor, intimating that all he had done or could do, was still unequal to what the Almighty had done for him. He was of middle stature, olive complexion, and venerable aspect; not learned but exceedingly eloquent, endowed with great natural capacity, generous to his friends, kind to the poor, comprehensive in discourse, cautious in advising, and in his speeches and replies, grave and witty. When Rinaldo degli Albizzi, at the beginning of his exile, sent to him to say, "the hen had laid," he replied, "she did ill to lay so far from the nest." Some other of the rebels gave him to understand they were "not dreaming." He said, "he believed it, for he had robbed them of their sleep." When Pope Pius was endeavoring to induce the different governments to join in an expedition against the Turks, he said, "he was an old man, and had undertaken the enterprise of a young one." To the Venetians ambassadors, who came to Florence with those of King Alfonso to complain of the republic, he uncovered his head, and asked them what color it was; they said, "white;" he replied, "it is so; and it will not be long before your senators have heads as white as mine." A few hours before his death, his wife asked him why he kept his eyes shut, and he said, "to get them in the way of it." Some citizens saying to him, after his return from exile, that he injured the city, and that it was offensive to God to drive so many religious persons out of it; he replied that, "it was better to injure the city, than to ruin it; that two yards of rose-colored cloth would make a gentleman, and that it required something more to direct a government than to play with a string of beads." These words gave occasion to his enemies to slander him, as a man who loved himself more than his country, and was more attached to this world than to the next. Many others of his sayings might be adduced, but we shall omit them as unnecessary. Cosmo was a friend and patron of learned men. He brought Argiripolo, a Greek by birth, and one of the most erudite of his time, to Florence, to instruct the youth in Hellenic literature. He entertained Marsilio Ficino, the reviver of the Platonic philosophy, in his own house; and being much attached to him, have him a residence near his palace at Careggi, that he might pursue the study of letters with greater convenience, and himself have an opportunity of enjoying his company. His prudence, his great wealth, the uses to which he applied it, and his splendid style of living, caused him to be beloved and respected in Florence, and obtained for him the highest consideration, not only among the princes and governments of Italy, but throughout all Europe. He thus laid a foundation for his descendants, which enabled them to equal him in virtue, and greatly surpass him in fortune; while the authority they possessed in Florence and throughout Christendom was not obtained without being merited. Toward the close of his life he suffered great affliction; for, of his two sons, Piero and Giovanni, the latter, of whom he entertained the greatest hopes, died; and the former was so sickly as to be unable to attend either to public or private business. On being carried from one apartment to another, after Giovanni's death, he remarked to his attendants, with a sigh, "This is too large a house for so small a family." His great mind also felt distressed at the idea that he had not extended the Florentine dominions by any valuable acquisition; and he regretted it the more, from imagining he had been deceived by Francesco Sforza, who, while count, had promised, that if he became lord of Milan, he would undertake the conquest of Lucca for the Florentines, a design, however, that was never realized; for the count's ideas changed upon his becoming duke; he resolved to enjoy in peace, the power he had acquired by war, and would not again encounter its fatigues and dangers, unless the welfare of his own dominions required it. This was a source of much annoyance to Cosmo, who felt he had incurred great expense and trouble for an ungrateful and perfidious friend. His bodily infirmities prevented him from attending either to public or private affairs, as he had been accustomed, and he consequently witnessed both going to decay; for Florence was ruined by her own citizens, and his fortune by his agents and children. He died, however, at the zenith of his glory and in the enjoyment of the highest renown. The city, and all the Christian princes, condoled with his son Piero for his loss. His funeral was conducted with the utmost pomp and solemnity, the whole city following his corpse to the tomb in the church of St.

Lorenzo, on which, by public decree, he was inscribed, "FATHER OF HIS COUNTRY." If, in speaking of Cosmo's actions, I have rather imitated the biographies of princes than general history, it need not occasion wonder; for of so extraordinary an individual I was compelled to speak with unusual praise.

CHAPTER II

The duke of Milan becomes lord of Genoa--The king of Naples and the duke of Milan endeavor to secure their dominions to their heirs--Jacopo Piccinino honorably received at Milan, and shortly afterward murdered at Naples--Fruitless endeavors of Pius II. to excite Christendom against the Turks--Death of Francesco Sforza, duke of Milan--Perfidious counsel given to Piero de' Medici by Diotisalvi Neroni--Conspiracy of Diotisalvi and others against Piero--Futile attempts to appease the disorders--Public spectacles--Projects of the conspirators against Piero de' Medici--Niccolo Fedini discloses to Piero the plots of his enemies.

While Florence and Italy were in this condition, Louis XI. of France was involved in very serious troubles with his barons, who, with the assistance of Francis, duke of Brittany, and Charles, duke of Burgundy, were in arms against him. This attack was so serious, that he was unable to render further assistance to John of Anjou in his enterprise against Genoa and Naples; and, standing in need of all the forces he could raise, he gave over Savona (which still remained in the power of the French) to the duke of Milan, and also intimated, that if he wished, he had his permission to undertake the conquest of Genoa. Francesco accepted the proposal, and with the influence afforded by the king's friendship, and the assistance of the Adorni, he became lord of Genoa. In acknowledgment of this benefit, he sent fifteen hundred horse into France for the king's service, under the command of Galeazzo, his eldest son. Thus Ferrando of Aragon and Francesco Sforza became, the latter, duke of Lombardy and prince of Genoa, and the former, sovereign of the whole kingdom of Naples. Their families being allied by marriage, they thought they might so confirm their power as to secure to themselves its enjoyment during life, and at their deaths, its unencumbered reversion to their heirs. To attain this end, they considered it necessary that the king should remove all ground of apprehension from those barons who had offended him in the war of John of Anjou, and that the duke should extirpate the adherents of the Bracceschi, the natural enemies of his family, who, under Jacopo Piccinino, had attained the highest reputation. The latter was now the first general in Italy, and possessing no territory, he naturally excited the apprehension of all who had dominions, and especially of the duke, who, conscious of what he had himself done, thought he could neither enjoy his own estate in safety, nor leave them with any degree of security to his son during Jacopo's lifetime. The king, therefore, strenuously endeavored to come to terms with his barons, and using his utmost ingenuity to secure them, succeeded in his object; for they perceived their ruin to be inevitable if they continued in war with their sovereign, though from submission and confidence in him, they would still have reason for apprehension. Mankind are always most eager to avoid a certain evil; and hence inferior powers are easily deceived by princes. The barons, conscious of the danger of continuing the war, trusted the king's promises, and having placed themselves in his hands, they were soon after destroyed in various ways, and under a variety of pretexts. This alarmed Jacopo Piccinino, who was with his forces at Sulmona; and to deprive the king of the opportunity of treating him similarly, he endeavored, by the mediation of his friends, to be reconciled with the duke, who, by the most liberal offers, induced Jacopo to visit him at Milan, accompanied by only a hundred horse.

Jacopo had served many years with his father and brother, first under Duke Filippo, and afterward under the Milanese republic, so that by frequent intercourse with the citizens he had acquired many friends and universal popularity, which present circumstances tended to increase; for the prosperity and newly acquired power of the Sforzeschi had occasioned envy, while Jacopo's misfortunes and long absence had given rise to compassion and a great desire to see him. These various feelings were displayed upon his arrival; for nearly all the nobility went to meet him; the streets through which he passed were filled with citizens, anxious to catch a glimpse of him, while shouts of "The Bracceschi! the Bracceschi!" resounded on all sides. These honors accelerated his ruin; for the duke's apprehensions increased his desire of destroying him; and to effect this with the least possible suspicion, Jacopo's marriage with Drusiana, the duke's natural daughter, was now celebrated. The duke then arranged with Ferrando to take him into pay, with the title of captain of his forces, and give him 100,000 florins for his maintenance. After this agreement, Jacopo, accompanied by a ducal ambassador and his wife Drusiana, proceeded to Naples, where he was honorably and joyfully received, and for many days entertained with every kind of festivity; but having asked permission to go to Sulmona, where his forces were, the king invited him to a banquet in the castle, at the conclusion of which he and his son Francesco were imprisoned, and shortly afterward put to death. It was thus our Italian princes, fearing those virtues in others which they themselves did not possess, extirpated them; and hence the country became a prey to the efforts of those by whom it was not long afterward oppressed and ruined.

At this time, Pope Pius II. having settled the affairs of Romagna, and witnessing a universal peace, thought it a suitable opportunity to lead the Christians against the Turks, and adopted measures similar to those which his predecessors had used. All the princes promised assistance either in men or money; while Matthias, king of Hungary, and Charles, duke of Burgundy, intimated their intention of joining the enterprise in person, and were by the pope appointed leaders of the expedition. The pontiff was so full of expectation, that he left Rome and proceeded to Ancona, where it had been arranged that the whole army should be assembled, and the Venetians engaged to send ships thither to convey the forces to Sclavonia. Upon the arrival of the pope in that city, there was soon such a concourse of people, that in a few days all the provisions it contained, or that could be procured from the neighborhood, were consumed, and famine began to impend. Besides this, there was no money to provide those who were in want of it, nor arms to furnish such as were without them. Neither Matthias nor Charles made their appearance. The Venetians sent a captain with some galleys, but rather for ostentation and the sake of keeping their word, than for the purpose of conveying troops. During this position of affairs, the pope, being old and infirm, died, and the assembled troops returned to their homes. The death of the pontiff occurred in 1465, and Paul II. of Venetian origin, was chosen to succeed him; and that nearly all the principalities of Italy might change their rulers about the same period, in the following year Francesco Sforza, duke of Milan, also died, having occupied the dukedom sixteen years, and Galleazzo, his son, succeeded him.

The death of this prince infused redoubled energy into the Florentine dissensions, and caused them to produce more prompt effects than they would otherwise have done. Upon the demise of Cosmo, his son Piero, being heir to the wealth and government of his father, called to his assistance Diotisalvi Neroni, a man of great influence and the highest reputation, in whom Cosmo reposed so much confidence that just before his death he recommended Piero to be wholly guided by him, both with regard to the government of the city and the management of his fortune. Piero acquired Diotisalvi with the opinion Cosmo entertained of him, and said that as he wished to obey his father, though now no more, as he always had while alive, he should consult him concerning both his patrimony and the city. Beginning with his private affairs, he caused an account of all his property, liabilities, and assets, to be placed in Diotisalvi's hands, that, with an entire acquaintance with the state of his affairs, he might be able to afford suitable advice, and the latter promised to use the utmost care. Upon examination of these accounts the affairs were found to be in great disorder, and Diotisalvi, instigated rather by his own ambition than by attachment to Piero or gratitude to Cosmo, thought he might without difficulty deprive him of both the reputation and the splendor which his father had left him as his inheritance. In order to realize his views, he waited upon Piero, and advised him to adopt a measure which, while it appeared quite correct in itself, and suitable to existing circumstances, involved a consequence destructive to his authority. He explained the disorder of his affairs, and the large amount of money it would be necessary to provide, if he wished to preserve his influence in the state and his reputation of wealth; and said there was no other means of remedying these disorders so just and available as to call in the sums which his father had lent to an infinite number of persons, both foreigners and citizens; for Cosmo, to acquire partisans in Florence and friends abroad, was extremely liberal of his money, and the amount of loans due to him was enormous. Piero thought the advice good, because he was only desirous to repossess his own property to meet the demands to which he was liable; but as soon as he had ordered those amounts to be recalled, the citizens, as if he had asked for something to which he had no kind of claim, took great offense, loaded him with opprobrious expressions, and accused him of being avaricious and ungrateful.

Diotisalvi, noticing the popular excitement against Piero, occasioned by his own advice, obtained an interview with Luca Pitti, Agnolo Acciajuoli, and Niccolo

Soderini, and they resolved to unite their efforts to deprive him both of the government and his influence. Each was actuated by a different motive; Luca Pitti wished to take the position Cosmo had occupied, for he was now become so great, that he disdained to submit to Piero; Diotisalvi Neroni, who knew Luca unfit to be at the head of a government, thought that of necessity on Piero's removal, the whole authority of the state would devolve upon himself; Niccolo Soderini desired the city to enjoy greater liberty, and for the laws to be equally binding upon all. Agnolo Acciajuoli was greatly incensed against the Medici, for the following reasons: his son, Raffaello, had some time before married Alessandra de' Bardi, and received with her a large dowry. She, either by her own fault or the misconduct of others, suffered much ill-treatment both from her father-in-law and her husband, and in consequence Lorenzo d' Ilarione, her kinsman, out of pity for the girl, being accompanied by several armed men, took her away from Agnolo's house. The Acciajuoli complained of the injury done them by the Bardi, and the matter was referred to Cosmo, who decided that the Acciajuoli should restore to Alessandra her fortune, and then leave it to her choice either to return to her husband or not. Agnolo thought Cosmo had not, in this instance, treated him as a friend; and having been unable to avenge himself on the father, he now resolved to do his utmost to ruin the son. These conspirators, though each was influenced by a different motive from the rest, affected to have only one object in view, which was that the city should be governed by the magistrates, and not be subjected to the counsels of a few individuals. The odium against Piero, and opportunities of injuring him, were increased by the number of merchants who failed about this time; for it was reported that he, in having, quite unexpectedly to all, resolved to call in his debts, had, to the disgrace and ruin of the city, caused them to become insolvent. To this was added his endeavor to obtain Clarice degli Orsini as wife of Lorenzo, his eldest son; and hence his enemies took occasion to say, it was quite clear, that as he despised a Florentine alliance, he no longer considered himself one of the people, and was preparing to make himself prince; for he who refuses his fellow-citizens as relatives, desires to make them slaves, and therefore cannot expect to have them as friends. The leaders of the sedition thought they had the victory in their power; for the greater part of the citizens followed them, deceived by the name of liberty which they, to give their purpose a graceful covering, adopted upon their ensigns.

In this agitated state of the city, some, to whom civil discord was extremely offensive, thought it would be well to endeavor to engage men's minds with some new occupation, because when unemployed they are commonly led by whoever chooses to excite them. To divert their attention from matters of government, it being now a year since the death of Cosmo, it was resolved to celebrate two festivals, similar to the most solemn observed in the city. At one of them was represented the arrival of the three kings from the east, led by the star which announced the nativity of Christ; which was conducted with such pomp and magnificence, that the preparations for it kept the whole city occupied many months. The other was a tournament (for so they call the exhibition of equestrian combats), in which the sons of the first families in the city took part with the most celebrated cavaliers of Italy. Among the most distinguished of the Florentine youth was Lorenzo, eldest son of Piero, who, not by favor, but by his own personal valor, obtained the principal prize. When these festivals were over, the citizens reverted to the same thoughts which had previously occupied them, and each pursued his ideas with more earnestness than ever. Serious differences and troubles were the result; and these were greatly increased by two circumstances: one of which was, that the authority of the balia had expired; the other, that upon the death of Duke Francesco, Galeazzo the new duke sent ambassadors to Florence, to renew the engagements of his father with the city, which, among other things, provided that every year a certain sum of money should be paid to the duke. The principal opponents of the Medici took occasion, from this demand, to make public resistance in the councils, on pretense that the alliance was made with Francesco and not Galeazzo; so that Francesco being dead, the obligation had ceased; nor was there any necessity to revive it, because Galeazzo did not possess his father's talents, and consequently they neither could nor ought to expect the same benefits from him; that if they had derived little advantage from Francesco, they would obtain still less from Galeazzo; and that if any citizen wished to hire him for his own purposes, it was contrary to civil rule, and inconsistent with the public liberty. Piero, on the contrary, argued that it would be very impolitic to lose such an alliance from mere avarice, and that there was nothing so important to the republic, and to the whole of Italy, as their alliance with the duke; that the Venetians, while they were united, could not hope either by feigned friendship or open war to injure the duchy; but as soon as they perceived the Florentines alienated from him they would prepare for hostilities, and, finding him young, new in the government, and without friends, they would, either by force or fraud, compel him to join them; in which case ruin of the republic would be inevitable.

The arguments of Piero were without effect, and the animosity of the parties began to be openly manifested in their nocturnal assemblies; the friends of the Medici meeting in the Crocetta, and their adversaries in the Pieta. The latter being anxious for Piero's ruin, had induced many citizens to subscribe their names as favorable to the undertaking. Upon one occasion, particularly when considering the course to be adopted, although all agreed that the power of the Medici ought to be reduced, different opinions were given concerning the means by which it should be effected; one party, the most temperate and reasonable, held that as the authority of the balia had ceased, they must take care to prevent its renewal; it would then be found to be the universal wish that the magistrates and councils should govern the city, and in a short time Piero's power would be visibly diminished, and, as a consequence of his loss of influence in the government, his commercial credit would also fail; for his affairs were in such a state, that if they could prevent him from using the public money his ruin must ensue. They would thus be in no further danger from him, and would succeed in the recovery of their liberty, without the death or exile of any individual; but if they attempted violence they would incur great dangers; for mankind are willing to allow one who falls of himself to meet his fate, but if pushed down they would hasten to his relief; so that if they adopted no extraordinary measures against him, he will have no reason for defense or aid; and if he were to seek them it would be greatly to his own injury, by creating such a general suspicion as would accelerate his ruin, and justify whatever course they might think proper to adopt. Many of the assembly were dissatisfied with this tardy method of proceeding; they thought delay would be favorable to him and injurious to themselves; for if they allowed matters to take their ordinary course, Piero would be in no danger whatever, while they themselves would incur many; for the magistrates who were opposed to him would allow him to rule the city, and his friends would make him a prince, and their own ruin would be inevitable, as happened in 1458; and though the advice they had just heard might be most consistent with good feeling, the present would be found to be the safest. That it would therefore be best, while the minds of men were yet excited against him, to effect his destruction.

It must be their plan to arm themselves, and engage the assistance of the marquis of Ferrara, that they might not be destitute of troops; and if a favorable Signory were drawn, they would be in condition to make use of them. They therefore determined to wait the formation of the new Signory, and be governed by circumstances.

Among the conspirators was Niccolo Fedini, who had acted as president of their assemblies. He, being induced by most certain hopes, disclosed the whole affair to Piero, and gave him a list of those who had subscribed their names, and also of the conspirators. Piero was alarmed on discovering the number and quality of those who were opposed to him; and by the advice of his friends he resolved to take the signatures of those who were inclined to favor him. Having employed one of his most trusty confidants to carry his design into effect, he found so great a disposition to change and instability, that many who had previously set down their names among the number of his enemies, now subscribed them in his favor.

CHAPTER III

Niccolo Soderini drawn Gonfalonier of Justice--Great hopes excited in consequence--The two parties take arms--The fears of the Signory--Their conduct with regard to Piero--Piero's reply to the Signory--Reform of government in favor of Piero de' Medici--Dispersion of his enemies--Fall of Lucca Pitti--Letter of Agnolo Acciajuoli to Piero de' Medici--Piero's answer--Designs of the Florentine exiles--They induce the Venetians to make war on Florence.

In the midst of these events, the time arrived for the renewal of the supreme magistracy; and Niccolo Soderini was drawn Gonfalonier of Justice. It was surprising to see by what a concourse, not only of distinguished citizens, but also of the populace, he was accompanied to the palace; and while on the way thither an olive wreath was placed upon his head, to signify that upon him depended the safety and liberty of the city. This, among many similar instances, serves to prove how undesirable it is to enter upon office or power exciting inordinate expectations; for, being unable to fulfil them (many looking for more than it is possible to perform), shame and disappointment are the ordinary results. Tommaso and Niccolo Soderini were brothers. Niccolo was the more ardent and spirited, Tommaso the wiser man; who, being very much the friend of Piero, and knowing that his brother desired nothing but the liberty of the city, and the stability of the republic, without injury to any, advised him to make new Squittini, by which means the election purses might be filled with the names of those favorable to his design. Niccolo took his brother's advice, and thus wasted the period of his magistracy in vain hopes, which his friends, the leading conspirators, allowed him to do from motives of envy; for they were unwilling that the government should be reformed by the authority of Niccolo, and thought they would be in time enough to effect their purpose under another gonfalonier. Thus the magistracy of Niccolo expired; and having commenced many things without completing aught, he retired from office with much less credit than when he had entered upon it.

This circumstance caused the aggrandizement of Piero's party, whose friends entertained stronger hopes, while those who had been neutral or wavering became his adherents; so that both sides being balanced, many months elapsed without any open demonstration of their particular designs. Piero's party continuing to gather strength, his enemies' indignation increased in proportion; and they now determined to effect by force what they either could not accomplish, or were unwilling to attempt by the medium of the magistrates, which was assassination of Piero, who lay sick at Careggi, and to this end order the marquis of Ferrara nearer to the city with his forces, that after Piero's death he might lead them into the piazza, and thus compel the Signory to form a government according to their own wishes; for though all might not be friendly, they trusted they would be able to induce those to submit by fear who might be opposed to them from principle.

Diotisalvi, the better to conceal his design, frequently visited Piero, conversed with him respecting the union of the city, and advised him to effect it. The conspirators' designs had already been fully disclosed to Piero; besides this, Domenico Martelli had informed him, that Francesco Neroni, the brother of Diotisalvi, had endeavored to induce him to join them, assuring him the victory was certain, and their object all but attained. Upon this, Piero resolved to take advantage of his enemies' tampering with the marquis of Ferrara, and be first in arms. He therefore intimated that he had received a letter from Giovanni Bentivogli, prince of Bologna, which informed him that the marquis of Ferrara was upon the river Albo, at the head of a considerable force, with the avowed intention of leading it to Florence; that upon this advice he had taken up arms; after which, in the midst of a strong force, he came to the city, when all who were disposed to support him, armed themselves also. The adverse party did the same, but not in such good order, being unprepared. The residence of Diotisalvi being near that of Piero, he did not think himself safe in it, but first went to the palace and begged the Signory would endeavor to induce Piero to lay down his arms, and thence to Luca Pitti, to keep him faithful in their cause. Niccolo Soderini displayed the most activity; for taking arms, and being followed by nearly all the plebeians in his vicinity, he proceeded to the house of Luca, and begged that he would mount his horse, and come to the piazza in support of the Signory, who were, he said, favorable, and that the victory would, undoubtedly, be on their side; that he should not stay in the house to be basely slain by their armed enemies, or ignominiously deceived by those who were unarmed; for, in that case, he would soon repent of having neglected an opportunity irrecoverably lost; that if he desired the forcible ruin of Piero, he might easily effect it; and that if he were anxious for peace, it would be far better to be in a condition to propose terms than to be compelled to accept any that might be offered. These words produced no effect upon Luca, whose mind was now quite made up; he had been induced to desert his party by new conditions and promises of alliance from Piero; for one of his nieces had been married to Giovanni Tornabuoni. He, therefore, advised Niccolo to dismiss his followers and return home, telling him he ought to be satisfied, if the city were governed by the magistrates, which would certainly be the case, and that all ought to lay aside their weapons; for the Signory, most of whom were friendly, would decide their differences. Niccolo, finding him impracticable, returned home; but before he left, he said, "I can do the city no good alone, but I can easily foresee the evils that will befall her. This resolution of yours will rob our country of her liberty; you will lose the government, I shall lose my property, and the rest will be exiled."

During this disturbance the Signory closed the palace and kept their magistrates about them, without showing favor to either party. The citizens, especially those who had followed Luca Pitti, finding Piero fully prepared and his adversaries unarmed, began to consider, not how they might injure him, but how, with least observation, glide into the ranks of his friends. The principal citizens, the leaders of both factions, assembled in the palace in the presence of the Signory, and spoke respecting the state of the city and the reconciliation of parties; and as the infirmities of Piero prevented him from being present, they, with one exception, unanimously determined to wait upon him at his house. Niccolo Soderini having first placed his children and his effects under the care of his brother Tommaso, withdrew to his villa, there to await the event, but apprehended misfortune to himself and ruin to his country. The other citizens coming into Piero's presence, one of them who had been appointed spokesman, complained of the disturbances that had arisen in the city, and endeavored to show, that those must be most to blame who had been first to take up arms; and not knowing what Piero (who was evidently the first to do so) intended, they had come in order to be informed of his design, and if it had in view the welfare of the city, they were desirous of supporting it. Piero replied, that not those who first take arms are the most to blame, but those who give the first occasion for it, and if they would reflect a little on their mode of proceeding toward himself, they would cease to wonder at what he had done; for they could not fail to perceive, that nocturnal assemblies, the enrollment of partisans, and attempts to deprive him both of his authority and his life, had caused him to take arms; and they might further observe, that as his forces had not quitted his own house, his design was evidently only to defend himself and not to injure others. He neither sought nor desired anything but safety and repose; neither had his conduct ever manifested a desire for ought else; for when the authority of the Balia expired, he never made any attempt to renew it, and was very glad the magistrates had governed the city and had been content. They might also remember that Cosmo and his sons could live respected in Florence, either with the Balia or without it, and that in 1458, it was not his family, but themselves, who had renewed it. That if they did not wish for it at present, neither did he; but this did not satisfy them; for he perceived that they thought it impossible to remain in Florence while he was there. It was entirely beyond all his anticipations that his own or his father's friends should think themselves unsafe with him in Florence, having always shown himself quiet and peaceable. He then addressed himself to Diotisalvi and his brothers, who were present, reminding them with grave indignation, of the benefits they had received from Cosmo, the confidence he had reposed in them and their subsequent ingratitude; and his words so strongly excited some present, that had he not interfered, they would certainly have torn the Neroni to pieces on the spot. He concluded by saying, that he should approve of any determination of themselves and the Signory; and that for his own part, he only desired peace and safety. After this, many things were discussed, but nothing determined, excepting generally, that it was necessary to reform the administration of the city and government.

The Gonfalon of Justice was then in the hands of Bernardo Lotti, a man not in the confidence of Piero, who was therefore disinclined to attempt aught while he was in office; but no inconvenience would result from the delay, as his magistracy was on the point of expiring. Upon the election of Signors for the months of September and October, 1466, Roberto Lioni was appointed to the supreme magistracy, and as soon as he assumed its duties, every requisite arrangement having been previously made, the people were called to the piazza, and a new Balia created, wholly in favor of Piero, who soon afterward filled all the offices of government according to his own pleasure. These transactions alarmed the leaders of the opposite faction, and Agnolo Acciajuoli fled to Naples, Diotisalvi Neroni and Niccolo Soderini to Venice. Luca Pitti remained in Florence, trusting to his new relationship and the promises of Piero. The refugees were declared rebels, and all the family of the Neroni were dispersed. Giovanni di Neroni, then archbishop of Florence, to avoid a greater evil, became a voluntary exile at Rome, and to many other citizens who fled, various places of banishment were appointed. Nor was this considered sufficient; for it was ordered that the citizens should go in solemn procession to thank God for the preservation of the government and the reunion of the city, during the performance of which, some were taken and tortured, and part of them afterward put to death and exiled. In this great vicissitude of affairs, there was not a more remarkable instance of the uncertainty of fortune than Luca Pitti, who soon found the difference between victory and defeat, honor and disgrace. His house now presented only a vast solitude, where previously crowds of citizens had assembled. In the streets, his friends and relatives, instead of accompanying, were afraid even to salute him. Some of them were deprived of the honors of government, others of their property, and all alike threatened. The superb edifices he had commenced were abandoned by the builders; the benefits that had been conferred upon him, where now exchanged for injuries, the honors for disgrace. Hence many of those who had presented him with articles of value now demanded them back again, as being only lent; and those who had been in the habit of extolling him as a man of surpassing excellence, now termed him violent and ungrateful. So that, when too late, he regretted not having taken the advice of Niccolo Soderini, and preferred an honorable death in battle, than to a life of ignominy among his victorious enemies.

The exiles now began to consider various means of recovering that citizenship which they had not been able to preserve. However, Agnolo Acciajuoli being at Naples, before he attempted anything else, resolved to sound Piero, and try if he could effect a reconciliation. For this purpose, he wrote to him in the following terms: "I cannot help laughing at the freaks of fortune, perceiving how, at her pleasure, she converts friends into enemies, and enemies into friends. You may remember that during your father's exile, regarding more the injury done to him than my own misfortunes, I was banished, and in danger of death, and never during Cosmo's life failed to honor and support your family; neither have I since his death ever entertained a wish to injure you. True, it is, that your own sickness, and the tender years of your sons, so alarmed me, that I judged it desirable to give such a form to the government, that after your death our country might not be ruined; and hence, the proceedings, which not against you, but for the safety of the state, have been adopted, which, if mistaken, will surely obtain forgiveness, both for the good design in view, and on account of my former services. Neither can I apprehend, that your house, having found me so long faithful, should now prove unmerciful, or that you could cancel the impression of so much merit for so small a fault." Piero replied: "Your laughing in your present abode is the cause why I do not weep, for were you to laugh in Florence, I should have to weep at Naples. I confess you were well disposed toward my father, and you ought to confess you were well paid for it; and the obligation is so much the greater on your part than on ours, as deeds are of greater value than words. Having been recompensed for your good wishes, it ought not to surprise you that you now receive the due reward of your bad ones. Neither will a pretense of your patriotism excuse you, for none will think the city less beloved or benefited by the Medici, than by the Acciajuoli. It, therefore, seems but just, that you should remain in dishonor at Naples, since you knew not how to live with honor at home."

Agnolo, hopeless of obtaining pardon, went to Rome, where, joining the archbishop and other refugees, they used every available means to injure the commercial credit of the Medici in that city. Their attempts greatly annoyed Piero; but by his friends' assistance, he was enabled to render them abortive. Diotisalvi Neroni and Niccolo Soderini strenuously urged the Venetian senate to make war upon their country, calculating, that in case of an attack, the government being new and unpopular, would be unable to resist. At this time there resided at Ferrara, Giovanni Francesco, son of Palla Strozzi, who, with his father, was banished from Florence in the changes of 1434. He possessed great influence, and was considered one of the richest merchants. The newly banished pointed out to Giovanni Francesco how easily they might return to their country, if the Venetians were to undertake the enterprise, and that it was most probable they would do so, if they had pecuniary assistance, but that otherwise it would be doubtful. Giovanni Francesco, wishing to avenge his own injuries, at once fell in with their ideas, and promised to contribute to the success of the attempt all the means in his power. On this they went to the Doge, and complained of the exile they were compelled to endure, for no other reason, they said, than for having wished their country should be subject to equal laws, and that the magistrates should govern, not a few private individuals; that Piero de' Medici, with his adherents, who were accustomed to act tyrannically, had secretly taken up arms, deceitfully induced them to lay their own aside, and thus, by fraud, expelled them from their country; that, not content with this, they made the Almighty himself a means of oppression to several, who, trusting to their promises, had remained in the city and were there betrayed; for, during public worship and solemn supplications, that the Deity might seem to participate in their treachery, many citizens had been seized, imprisoned, tortured, and put to death; thus affording to the world a horrible and impious precedent. To avenge themselves for these injuries, they knew not where to turn with so much hope of success as to the senate, which, having always enjoyed their liberty, ought to compassionate those who had lost it. They therefore called upon them as free men to assist them against tyrants; as pious, against the wicked; and would remind the Venetians, that it was the family of the Medici who had robbed them of their dominions in Lombardy, contrary to the wish of the other citizens, and who, in opposition to the interests of the senate, had favored and supported Francesco, so, that if the exiles' distresses could not induce them to undertake the war, the just indignation of the people of Venice, and their desire of vengeance ought to prevail.

CHAPTER IV

War between the Venetians and the Florentines--Peace re-established--Death of Niccolo Soderini--His character--Excesses in Florence--Various external events from 1468 to 1471--Accession of Sixtus IV.--His character--Grief of Piero de' Medici for the violence committed in Florence--His speech to the principal citizens--Plans of Piero de' Medici for the restoration of order--His death and character--Tommaso Soderini, a citizen of great reputation, declares himself in favor of the Medici--Disturbances at Prato occasioned by Bernardo Nardi.

The concluding words of the Florentine exiles produced the utmost excitement among the Venetian senators, and they resolved to send Bernardo Coglione, their general, to attack the Florentine territory. The troops were assembled, and joined by Ercole da Esti, who had been sent by Borgo, marquis of Ferrara. At the commencement of hostilities, the Florentines not being prepared, their enemies burned the Borgo of Dovadola, and plundered the surrounding country. But having expelled the enemies of Piero, renewed their league with Galeazzo, duke of Milan, and Ferrando, king of Naples, they appointed to the command of their forces Federigo, count of Urbino; and being thus on good terms with their friends, their enemies occasioned them less anxiety. Ferrando sent Alfonso, his eldest son, to their aid, and Galeazzo came in person, each at the head of a suitable force, and all assembled at Castrocaro, a fortress belonging to the Florentines, and situated among the roots of the Appennines which descend from Tuscany to Romagna. In the meantime, the enemy withdrew toward Imola. A few slight skirmishes took place between the armies; yet, in accordance with the custom of the times, neither of them acted on the offensive, besieged any town, or gave the other an opportunity of coming to a general engagement; but each kept within their tents, and conducted themselves with most remarkable cowardice. This occasioned general dissatisfaction among the Florentines; for they found themselves involved in an expensive war, from which no advantage could be derived. The magistrates complained of these spiritless proceedings to those who had been appointed commissaries to the expedition; but they replied, that the entire evil was chargeable upon the Duke Galeazzo, who possessing great authority and little experience, was unable to suggest useful measures, and unwilling to take the advice of those who were more capable; and therefore any demonstration of courage or energy would be impracticable so long as he remained with the army. Hereupon the Florentines intimated to the duke, that his presence with the force was in many ways advantageous and beneficial, and of itself sufficient to alarm the enemy; but they considered his own safety and that of his dominions, much more important than their own immediate convenience; because so long as the former were safe, the Florentines had nothing to fear, and all would go well; but if his dominions were to suffer, they might then apprehend all kinds of misfortune. They assured him they did not think it prudent for him to be absent so long from Milan, having recently succeeded to the government, and being surrounded by many powerful enemies and suspected neighbors; while any who were desirous of plotting against him, had an opportunity of doing so with impunity. They would, therefore, advise him to return to his territories, leaving part of his troops with them for the use of the expedition. This advice pleased Galeazzo, who, in consequence, immediately withdrew to Milan. The Florentine generals being now left without any hindrance, to show that the cause assigned for their inaction was the true one, pressed the enemy more closely, so that they came to a regular engagement, which continued half a day, without either party yielding. Some horses were wounded and prisoners taken, but no death occurred. Winter having arrived, and with it the usual time for armies to retire into quarters, Bartolommeo Coglione withdrew to Ravenna, the Florentine forces into Tuscany, and those of the king and duke, each to the territories of their sovereign. As this attempt had not occasioned any tumult in Florence, contrary to the rebels' expectation, and the troops they had hired were in want of pay, terms of peace were proposed, and easily arranged. The revolted Florentines, thus deprived of hope, dispersed themselves in various places. Diotisalvi Neroni withdrew to Ferrara, where he was received and entertained by the Marquis Borso. Niccolo Soderini went to

Ravenna, where, upon a small pension allowed by the Venetians, he grew old and died. He was considered a just and brave man, but over-cautious and slow to determine, a circumstance which occasioned him, when Gonfalonier of Justice, to lose the opportunity of victory which he would have gladly recovered when too late.

Upon the restoration of peace, those who remained victorious in Florence, as if unable to convince themselves they had conquered, unless they oppressed not merely their enemies, but all whom they suspected, prevailed upon Bardo Altoviti, then Gonfalonier of Justice, to deprive many of the honors of government, and to banish several more. They exercised their power so inconsiderately, and conducted themselves in such an arbitrary manner, that it seemed as if fortune and the Almighty had given the city up to them for a prey. Piero knew little of these things, and was unable to remedy even the little he knew, on account of his infirmities; his body being so contracted that he could use no faculty but that of speech. All he could do was to admonish the leading men, and beg they would conduct themselves with greater moderation, and not by their violence effect their country's ruin. In order to divert the city, he resolved to celebrate the marriage of his son Lorenzo with Clarice degli Orsini with great splendor; and it was accordingly solemnized with all the display suitable to the exalted rank of the parties. Feasts, dancing, and antique representations occupied many days; at the conclusion of which, to exhibit the grandeur of the house of Medici and of the government, two military spectacles were presented, one performed by men on horseback, who went through the evolutions of a field engagement, and the other representing the storming of a town; everything being conducted with admirable order and the greatest imaginable brilliancy.

During these transactions in Florence, the rest of Italy, though at peace, was filled with apprehension of the power of the Turks, who continued to attack the Christians, and had taken Negropont, to the great disgrace and injury of the Christian name. About this time died Borso, marquis of Ferrara, who was succeeded by his brother Ercole. Gismondo da Rimini, the inveterate enemy of the church also expired, and his natural brother Roberto, who was afterward one of the best generals of Italy, succeeded him. Pope Paul died, and was succeeded by Sixtus IV. previously called Francesco da Savona, a man of the very lowest origin, who by his talents had become general of the order of St. Francis, and afterward cardinal. He was the first who began to show how far a pope might go, and how much that which was previously regarded as sinful lost its iniquity when committed by a pontiff. Among others of his family were Piero and Girolamo, who, according to universal belief, were his sons, though he designated them by terms reflecting less scandal on his character. Piero being a priest, was advanced to the dignity of a cardinal, with the title of St. Sixtus. To Girolamo he gave the city of Furli, taken from Antonio Ordelaffi, whose ancestors had held that territory for many generations. This ambitious method of procedure made him more regarded by the princes of Italy, and all sought to obtain his friendship. The duke of Milan gave his natural daughter Caterina to Girolamo, with the city of Imola, which he had taken from Taddeo degli Alidossi, as her portion. New matrimonial alliances were formed between the duke and king Ferrando; Elisabetta, daughter of Alfonso, the king's eldest son, being united to Giovan Galeazzo, the eldest son of the duke.

Italy being at peace, the principal employment of her princes was to watch each other, and strengthen their own influence by new alliances, leagues, or friendships. But in the midst of this repose, Florence endured great oppression from her principal citizens, and the infirmities of Piero incapacitated him from restraining their ambition. However, to relieve his conscience, and, if possible, to make them ashamed of their conduct, he sent for them to his house, and addressed them in the following words: "I never thought a time would come when the behavior of my friends would compel me to esteem and desire the society of my enemies, and wish that I had been defeated rather than victorious; for I believed myself to be associated with those who would set some bounds to their avarice, and who, after having avenged themselves on their enemies, and lived in their country with security and honor, would be satisfied. But now I find myself greatly deceived, unacquainted with the ambition of mankind, and least of all with yours; for, not satisfied with being masters of so great a city, and possessing among yourselves those honors, dignities, and emoluments which used to be divided among many citizens; not contented with having shared among a few the property of your enemies, or with being able to oppress all others with public burdens, while you yourselves are exempt from them, and enjoy all the public offices of profit you must still further load everyone with ill usage. You plunder your neighbors of their wealth; you sell justice; you evade the law; you oppress the timid and exalt the insolent. Nor is there, throughout all Italy, so many and such shocking examples of violence and avarice as in this city. Has our country fostered us only to be her destroyer? Have we been victorious only to effect her ruin? Has she honored us that we may overwhelm her with disgrace? Now, by that faith which is binding upon all good men, I promise you, that if you still conduct yourselves so as to make me regret my victory, I will adopt such measures as shall cause you bitterly to repent of having misused it." The reply of the citizens accorded with the time and circumstances, but they did not forego their evil practices; so that, in consequence, Piero sent for Agnolo Acciajuoli to come secretly to Cafaggiolo, and discussed with him at great length the condition of the city; and doubtless, had he not been prevented by death, he would have called home the exiles as a check upon the rapine of the opposite party. But these honorable designs were frustrated; for, sinking under bodily infirmities and mental anguish, he expired in the fifty-third year of his age. His goodness and virtue were not duly appreciated by his country, principally from his having, until almost the close of his life, been associated with Cosmo, and the few years he survived being spent in civil discord and constant debility. Piero was buried in the church of St. Lorenzo, near his father, and his obsequies were performed with all the pomp and solemnity due to his exalted station. He left two sons, Lorenzo and Guiliano, whose extreme youth excited alarm in the minds of thinking men, though each gave hopes of future usefulness to the republic.

Among the principal citizens in the government of Florence, and very superior to the rest, was Tommaso Soderini, whose prudence and authority were well known not only at home, but throughout Italy. After Piero's death, the whole city looked up to him; many citizens waited upon him at his own house, as the head of the government, and several princes addressed him by letter; but he, impartially estimating his own fortune and that of the house of Medici, made no reply to the princes' communications, and told the citizens, it was not his house, but that of the Medici they ought to visit. To demonstrate by his actions the sincerity and integrity of his advice he assembled all the heads of noble families in the convent of St. Antonio, whither he also brought Lorenzo and Guiliano de' Medici, and in a long and serious speech upon the state of the city, the condition of Italy, and the views of her princes, he assured them, that if they wished to live in peace and unity in Florence, free both from internal dissensions and foreign wars, it would be necessary to respect the sons of Piero and support the reputation of their house; for men never regret their continuance in a course sanctioned by custom while new methods are soon adopted and as speedily set aside; and it has always been found easier to maintain a power which by its continuance has outlived envy, than to raise a new one, which innumerable unforeseen causes may overthrow. When Tommaso had concluded, Lorenzo spoke, and, though young, with such modesty and discretion that all present felt a presentiment of his becoming what he afterward proved to be; and before the citizens departed they swore to regard the youths as their sons, and the brothers promised to look upon them as their parents. After this, Lorenzo and Guiliano were honored as princes, and resolved to be guided by the advice of Tommaso Soderini.

While profound tranquillity prevailed both at home and abroad, no wars disturbing the general repose, there arose an unexpected disturbance, which came like a presage of future evils. Among the ruined families of the party of Luca Pitti, was that of the Nardi; for Salvestro and his brothers, the heads of the house, were banished and afterward declared rebels for having taken part in the war under Bartolommeo Coglione. Bernardo, the brother of Salvestro, was young, prompt, and bold, and on account of his poverty being unable to alleviate the sorrows of exile, while the peace extinguished all hopes of his return to the city, he determined to attempt some means of rekindling the war; for a trifling commencement often produces great results, and men more readily prosecute what is already begun than originate new enterprises. Bernardo had many acquaintances at Prato, and still more in the district of Pistoia, particularly among the Palandra, a family which, though rustic, was very numerous, and, like the rest of the Pistolesi, brought up to slaughter and war. These he knew to be discontented, on account of the Florentine magistrates having endeavored, perhaps too severely, to check their partiality for inveterate feuds and consequence bloodshed. He was also aware that the people of Prato considered themselves injured by the pride and avarice of their governors, and that some were ill disposed toward Florence; therefore all things considered, he hoped to be able to kindle a fire in Tuscany (should Prato rebel) which would be fostered by so many, that those who might wish to extinguish it would fail in the attempt. He communicated his ideas to Diotisalvi Neroni, and asked him, in case they should succeed in taking possession of Prato, what assistance might be expected from the princes of Italy, by his means? Diotisalvi considered the enterprise as imminently dangerous, and almost impracticable; but since it presented a fresh chance of attaining his object, at the risk of others, he advised him to proceed, and promised certain assistance from Bologna and Ferrara, if he could retain Prato not less than fifteen days. Bernardo, whom this promise inspired with a lively hope of success, proceeded secretly to Prato, and communicated with those most disposed to favor him, among whom were the Palandra; and having arranged the time and plan, informed Diotisalvi of what had been done.

CHAPTER V

Bernardo takes possession of Prato, but is not assisted by the inhabitants--He is taken, and the tumult appeased--Corruption of Florence--The duke of Milan in Florence--The church of Santo Spirito destroyed by fire--The rebellion of Volterra, and the cause of it--Volterra reduced to obedience by force, in accordance with the advice of Lorenzo de' Medici--Volterra pillaged.

Cesare Petrucci held the office of Provost of Prato for the Florentine people, at this period. It is customary with governors of towns, similarly situated, to keep the keys of the gates near their persons; and whenever, in peaceful times, they are required by any of the inhabitants, for entrance or exit, they are usually allowed to be taken. Bernardo was aware of this custom, and about daybreak, presented himself at the gate which looks toward Pistoia, accompanied by the Palandra and about one hundred persons, all armed. Their confederates within the town also armed themselves, and one of them asked the governor for the keys, alleging, as a pretext, that some one from the country wished to enter. The governor not entertaining the slightest suspicion, sent a servant with them. When at a convenient distance, they were taken by the conspirators, who, opening the gates, introduced Bernardo and his followers. They divided themselves into two parties, one of which, led by Salvestro, an inhabitant of Prato, took possession of the citadel; the other following Bernardo, seized the palace, and placed Cesare with all his family in the custody of some of their number. They then raised the cry of liberty, and proceeded through the town. It was now day, and many of the inhabitants hearing the disturbance, ran to the piazza where, learning that the fortress and the palace were taken and the governor with all his people made prisoners, they were utterly astonished, and could not imagine how it had occurred. The eight citizens, possessing the supreme authority, assembled in their palace to consider what was best to be done. In the meantime, Bernardo and his followers, on going round the town, found no encouragement, and being told that the Eight had assembled, went and declared the nature of their enterprise, which he said was to deliver the country from slavery, reminding them how glorious it would be for those who took arms to effect such an honorable object, for they would thus obtain permanent repose and everlasting fame. He called to recollection their ancient liberty and present condition, and assured them of certain assistance, if they would only, for a few days, aid in resisting the forces the Florentines might send against them. He said he had friends in Florence who would join them as soon as they found the inhabitants resolved to support him. His speech did not produce the desired effect upon the Eight, who replied that they knew not whether Florence was free or enslaved, for that was a matter which they were not called upon to decide; but this they knew very well, that for their own part, they desired no other liberty than to obey the magistrates who governed Florence, from whom they had never received any injury sufficient to make them desire a change. They therefore advised him to set the governor at liberty, clear the place of his people, and, as quickly as possible, withdraw from the danger he had so rashly incurred. Bernardo was not daunted by these words, but determined to try whether fear could influence the people of Prato, since entreaties produced so little effect. In order to terrify them, he determined to put Cesare to death, and having brought him out of prison, ordered him to be hanged at the windows of the palace. He was already led to the spot with a halter around his neck, when seeing Bernardo giving directions to hasten his end, he turned to him, and said: "Bernardo, you put me to death, thinking that the people of Prato will follow you; but the direct contrary will result; for the respect they have for the rectors which the Florentine people send here is so great, that as soon as they witness the injury inflicted upon me, they will conceive such a disgust against you as will inevitably effect your ruin. Therefore, it is not by my death, but by the preservation of my life, that you can attain the object you have in view; for if I deliver your commands, they will be much more readily obeyed, and following your directions, we shall soon attain the completion of your design." Bernardo, whose mind was not fertile in expedients, thought the advice good, and commanded Cesare, on being conducted to a veranda which looked upon the piazza, to order the people of Prato to obey him, and having done which, Cesare was led back to prison.

The weakness of the conspirators was obvious; and many Florentines residing in the town, assembled together, among whom, Giorgio Ginori, a knight of Rhodes, took arms first against them, and attacked Bernardo, who traversed the piazza, alternately entreating and threatening those who refused to obey him, and being surrounded by Giorgio's followers, he was wounded and made prisoner. This being done, it was easy to set the governor at liberty and subdue the rest, who being few, and divided into several parties, were nearly all either secured or slain. An exaggerated report of these transactions reached Florence, it being told there that Prato was taken, the governor and his friends put to death, and the place filled with the enemy; and that Pistoia was also in arms, and most of the citizens in the conspiracy. In consequence of this alarming account, the palace as quickly filled with citizens, who consulted with the Signory what course ought to be adopted. At this time, Roberto da San Severino, one of the most distinguished generals of this period, was at Florence, and it was therefore determined to send him, with what forces could be collected, to Prato, with orders that he should approach the place, particularly observe what was going on, and provide such remedies as the necessity of the case and his own prudence should suggest. Roberto had scarcely passed the fortress of Campi, when he was met by a messenger from the governor, who informed him that Bernardo was taken, his followers either dispersed or slain, and everything restored to order. He consequently returned to Florence, whither Bernardo was shortly after conveyed, and when questioned by the magistracy concerning the real motives of such a weak conspiracy, he said, he had undertaken it, because, having resolved to die in Florence rather than live in exile, he wished his death to be accompanied by some memorable action.

This disturbance having been raised and quelled almost at the same time, the citizens returned to their accustomed mode of life, hoping to enjoy, without anxiety, the state they had now established and confirmed. Hence arose many of those evils which usually result from peace; for the youth having become more dissolute than before, more extravagant in dress, feasting, and other licentiousness, and being without employment, wasted their time and means on gaming and women; their principal study being how to appear splendid in apparel, and attain a crafty shrewdness in discourse; he who could make the most poignant remark being considered the wisest, and being most respected. These manners derived additional encouragement from the followers of the duke of Milan, who, with his duchess and the whole ducal court, as it was said, to fulfill a vow, came to Florence, where he was received with all the pomp and respect due to so great a prince, and one so intimately connected with the Florentine people. Upon this occasion the city witnessed an unprecedented exhibition; for, during Lent, when the church commands us to abstain from animal food, the Milanese, without respect for either God or his church, ate of it daily. Many spectacles were exhibited in honor of the duke, and among others, in the temple of Santo Spirito, was represented the descent of the Holy Ghost among the apostles; and in consequence of the numerous fires used upon the occasion, some of the woodwork became ignited, and the church was completely destroyed by the flames. Many thought that the Almighty being offended at our misconduct, took this method of signifying his displeasure. If, therefore, the duke found the city full of courtly delicacies, and customs unsuitable to well-regulated conduct, he left it in a much worse state. Hence the good citizens thought it necessary to restrain these improprieties, and made a law to put a stop to extravagance in dress, feasts, and funerals.

In the midst of this universal peace, a new and unexpected disturbance arose in Tuscany. Certain citizens of Volterra had discovered an alum-mine in their district, and being aware of the profit derivable from it, in order to obtain the means of working and securing it, they applied to some Florentines, and allowed them to share in the profits. This, as is frequently the case with new undertakings, at first excited little attention from the people of Volterra; but in time, finding the profits derived from it had become considerable, they fruitlessly endeavored to effect what at first might have been easily accomplished. They began by agitating the question in their councils, declaring it grossly improper that a source of wealth discovered in the public lands should be converted to the emolument of private individuals. They next sent advocates to Florence, and the question was referred to the consideration of certain citizens, who, either through being bribed by the party in possession, or from a sincere conviction, declared the aim of the people of Volterra to be unjust in desiring to deprive their citizens of the fruit of their labor; and decided that the alum-pit was the rightful property of those who had hitherto wrought it; but, at the same time, recommended them to pay an annual sum by way of acknowledgment to the city. This answer instead of abating, served only to increase the animosities and tumult in Volterra, and absorbed entire attention both in the councils and throughout the city; the people demanding the restitution of what they considered their due, and the proprietors insisting upon their right to retain what they had originally acquired, and what had been subsequently been confirmed to them by the decision of the Florentines. In the midst of these disturbances, a respectable citizen, named Il Pecorino, was killed, together with several others, who had embraced the same side, whose houses were also plundered and burned; and the fury of the mob rose to such a height, that they were with difficulty restrained from putting the Florentine rectors to death.

After the first outrage, the Volterrani immediately determined to send ambassadors to Florence, who intimated, that if the Signory would allow them their ancient privileges, the city would remain subject to them as formerly. Many and various were the opinions concerning the reply to be made. Tommaso Soderini advised that they should accept the submission of the people of Volterra, upon any conditions with which they were disposed to make it; for he considered it unreasonable and unwise to kindle a flame so near home that it might burn their own dwelling; he suspected the pope's ambition, and was apprehensive of the power of the king; nor could he confide in the friendship either of the duke or the Venetians, having no assurance of the sincerity of the latter, or the valor of the former. He concluded by quoting that trite proverb, "Meglio un magro accordo che una grassa vittoria."[2] On the other hand, Lorenzo de' Medici, thinking this an opportunity for exhibiting his prudence and wisdom, and being strenuously supported by those who envied the influence of Tommaso Soderini, resolved to march against them, and punish the arrogance of the people of Volterra with arms; declaring that if they were not made a striking example, others would, without the least fear or respect, upon every slight occasion, adopt a similar course. The enterprise being resolved on, the Volterrani were told that they could not demand the observance of conditions which they themselves had broken, and therefore must either submit to the direction of the Signory or expect war. With this answer they returned to their city, and prepared for its defense; fortifying the place, and sending to all the princes of Italy to request assistance, none of whom listened to them, except the Siennese

2   A lean peace is better than a fat victory.

and the lord of Piombino, who gave them some hope of aid. The Florentines on the other hand, thinking success dependent principally upon celerity, assembled ten thousand foot and two thousand horse, who, under the command of Federigo, lord of Urbino, marched into the country of Volterra and quickly took entire possession of it. They then encamped before the city, which, being in a lofty situation, and precipitous on all sides, could only be approached by a narrow pass near the church of St. Alessandro. The Volterrani had engaged for their defense about one thousand mercenaries, who, perceiving the great superiority of the Florentines, found the place untenable, and were tardy in their defensive operations, but indefatigable in the constant injuries they committed upon the people of the place. Thus these poor citizens were harassed by the enemy without, and by their own soldiery within; so, despairing of their safety, they began to think of a capitulation; and, being unable to obtain better terms, submitted to the discretion of the Florentine commissaries, who ordered the gates to be opened, and introduced the greater part of their forces. They then proceeded to the palace, and commanded the priors to retire to their homes; and, on the way thither, one of them was in derision stripped by the soldiers. From this beginning (so much more easily are men predisposed to evil than to good) originated the pillage and destruction of the city; which for a whole day suffered the greatest horrors, neither women nor sacred places being spared; and the soldiery, those engaged for its defense as well as its assailants, plundered all that came within their reach. The news of this victory was received with great joy at Florence, and as the expedition had been undertaken wholly by the advice of Lorenzo, he acquired great reputation. Upon which one of the intimate friends of Tommaso Soderini, reminding him of the advice he had given, asked him what he thought of the taking of Volterra; to which he replied, "To me the place seems rather lost than won; for had it been received on equitable terms, advantage and security would have been the result; but having to retain it by force it will in critical junctures, occasion weakness and anxiety, and in times of peace, injury and expense."

CHAPTER VI

Origin of the animosity between Sixtus IV. and Lorenzo de' Medici--Carlo di Braccio da Perugia attacks the Siennese--Carlo retires by desire of the Florentines--Conspiracy against Galeazzo, duke of Milan--His vices--He is slain by the conspirators--Their deaths.

The pope, anxious to retain the territories of the church in obedience, had caused Spoleto to be sacked for having, through internal factions, fallen into rebellion. Citta di Castello being in the same state of contumacy, he besieged that place; and Niccolo Vitelli its prince, being on intimate terms with Lorenzo de' Medici, obtained assistance from him, which, though inadequate, was quite enough to originate that enmity between Sixtus IV. and the Medici afterward productive of such unhappy results. Nor would this have been so long in development had not the death of Frate Piero, cardinal of St. Sixtus, taken place; who, after having traveled over Italy and visited Venice and Milan (under the pretense of doing honor to the marriage of Ercole, marquis of Ferrara), went about sounding the minds of the princes, to learn how they were disposed toward the Florentines. But upon his return he died, not without suspicion of having been poisoned by the Venetians, who found they would have reason to fear Sixtus if he were allowed to avail himself of the talents and exertions of Frate Piero. Although of very low extraction, and meanly brought up within the walls of a convent, he had no sooner attained the distinction of the scarlet hat, than he exhibited such inordinate pride and ambition, that the pontificate seemed too little for him, and he gave a feast in Rome which would have seemed extraordinary even for a king, the expense exceeding twenty thousand florins. Deprived of this minister, the designs of Sixtus proceeded with less promptitude. The Florentines, the duke, and the Venetians having renewed their league, and allowed the pope and the king to join them if they thought proper, the two latter also entered into a league, reserving an opening for the others if they were desirous to become parties to it. Italy was thus divided in two factions; for circumstances daily arose which occasioned ill feeling between the two leagues; as occurred with respect to the island of Cyprus, to which Ferrando laid claim, and the Venetians occupied. Thus the pope and the king became more closely united. Federigo, prince of Urbino, was at this time one of the first generals of Italy; and had long served the Florentines. In order, if possible, to deprive the hostile league of their captain, the pope advised, and the king requested him to pay a visit to them. To the surprise and displeasure of the Florentines, Federigo complied; for they thought the same fate awaited him as had befallen Niccolo Piccinino. However, the result was quite different; for he returned from Naples and Rome greatly honored, and with the appointment of general to their forces. They also endeavored to gain over to their interest the lords of Romagna and the Siennese, that they might more easily injure the Florentines, who, becoming aware of these things, used their utmost endeavors to defend themselves against the ambition of their enemies; and having lost Federigo d'Urbino, they engaged Roberto da Rimino in his place, renewed the league with the Perugini and formed one with the prince of Faenza. The pope and the king assigned, as the reasons of their animosity against the Florentines, that they wished to withdraw them from the Venetian alliance, and associate them with their own league; for the pope did not think the church could maintain her reputation, nor the Count Girolamo retain the states of Romagna, while the Florentines and the Venetians remained united. The Florentines conjectured their design was to set them at enmity with the Venetians, not so much for the sake of gaining their friendship as to be able the more easily to injure them. Two years passed away in these jealousies and discontents before any disturbance broke out; but the first which occurred, and that but trivial, took place in Tuscany.

Braccio of Perugia, whom we have frequently mentioned as one of the most distinguished warriors of Italy, left two sons, Oddo and Carlo; the latter was of tender years; the former, as above related, was slain by the people of Val di Lamona; but Carlo, when he came to mature age, was by the Venetians, out of respect for the memory of his father, and the hopes they entertained from himself, received among the condottieri of their republic. The term of his engagement having expired, he did not design to renew it immediately, but resolved to try if, by his own influence and his father's reputation, he could recover possession of Perugia. To this the Venetians willingly consented, for they usually extended their dominion by any changes that occurred in the neighboring states. Carlo consequently came into Tuscany, but found more difficulties in his attempt upon Perugia than he had anticipated, on account of its being allied with the Florentines; and desirous of doing something worthy of memory, he made war upon the Siennese, alleging them to be indebted to him for services performed by his father in the affairs of that republic, and attacked them with such impetuosity as to threaten the total overthrow of their dominion. The Siennese, ever ready to suspect the Florentines, persuaded themselves that this outrage had been committed with their cognizance, and made heavy complaints to the pope and the king against them. They also sent ambassadors to Florence to complain of the injuries they had suffered, and adroitly intimated, that if Carlo had not been secretly supported he could not have made war upon them with such perfect security. The Florentines denied all participation in the proceedings of Carlo, expressed their most earnest wish to do everything in their power to put a stop to them, and allowed the ambassadors to use whatever terms they pleased in the name of the Signory, to command him to desist. Carlo complained that the Florentines, by their unwillingness to support him, had deprived themselves of a most valuable acquisition and him of great glory; for he could have insured them the possession of the whole territory in a short time, from the want of courage in the people and the ineffectual provision they had made for their defense. He then withdrew to his engagement under the Venetians; but the Siennese, although delivered from such imminent peril by the Florentines, were still very indignant against them; considering themselves under no obligation to those who had delivered them from an evil to which they had first exposed them.

While the transactions between the king and the pope were in progress, and those in Tuscany in the manner we have related, an event of greater importance occurred in Lombardy. Cola Montano, a learned and ambitious man, taught the Latin language to the youth of the principal families in Milan. Either out of hatred to the character and manners of the duke, or from some other cause, he constantly deprecated the condition of those who live under a bad prince; calling those glorious and happy who had the good fortune to be born and live in a republic. He endeavored to show that the most celebrated men had been produced in republics, and not reared under princes; that the former cherish virtue, while the latter destroy it; the one deriving advantage from virtuous men, while the latter naturally fear them. The youths with whom he was most intimate were Giovanni Andrea Lampognano, Carlo Visconti, and Girolamo Ogliato. He frequently discussed with them the faults of their prince, and the wretched condition of those who were subject to him; and by constantly inculcating his principles, acquired such an ascendancy over their minds as to induce them to bind themselves by oath to effect the duke's destruction, as soon as they became old enough to attempt it. Their minds being fully occupied with this design, which grew with their years, the duke's conduct and their own private injuries served to hasten its execution. Galeazzo was licentious and cruel, of both which vices he had given such repeated proofs, that he became odious to all. Not content with corrupting the wives of the nobility, he also took pleasure in making it notorious; nor was he satisfied with murdering individuals unless he effected their deaths by some unusual cruelty. He was suspected of having destroyed his own mother; for, not considering himself prince while she was present, he conducted himself in such a manner as induced her to withdraw from his court, and, travelling toward Cremona, which she obtained as part of her marriage portion, she was seized with a sudden illness, and died upon the road; which made many think her son had caused her death. The duke had dishonored both Carlo and Girolamo in respect to their wives or other female relatives, and had refused to concede to Giovanandrea possession of the monastery of Miramondo, of which he had obtained a grant from the pope for a near relative. These private injuries increased the young men's desire for vengeance, and the deliverance of their country from so many evils; trusting that whenever they should succeed in destroying the duke, many of the nobility and all the people would rise in their defense. Being resolved upon their undertaking, they were often together, which, on account of their long intimacy, did not excite any suspicion. They frequently discussed the subject; and in order to familiarize their minds with the deed itself, they practiced striking each other in the breast and in the side with the sheathed daggers intended to be used for the purpose. On considering the most suitable time and place, the castle seemed insecure; during the chase, uncertain and dangerous; while going about the city for his own amusement, difficult if not impracticable; and, at a banquet, of doubtful result. They, therefore, determined to kill him upon the occasion of some procession or public festivity when there would be no doubt of his presence, and where they might, under various pretexts, assemble their friends. It was also resolved that if one of their number were prevented from attending, on any account whatever, the rest should put him to death in the midst of their armed enemies.

It was now the close of the year 1476, near Christmas, and as it was customary for the duke to go upon St. Stephen's day, in great solemnity, to the church of that martyr, they considered this the most suitable opportunity for the execution of their design. Upon the morning of that day they ordered some of their most trusty friends and servants to arm, telling them they wished to go to the assistance of Giovanandrea, who, contrary to the wish of some of his neighbors, intended to turn a watercourse into his estate; but that before they went they wished to take leave of the prince. They also assembled, under various pretenses, other friends and relatives, trusting that when the deed was accomplished, everyone would join them in the completion of their enterprise. It was their intention, after the duke's death, to collect their followers together and proceed to those parts of the city where they imagined the plebeians would be most disposed to take arms against the duchess and the principal ministers of state, and they thought the people, on account of the famine which then prevailed, would easily be induced to follow them; for it was their design to give up the houses of Cecco Simonetta, Giovanni Botti, and Francesco Lucani, all leading men in the government, to be plundered, and by this means gain over the populace and restore liberty to the community. With these ideas, and with minds resolved upon their execution, Giovanandrea, together with the rest, were early at the church, and heard mass together; after which, Giovanandrea, turning to a statue of St. Ambrose, said, "O patron of our city! thou knowest our intention, and the end we would attain, by so many dangers; favor our enterprise, and prove, by protecting the oppressed, that tyranny is offensive to thee." To the duke, on the other hand, when intending to go to the church, many omens occurred of his approaching death; for in the morning, having put on a cuirass, as was his frequent custom, he immediately took it off again, either because it inconvenienced him, or that he did not like its appearance. He then wished to hear mass in the castle, and found that the priest who officiated in the chapel had gone to St. Stephen's, and had taken with him the sacred utensils. On this he desired the service to be performed by the bishop of Como, who acquainted him with preventing circumstances. Thus, almost compelled, he determined to go to the church; but before his departure, caused his sons, Giovan Galeazzo and Ermes, to be brought to him, whom he embraced and kissed several times, seeming reluctant to part with them. He then left the castle, and, with the ambassadors of Ferrara and Mantua on either hand, proceeded to St. Stephen's. The conspirators, to avoid exciting suspicion, and to escape the cold, which was very severe, had withdrawn to an apartment of the archpriest, who was a friend of theirs, but hearing the duke's approach, they came into the church, Giovanandrea and Girolamo placing themselves upon the right hand of the entrance, and Carlo on the left. Those who led the procession had already entered, and were followed by the duke, surrounded by such a multitude as is usual on similar occasions. The first attack was made by Lampognano and Girolamo, who, pretending to clear the way for the prince, came close to him, and grasping their daggers, which, being short and sharp, were concealed in the sleeves of their vests, struck at him. Lampognano gave him two wounds, one in the belly, the other in the throat. Girolamo struck him in the throat and breast. Carlo Visconti, being nearer the door, and the duke having passed, could not wound him in front: but with two strokes, transpierced his shoulder and spine. These six wounds were inflicted so instantaneously, that the duke had fallen before anyone was aware of what had happened, and he expired, having only once ejaculated the name of the Virgin, as if imploring her assistance. A great tumult immediately ensued, several swords were drawn, and as often happens in sudden emergencies, some fled from the church, and others ran toward the scene of tumult, both without any definite motive or knowledge of what had occurred. Those, however, who were nearest the duke and had seen him slain, recognizing the murderers, pursued them. Giovanandrea, endeavoring to make his way out of the church, proceeded among the women, who being numerous, and according to their custom, seated upon the ground, was prevented in his progress by their apparel, and being overtaken, he was killed by a Moor, one of the duke's footmen. Carlo was slain by those immediately around him. Girolamo Olgiato passed through the crowd, and got out of the church; but seeing his companions dead, and not knowing where else to go, he proceeded home, where his father and brothers refused to receive him; his mother only, having compassion on her son recommended him to a priest, an old friend of the family, who, disguising him in his own apparel, led him to his house. Here he remained two days, not without hope that some disturbance might arise in Milan which would contribute to his safety. This not occurring, and apprehensive that his hiding place would be discovered, he endeavored to escape in disguise, but being observed, he was given over to justice, and disclosed all the particulars of the conspiracy. Girolamo was twenty-three years of age, and exhibited no less composure at his death than resolution in his previous conduct, for being stripped of his apparel, and in the hands of the executioner, who stood by with the sword unsheathed, ready to deprive him of life, he repeated the following words, in the Latin tongue, in which he was well versed: "Mors acerba, fama perpetua, stabit vetus memoria facti."

The enterprise of these unfortunate young men was conducted with secrecy and executed with resolution; and they failed for want of the support of those whom they expected would rise in their defense. Let princes therefore learn to live, so as to render themselves beloved and respected by their subjects, that none may have hope of safety after having destroyed them; and let others see how vain is the expectation which induces them to trust so much to the multitude, as to believe, that even when discontented, they will either embrace or ward off their dangers. This event spread consternation all over Italy; but those which shortly afterward occurred in Florence caused much more alarm, and terminated a peace of twelve years' continuance, as will be shown in the following book; which, having commenced with blood and horror, will have a melancholy and tearful conclusion.

BOOK VIII

CHAPTER I

State of the family of the Medici at Florence--Enmity of Sixtus IV. toward Florence--Differences between the family of the Pazzi and that of the Medici--Beginning of the conspiracy of the Pazzi--Arrangements to effect the design of the conspiracy--Giovanni Batista da Montesecco is sent to Florence--The pope joins the conspiracy--The king of Naples becomes a party to it--Names of the conspirators--The conspirators make many ineffectual attempts to kill Lorenzo and Giuliano de' Medici--The final arrangement--Order of the conspiracy.

This book, commencing between two conspiracies, the one at Milan already narrated, the other yet to be recorded, it would seem appropriate, and in accordance with our usual custom, were we to treat of the nature and importance of these terrible demonstrations. This we should willingly do had we not discussed the matter elsewhere, or could it be comprised in few words. But requiring much consideration, and being already noticed in another place, it will be omitted, and we shall proceed with our narrative. The government of the Medici having subdued all its avowed enemies in order to obtain for that family undivided authority, and distinguish them from other citizens in their relation to the rest, found it necessary to subdue those who secretly plotted against them. While Medici contended with other families, their equals in authority and reputation, those who envied their power were able to oppose them openly without danger of being suppressed at the first demonstration of hostility; for the magistrates being free, neither party had occasion to fear, till one or other of them was overcome. But after the victory of 1466, the government became so entirely centred in the Medici, and they acquired so much authority, that discontented spirits were obliged either to suffer in silence, or, if desirous to destroy them, to attempt it in secrecy, and by clandestine means; which plots rarely succeed and most commonly involve the ruin of those concerned in them, while they frequently contribute to the aggrandizement of those against whom they are directed. Thus the prince of a city attacked by a conspiracy, if not slain like the duke of Milan (which seldom happens), almost always attains to a greater degree of power, and very often has his good disposition perverted to evil. The proceedings of his enemies give him cause for fear; fear suggests the necessity of providing for his own safety, which involves the injury of others; and hence arise animosities, and not unfrequently his ruin. Thus these conspiracies quickly occasion the destruction of their contrivers, and, in time, inevitably injure their primary object.

Italy, as we have seen above, was divided into two factions; the pope and the king on one side; on the other, the Venetians, the duke, and the Florentines. Although the flames of war had not yet broken out, every day gave rise to some new occasion for rekindling them; and the pope, in particular, in all his plans endeavored to annoy the Florentine government. Thus Filippo de' Medici, archbishop of Pisa, being dead, Francesco Salviati, a declared enemy of the Medici, was appointed his successor, contrary to the wish of the Signory of Florence, who being unwilling to give him possession, there arose between them and the pope many fresh grounds of offense, before the matter was settled. Besides this, he conferred, at Rome, many favors upon the family of the Pazzi, and opposed that of the Medici, whenever an opportunity offered. The Pazzi were at this time, both on account of nobility of birth and their great wealth, the most brilliant in France. The head of this family was Jacopo, whom the people, on account of his distinguished pre-eminence, had made a knight. He had no children, except one natural daughter, but many nephews, sons of his brothers Piero and Antonio, the first of whom were Guglielmo, Francesco, Rinato, Giovanni, and then, Andrea, Niccolo, and Galeotto. Cosmo de' Medici, noticing the riches and rank of this family, had given his granddaughter, Bianca, to Guglielmo, hoping by this marriage to unite the houses, and obviate those enmities and dissensions so frequently occasioned by jealousy. However (so uncertain and fallacious are our expectations), very different feelings were thus originated;

for Lorenzo's advisers pointed out to him how dangerous it was, and how injurious to his authority, to unite in the same individuals so much wealth and power. In consequence, neither Jacopo nor his nephews obtained those degrees of honor, which in the opinion of other citizens were their due. This gave rise to anger in the Pazzi, and fear on the part of the Medici; as the former of these increased, so did the latter; and upon all occasions, when the Pazzi came in competition with other citizens, their claims to distinction, however strong, were set aside by the magistracy. Francesco de' Pazzi, being at Rome, the Council of Eight, upon some trivial occasion, compelled him to return, without treating him with the respect usually observed toward great citizens, so that the Pazzi everywhere bitterly complained of the ill usage they experienced, and thus excited suspicion in others, and brought down greater evils upon themselves. Giovanni de' Pazzi had married the daughter of Giovanni Buonromei, a very wealthy man, whose riches on his decease, without other children, came to his daughter. His nephew, Carlo, however, took possession of part, and the question being litigated, a law was passed, by virtue of which the wife of Giovanni de' Pazzi was robbed of her inheritance, and it was given to Carlo. In this piece of injustice the Pazzi at once recognized the influence of the Medici. Giuliano de' Medici often complained to his brother Lorenzo of the affair, saying he was afraid that by grasping at too much they would lose all.

Lorenzo, flushed with youth and power, would assume the direction of everything, and resolved that all transactions should bear an impress of his influence. The Pazzi, with their nobility and wealth unable to endure so many affronts, began to devise some means of vengeance. The first who spoke of any attempt against the Medici, was Francesco, who, being more sensitive and resolute than the others, determined either to obtain what was withheld from him, or lose what he still possessed. As the government of Florence gave him great offense, he resided almost constantly at Rome, where, like other Florentine merchants, he conducted extensive commercial operations; and being a most intimate friend of Count Girolamo, they frequently complained to each other of the conduct of the Medici. After a while they began to think that for the count to retain his estates, or the Pazzi their rights in the city, it would be necessary to change the government of Florence; and this they considered could not be done without the death of Giuliano and Lorenzo. They imagined the pope and the king would be easily induced to consent, because each could be convinced of the facility of the enterprise. Having acquired these ideas, they communicated them to Francesco Salviati, archbishop of Pisa, who, being ambitious and recently offended by the Medici, willingly adopted their views. Considering their next step, they resolved, in order to facilitate the design, to obtain the consent of Jacopo de' Pazzi, without whose concurrence they feared it would be impracticable. With this view, it was resolved that Francesco de' Pazzi should go to Florence, while the archbishop and the count were to remain at Rome, to be ready to communicate with the pope when a suitable opportunity occurred. Francesco found Jacopo de' Pazzi more cautious and difficult to persuade than he could have wished, and on imparting this to his friends at Rome, it was thought he desired the sanction of some greater authority to induce him to adopt their views. Upon this, the archbishop and the count communicated the whole affair to Giovanni Batista da Montesecco, a leader of the papal forces, possessing military reputation, and under obligations to the pope and the count. To him the affair seemed difficult and dangerous, while the archbishop endeavored to obviate his objections by showing how much assistance the pope and the king would lend to the enterprise; the hatred of the Florentines toward the Medici, the numerous friends the Salviati and the Pazzi would bring with them, the readiness with which the young men might be slain, on account of their going about the city unaccompanied and without suspicion, and the facility with which the government might then be changed. These things Giovanni Batista did not in reality believe, for he had heard from many Florentines quite contrary statements.

While occupied with these deliberations, Carlo, lord of Faenza, was taken ill, and tears were entertained for his life. This circumstance seemed to the archbishop and the count to offer an opportunity for sending Giovanni Batista to Florence, and thence to Romagna, under pretence of recovering certain territories belonging to the latter, of which the lord of Faenza had taken possession. The count therefore commissioned Giovanni Batista to have an interview with Lorenzo de' Medici, and on his part request his advice how to proceed with respect to the affair of Romagna; that he should then see Francesco de' Pazzi, and in conjunction with him endeavor to induce his uncle Jacopo to adopt their ideas. To render the pope's authority available in their behalf, Giovanni Batista was ordered, before his departure, to communicate with the pontiff, who offered every means at his disposal in favor of their enterprise. Giovanni Batista, having arrived at Florence, obtained an interview with Lorenzo, by whom he was most graciously received; and with regard to the advice he was commissioned to ask, obtained a wise and friendly answer; so that he was astonished at finding him quite a different character from what he had been represented, and considered him to possess great sagacity, an affectionate heart, and most amicably disposed toward the count. He found Francesco de' Pazzi had gone to Lucca, and spoke to Jacopo, who was at first quite opposed to their design, but before they parted the pope's authority seemed to have influenced him; for he told Giovanni Batista, that he might go to Romagna, and that before his return Francesco would be with him, and they would then consult more particularly upon the subject. Giovanni Batista proceeded to Romagna, and soon returned to Florence. After a pretended consultation with Lorenzo, upon the count's affairs, he obtained an interview with Francesco and Jacopo de' Pazzi, when the latter gave his consent to their enterprise. They then discussed the means of carrying it into effect. Jacopo de' Pazzi was of opinion that it could not be effected while both the brothers remained at Florence; and therefore it would be better to wait till Lorenzo went to Rome, whither it was reported he had an intention of going; for then their object would be more easily attained. Francesco de' Pazzi had no objection to Lorenzo being at Rome, but if he were to forego the journey, he thought that both the brothers might be slain, either at a marriage, or at a play, or in a church. With regard to foreign assistance, he supposed the pope might assemble forces for the conquest of the fortress of Montone, being justified in taking it from Count Carlo, who had caused the tumults already spoken of in Sienna and Perugia.

Still no definite arrangement was made; but it was resolved that Giovanni Batista and Francesco de' Pazzi should go to Rome and settle everything with the pontiff. The matter was again debated at Rome; and at length it was concluded that besides an expedition against Montone, Giovan Francesco da Tolentino, a leader of the papal troops, should go into Romagna, and Lorenzo da Castello to the Val di Tavere; that each, with the forces of the country, should hold himself in readiness to perform the commands of the archbishop de' Salviati and Francesco de Pazzi, both of whom were to come to Florence, and provide for the execution of their design, with the assistance of Giovanni Batista da Montesecco. King Ferrando promised, by his ambassador, to contribute all in his power to the success of their undertaking.

Francesco de' Pazzi and the archbishop having arrived at Florence, prevailed upon Jacopo di Poggio, a well educated youth, but ambitious and very desirous of change, to join them, and two others, each of the name of Jacopo Salviati, one a brother, the other a kinsman, of the archbishop. They also gained over Bernardo Bandini and Napoleone Franzeni, two bold young men, under great obligations to the family of the Pazzi. Besides those already mentioned, they were joined by Antonio da Volterra and a priest named Stefano, who taught Latin to the daughter of Jacopo de' Pazzi. Rinato de' Pazzi, a grave and prudent man, being quite aware of the evils resulting from such undertakings, refused all participation in the conspiracy; he held it in abhorrence, and as much as possible, without betraying his kinsmen, endeavored to counteract it.

The pope had sent Raffaello di Riario, a nephew of Count Girolamo, to the college of Pisa, to study canon law, and while there, had advanced him to the dignity of a cardinal. The conspirators determined to bring this cardinal to Florence, as they would thus be better able to conceal their design, since any persons requisite to be introduced into the city might easily be made to appear as a part of his retinue, and his arrival might facilitate the completion of their enterprise. The cardinal came, and was received by Jacopo de' Pazzi at his villa of Montughi, near Florence. By his means it was also intended to bring together Giuliano and Lorenzo, and whenever this happened, to put them both to death. They therefore invited them to meet the cardinal at their villa of Fiesole; but Giuliano, either intentionally or through some preventing cause, did not attend; and this design having failed, they thought that if asked to an entertainment at Florence, both brothers would certainly be present. With this intention they appointed Sunday, the twenty-sixth of April, 1478, to give a great feast; and, resolving to assassinate them at table, the conspirators met on the Saturday evening to arrange all proceedings for the following day. In the morning it was intimated to Francesco that Giuliano would be absent; on which the conspirators again assembled and finding they could no longer defer the execution of their design, since it would be impossible among so many to preserve secrecy, they determined to complete it in the cathedral church of Santa Reparata, where the cardinal attending, the two brothers would be present as usual. They wished Giovanni Batista da Montesecco to undertake the murder of Lorenzo, while that of Giuliano was assigned to Francesco de' Pazzi and Bernardo Bandini. Giovanni

Batista refused, either because his familiarity with Lorenzo had created feelings in his favor, or from some other reason, saying he should not have resolution sufficient to commit such a deed in a church, and thus add sacrilege to treachery. This caused the failure of their undertaking; for time pressing, they were compelled to substitute Antonio da Volterra and Stefano, the priest, two men, who, from nature and habit, were the most unsuitable of any; for if firmness and resolution joined with experience in bloodshed be necessary upon any occasion, it is on such as these; and it often happens that those who are expert in arms, and have faced death in all forms on the field of battle, still fail in an affair like this. Having now decided upon the time, they resolved that the signal for the attack should be the moment when the priest who celebrated high mass should partake of the sacrament, and that, in the meantime, the Archbishop de' Salviati, with his followers, and Jacopo di Poggio, should take possession of the palace, in order that the Signory, after the young men's death, should voluntarily, or by force, contribute to their assistance.

CHAPTER II

Giuliano de' Medici slain--Lorenzo escapes--The archbishop Salviati endeavors to seize the palace of the Signory--He is taken and hanged--The enterprise of the conspirators entirely fails--Manifestations of the Florentines in favor of Lorenzo de' Medici--The conspirators punished--The funeral of Giuliano--The pope and the king of Naples make war upon the Florentines--Florence excommunicated--Speech of Lorenzo de' Medici to the citizens of Florence.

The conspirators proceeded to Santa Reparata, where the cardinal and Lorenzo had already arrived. The church was crowded, and divine service commenced before Giuliano's arrival. Francesco de' Pazzi and Bernardo Bandini, who were appointed to be his murderers, went to his house, and finding him, they, by earnest entreaties, prevailed upon him to accompany them. It is surprising that such intense hatred, and designs so full of horror as those of Francesco and Bernardo, could be so perfectly concealed; for while conducting him to the church, and after they had reached it, they amused him with jests and playful discourse. Nor did Francesco forget, under pretense of endearment, to press him in his arms, so as to ascertain whether under his apparel he wore a cuirass or other means of defense. Giuliano and Lorenzo were both aware of the animosity of the Pazzi, and their desire to deprive them of the government; but they felt assured that any design would be attempted openly, and in conjunction with the civil authority. Thus being free from apprehension for their personal safety both affected to be on friendly terms with them. The murderers being ready, each in his appointed station, which they could retain without suspicion, on account of the vast numbers assembled in the church, the preconcerted moment arrived, and Bernardo Bandini, with a short dagger provided for the purpose, struck Giuliano in the breast, who, after a few steps, fell to the earth. Francesco de' Pazzi threw himself upon the body and covered him with wounds; while, as if blinded by rage, he inflicted a deep incision upon his own leg. Antonio and Stefano, the priest, attacked Lorenzo, and after dealing many blows, effected only a slight incision in the throat; for either their want of resolution, the activity of Lorenzo, who, finding himself attacked, used his arms in his own defense, or the assistance of those by whom he was surrounded, rendered all attempts futile. They fled and concealed themselves, but being subsequently discovered, were put to death in the most ignominious manner, and their bodies dragged about the city. Lorenzo, with the friends he had about him, took refuge in the sacristy of the church. Bernardo Bandini, after Giuliano's death, also slew Francesco Nori, a most intimate friend of the Medici, either from some previous hatred or for having endeavored to render assistance to Giuliano; and not content with these murders, he ran in pursuit of Lorenzo, intending, by his own promptitude, to make up for the weakness and inefficiency of the others; but finding he had taken refuge in the vestry, he was prevented.

In the midst of these violent and fearful deeds, during which the uproar was so terrible, that it seemed almost sufficient to bring the church down upon its inmates, the cardinal Riario remained close to the altar, where he was with difficulty kept in safety by the priests, until the Signory, upon the abatement of the disturbance, could conduct him to their palace, where he remained in the utmost terror till he was set at liberty.

There were at this time in Florence some people of Perugia, whom party feuds had compelled to leave their homes; and the Pazzi, by promising to restore them to their country, obtained their assistance. The Archbishop de' Salviati, going to seize the palace, together with Jacopo di Poggio, and the Salviati, his friends, took these Perugini with him. Having arrived, he left part of his people below, with orders that when they heard a noise they should make themselves masters of the entrance, while himself, with the greater part of the Perugini, proceeded above, and finding the Signory at dinner (for it was now late), was admitted after a short delay, by Cesare Petrucci, the Gonfalonier of Justice. He entered with only a few of his followers, the greater part of them being shut up in the cancelleria into which they had gone, whose doors were so contrived, that upon closing they could not be opened from either side, without the key. The archbishop being with the gonfalonier, under pretense of having something to communicate on the part of the pope, addressed him in such an incoherent and hesitating manner, that the gonfalonier at once suspected him, and rushing out of the chamber to call assistance, found Jacopo di Poggio, whom he seized by the hair of the head, and gave into the custody of his attendants. The Signory hearing the tumult, snatched such arms as they could at the moment obtain, and all who had gone up with the archbishop, part of them being shut up, and part overcome with terror, were immediately slain or thrown alive out of the windows of the palace, at which the archbishop, the two Jacopi Salviati, and Jacopodi Poggio were hanged. Those whom the archbishop left below, having mastered the guard and taken possession of the entrance occupied all the lower floors, so that the citizens, who in the uproar, hastened to the palace, were unable to give either advice or assistance to the Signory.

Francesco de' Pazzi and Bernardo Bandini, perceiving Lorenzo's escape, and the principal agent in the enterprise seriously wounded, became immediately conscious of the imminent peril of their position. Bernardo, using the same energy in his own behalf that had served him against the Medici, finding all lost, saved himself by flight. Francesco, wounded as he was, got to his house, and endeavored to get on horseback, for it had been arranged they should ride through the city and call the people to arms and liberty; but he found himself unable, from the nature of his wound, and, throwing himself naked upon his bed, begged Jacopo de' Pazzi to perform the part for which he was himself incapacitated. Jacopo, though old and unaccustomed to such business, by way of making a last effort, mounted his horse, and, with about a hundred armed followers, collected without previous preparation, hastened to the piazza of the palace, and endeavored to assemble adherents by cries of "people," and "liberty;" but the former, having been rendered deaf by the fortune and liberty of the Medici, the latter was unknown in Florence, and he found no followers. The signors, who held the upper part of the palace, saluted him with stones and threats. Jacopo, while hesitating, was met by Giovanni Seristori, his brother-in-law, who upbraided him with the troubles he had occasioned, and then advised him to go home, for the people and liberty were as dear to other citizens as to himself. Thus deprived of every hope, Lorenzo being alive, Francesco seriously wounded, and none disposed to follow him, not knowing what to do, he resolved, if possible, to escape by flight; and, accompanied by those whom he had led into the piazza, left Florence with the intention of going into Romagna.

In the meantime the whole city was roused to arms, and Lorenzo de' Medici, accompanied by a numerous escort, returned to his house. The palace was recovered from its assailants, all of whom were either slain or made prisoners. The name of the Medici echoed everywhere, and portions of dead bodies were seen borne on spears and scattered through the streets; while everyone was transported with rage against the Pazzi, and pursued them with relentless cruelty. The people took possession of their houses, and Francesco, naked as they found him, was led to the palace, and hanged beside the archbishop and the rest. He could not be induced, by any injurious words or deeds, to utter a syllable, but regarding those around with a steady look, he silently sighed. Guglielmo de' Pazzi, brother-in-law to Lorenzo, fled to the latter's house, and by his innocence and the intercession of his wife, Bianca, he escaped death. There was not a citizen of any rank whatever who did not, upon this occasion, wait upon Lorenzo with an offer of his services; so great were the popularity and good fortune which this family had acquired by their liberality and prudence. Rinato de' Pazzi was at his villa when the event took place, and on being informed of it, he endeavored to escape in disguise, but was arrested upon the road and brought to Florence. Jacopo de' Pazzi was taken while crossing the mountains of Romagna, for the inhabitants of these parts having heard what had occurred, and seeing him in flight, attacked and brought him back to the city; nor could he, though he frequently endeavored, prevail with them to put him to death upon the road. Jacopo and Rinato were condemned within four days after the murder of Giuliano. And though so many deaths had been inflicted that the roads were covered with fragments of human bodies, not one excited a feeling of regret, except that of Rinato; for he was considered a wise and good man, and possessed none of the pride for which the rest of his family were notorious. As if to mark the event by some extraordinary circumstance, Jacopo de' Pazzi, after having been buried in the tomb of his ancestors, was disinterred like an excommunicated person, and thrown into a hole at the outside of the city walls; from this grave he was taken, and with the halter in which he had been hanged, his body was dragged naked through the city, and, as if unfit for sepulture on earth, thrown by the populace into the Arno, whose waters were then very high. It was an awful instance of the instability of fortune, to see so wealthy a man, possessing the utmost earthly felicity, brought down to such a depth of misery, such utter ruin and extreme degradation. It is said he had vices, among which were gaming and profane swearing, to which he was very much addicted; but these seem more than balanced by his numerous charities, for he relieved many in distress, and bestowed much money for pious uses. It may also be recorded in his favor, that upon the Saturday preceding the death of Giuliano, in order that none might suffer from his misfortunes, he discharged all his debts; and whatever property he possessed belonging to others, either in his own house or his place of business, he was particularly careful to return to its owners. Giovanni Batista da Montesecco, after a long examination, was beheaded; Napoleone Franzesi escaped punishment by flight; Giulielmo de' Pazzi was banished, and such of his cousins as remained alive were imprisoned in the fortress of Volterra. The disturbances being over, and the conspirators punished, the funeral obsequies of Giuliano were performed amid universal lamentation; for he possessed all the liberality and humanity that could be wished for in one of his high station. He left a natural son, born some months after his death, named Giulio, who was endowed with that virtue and felicity with which the whole world is now acquainted; and of which we shall speak at length when we come to our own times, if God spare us. The people who had assembled in favor of the Pazzi under Lorenzo da Castello in the Val di Tavere, and under Giovan Francesco da Tolentino in Romagna, approached Florence, but having heard of the failure of the conspiracy, they returned home.

The changes desired by the pope and the king in the government of Florence, not having taken place, they determined to effect by war what they had failed to accomplish by treachery; and both assembled forces with all speed to attack the Florentine states; publicly declaring that they only wished the citizens to remove Lorenzo de' Medici, who alone of all the Florentines was their enemy. The king's forces had already passed the Tronto, and the pope's were in Perugia; and that the citizens might feel the effect of spiritual as well as temporal weapons, the pontiff excommunicated and anathematized them. Finding themselves attacked by so many armies, the Florentines prepared for their defense with the utmost care. Lorenzo de' Medici, as the enemy's operations were said to be directed against himself alone, resolved first of all to assemble the Signory, and the most influential citizens, in the palace, to whom, being above three hundred in number, he spoke as follows:-- "Most excellent signors, and you, magnificent citizens, I know not whether I have more occasion to weep with you for the events which have recently occurred, or to rejoice in the circumstances with which they have been attended. Certainly, when I think with what virulence of united deceit and hatred I have been attacked, and my brother murdered, I cannot but mourn and grieve from my heart, from my very soul. Yet when I consider with what promptitude, anxiety, love, and unanimity of the whole city my brother has been avenged and myself defended, I am not only compelled to rejoice, but feel myself honored and exalted; for if experience has shown me that I had more enemies than I apprehended, it has also proved that I possess more warm and resolute friends than I could ever have hoped for. I must therefore grieve with you for the injuries others have suffered, and rejoice in the attachment you have exhibited toward myself; but I feel more aggrieved by the injuries committed, since they are so unusual, so unexampled, and (as I trust you believe) so undeserved on our part. Think, magnificent citizens, to what a dreadful point ill fortune has reduced our family, when among friends, amidst our own relatives, nay, in God's holy temple, we have found our greatest foes. Those who are in danger turn to their friends for assistance; they call upon their relatives for aid; but we found ours armed, and resolved on our destruction. Those who are persecuted, either from public or private motives, flee for refuge to the altars; but where others are safe, we are assassinated; where parricides and assassins are secure, the Medici find their murderers. But God, who has not hitherto abandoned our house, again saved us, and has undertaken the defense of our just cause. What injury have we done to justify so intense desire of our destruction? Certainly those who have shown themselves so much our enemies, never received any private wrong from us; for, had we wished to injure them, they would not have had an opportunity of injuring us. If they attribute public grievances to ourselves (supposing any had been done to them), they do the greater injustices to you, to this palace, to the majesty of this government, by assuming that on our account you would act unfairly to any of your citizens; and such a supposition, as we all know, is contradicted by every view of the circumstances; for we, had we been able, and you, had we wished it, would never have contributed to so abominable a design. Whoever inquires into the truth of these matters, will find that our family has always been exalted by you, and from this sole cause, that we have endeavored by kindness, liberality, and beneficence, to do good to all; and if we have honored strangers, when did we ever injure our relatives? If our enemies' conduct has been adopted, to gratify their desire for power (as would seem to be the case from their having taken possession of the palace and brought an armed force into the piazza), the infamous, ambitious, and detestable motive is at once disclosed. If they were actuated by envy and hatred of our authority, they offend you rather than us; for from you we have derived all the influence we possess. Certainly usurped power deserves to be detested; but not distinctions conceded for acts of kindness, generosity, and magnificence. And you all know that our family never attained any rank to which this palace and your united consent did not raise it. Cosmo, my grandfather, did not return from exile with arms and violence, but by your unanimous desire and approbation. It was not my father, old and inform, who defended the government against so many enemies, but yourselves by your authority and benevolence defended him; neither could I, after his death, being then a boy, have maintained the position of my house except by your favor and advice. Nor should we ever be able to conduct the affairs of this republic, if you did not contribute to our support. Therefore, I know not the reason of their hatred toward us, or what just cause they have of envy. Let them direct their enmity against their own ancestors, who, by their pride and avarice, lost the reputation which ours, by very opposite conduct, were enabled to acquire. But let it be granted we have greatly injured them, and that they are justified in seeking our ruin; why do they come and take possession of the palace? Why enter into league with the pope and the king, against the liberties of this republic? Why break the long-continued peace of Italy? They have no excuse for this; they ought to confine their vengeance to those who do them wrong, and not confound private animosities with public grievances. Hence it is that since their defeat our misfortune is the greater; for on their account the pope and the king make war upon us, and this war, they say, is directed against my family and myself. And would to God that this were true; then the remedy would be sure and unfailing, for I would not be so base a citizen as to prefer my own safety to yours; I would at once resolve to ensure your security, even though my own destruction were the immediate and inevitable consequence. But as the wrongs committed by princes are usually concealed under some less offensive covering, they have adopted this plea to hide their more abominable purpose. If, however, you think otherwise, I am in your hands; it is with you to do with me what you please. You are my fathers, my protectors, and whatever you command me to do I will perform most willingly; nor will I ever refuse, when you find occasion to require it, to close the war with my own blood which was commenced with that of my brother." While Lorenzo spoke, the citizens were unable to refrain from tears, and the sympathy with which he had been heard was extended to their reply, delivered by one of them in the name of the rest, who said that the city acknowledged many advantages derived from the good qualities of himself and his family; and encouraged them to hope that with as much promptitude as they had used in his defense, and in avenging his brother's death, they would secure to him his influence in the government, which he should never lose while they retained possession of the country. And that their deeds might correspond with their words, they immediately appointed a number of armed men, as a guard for the security of his person against domestic enemies.

CHAPTER III

The Florentines prepare for war against the pope--They appeal to a future council--Papal and Neapolitan movements against the Florentines--The Venetians refuse to assist the Florentines--Disturbances in Milan--Genoa revolts from the duke--Futile endeavors to effect peace with the pope--The Florentines repulse their enemies from the territory of Pisa--They attack the papal states--The papal forces routed upon the borders of the Lake of Perugia.

The Florentines now prepared for war, by raising money and collecting as large a force as possible. Being in league with the duke of Milan and the Venetians, they applied to both for assistance. As the pope had proved himself a wolf rather than a shepherd, to avoid being devoured under false accusations, they justified their cause with all available arguments, and filled Italy with accounts of the treachery practiced against their government, exposing the impiety and injustice of the pontiff, and assured the world that the pontificate which he had wickedly attained, he would as impiously fill; for he had sent those whom he had advanced to the highest order of prelacy, in the company of traitors and parricides, to commit the most horrid treachery in the church in the midst of divine service and during the celebration of the holy sacrament, and that then, having failed to murder the citizens, change the government, and plunder the city, according to his intention, he had suspended the performance of all religious offices, and injuriously menaced and injured the republic with pontifical maledictions. But if God was just, and violence was offensive to him, he would be displeased with that of his viceregent, and allow his injured people who were not admitted to communion with the latter, to offer up their prayers to himself. The Florentines, therefore, instead of receiving or obeying the interdict, compelled the priests to perform divine service, assembled a council in Florence of all the Tuscan prelates under their jurisdiction, and appealed against the injuries suffered from the pontiff to a future general council.

The pope did not neglect to assign reasons in his own justification, and maintained it was the duty of a pontiff to suppress tyranny, depress the wicked, and exalt the good; and that this ought to be done by every available means; but that secular princes had no right to detain cardinals, hang bishops, murder, mangle, and drag about the bodies of priests, destroying without distinction the innocent with the guilty.

Notwithstanding these complaints and accusations, the Florentines restored to the pope the cardinal whom they had detained, in return for which he immediately assailed them with his own forces and those of the king. The two armies, under the command of Alfonso, eldest son of Ferrando, and duke of Calabria, who had as his general, Federigo, count of Urbino, entered the Chianti, by permission of the Siennese, who sided with the enemy, occupied Radda with many other fortresses, and having plundered the country, besieged the Castellina. The Florentines were greatly alarmed at these attacks, being almost destitute of forces, and finding their friends slow to assist; for though the duke sent them aid, the Venetians denied all obligation to support the Florentines in their private quarrels, since the animosities of individuals were not to be defended at the public expense. The Florentines, in order to induce the Venetians to take a more correct view of the case, sent Tommaso Soderini as their ambassador to the senate, and, in the meantime, engaged forces, and appointed Ercole, marquis of Ferrara, to the command of their army. While these preparations were being made, the Castellina was so hard pressed by the enemy, that the inhabitants, despairing of relief, surrendered, after having sustained a siege of forty-two days. The enemy then directed their course toward Arezzo, and encamped before San Savino. The Florentine army being now in order, went to meet them, and having approached within three miles, caused such annoyance, that Federigo d'Urbino demanded a truce for a few days, which was granted, but proved so disadvantageous to the Florentines, that those who had made the request were astonished at having obtained it; for, had it been refused, they would have been compelled to retire in disgrace. Having gained these few days to recruit themselves, as soon as they were expired, they took the castle in the presence of their enemies. Winter being now come, the forces of the pope and king retired for convenient quarters to the Siennese territory. The Florentines also withdrew to a more commodious situation, and the marquis of Ferrara, having done little for himself and less for others, returned to his own territories.

At this time, Genoa withdrew from the dominion of Milan, under the following circumstances. Galeazzo, at his death, left a son, Giovan Galeazzo, who being too young to undertake the government, dissensions arose between Sforza, Lodovico, Ottaviano, and Ascanio, his uncles, and the lady Bona, his mother, each of whom desired the guardianship of the young duke. By the advice and mediation of Tommaso Soderini, who was then Florentine ambassador at the court of Milan, and of Cecco Simonetta, who had been secretary to Galeazzo, the lady Bona prevailed. The uncles fled, Ottaviano was drowned in crossing the Adda; the rest were banished to various places, together with Roberto da San Severino, who in these disputes had deserted the duchess and joined the uncles of the duke. The troubles in Tuscany, which immediately followed, gave these princes hope that the new state of things would present opportunities for their advantage; they therefore quitted the places to which their exile limited them, and each endeavored to return home. King Ferrando, finding the Florentines had obtained assistance from none but the Milanese, took occasion to give the duchess so much occupation in her own government, as to render her unable to contribute to their assistance. By means of Prospero Adorno, the Signor Roberto, and the rebellious uncles of the duke, he caused Genoa to throw off the Milanese yoke. The Castelletto was the only place left; confiding in which, the duchess sent a strong force to recover the city, but it was routed by the enemy; and perceiving the danger which might arise to her son and herself if the war were continued, Tuscany being in confusion, and the Florentines, in whom alone she had hope, themselves in trouble, she determined, as she could not retain Genoa in subjection, to secure it as an ally; and agreed with Battistino Fregoso, the enemy of Prospero Adorno, to give him the Castelletto, and make him prince of Genoa, on condition that he should expel Prospero, and do nothing in favor of her son's uncles. Upon this agreement, Battistino, by the assistance of the Castelletto and of his friends, became lord of Genoa; and according to the custom of the city, took the title of Doge. The Sforzeschi and the Signor Roberto, being thus expelled by the Genoese, came with their forces into Lunigiana, and the pope and the king, perceiving the troubles of Lombardy to be composed, took occasion with them to annoy Tuscany in the Pisan territory, that the Florentines might be weakened by dividing their forces. At the close of winter they ordered Roberto da San Severino to leave Lunigiana and march thither, which he did, and with great tumult plundered many fortresses, and overran the country around Pisa.

At this time, ambassadors came to Florence from the emperor, the king of France, and the king of Hungary, who were sent by their princes to the pontiff. They solicited the Florentines also to send ambassadors to the pope, and promised to use their utmost exertion to obtain for them an advantageous peace. The Florentines did not refuse to make trial, both for the sake of publicly justifying their proceedings, and because they were really desirous of peace. Accordingly, the ambassadors were sent, but returned without coming to any conclusion of their differences. The Florentines, to avail themselves of the influence of the king of France, since they were attacked by one part of the Italians and abandoned by the other, sent to him as their ambassador, Donato Acciajuoli, a distinguished Latin and Greek scholar, whose ancestors had always ranked high in the city, but while on his journey he died at Milan. To relieve his surviving family and pay a deserved tribute to his memory, he was honorably buried at the public expense, provision was made for his sons, and suitable marriage portions given to his daughters, and Guid' Antonio Vespucci, a man well acquainted with pontifical and imperial affairs, was sent as ambassador to the king in his stead.

The attack of Signor Roberto upon the Pisan territory, being unexpected, greatly perplexed the Florentines; for having to resist the foe in the direction of Sienna, they knew not how to provide for the places about Pisa. To keep the Lucchese faithful, and prevent them from furnishing the enemy either with money or provisions, they sent as ambassador Piero di Gino Capponi, who was received with so much jealousy, on account of the hatred which that city always cherishes against the Florentines from former injuries and constant fear, that he was on many occasions in danger of being put to death by the mob; and thus his mission gave fresh cause of animosity rather than of union. The Florentines recalled the marquis of Ferrara, and engaged the marquis of Mantua; they also as earnestly requested the Venetians to send them Count Carlo, son of Braccio, and Deifobo, son of Count Jacopo, and after many delays, they complied; for having made a truce with the Turks, they had no excuse to justify a refusal, and could not break through the obligation of the League without the utmost disgrace. The counts, Carlo and Deifobo, came with a good force, and being joined by all that could be spared from the army, which, under the marquis of Ferrara, held in check the duke of Calabria, proceeded toward Pisa, to meet Signor Roberto, who was with his troops near the river Serchio, and who, though he had expressed his intention of awaiting their arrival, withdrew to the camp at Lunigiana, which he had quitted upon coming into the Pisan territory, while Count Carlo recovered all the places that had been taken by the enemy in that district.

The Florentines, being thus relieved from the attack in the direction of Pisa, assembled the whole force between Colle and Santo Geminiano. But the army, on the arrival of Count Carlo, being composed of Sforzeschi and Bracceschi, their hereditary feuds soon broke forth, and it was thought that if they remained long in company, they would turn their arms against each other. It was therefore determined, as the smaller evil, to divide them; to send one party, under Count Carlo, into the district of Perugia, and establish the other at Poggibonzi, where they formed a strong encampment in order to prevent the enemy from penetrating the Florentine territory. By this they also hoped to compel the enemy to divide their forces; for Count Carlo was understood to have many partisans in Perugia, and it was therefore expected, either that he would occupy the place, or that the pope would be compelled to send a large body of men for its defense. To reduce the pontiff to greater necessity, they ordered Niccolo Vitelli, who had been expelled from Citta di Castello, where his enemy Lorenzo Vitelli commanded, to lead a force against that place, with the view of driving out his adversary and withdrawing it from obedience to the pope. At the beginning of the campaign, fortune seemed to favor the Florentines; for Count Carlo made rapid advances in the Perugino, and Niccolo Vitelli, though unable to enter Castello, was superior in the field, and plundered the surrounding country without opposition. The forces also, at Poggibonzi, constantly overran the country up to the walls of Sienna. These hopes, however, were not realized; for in the first place, Count Carlo died, while in the fullest tide of success; though the consequences of this would have been less detrimental to the Florentines, had not the victory to which it gave occasion, been nullified by the misconduct of others. The death of the count being known, the forces of the church, which had already assembled in Perugia, conceived hopes of overcoming the Florentines, and encamped upon the lake, within three miles of the enemy. On the other side, Jacopo Guicciardini, commissary to the army, by the advice of Roberto da Rimino, who, after the death of Count Carlo, was the principal commander, knowing the ground of their sanguine expectations, determined to meet them, and coming to an engagement near the lake, upon the site of the memorable rout of the Romans, by Hannibal, the Carthaginian general, the papal forces were vanquished. The news of the victory, which did great honor to the commanders, diffused universal joy at Florence, and would have ensured a favorable termination of the campaign, had not the disorders which arose in the army at Poggibonzi thrown all into confusion; for the advantage obtained by the valor of the one, was more than counterbalanced by the disgraceful proceedings of the other. Having made considerable booty in the Siennese territory, quarrels arose about the division of it between the marquis of Mantua and the marquis of Ferrara, who, coming to arms, assailed each other with the utmost fury; and the Florentines seeing they could no longer avail themselves of the services of both, allowed the marquis of Ferrara and his men to return home.

CHAPTER IV

The duke of Calabria routs the Florentine army at Poggibonzi--Dismay in Florence on account of the defeat--Progress of the duke of Calabria--The Florentines wish for peace--Lorenzo de' Medici determines to go to Naples to treat with the king--Lodovico Sforza, surnamed the Moor, and his brothers, recalled to Milan--Changes in the government of that city in consequence--The Genoese take Serezana--Lorenzo de' Medici arrives at Naples--Peace concluded with the king--The pope and the Venetians consent to the peace--The Florentines in fear of the duke of Calabria--Enterprises of the Turks--They take Otranto--The Florentines reconciled with the pope--Their ambassadors at the papal court--The pope's reply to the ambassadors--The king of Naples restores to the Florentines all the fortresses he had taken.

The army being thus reduced, without a leader, and disorder prevailing in every department, the duke of Calabria, who was with his forces near Sienna, resolved to attack them immediately. The Florentines, finding the enemy at hand, were seized with a sudden panic; neither their arms, nor their numbers, in which they were superior to their adversaries, nor their position, which was one of great strength, could give them confidence; but observing the dust occasioned by the enemy's approach, without waiting for a sight of them, they fled in all directions, leaving their ammunition, carriages, and artillery to be taken by the foe. Such cowardice and disorder prevailed in the armies of those times, that the turning of a horse's head or tail was sufficient to decide the fate of an expedition. This defeat loaded the king's troops with booty, and filled the Florentines with dismay; for the city, besides the war, was afflicted with pestilence, which prevailed so extensively, that all who possessed villas fled to them to escape death. This occasioned the defeat to be attended with greater horror; for those citizens whose possessions lay in the Val di Pesa and the Val d'Elsa, having retired to them, hastened to Florence with all speed as soon as they heard of the disaster, taking with them not only their children and their property, but even their laborers; so that it seemed as if the enemy were expected every moment in the city. Those who were appointed to the management of the war, perceiving the universal consternation, commanded the victorious forces in the Perugino to give up their enterprise in that direction, and march to oppose the enemy in the Val d'Elsa, who, after their victory, plundered the country without opposition; and although the Florentine army had so closely pressed the city of Perugia that it was expected to fall into their hands every instant, the people preferred defending their own possessions to endeavoring to seize those of others. The troops, thus withdrawn from the pursuit of their good fortune, were marched to San Casciano, a castle within eight miles of Florence; the leaders thinking they could take up no other position till the relics of the routed army were assembled. On the other hand, the enemy being under no further restraint at Perugia, and emboldened by the departure of the Florentines, plundered to a large amount in the districts of Arezzo and Cortona; while those who under Alfonso, duke of Calabria, had been victorious near Poggibonzi, took the town itself; sacked Vico and Certaldo, and after these conquests and pillagings encamped before the fortress of Colle, which was considered very strong; and as the garrison was brave and faithful to the Florentines, it was hoped they would hold the enemy at bay till the republic was able to collect its forces. The Florentines being at Santo Casciano, and the enemy continuing to use their utmost exertions against Colle, they determined to draw nearer, that the inhabitants might be more resolute in their defense, and the enemy assail them less boldly. With this design they removed their camp from Santo Casciano to Santo Geminiano, about five miles from Colle, and with light cavalry and other suitable forces were able every day to annoy the duke's camp. All this, however, was insufficient to relieve the people of Colle; for, having consumed their provisions, they were compelled to surrender on the thirteenth of November, to the great grief of the Florentines, and joy of the enemy, more especially of the Siennese, who, besides their habitual hatred of the Florentines, had a particular animosity against the people of Colle.

It was now the depth of winter, and the weather so unsuitable for war, that the pope and the king, either designing to hold out a hope of peace, or more quietly to enjoy the fruit of their victories, proposed a truce for three months to the Florentines, and allowed them ten days to consider the reply. The offer was eagerly accepted; but as wounds are well known to be more painful after the blood cools than when they were first received, this brief repose awakened the Florentines to a consciousness of the miseries they had endured; and the citizens openly laid the blame upon each other, pointing out the errors committed in the management of the war, the expenses uselessly incurred, and the taxes unjustly imposed. These matters were boldly discussed, not only in private circles, but in the public councils; and one individual even ventured to turn to Lorenzo de' Medici, and say, "The city is exhausted, and can endure no more war; it is therefore necessary to think of peace." Lorenzo was himself aware of the necessity, and assembled the friends in whose wisdom and fidelity he had the greatest confidence, when it was at once concluded, that as the Venetians were lukewarm and unfaithful, and the duke in the power of his guardians, and involved in domestic difficulties, it would be desirable by some new alliance to give a better turn to their affairs. They were in doubt whether to apply to the king or to the pope; but having examined the question in all sides, they preferred the friendship of the king as more suitable and secure; for the short reigns of the pontiffs, the changes ensuing upon each succession, the disregard shown by their church toward temporal princes, and the still greater want of respect for them exhibited in her determinations, render it impossible for a secular prince to trust a pontiff, or safely to share his fortune; for an adherent of the pope will have a companion in victory, but in defeat must stand alone, while the pontiff is sustained by his spiritual power and influence. Having therefore decided that the king's friendship would be of the greatest utility to them, they thought it would be most easily and certainly obtained by Lorenzo's presence; for in proportion to the confidence they evinced toward him, the greater they imagined would be the probability of removing his impressions of past enmities. Lorenzo having resolved to go to Naples, recommended the city and government to the care of Tommaso Soderini, who was at that time Gonfalonier of Justice. He left Florence at the beginning of December, and having arrived at Pisa, wrote to the government to acquaint them with the cause of his departure. The Signory, to do him honor, and enable him the more effectually to treat with the king, appointed him ambassador from the Florentine people, and endowed him with full authority to make such arrangements as he thought most useful for the republic.

At this time Roberto da San Severino, with Lodovico and Ascanio (Sforza their elder brother being dead) again attacked Milan, in order to recover the government. Having taken Tortona, and the city and the whole state being in arms, the duchess Bona was advised to restore the Sforzeschi, and to put a stop to civil contentions by admitting them to the government. The person who gave this advice was Antonio Tassino, of Ferrara, a man of low origin, who, coming to Milan, fell into the hands of the duke Galeazzo, and was given by him to his duchess for her valet. He, either from his personal attractions, or some secret influence, after the duke's death attained such influence over the duchess, that he governed the state almost at his will. This greatly displeased the minister Cecco, whom prudence and long experience had rendered invaluable; and who, to the utmost of his power, endeavored to diminish the authority of Tassino with the duchess and other members of the government. The latter, aware of this, to avenge himself for the injury, and secure defenders against Cecco, advised the duchess to recall the Sforzeschi, which she did, without communicating her design to the minister, who, when it was done, said to her, "You have taken a step which will deprive me of my life, and you of the government." This shortly afterward took place; for Cecco was put to death by Lodovico, and Tassino, being expelled from the dukedom, the duchess was so enraged that she left Milan, and gave up the care of her son to Lodovico, who, becoming sole governor of the dukedom, caused, as will be hereafter seen, the ruin of Italy.

Lorenzo de' Medici had set out for Naples, and the truce between the parties was in force, when, quite unexpectedly, Lodovico Fregoso, being in correspondence with some persons of Serezana, entered the place by stealth, took possession of it with an armed force, and imprisoned the Florentine governor. This greatly offended the Signory, for they thought the whole had been concerted with the connivance of King Ferrando. They complained to the duke of Calabria, who was with the army at Sienna, of a breach of the truce; and he endeavored to prove, by letters and embassies, that it had occurred without either his own or his father's knowledge. The Florentines, however, found themselves in a very awkward predicament, being destitute of money, the head of the republic in the power of the king, themselves engaged in a long-standing war with the latter and the pope, in a new one with the

Genoese, and entirely without friends; for they had no confidence in the Venetians, and on account of its changeable and unsettled state they were rather apprehensive of Milan. They had thus only one hope, and that depended upon Lorenzo's success with the king.

Lorenzo arrived at Naples by sea, and was most honorably received, not only by Ferrando, but by the whole city, his coming having excited the greatest expectation; for it being generally understood that the war was undertaken for the sole purpose of effecting his destruction, the power of his enemies invested his name with additional lustre. Being admitted to the king's presence, he spoke with so much propriety upon the affairs of Italy, the disposition of her princes and people, his hopes from peace, his fears of the results of war, that Ferrando was more astonished at the greatness of his mind, the promptitude of his genius, his gravity and wisdom, than he had previously been at his power. He consequently treated him with redoubled honor, and began to feel compelled rather to part with him as a friend, than detain him as an enemy. However, under various pretexts he kept Lorenzo from December till March, not only to gain the most perfect knowledge of his own views, but of those of his city; for he was not without enemies, who would have wished the king to detain and treat him in the same manner as Jacopo Piccinino; and, with the ostensible view of sympathizing for him, pointed out all that would, or rather that they wished should, result from such a course; at the same time opposing in the council every proposition at all likely to favor him. By such means as these the opinion gained ground, that if he were detained at Naples much longer, the government of Florence would be changed. This caused the king to postpone their separation more than he would have otherwise done, to see if any disturbance were likely to arise. But finding everything go quietly on, Ferrando allowed him to depart on the sixth of March, 1479, having, with every kind of attention and token of regard, endeavored to gain his affection, and formed with him a perpetual alliance for their mutual defense. Lorenzo returned to Florence, and upon presenting himself before the citizens, the impressions he had created in the popular mind surrounded him with a halo of majesty brighter than before. He was received with all the joy merited by his extraordinary qualities and recent services, in having exposed his own life to the most imminent peril, in order to restore peace to his country. Two days after his return, the treaty between the republic of Florence and the king, by which each party bound itself to defend the other's territories, was published. The places taken from the Florentines during the war were to be taken up at the discretion of the king; the Pazzi confined in the tower of Volterra were to be set at liberty, and a certain sum of money, for a limited period, was to be paid to the duke of Calabria.

As soon as this peace was publicly known, the pope and the Venetians were transported with rage; the pope thought himself neglected by the king; the Venetians entertained similar ideas with regard to the Florentines, and complained that, having been companions in the war, they were not allowed to participate in the peace. Reports of this description being spread abroad, and received with entire credence at Florence, caused a general fear that the peace thus made would give rise to greater wars; and therefore the leading members of the government determined to confine the consideration of the most important affairs to a smaller number, and formed a council of seventy citizens, in whom the principal authority was invested. This new regulation calmed the minds of those desirous of change, by convincing them of the futility of their efforts. To establish their authority, they in the first place ratified the treaty of peace with the king, and sent as ambassadors to the pope Antonio Ridolfi and Piero Nasi. But, notwithstanding the peace, Alfonso, duke of Calabria, still remained at Sienna with his forces, pretending to be detained by discords among the citizens, which, he said, had risen so high, that while he resided outside the city they had compelled him to enter and assume the office of arbitrator between them. He took occasion to draw large sums of money from the wealthiest citizens by way of fines, imprisoned many, banished others, and put some to death; he thus became suspected, not only by the Siennese but by the Florentines, of a design to usurp the sovereignty of Sienna; nor was any remedy then available, for the republic had formed a new alliance with the king, and were at enmity with the pope and the Venetians. This suspicion was entertained not only by the great body of the Florentine people, who were subtle interpreters of appearances, but by the principal members of the government; and it was agreed, on all hands, that the city never was in so much danger of losing her liberty. But God, who in similar extremities has always been her preserver, caused an unhoped-for event to take place, which gave the pope, the king, and the Venetians other matters to think of than those in Tuscany.

The Turkish emperor, Mahomet II. had gone with a large army to the siege of

Rhodes, and continued it for several months; but though his forces were numerous, and his courage indomitable, he found them more than equalled by those of the besieged, who resisted his attack with such obstinate valor, that he was at last compelled to retire in disgrace. Having left Rhodes, part of his army, under the Pasha Achmet, approached Velona, and, either from observing the facility of the enterprise, or in obedience to his sovereign's commands, coasting along the Italian shores, he suddenly landed four thousand soldiers, and attacked the city of Otranto, which he easily took, plundered, and put all the inhabitants to the sword. He then fortified the city and port, and having assembled a large body of cavalry, pillaged the surrounding country. The king, learning this, and aware of the redoubtable character of his assailant, immediately sent messengers to all the surrounding powers, to request assistance against the common enemy, and ordered the immediate return of the duke of Calabria with the forces at Sienna.

This attack, however it might annoy the duke and the rest of Italy, occasioned the utmost joy at Florence and Sienna; the latter thinking it had recovered its liberty, and the former that she had escaped a storm which threatened her with destruction. These impressions, which were not unknown to the duke, increased the regret he felt at his departure from Sienna; and he accused fortune of having, by an unexpected and unaccountable accident, deprived him of the sovereignty of Tuscany. The same circumstance changed the disposition of the pope; for although he had previously refused to receive any ambassador from Florence, he was now so mollified as to be anxious to listen to any overtures of peace; and it was intimated to the Florentines, that if they would condescend to ask the pope's pardon, they would be sure of obtaining it. Thinking it advisable to seize the opportunity, they sent twelve ambassadors to the pontiff, who, on their arrival, detained them under different pretexts before he would admit them to an audience. However, terms were at length settled, and what should be contributed by each in peace or war. The messengers were then admitted to the feet of the pontiff, who, with the utmost pomp, received them in the midst of his cardinals. They apologized for past occurrences; first showing they had been compelled by necessity, then blaming the malignity of others, or the rage of the populace, and their just indignation, and enlarging on the unfortunate condition of those who are compelled either to fight or die; saying, that since every extremity is endured in order to avoid death, they had suffered war, interdicts, and other inconveniences, brought upon them by recent events, that their republic might escape slavery, which is the death of free cities. However, if in their necessities they had committed any offense, they were desirous to make atonement, and trusted in his clemency, who, after the example of the blessed Redeemer, would receive them into his compassionate arms.

The pope's reply was indignant and haughty. After reiterating all the offenses against the church during the late transactions, he said that, to comply with the precepts of God, he would grant the pardon they asked, but would have them understand, that it was their duty to obey; and that upon the next instance of their disobedience, they would inevitably forfeit, and that most deservedly, the liberty which they had just been upon the point of losing; for those merit freedom who exercise themselves in good works and avoid evil; that liberty, improperly used, injures itself and others; that to think little of God, and less of his church, is not the part of a free man, but a fool, and one disposed to evil rather than good, and to effect whose correction is the duty not only of princes but of every Christian; so that in respect of the recent events, they had only themselves to blame, who, by their evil deeds, had given rise to the war, and inflamed it by still worse actions, it having been terminated by the kindness of others rather than by any merit of their own. The formula of agreement and benediction was then read; and, in addition to what had already been considered and agreed upon between the parties, the pope said, that if the Florentines wished to enjoy the fruit of his forgiveness, they must maintain fifteen galleys, armed, and equipped, at their own expense, as long as the Turks should make war upon the kingdom of Naples. The ambassadors complained much of this burden in addition to the arrangement already made, but were unable to obtain any alleviation. However, after their return to Florence, the Signory sent, as ambassador to the pope, Guidantonio Vespucci, who had recently returned from France, and who by his prudence brought everything to an amicable conclusion, obtained many favors from the pontiff, which were considered as presages of a closer reconciliation.

Having settled their affairs with the pope, Sienna being free, themselves released from the fear of the king, by the departure of the duke of Calabria from Tuscany, and the war with the Turks still continuing, the Florentines pressed the king to restore their fortresses, which the duke of Calabria, upon quitting the country, had left in the hands of the Siennese. Ferrando, apprehensive that if he refused, they would withdraw from the alliance with him, and by new wars with the Siennese deprive him of the assistance he hoped to obtain from the pope and other Italian powers, consented that they should be given up, and by new favors endeavored to attach the Florentines to his interests. It is thus evident, that force and necessity, not deeds and obligations, induce princes to keep faith.

The castles being restored, and this new alliance established, Lorenzo de' Medici recovered the reputation which first the war and then the peace, when the king's designs were doubtful, had deprived him of; for at this period there was no lack of those who openly slandered him with having sold his country to save himself, and said, that in war they had lost their territories, and in peace their liberty. But the fortresses being recovered, an honorable treaty ratified with the king, and the city restored to her former influence, the spirit of public discourse entirely changed in Florence, a place greatly addicted to gossip, and in which actions are judged by the success attending them, rather than by the intelligence employed in their direction; therefore, the citizens praised Lorenzo extravagantly, declaring that by his prudence he had recovered in peace, what unfavorable circumstances had taken from them in war, and that by his discretion and judgment he had done more than the enemy with all the force of their arms.

CHAPTER V

New occasions of war in Italy--Differences between the marquis of Ferrara, and the Venetians--The king of Naples and the Florentines attack the papal states--The pope's defensive arrangements--The Neapolitan army routed by the papal forces--Progress of the Venetians against the marquis of Ferrara--The pope makes peace, and enters into a league against the Venetians--Operations of the League against the Venetians--The Venetians routed at Bondeno--Their losses--Disunion among the League--Lodovico Sforza makes peace with the Venetians--Ratified by the other parties.

The invasion of the Turks had deferred the war which was about to break forth from the anger of the pope and the Venetians at the peace between the Florentines and the king. But as the beginning of that invasion was unexpected and beneficial, its conclusion was equally unlooked for and injurious; for Mahomet dying suddenly, dissensions arose among his sons, and the forces which were in Puglia being abandoned by their commander, surrendered Otranto to the king. The fears which restrained the pope and the Venetians being thus removed, everyone became apprehensive of new troubles. On the one hand, was the league of the pope and the Venetians, and with them the Genoese, Siennese, and other minor powers; on the other, the Florentines, the king, and the duke, with whom were the Bolognese and many princes. The Venetians wished to become lords of Ferrara, and thought they were justified by circumstances in making the attempt, and hoping for a favorable result. Their differences arose thus: the marquis of Ferrara affirmed he was under no obligation to take salt from the Venetians, or to admit their governor; the terms of convention between them declaring, that after seventy years, the city was to be free from both impositions. The Venetians replied, that so long as he held the Polesine, he was bound to receive their salt and their governor. The marquis refusing his consent, the Venetians considered themselves justified in taking arms, and that the present moment offered a suitable opportunity; for the pope was indignant against the Florentines and the king; and to attach the pope still further, the Count Girolamo, who was then at Venice, was received with all possible respect; first admitted to the privileges of a citizen, and then raised to the rank of a senator, the highest distinctions the Venetian senate can confer. To prepare for the war, they levied new taxes, and appointed to the command of the forces, Roberto da San Severino, who being offended with Lodovico, governor of Milan, fled to Tortona, whence, after occasioning some disturbances, he went to Genoa, and while there, was sent for by the Venetians, and placed at the head of their troops.

These circumstances becoming known to the opposite league, induced it also to provide for war. The duke of Milan appointed as his general, Federigo d'Urbino; the Florentines engaged Costanzo, lord of Pesaro; and to sound the disposition of the pope, and know whether the Venetians made war against Ferrara with his consent or not, King Ferrando sent Alfonso, duke of Calabria, with his army across the Tronto, and asked the pontiff's permission to pass into Lombardy to assist the marquis, which was refused in the most peremptory manner. The Florentines and the king, no longer doubtful about the pope's intentions, determined to harass him, and thus either compel him to take part with them, or throw such obstacles in his way, as would prevent him from helping the Venetians, who had already taken the field, attacked the marquis, overran his territory, and encamped before Figaruolo, a fortress of the greatest importance. In pursuance of the design of the Florentines and the king, the duke of Calabria, by the assistance of the Colonna family (the Orsini had joined the pope), plundered the country about Rome and committed great devastation; while the Florentines, with Niccolo Vitelli, besieged and took Citta di Castello, expelling Lorenzo Vitelli, who held it for the pope, and placing Niccolo in it as prince.

The pope now found himself in very great straits; for the city of Rome was disturbed by factions and the country covered with enemies. But acting with courage and resolution, he appointed Roberto da Rimino to take the command of his forces; and having sent for him to Rome, where his troops were assembled, told him how great would be the honor, if he could deliver the church from the king's forces, and the troubles in which it was involved; how greatly indebted, not only himself, but all his successors would be, and, that not mankind merely, but God himself would be under obligations to him. The magnificent Roberto, having considered the forces and preparations already made, advised the pope to raise as numerous a body of infantry as possible, which was done without delay. The duke of Calabria was at hand, and constantly harassed the country up to the very gates of Rome, which so roused the indignation of the citizens, that many offered their assistance to Roberto, and all were thankfully received. The duke, hearing of these preparations, withdrew a short distance from the city, that in the belief of finding him gone, the magnificent Roberto would not pursue him, and also in expectation of his brother Federigo, whom their father had sent to him with additional forces. But Roberto, finding himself nearly equal to the duke in cavalry, and superior in infantry, marched boldly out of Rome and took a position within two miles of the enemy. The duke, seeing his adversaries close upon him, found he must either fight or disgracefully retire. To avoid a retreat unbecoming a king's son, he resolved to face the enemy; and a battle ensued which continued from morning till midday. In this engagement, greater valor was exhibited on both sides than had been shown in any other during the last fifty years, upward of a thousand dead being left upon the field. The troops of the church were at length victorious, for her numerous infantry so annoyed the ducal cavalry, that they were compelled to retreat, and Alfonso himself would have fallen into the hands of the enemy, had he not been rescued by a body of Turks, who remained at Otranto, and were at that time in his service. The lord of Rimino, after this victory, returned triumphantly to Rome, but did not long enjoy the fruit of his valor; for having, during the heat of the engagement, taken a copious draught of water, he was seized with a flux, of which he very shortly afterward died. The pope caused his funeral to be conducted with great pomp, and in a few days, sent the Count Girolamo toward Citta di Castello to restore it to Lorenzo, and also endeavor to gain Rimino, which being by Roberto's death left to the care of his widow and a son who was quite a boy, his holiness thought might be easily won; and this certainly would have been the case, if the lady had not been defended by the Florentines, who opposed him so effectually, as to prevent his success against both Castello and Rimino.

While these things were in progress at Rome and in Romagna, the Venetians took possession of Figaruolo and crossed the Po with their forces. The camp of the duke of Milan and the marquis was in disorder; for the count of Urbino having fallen ill, was carried to Bologna for his recovery, but died. Thus the marquis's affairs were unfortunately situated, while those of the Venetians gave them increasing hopes of occupying Ferrara. The Florentines and the king of Naples used their utmost endeavors to gain the pope to their views; and not having succeeded by force, they threatened him with the council, which had already been summoned by the emperor to assemble at Basle; and by means of the imperial ambassadors, and the co-operation of the leading cardinals, who were desirous of peace, the pope was compelled to turn his attention toward effecting the pacification of Italy. With this view, at the instigation of his fears, and with the conviction that the aggrandizement of the Venetians would be the ruin of the church and of Italy, he endeavored to make peace with the League, and sent his nuncios to Naples, where a treaty was concluded for five years, between the pope, the king, the duke of Milan, and the Florentines, with an opening for the Venetians to join them if they thought proper. When this was accomplished, the pope intimated to the Venetians, that they must desist from war against Ferrara. They refused to comply, and made preparations to prosecute their design with greater vigor than they had hitherto done; and having routed the forces of the duke and the marquis at Argenta, they approached Ferrara so closely as to pitch their tents in the marquis's park.

The League found they must no longer delay rendering him efficient assistance, and ordered the duke of Calabria to march to Ferrara with his forces and those of the pope, the Florentine troops also moving in the same direction. In order to direct the operations of the war with greater efficiency, the League assembled a diet at Cremona, which was attended by the pope's legate, the Count Girolamo, the duke of Calabria, the Signor Lodovico Sforza, and Lorenzo de' Medici, with many other Italian princes; and when the measures to be adopted were fully discussed, having decided that the best way of relieving Ferrara would be to effect a division of the enemy's forces, the League desired Lodovico to attack the Venetians on the side of Milan, but this he declined, for fear of bringing a war upon the duke's territories, which it would be difficult to quell. It was therefore resolved to proceed with the united forces of the League to Ferrara, and having assembled four thousand cavalry and eight thousand infantry, they went in pursuit of the Venetians, whose force amounted to two thousand two hundred men at arms, and six thousand foot. They first attacked the Venetian flotilla, then lying upon the river Po, which they routed with the loss of above two hundred vessels, and took prisoner Antonio Justiniano, the purveyor of the fleet. The Venetians, finding all Italy united against them, endeavored to support their reputation by engaging in their service the duke of Lorraine, who joined them with two hundred men at arms: and having suffered so great a destruction of their fleet, they sent him, with part of their army, to keep their enemies at bay, and Roberto da San Severino to cross the Adda with the remainder, and proceed to Milan, where they were to raise the cry of "The duke and the Lady Bona," his mother; hoping by this means to give a new aspect to affairs there, believing that Lodovico and his government were generally unpopular. This attack at first created great consternation, and roused the citizens in arms; but eventually produced consequences unfavorable to the designs of the Venetians; for Lodovico was now desirous to undertake what he had refused to do at the entreaty of his allies. Leaving the marquis of Ferrara to the defense of his own territories, he, with four thousand horse and two thousand foot, and joined by the duke of Calabria with twelve thousand horse and five thousand foot, entered the territory of Bergamo, then Brescia, next that of Verona, and, in defiance of the Venetians, plundered the whole country; for it was with the greatest difficulty that Roberto and his forces could save the cities themselves. In the meantime, the marquis of Ferrara had recovered a great part of his territories; for the duke of Lorraine, by whom he was attacked, having only at his command two thousand horse and one thousand foot, could not withstand him. Hence, during the whole of 1483, the affairs of the League were prosperous.

  The winter having passed quietly over, the armies again took the field. To produce the greater impression upon the enemy, the League united their whole force, and would easily have deprived the Venetians of all they possessed in Lombardy, if the war had been conducted in the same manner as during the preceding year; for by the departure of the duke of Lorraine, whose term of service had expired, they were reduced to six thousand horse and five thousand foot, while the allies had thirteen thousand horse and five thousand foot at their disposal. But, as is often the case where several of equal authority are joined in command, their want of unity decided the victory to their enemies. Federigo, marquis of Mantua, whose influence kept the duke of Calabria and Lodovico Sforza within bounds, being dead, differences arose between them which soon became jealousies. Giovan Galeazzo, duke of Milan, was now of an age to take the government on himself, and had married the daughter of the duke of Calabria, who wished his son-in-law to exercise the government and not Lodovico; the latter, being aware of the duke's design, studied to prevent him from effecting it. The position of Lodovico being known to the Venetians, they thought they could make it available for their own interests; and hoped, as they had often before done, to recover in peace all they had lost by war; and having secretly entered into treaty with Lodovico, the terms were concluded in August, 1484. When this became known to the rest of the allies, they were greatly dissatisfied, principally because they found that the places won from the Venetians were to be restored; that they were allowed to keep Rovigo and the Polesine, which they had taken from the marquis of Ferrara, and besides this retain all the pre-eminence and authority over Ferrara itself which they had formerly possessed. Thus it was evident to everyone, they had been engaged in a war which had cost vast sums of money, during the progress of which they had acquired honor, and which was concluded with disgrace; for the places wrested from the enemy were restored without themselves recovering those they had lost. They were, however, compelled to ratify the treaty, on account of the unsatisfactory state of their finances, and because the faults and ambition of others had rendered them unwilling to put their fortunes to further proof.

CHAPTER VI

Affairs of the pope--He is reconciled to Niccolo Vitelli--Discords between the Colonnesi and the Orsini--Various events--The war of Serezana--Genoa occupied by her archbishop--Death of Sixtus IV.--Innocent VIII. elected--Agostino Fregoso gives Serezana to the bank of St. Giorgio--Account of the bank of St. Giorgio--War with the Genoese for Serezana--Stratagem of the Florentines to attack Pietra Santa--Difficulties and final surrender of Pietra Santa--The Lucchese lay claim to Pietra Santa--The city of L'Aquila revolts against the king of Naples--War between him and the pope--The Florentines take the king's party--Peace between the pope and the king.

During these events in Lombardy, the pope sent Lorenzo to invest Citta di Castello, for the purpose of expelling Niccolo Vitelli, the place having been abandoned to him by the League, for the purpose of inducing the pontiff to join them. During the siege, Niccolo's troops were led out against the papal forces and routed them. Upon this the pope recalled the Count Girolamo from Lombardy with orders first to recruit his army at Rome, and then proceed against Citta di Castello. But thinking afterward, that it would be better to obtain Niccolo Vitello as his friend than to renew hostilities with him, an arrangement was entered into by which the latter retained Citta di Castello, and the pope pacified Lorenzo as well as he could. He was induced to both these measures rather by his apprehension of fresh troubles than by his love of peace, for he perceived dissensions arising between the Colonessi and the Orsini.

In the war between the king of Naples and the pope, the former had taken the district of Tagliacozzo from the Orsini, and given it to the Colonnesi, who had espoused his cause. Upon the establishment of peace, the Orsini demanded its restoration by virtue of the treaty. The pope had frequently intimated to the Colonnesi that it ought to be restored; but they, instead of complying with the entreaties of the Orsini, or being influenced by the pope's threats, renewed hostilities against the former. Upon this the pontiff, unable to endure their insolence, united his own forces with those of the Orsini, plundered the houses they possessed in Rome, slew or made prisoners all who defended them, and seized most of their fortresses. So that when these troubles were composed, it was rather by the complete subjugation of one party than from any desire for peace in the other.

Nor were the affairs of Genoa or of Tuscany in repose, for the Florentines kept the Count Antonio da Marciano on the borders of Serezana; and while the war continued in Lombardy, annoyed the people of Serezana by inroads and light skirmishes. Battistino Fregoso, doge of Genoa, trusting to Pagolo Fregoso, the archbishop, was taken prisoner, with his wife and children, by the latter, who assumed the sovereignty of the city. The Venetian fleet had attacked the kingdom of Naples, taken Gallipoli, and harassed the neighboring places. But upon the peace of Lombardy, all tumults were hushed except those of Tuscany and Rome; for the pope died in five days after its declaration, either in the natural course of things, or because his grief for peace, to which he was always opposed, occasioned his end.

Upon the decease of the pontiff, Rome was immediately in arms. The Count Girolamo withdrew his forces into the castle; and the Orsini feared the Colonnesi would avenge the injuries they had recently sustained. The Colonnesi demanded the restitution of their houses and castles, so that in a few days robberies, fires, and murders prevailed in several parts of the city. The cardinals entreated the count to give the castle into the hands of the college, withdraw his troops, and deliver Rome from the fear of his forces, and he, by way of ingratiating himself with the future pontiff obeyed, and retired to Imola. The cardinals, being thus divested of their fears, and the barons hopeless of assistance in their quarrels, proceeded to create a new pontiff, and after some discussion, Giovanni Batista Cibo, a Genoese, cardinal of Malfetta, was elected, and took the name of Innocent VIII. By the mildness of his disposition (for he was peaceable and humane) he caused a cessation of hostilities, and for the present restored peace to Rome.

The Florentines, after the pacification of Lombardy, could not remain quiet; for it appeared disgraceful that a private gentleman should deprive them of the fortress of Serezana; and as it was allowed by the conditions of peace, not only to demand lost places, but to make war upon any who should impede their restoration, they immediately provided men and money to undertake its recovery. Upon this, Agostino Fregoso, who had seized Serezana, being unable to defend it, gave the fortress to the Bank of St. Giorgio. As we shall have frequent occasion to speak of St. Giorgio and the Genoese, it will not be improper, since Genoa is one of the principal cities of Italy, to give some account of the regulations and usages prevailing there. When the Genoese had made peace with the Venetians, after the great war, many years ago, the republic, being unable to satisfy the claims of those who had advanced large sums of money for its use, conceded to them the revenue of the Dogano or customhouse, so that each creditor should participate in the receipts in proportion to his claim, until the whole amount should be liquidated, and as a suitable place for their assembling, the palace over the Dogano was assigned for their use. These creditors established a form of government among themselves, appointing a council of one hundred persons for the direction of their affairs, and a committee of eight, who, as the executive body, should carry into effect the determinations of the council. Their credits were divided into shares, called Luoghi, and they took the title of the Bank, or Company of St. Giorgio. Having thus arranged their government, the city fell into fresh difficulties, and applied to San Giorgio for assistance, which, being wealthy and well managed, was able to afford the required aid. On the other hand, as the city had at first conceded the customs, she next began to assign towns, castles, or territories, as security for moneys received; and this practice has proceeded to such a length, from the necessities of the state, and the accommodation by the San Giorgio, that the latter now has under its administration most of the towns and cities in the Genoese dominion. These the Bank governs and protects, and every year sends its deputies, appointed by vote, without any interference on the part of the republic. Hence the affections of the citizens are transferred from the government to the San Giorgio, on account of the tyranny of the former, and the excellent regulations adopted by the latter. Hence also originate the frequent changes of the republic, which is sometimes under a citizen, and at other times governed by a stranger; for the magistracy, and not the San Giorgio, changes the government. So when the Fregosi and the Adorni were in opposition, as the government of the republic was the prize for which they strove, the greater part of the citizens withdrew and left it to the victor. The only interference of the Bank of St. Giorgio is when one party has obtained a superiority over the other, to bind the victor to the observance of its laws, which up to this time have not been changed; for as it possesses arms, money, and influence, they could not be altered without incurring the imminent risk of a dangerous rebellion. This establishment presents an instance of what in all the republics, either described or imagined by philosophers, has never been thought of; exhibiting within the same community, and among the same citizens, liberty and tyranny, integrity and corruption, justice and injustice; for this establishment preserves in the city many ancient and venerable customs; and should it happen (as in time it easily may) that the San Giorgio should have possession of the whole city, the republic will become more distinguished than that of Venice.

Agostino Fregoso conceded Serezana to the San Giorgio, which readily accepted it, undertook its defense, put a fleet to sea, and sent forces to Pietra Santa to prevent all attempts of the Florentines, whose camp was in the immediate vicinity. The Florentines found it would be essentially necessary to gain possession of Pietra Santa, for without it the acquisition of Serezana lost much of its value, being situated between the latter place and Pisa; but they could not, consistently with the treaty, besiege it, unless the people of Pietra Santa, or its garrison, were to impede their acquisition of Serezana. To induce the enemy to do this, the Florentines sent from Pisa to the camp a quantity of provisions and military stores, accompanied by a very weak escort; that the people of Pietra Santa might have little cause for fear, and by the richness of the booty be tempted to the attack. The plan succeeded according to their expectation; for the inhabitants of Pietra Santa, attracted by the rich prize took possession of it.

This gave legitimate occasion to the Florentines to undertake operations against them; so leaving Serezana they encamped before Pietra Santa, which was very populous, and made a gallant defense. The Florentines planted their artillery in the plain, and formed a rampart upon the hill, that they might also attack the place on that side. Jacopo Guicciardini was commissary of the army; and while the siege of Pietra Santa was going on, the Genoese took and burned the fortress of Vada, and, landing their forces, plundered the surrounding country. Biongianni Gianfigliazzi was sent against them, with a body of horse and foot, and checked their audacity, so that they pursued their depredations less boldly. The fleet continuing its efforts went to Livorno, and by pontoons and other means approached the new tower, playing their artillery upon it for several days, but being unable to make any impression they withdrew.

In the meantime the Florentines proceeded slowly against Pietra Santa, and the enemy taking courage attacked and took their works upon the hill. This was effected with so much glory, and struck such a panic into the Florentines, that they were almost ready to raise the siege, and actually retreated a distance of four miles; for their generals thought that they would retire to winter quarters, it being now October, and make no further attempt till the return of spring.

When the discomfiture was known at Florence, the government was filled with indignation; and, to impart fresh vigor to the enterprise, and restore the reputation of their forces, they immediately appointed Antonio Pucci and Bernardo del Neri commissaries, who, with vast sums of money, proceeded to the army, and intimated the heavy displeasure of the Signory, and of the whole city, if they did not return to the walls; and what a disgrace, if so large an army and so many generals, having only a small garrison to contend with, could not conquer so poor and weak a place. They explained the immediate and future advantages that would result from the acquisition, and spoke so forcibly upon the subject, that all became anxious to renew the attack. They resolved, in the first place, to recover the rampart upon the hill; and here it was evident how greatly humanity, affability, and condescension influence the minds of soldiers; for Antonio Pucci, by encouraging one and promising another, shaking hands with this man and embracing that, induced them to proceed to the charge with such impetuosity, that they gained possession of the rampart in an instant. However, the victory was not unattended by misfortune, for Count Antonio da Marciano was killed by a cannon shot. This success filled the townspeople with so much terror, that they began to make proposals for capitulation; and to invest the surrender with imposing solemnity, Lorenzo de' Medici came to the camp, when, after a few days, the fortress was given up. It being now winter, the leaders of the expedition thought it unadvisable to make any further effort until the return of spring, more particularly because the autumnal air had been so unhealthy that numbers were affected by it. Antonio Pucci and Biongianni Gianfigliazzi were taken ill and died, to the great regret of all, so greatly had Antonio's conduct at Pietra Santa endeared him to the army.

Upon the taking of Pietra Santa, the Lucchese sent ambassadors to Florence, to demand its surrender to their republic, on account of its having previously belonged to them, and because, as they alleged, it was in the conditions that places taken by either party were to be restored to their original possessors. The Florentines did not deny the articles, but replied that they did not know whether, by the treaty between themselves and the Genoese, which was then under discussion, it would have to be given up or not, and therefore could not reply to that point at present; but in case of its restitution, it would first be necessary for the Lucchese to reimburse them for the expenses they had incurred and the injury they had suffered, in the death of so many citizens; and that when this was satisfactorily arranged, they might entertain hopes of obtaining the place.

The whole winter was consumed in negotiations between the Florentines and Genoese, which, by the pope's intervention, were carried on at Rome; but not being concluded upon the return of spring, the Florentines would have attacked Serezana had they not been prevented by the illness of Lorenzo de' Medici, and the war between the pope and King Ferrando; for Lorenzo was afflicted not only by the gout, which seemed hereditary in his family, but also by violent pains in the stomach, and was compelled to go the baths for relief.

The more important reason was furnished by the war, of which this was the origin. The city of L'Aquila, though subject to the kingdom of Naples, was in a manner free; and the Count di Montorio possessed great influence over it. The duke of Calabria was upon the banks of the Tronto with his men-at-arms, under pretense of appeasing some disturbances among the peasantry; but really with a design of reducing L'Aquila entirely under the king's authority, and sent for the Count di Montorio, as if to consult him upon the business he pretended then to have in hand. The count obeyed without the least suspicion, and on his arrival was made prisoner by the duke and sent to Naples. When this circumstance became known at L'Aquila, the anger of the inhabitants arose to the highest pitch; taking arms they killed Antonio Cencinello, commissary for the king, and with him some inhabitants known partisans of his majesty. The L'Aquilani, in order to have a defender in their rebellion, raised the banner of the church, and sent envoys to the pope, to submit their city and themselves to him, beseeching that he would defend them as his own subjects against the tyranny of the king. The pontiff gladly undertook their defense, for he had both public and private reasons for hating that monarch; and

Signor Roberto of San Severino, an enemy of the duke of Milan, being disengaged, was appointed to take the command of his forces, and sent for with all speed to Rome. He entreated the friends and relatives of the Count di Montorio to withdraw their allegiance from the king, and induced the princes of Altimura, Salerno, and Bisignano to take arms against him. The king, finding himself so suddenly involved in war, had recourse to the Florentines and the duke of Milan for assistance. The Florentines hesitated with regard to their own conduct, for they felt all the inconvenience of neglecting their own affairs to attend to those of others, and hostilities against the church seemed likely to involve much risk. However, being under the obligation of a League, they preferred their honor to convenience or security, engaged the Orsini, and sent all their own forces under the Count di Pitigliano toward Rome, to the assistance of the king. The latter divided his forces into two parts; one, under the duke of Calabria, he sent toward Rome, which, being joined by the Florentines, opposed the army of the church; with the other, under his own command, he attacked the barons, and the war was prosecuted with various success on both sides. At length, the king, being universally victorious, peace was concluded by the intervention of the ambassadors of the king of Spain, in August, 1486, to which the pope consented; for having found fortune opposed to him he was not disposed to tempt it further. In this treaty all the powers of Italy were united, except the Genoese, who were omitted as rebels against the republic of Milan, and unjust occupiers of territories belonging to the Florentines. Upon the peace being ratified, Roberto da San Severino, having been during the war a treacherous ally of the church, and by no means formidable to her enemies, left Rome; being followed by the forces of the duke and the Florentines, after passing Cesena, found them near him, and urging his flight reached Ravenna with less than a hundred horse. Of his forces, part were received into the duke's service, and part were plundered by the peasantry. The king, being reconciled with his barons, put to death Jacopo Coppola and Antonello d'Aversa and their sons, for having, during the war, betrayed his secrets to the pope.

CHAPTER VII

The pope becomes attached to the Florentines--The Genoese seize Serezanello--They are routed by the Florentines--Serezana surrenders--Genoa submits to the duke of Milan--War between the Venetians and the Dutch--Osimo revolts from the church--Count Girolamo Riario, lord of Furli, slain by a conspiracy--Galeotto, lord of Faenza, is murdered by the treachery of his wife--The government of the city offered to the Florentines--Disturbances in Sienna--Death of Lorenzo de' Medici--His eulogy--Establishment of his family--Estates bought by Lorenzo--His anxiety for the defense of Florence--His taste for arts and literature--The university of Pisa--The estimation of Lorenzo by other princes.

The pope having observed in the course of the war, how promptly and earnestly the Florentines adhered to their alliances, although he had previously been opposed to them from his attachment to the Genoese, and the assistance they had rendered to the king, now evinced a more amicable disposition, and received their ambassadors with greater favor than previously. Lorenzo de' Medici, being made acquainted with this change of feeling, encouraged it with the utmost solicitude; for he thought it would be of great advantage, if to the friendship of the king he could add that of the pontiff. The pope had a son named Francesco, upon whom designing to bestow states and attach friends who might be useful to him after his own death, saw no safer connection in Italy than Lorenzo's, and therefore induced the latter to give him one of his daughters in marriage. Having formed this alliance, the pope desired the Genoese to concede Serezana to the Florentines, insisting that they had no right to detain what Agostino had sold, nor was Agostino justified in making over to the Bank of San Giorgio what was not his own. However, his holiness did not succeed with them; for the

Genoese, during these transactions at Rome, armed several vessels, and, unknown to the Florentines, landed three thousand foot, attacked Serezanello, situated above Serezana, plundered and burnt the town near it, and then, directing their artillery against the fortress, fired upon it with their utmost energy. This assault was new and unexpected by the Florentines, who immediately assembled their forces under Virginio Orsino, at Pisa, and complained to the pope, that while he was endeavoring to establish peace, the Genoese had renewed their attack upon them. They then sent Piero Corsini to Lucca, that by his presence he might keep the city faithful; and Pagolantonio Soderini to Venice, to learn how that republic was disposed. They demanded assistance of the king and of Signor Lodovico, but obtained it from neither; for the king expressed apprehensions of the Turkish fleet, and Lodovico made excuses, but sent no aid. Thus the Florentines in their own wars are almost always obliged to stand alone, and find no friends to assist them with the same readiness they practice toward others. Nor did they, on this desertion of their allies (it being nothing new to them) give way to despondency; for having assembled a large army under Jacopo Guicciardini and Pietro Vettori, they sent it against the enemy, who had encamped upon the river Magra, at the same time pressing Serezanello with mines and every species of attack. The commissaries being resolved to relieve the place, an engagement ensued, when the Genoese were routed, and Lodovico dal Fiesco, with several other principal men, made prisoners. The Serezanesi were not so depressed at their defeat as to be willing to surrender, but obstinately prepared for their defense, while the Florentine commissaries proceeded with their operations, and instances of valor occurred on both sides. The siege being protracted by a variety of fortune, Lorenzo de' Medici resolved to go to the camp, and on his arrival the troops acquired fresh courage, while that of the enemy seemed to fail; for perceiving the obstinacy of the Florentines' attack, and the delay of the Genoese in coming to their relief, they surrendered to Lorenzo, without asking conditions, and none were treated with severity except two or three who were leaders of the rebellion. During the siege, Lodovico had sent troops to Pontremoli, as if with an intention of assisting the Florentines; but having secret correspondence in Genoa, a party was raised there, who, by the aid of these forces, gave the city to the duke of Milan.

At this time the Dutch made war upon the Venetians, and Boccolino of Osimo, in the Marca, caused that place to revolt from the pope, and assumed the sovereignty. After a variety of fortune, he was induced to restore the city to the pontiff and come to Florence, where, under the protection of Lorenzo de' Medici, by whose advice he had been prevailed upon to submit, he lived long and respected. He afterward went to Milan, but did not experience such generous treatment; for Lodovico caused him to be put to death. The Venetians were routed by the Dutch, near the city of Trento, and Roberto da S. Severino, their captain, was slain. After this defeat, the Venetians, with their usual good fortune, made peace with the Dutch, not as vanquished, but as conquerors, so honorable were the terms they obtained.

About this time, there arose serious troubles in Romagna. Francesco d'Orso, of Furli, was a man of great authority in that city, and became suspected by the count Girolamo, who often threatened him. He consequently, living under great apprehensions, was advised by his friends to provide for his own safety, by the immediate adoption of such a course as would relieve him from all further fear of the count. Having considered the matter and resolved to attempt it, they fixed upon the market day, at Furli, as most suitable for their purpose; for many of their friends being sure to come from the country, they might make use of their services without having to bring them expressly for the occasion. It was the month of May, when most Italians take supper by daylight. The conspirators thought the most convenient hour would be after the count had finished his repast; for his household being then at their meal, he would remain in the chamber almost alone. Having fixed upon the hour, Francesco went to the count's residence, left his companions in the hall, proceeded to his apartment, and desired an attendant to say he wished for an interview. He was admitted, and after a few words of pretended communication, slew him, and calling to his associates, killed the attendant. The governor of the place coming by accident to speak with the count, and entering the apartment with a few of his people, was also slain. After this slaughter, and in the midst of a great tumult, the count's body was thrown from the window, and with the cry of "church and liberty," they roused the people (who hated the avarice and cruelty of the count) to arms, and having plundered his house, made the Countess Caterina and her children prisoners. The fortress alone had to be taken to bring the enterprise to a successful issue; but the Castellan would not consent to its surrender. They begged the countess would desire him to comply with their wish, which she promised to do, if they would allow her to go into the fortress, leaving her children as security for the performance of her promise. The conspirators trusted her, and permitted her to enter; but as soon as she was within, she threatened them with death and every kind of torture in revenge for the murder of her husband; and upon their menacing her with the death of her children, she said she had the means of getting more. Finding they were not supported by the pope, and that Lodovico Sforza, uncle to the countess, had sent forces to her assistance, the conspirators became terrified, and taking with them whatever property they could carry off, they fled to Citta di Castello. The countess recovered the state, and avenged the death of her husband with the utmost cruelty. The Florentines hearing of the count's death, took occasion to recover the fortress of Piancaldoli, of which he had formerly deprived them, and, on sending some forces, captured it; but Cecco, the famous engineer, lost his life during the siege.

To this disturbance in Romagna, another in that province, no less important, has to be added. Galeotto, lord of Faenza, had married the daughter of Giovanni Bentivogli, prince of Bologna. She, either through jealousy or ill treatment by her husband, or from the depravity of her own nature, hated him to such a degree, that she determined to deprive him of his possessions and his life; and pretending sickness, she took to her bed, where, having induced Galeotto to visit her, he was slain by assassins, whom she had concealed for that purpose in the apartment. She had acquainted her father with her design, and he hoped, on his son-in-law's death, to become lord of Faenza. A great tumult arose as soon as the murder was known, the widow, with an infant son, fled into the fortress, the people took up arms, Giovanni Bentivogli, with a condottiere of the duke of Milan, named Bergamino, engaged for the occasion, entered Faenza with a considerable force, and Antonio Boscoli, the Florentine commissary, was also there. These leaders being together, and discoursing of the government of the place, the men of Val di Lamona, who had risen unanimously upon learning what had occurred, attacked Giovanni and Bergamino, the latter of whom they slew, made the former prisoner, and raising the cry of "Astorre and the Florentines," offered the city to the commissary. These events being known at Florence, gave general offense; however, they set Giovanni and his daughter at liberty, and by the universal desire of the people, took the city and Astorre under their protection. Besides these, after the principal differences of the greater powers were composed, during several years tumults prevailed in Romagna, the Marca, and Sienna, which, as they are unimportant, it will be needless to recount. When the duke of Calabria, after the war of 1478, had left the country, the distractions of Sienna became more frequent, and after many changes, in which, first the plebeians, and then the nobility, were victorious, the latter and length maintained the superiority, and among them Pandolfo and Jacopo Petrucci obtained the greatest influence, so that the former being distinguished for prudence and the latter for resolution, they became almost princes in the city.

The Florentines after the war of Serezana, lived in great prosperity until 1492, when Lorenzo de' Medici died; for he having put a stop to the internal wars of Italy, and by his wisdom and authority established peace, turned his thoughts to the advancement of his own and the city's interests, and married Piero, his eldest son, to Alfonsina, daughter of the Cavaliere Orsino. He caused Giovanni, his second son, to be raised to the dignity of cardinal. This was the more remarkable from its being unprecedented; for he was only fourteen years of age when admitted to the college; and became the medium by which his family attained to the highest earthly glory. He was unable to make any particular provision for Guiliano, his third son, on account of his tender years, and the shortness of his own life. Of his daughters, one married Jacopo Salviati; another, Francesco Cibo; the third, Piero Ridolfi; and the fourth, whom, in order to keep his house united, he had married to Giovanni de' Medici, died. In his commercial affairs he was very unfortunate, from the improper conduct of his agents, who in all their proceedings assumed the deportment of princes rather than of private persons; so that in many places, much of his property was wasted, and he had to be relieved by his country with large sums of money. To avoid similar inconvenience, he withdrew from mercantile pursuits, and invested his property in land and houses, as being less liable to vicissitude. In the districts of Prato, Pisa, and the Val di Pesa, he purchased extensively, and erected buildings, which for magnificence and utility, were quite of regal character. He next undertook the improvement of the city, and as many parts were unoccupied by buildings, he caused new streets to be erected in them, of great beauty, and thus enlarged the accommodation of the inhabitants. To enjoy his power in security and repose, and conquer or resist his enemies at a distance, in the direction of Bologna he fortified the castle of Firenzuola, situated in the midst of the Appennines; toward Sienna he commenced the restoration and fortification of the Poggio Imperiale; and he shut out the enemy in the direction of Genoa, by the acquisition of Pietra Santa and Serezana. For the greater safety of the city, he kept in pay the Baglioni, at Perugia, and the Vitelli, at Citta di Castello, and held the government of Faenza wholly in his own power; all which greatly contributed to the repose and prosperity of Florence. In peaceful times, he frequently entertained the people with feasts, and exhibitions of various events and triumphs of antiquity; his object being to keep the city abundantly supplied, the people united, and the nobility honored. He was a great admirer of excellence in the arts, and a patron of literary men, of which Agnolo da Montepulciano, Cristofero Landini, and Demetrius Chalcondylas, a Greek, may afford sufficient proofs. On this account, Count Giovanni della Mirandola, a man of almost supernatural genius, after visiting every court of Europe, induced by the munificence of Lorenzo, established his abode at Florence. He took great delight in architecture, music, and poetry, many of his comments and poetical compositions still remaining. To facilitate the study of literature to the youth of Florence, he opened a university at Pisa, which was conducted by the most distinguished men in Italy. For Mariano da Chinazano, a friar of the order of St. Augustine, and an excellent preacher, he built a monastery in the neighborhood of Florence. He enjoyed much favor both from fortune and from the Almighty; all his enterprises were brought to a prosperous termination, while his enemies were unfortunate; for, besides the conspiracy of the Pazzi, an attempt was made to murder him in the Carmine, by Batista Frescobaldi, and a similar one by Baldinetto da Pistoja, at his villa; but these persons, with their confederates, came to the end their crimes deserved. His skill, prudence, and fortune, were acknowledged with admiration, not only by the princes of Italy, but by those of distant countries; for Matthias, king of Hungary, gave him many proofs of his regard; the sultan sent ambassadors to him with valuable presents, and the Turkish emperor placed in his hands Bernardo Bandini, the murderer of his brother. These circumstances raised his fame throughout Italy, and his reputation for prudence constantly increased; for in council he was eloquent and acute, wise in determination, and prompt and resolute in execution. Nor can vices be alleged against him to sully so many virtues; though he was fond of women, pleased with the company of facetious and satirical men, and amused with the games of the nursery, more than seemed consistent with so great a character; for he was frequently seen playing with his children, and partaking of their infantine sports; so that whoever considers this gravity and cheerfulness, will find united in him dispositions which seem almost incompatible with each other. In his later years, he was greatly afflicted; besides the gout, he was troubled with excruciating pains in the stomach, of which he died in April, 1492, in the forty-fourth year of his age; nor was there ever in Florence, or even in Italy, one so celebrated for wisdom, or for whose loss such universal regret was felt. As from his death the greatest devastation would shortly ensue, the heavens gave many evident tokens of its approach; among other signs, the highest pinnacle of the church of Santa Reparata was struck with lightning, and great part of it thrown down, to the terror and amazement of everyone. The citizens and all the princes of Italy mourned for him, and sent their ambassadors to Florence, to condole with the city on the occasion; and the justness of their grief was shortly after apparent; for being deprived of his counsel, his survivors were unable either to satisfy or restrain the ambition of Lodovico Sforza, tutor to the duke of Milan; and hence, soon after the death of Lorenzo, those evil plants began to germinate, which in a little time ruined Italy, and continue to keep her in desolation.

www.bookjungle.com email: sales@bookjungle.com fax: 630-214-0564 mail: Book Jungle PO Box 2226 Champaign, IL 61825

The Codes Of Hammurabi And Moses
W. W. Davies

The discovery of the Hammurabi Code is one of the greatest achievements of archaeology, and is of paramount interest, not only to the student of the Bible, but also to all those interested in ancient history...

Religion   **ISBN:** *1-59462-338-4*   Pages: 132
MSRP $12.95   QTY

The Theory of Moral Sentiments
Adam Smith

This work from 1749. contains original theories of conscience amd moral judgment and it is the foundation for systemof morals.

Philosophy   **ISBN:** *1-59462-777-0*   Pages: 536
MSRP $19.95   QTY

Jessica's First Prayer
Hesba Stretton

In a screened and secluded corner of one of the many railway-bridges which span the streets of London there could be seen a few years ago, from five o'clock every morning until half past eight, a tidily set-out coffee-stall, consisting of a trestle and board, upon which stood two large tin cans, with a small fire of charcoal burning under each so as to keep the coffee boiling during the early hours of the morning when the work-people were thronging into the city on their way to their daily toil...

Childrens   **ISBN:** *1-59462-373-2*   Pages: 84
MSRP $9.95   QTY

My Life and Work
Henry Ford

Henry Ford revolutionized the world with his implementation of mass production for the Model T automobile. Gain valuable business insight into his life and work with his own auto-biography... "We have only started on our development of our country we have not as yet, with all our talk of wonderful progress, done more than scratch the surface. The progress has been wonderful enough but..."

Biographies/   **ISBN:** *1-59462-198-5*   Pages: 300
MSRP $21.95   QTY

www.bookjungle.com *email: sales@bookjungle.com fax: 630-214-0564 mail: Book Jungle PO Box 2226 Champaign, IL 61825*

The Art of Cross-Examination
Francis Wellman

QTY

I presume it is the experience of every author, after his first book is published upon an important subject, to be almost overwhelmed with a wealth of ideas and illustrations which could readily have been included in his book, and which to his own mind, at least, seem to make a second edition inevitable. Such certainly was the case with me; and when the first edition had reached its sixth impression in five months, I rejoiced to learn that it seemed to my publishers that the book had met with a sufficiently favorable reception to justify a second and considerably enlarged edition. ...

Reference   ISBN: *1-59462-647-2*   Pages:412 MSRP *$19.95*

On the Duty of Civil Disobedience
Henry David Thoreau

QTY

Thoreau wrote his famous essay, On the Duty of Civil Disobedience, as a protest against an unjust but popular war and the immoral but popular institution of slave-owning. He did more than write—he declined to pay his taxes, and was hauled off to gaol in consequence. Who can say how much this refusal of his hastened the end of the war and of slavery ?

Law   ISBN: *1-59462-747-9*   Pages:48 MSRP *$7.45*

Dream Psychology Psychoanalysis for Beginners
Sigmund Freud

QTY

Sigmund Freud, born Sigismund Schlomo Freud (May 6, 1856 - September 23, 1939), was a Jewish-Austrian neurologist and psychiatrist who co-founded the psychoanalytic school of psychology. Freud is best known for his theories of the unconscious mind, especially involving the mechanism of repression; his redefinition of sexual desire as mobile and directed towards a wide variety of objects; and his therapeutic techniques, especially his understanding of transference in the therapeutic relationship and the presumed value of dreams as sources of insight into unconscious desires.

Psychology   ISBN: *1-59462-905-6*   Pages:196 MSRP *$15.45*

The Miracle of Right Thought
Orison Swett Marden

QTY

Believe with all of your heart that you will do what you were made to do. When the mind has once formed the habit of holding cheerful, happy, prosperous pictures, it will not be easy to form the opposite habit. It does not matter how improbable or how far away this realization may see, or how dark the prospects may be, if we visualize them as best we can, as vividly as possible, hold tenaciously to them and vigorously struggle to attain them, they will gradually become actualized, realized in the life. But a desire, a longing without endeavor, a yearning abandoned or held indifferently will vanish without realization.

Self Help   ISBN: *1-59462-644-8*   Pages:360 MSRP *$25.45*

www.bookjungle.com *email: sales@bookjungle.com fax: 630-214-0564 mail: Book Jungle PO Box 2226 Champaign, IL 61825*

QTY

☐	**The Rosicrucian Cosmo-Conception Mystic Christianity** by *Max Heindel* *The Rosicrucian Cosmo-conception is not dogmatic, neither does it appeal to any other authority than the reason of the student. It is: not controversial, but is: sent forth in the, hope that it may help to clear...* New Age/Religion Pages 646	ISBN: 1-59462-188-8	$38.95
☐	**Abandonment To Divine Providence** by *Jean-Pierre de Caussade* *"The Rev. Jean Pierre de Caussade was one of the most remarkable spiritual writers of the Society of Jesus in France in the 18th Century. His death took place at Toulouse in 1751. His works have gone through many editions and have been republished..."* Inspirational/Religion Pages 400	ISBN: 1-59462-228-0	$25.95
☐	**Mental Chemistry** by *Charles Haanel* *Mental Chemistry allows the change of material conditions by combining and appropriately utilizing the power of the mind. Much like applied chemistry creates something new and unique out of careful combinations of chemicals the mastery of mental chemistry...* New Age Pages 354	ISBN: 1-59462-192-6	$23.95
☐	**The Letters of Robert Browning and Elizabeth Barret Barrett 1845-1846 vol II** by *Robert Browning* and *Elizabeth Barrett* Biographies Pages 596	ISBN: 1-59462-193-4	$35.95
☐	**Gleanings In Genesis (volume I)** by *Arthur W. Pink* *Appropriately has Genesis been termed "the seed plot of the Bible" for in it we have, in germ form, almost all of the great doctrines which are afterwards fully developed in the books of Scripture which follow...* Religion/Inspirational Pages 420	ISBN: 1-59462-130-6	$27.45
☐	**The Master Key** by *L. W. de Laurence* *In no branch of human knowledge has there been a more lively increase of the spirit of research during the past few years than in the study of Psychology, Concentration and Mental Discipline. The requests for authentic lessons in Thought Control, Mental Discipline and...* New Age/Business Pages 422	ISBN: 1-59462-001-6	$30.95
☐	**The Lesser Key Of Solomon Goetia** by *L. W. de Laurence* *This translation of the first book of the "Lernegton" which is now for the first time made accessible to students of Talismanic Magic was done, after careful collation and edition, from numerous Ancient Manuscripts in Hebrew, Latin, and French...* New Age/Occult Pages 92	ISBN: 1-59462-092-X	$9.95
☐	**Rubaiyat Of Omar Khayyam** by *Edward Fitzgerald* *Edward Fitzgerald, whom the world has already learned, in spite of his own efforts to remain within the shadow of anonymity, to look upon as one of the rarest poets of the century, was born at Bredfield, in Suffolk, on the 31st of March, 1809. He was the third son of John Purcell...* Music Pages 172	ISBN: 1-59462-332-5	$13.95
☐	**Ancient Law** by *Henry Maine* *The chief object of the following pages is to indicate some of the earliest ideas of mankind, as they are reflected in Ancient Law, and to point out the relation of those ideas to modern thought.* Religiom/History Pages 452	ISBN: 1-59462-128-4	$29.95
☐	**Far-Away Stories** by *William J. Locke* *"Good wine needs no bush, but a collection of mixed vintages does. And this book is just such a collection. Some of the stories I do not want to remain buried for ever in the museum files of dead magazine-numbers an author's not unpardonable vanity..."* Fiction Pages 272	ISBN: 1-59462-129-2	$19.45
☐	**Life of David Crockett** by *David Crockett* *"Colonel David Crockett was one of the most remarkable men of the times in which he lived. Born in humble life, but gifted with a strong will, an indomitable courage, and unremitting perseverance...* Biographies/New Age Pages 424	ISBN: 1-59462-250-7	$27.45
☐	**Lip-Reading** by *Edward Nitchie* *Edward B. Nitchie, founder of the New York School for the Hard of Hearing, now the Nitchie School of Lip-Reading, Inc, wrote "LIP-READING Principles and Practice". The development and perfecting of this meritorious work on lip-reading was an undertaking...* How-to Pages 400	ISBN: 1-59462-206-X	$25.95
☐	**A Handbook of Suggestive Therapeutics, Applied Hypnotism, Psychic Science** by *Henry Munro* Health/New Age/Health/Self-help Pages 376	ISBN: 1-59462-214-0	$24.95
☐	**A Doll's House: and Two Other Plays** by *Henrik Ibsen* *Henrik Ibsen created this classic when in revolutionary 1848 Rome. Introducing some striking concepts in playwriting for the realist genre, this play has been studied the world over.* Fiction/Classics/Plays 308	ISBN: 1-59462-112-8	$19.95
☐	**The Light of Asia** by *sir Edwin Arnold* *In this poetic masterpiece, Edwin Arnold describes the life and teachings of Buddha. The man who was to become known as Buddha to the world was born as Prince Gautama of India but he rejected the worldly riches and abandoned the reigns of power when...* Religion/History/Biographies Pages 170	ISBN: 1-59462-204-3	$13.95
☐	**The Complete Works of Guy de Maupassant** by *Guy de Maupassant* *"For days and days, nights and nights, I had dreamed of that first kiss which was to consecrate our engagement, and I knew not on what spot I should put my lips..."* Fiction/Classics Pages 240	ISBN: 1-59462-157-8	$16.95
☐	**The Art of Cross-Examination** by *Francis L. Wellman* *Written by a renowned trial lawyer, Wellman imparts his experience and uses case studies to explain how to use psychology to extract desired information through questioning.* How-to/Science/Reference Pages 408	ISBN: 1-59462-309-0	$26.95
☐	**Answered or Unanswered?** by *Louisa Vaughan* *Miracles of Faith in China* Religion Pages 112	ISBN: 1-59462-248-5	$10.95
☐	**The Edinburgh Lectures on Mental Science (1909)** by *Thomas* *This book contains the substance of a course of lectures recently given by the writer in the Queen Street Hall, Edinburgh. Its purpose is to indicate the Natural Principles governing the relation between Mental Action and Material Conditions...* New Age/Psychology Pages 148	ISBN: 1-59462-008-3	$11.95
☐	**Ayesha** by *H. Rider Haggard* *Verily and indeed it is the unexpected that happens! Probably if there was one person upon the earth from whom the Editor of this, and of a certain previous history, did not expect to hear again...* Classics Pages 380	ISBN: 1-59462-301-5	$24.95
☐	**Ayala's Angel** by *Anthony Trollope* *The two girls were both pretty, but Lucy who was twenty-one who supposed to be simple and comparatively unattractive, whereas Ayala was credited, as her Bombwhat romantic name might show, with poetic charm and a taste for romance. Ayala when her father died was nineteen...* Fiction Pages 484	ISBN: 1-59462-352-X	$29.95
☐	**The American Commonwealth** by *James Bryce* *An interpretation of American democratic political theory. It examines political mechanics and society from the perspective of Scotsman James Bryce* Politics Pages 572	ISBN: 1-59462-286-8	$34.45
☐	**Stories of the Pilgrims** by *Margaret P. Pumphrey* *This book explores pilgrims religious oppression in England as well as their escape to Holland and eventual crossing to America on the Mayflower, and their early days in New England...* History Pages 268	ISBN: 1-59462-116-0	$17.95

www.bookjungle.com email: sales@bookjungle.com fax: 630-214-0564 mail: Book Jungle PO Box 2226 Champaign, IL 61825

QTY

The Fasting Cure *by Sinclair Upton* ISBN: *1-59462-222-1* **$13.95**
In the Cosmopolitan Magazine for May, 1910, and in the Contemporary Review (London) for April, 1910, I published an article dealing with my experiences in fasting. I have written a great many magazine articles, but never one which attracted so much attention... *New Age/Self Help/Health Pages 164*

Hebrew Astrology *by Sepharial* ISBN: *1-59462-308-2* **$13.45**
In these days of advanced thinking it is a matter of common observation that we have left many of the old landmarks behind and that we are now pressing forward to greater heights and to a wider horizon than that which represented the mind-content of our progenitors... *Astrology Pages 144*

Thought Vibration or The Law of Attraction in the Thought World ISBN: *1-59462-127-6* **$12.95**
by William Walker Atkinson *Psychology/Religion Pages 144*

Optimism *by Helen Keller* ISBN: *1-59462-108-X* **$15.95**
Helen Keller was blind, deaf, and mute since 19 months old, yet famously learned how to overcome these handicaps, communicate with the world, and spread her lectures promoting optimism. An inspiring read for everyone... *Biographies/Inspirational Pages 84*

Sara Crewe *by Frances Burnett* ISBN: *1-59462-360-0* **$9.45**
In the first place, Miss Minchin lived in London. Her home was a large, dull, tall one, in a large, dull square, where all the houses were alike, and all the sparrows were alike, and where all the door-knockers made the same heavy sound... *Childrens/Classic Pages 88*

The Autobiography of Benjamin Franklin *by Benjamin Franklin* ISBN: *1-59462-135-7* **$24.95**
The Autobiography of Benjamin Franklin has probably been more extensively read than any other American historical work, and no other book of its kind has had such ups and downs of fortune. Franklin lived for many years in England, where he was agent... *Biographies/History Pages 332*

Name	
Email	
Telephone	
Address	
City, State ZIP	

☐ Credit Card   ☐ Check / Money Order

Credit Card Number	
Expiration Date	
Signature	

Please Mail to: Book Jungle
PO Box 2226
Champaign, IL 61825
or Fax to: 630-214-0564

ORDERING INFORMATION

web: www.bookjungle.com
email: sales@bookjungle.com
fax: 630-214-0564
mail: Book Jungle PO Box 2226 Champaign, IL 61825
or PayPal *to sales@bookjungle.com*

Please contact us for bulk discounts

DIRECT-ORDER TERMS

20% Discount if You Order Two or More Books
Free Domestic Shipping!
Accepted: Master Card, Visa, Discover, American Express

www.ingramcontent.com/pod-product-compliance
Lightning Source LLC
Chambersburg PA
CBHW082033230426
43670CB00016B/2642